The Bridge
Gray Church,
S. Dunstan in the East,
Belinsgate,
Custome house,
The Tower,

31 Tower wharfe
32 S. Catharins
33 S. Olaffe,
34 S. Marie Overis,
35 Winchester house
36 The Globe,

37 Bear Garden
38 The Swan,
39 Harrowe on the Hill,
40 Hamsted,
41 Hygate,
42 Hackney,

43 Poutney,
44 Ell Ships
45 Gally Fufte,
46 Cool harbour,

Elizabethan Backgrounds

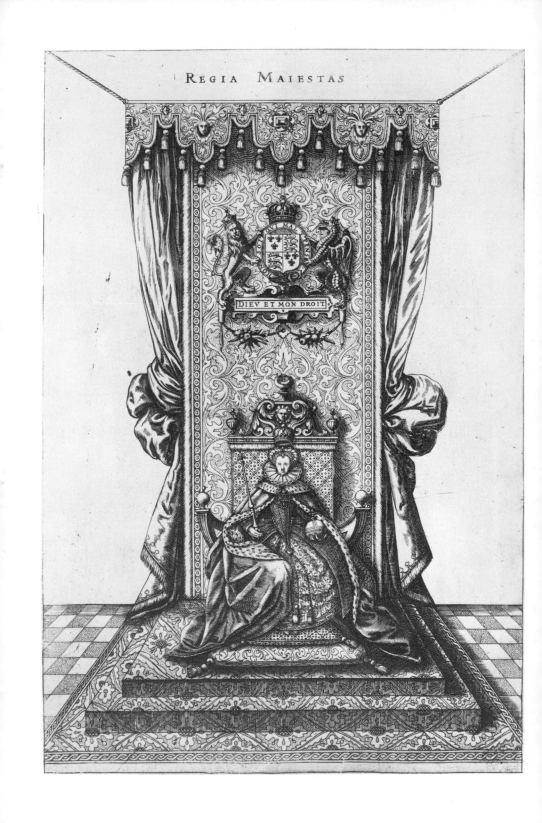

DIEV ET MON DROIT

Elizabethan
Backgrounds

Historical Documents of the Age of Elizabeth I

newly edited, with introductions,

by Arthur F. Kinney

ARCHON BOOKS

1975

Library of Congress Cataloging in Publication Data

Kinney, Arthur F.   1933-   comp.
 Elizabethan backgrounds.

 CONTENTS: Proclamation of accession (1558).—The
Quene's Majestie's passage (1559).—Proclamation for peace
between England, France, and Scotland (1559). [etc.]
 1. Great Britain — History — Elizabeth, 1558-1603 —
Sources.   I. Title.   II. Series.
DA350.K56   942.05′5   74-924
ISBN 0-208-01424-1

©1975 by Arthur F. Kinney
First published 1975 as an Archon Book,
an imprint of The Shoe String Press, Inc.,
Hamden, Connecticut 06514

For my parents
Arthur Frederick Kinney, 1898—, and
Gladys Mudge Kinney, 1899—

Printed in the United States of America

Contents

Illustrations

frontispiece Detail of throne. See illustration 5.
[following page 212]

1. Queen Elizabeth: The "Darnley" portrait.
2. The second great seal of Queen Elizabeth I.
3. Elizabeth's coronation procession.
4. The Queen's route to her coronation.
5. Queen Elizabeth enthroned before Parliament.
6. (top) William Cecil.
7. (bottom) Robert Devereux.
8. A map of London and Westminster in 1563.
9. "A true plan of the City of Excester" in the sixteenth century.
10. (left) The procession of Queen Elizabeth I.
11. The execution of Mary Stuart.
12. Resolution to pursue the Armada.
13. Opening formations during the Spanish Armada.
14. Map illustrating the seige of Kinsale, 1601-02.
15. The Aging Queen.
16. Queen Elizabeth's funeral procession.
17. The Queen in effigy.

front end leaves London in the time of Elizabeth I.
back end leaves Part of Westminster.

    (*End leaves reproduced with permission of the Henry E. Huntington Library and Art Gallery.*)

Preface

Of all the forms and methods of historical representation, the best is said to be that which echoes original voices. But it is not echoes we hear in this and its fellow-volumes; it is the original voices themselves. They speak in no borrowed accents; no interpreter mars their meaning; no medium muffles their tones. History is a glass through which we behold the past; but the glass is coloured by the historians's mind, and we see through it sometimes darkly. Contemporary writings are a glass of truth, a mirror of the age in which they are written.

So A. F. Pollard in the introduction to his *Tudor Tracts 1532-1588* (Westminster, 1903), a reworking of the Reverend Edward A. Arber's *An English Garner* (Westminster, 1880-1897). Pollard might further have recalled that the age he was examining presented a number of "mirrors," among them both the "magical perspective" of Robert Greene's black magician Roger Bacon—which allowed one to peer into the private activities of those far away for one's own private purposes—and Ophelia's "glass of fashion, and the mold of form" which might be "quite, quite down"—such models of excellence, that is, as Hamlet who might be observed in a time of undoing and so reflect neither the truth nor an ideal but rather a misleading, because unrepresentative, moment. In the works I have collected here the Elizabethans were aware of these other mirrors—at least some of their writers were—for they shaped their eye-witness accounts and their journal records to a schoolbook theme, to an outburst of passionate commentary, or to the useful ends of persuasion as often as they used proclamation and pamphlet to record an event objectively. They understood that truth is not merely fact, but perceived fact; and the form of their truths often itself tells a story which, dark as any intervening historian's, still guides us on the path towards the "glass of truth" which gives us now some understanding of their colorful and complex age.

We need whatever aid the age itself can give us. At first the age of Elizabeth may seem simple, even medieval in its thought and behavior. We hear Shakespeare's Ulysses praising natural order and *status quo* and warning us against taking "degree" away and untuning the string of the cosmos and of life, for "hark what discord follows." We recall that Sir Thomas Smith in his admirable *De republica Anglorum* (1585) examines his government as one based on social and political inequality (or "degree"): "A gentleman must go like a gentleman, a yeoman like a yeoman, a rascal like a rascal." This is all very well until we remember that this was the period when an illegitimate bastard laid claim to the throne (though her perfectly legitimate first cousin, soon the ruler in two other countries, offered to take over for her) and that the man who served in effect as her Prime Minister fabricated his genealogy so he could be a "respectable" peer of the realm. We recall Elizabeth's religious settlement, as we term it, was really nationalistic and laic. We consider that the Elizabethan custom of putting the country before the self was voiced even by some of the most startlingly individualistic persons in English history: Raleigh, Leicester, Essex, Drake, Hakluyt, Mary Stuart, Bacon, even Burghley and the Queen herself. Indeed, Elizabeth's reign now seems bound in by paradoxes: a high love of the arts alongside delight in base cruelty; an active pursuit of peace and the fostering of rebellion; the notion— crudely apparent in reports Hakluyt collected—of colonization for spreading the gospel cloaking more determined ends of imperialism; heroism lending often as not a kind of desperation that produced a madman Somerville for every Egerton, an Essex for every Mountjoy, a Leicester for every Burghley, a Throckmorton for every Walsingham, a Wentworth for every Bacon. The antipodes bend to make their circumference; antipathies merge. As Trevelyan once noted, Elizabethan England is that unique place and concept "at once insular and oceanic."

The nineteen rather diverse works freshly edited for this volume help us to make sense out of an apparent chaos. They all contribute as they grope separately and together towards an increasing sense of national consciousness. For that is often what links them. This was, after all, the period when the land was united through instituting common law and giving increased respect to a more representative House of Commons; the economic age when the clothing industry was nationally organized and the relation of local trade, regional trade, international trade and economic health was systematically considered; the time when a singular church was developed as a careful and tolerant umbrella for a wide area of shared and independent ways of conscience; the years when English triumphed as a literary language and the printed book and growing literate public first reached appreciable numbers; and—perhaps most importantly—the era of the progresses in state of a Queen who journeyed through home counties and distant sections of her land welding together a varied, often semi-isolated people through their honoring and loving her as a symbol of their pride and identity as a nation. The works presented here are important—to repeat—because they are windows into men's minds if not into their souls, and they allow us to see a nation coming into being. They do something more: in reproducing for our bookstores what the Englishman of the sixteenth century would find displayed in the bookstalls along the yard of Paul's, this collection allows us to see clearly reflected the "popular mind" by letting us read what her people chose to read, letting us see what they chose to write and how they organized and phrased it. If we gaze beyond this to see common threads, if we look behind statements to discover possible motivations, we come as close as I suspect we ever will to the England of Elizabeth I. The purpose of *Elizabethan Backgrounds*, then, is twofold: it is intended to introduce us to a unique and essential period of English historical and cultural achievement and to remain as a reference tool for understanding the thought and reasoning, the "habits of mind," of that age.

In light of this double purpose, I have read a good part of the STC collection which is still extant; and I have chosen for editing—where I could—those documents which seemed to me to be representative rather than exceptional, from witnesses rather than later narrators; and I have tried to include several works dealing with the major historical events, the thought, and the governmental operations of the Elizabethan period. Other topics—such as religion, education, science, commerce, exploration, social manners and customs, sports, and the fine arts—await similar collections.

A word about the texts themselves: I have chosen only those which are brief enough to be included in their entirety, since their organization and total content form a part of their meaning. I have used as copy-texts the first Elizabethan edition; and I have considered only books printed in English and issued originally in Elizabeth's reign, between November 17, 1558, and March 24, 1603, with one exception: the "homily of obedience," first written and published during Edward's reign in the first book of *Certayne Sermons*, was altered at Elizabeth's command, and it is the altered Elizabethan version which is included here. I have tried to choose works widely distributed: common knowledge with some kind of common appeal. I have, moreover, incorporated only works of non-fiction prose—works, therefore, that Elizabethans would have thought informative and instructive as well as (or instead of) entertaining. Literary scholars have, for the most part, already preserved for us in careful old-spelling editions the best of the Elizabethan poetry, drama, romance, and memoirs.

I have retained the old-spelling because it is part of the authenticity which I have tried to preserve as my first principle. My only changes have been in the regularization of *u* and *v*; the addition of an omitted nasal and the elimination of the tilde; the extending of the abbreviations *&*, *w*ͭ, *y*ͭ, and *y*ͭ for *and, with, the* and *that*; the joining of words compound in meaning; the modernization of possessives; and emendations of obvious printers' errors. I have provided some glosses although, as Dr. Johnson remarked, I will have noted too much for some, too little for others, and pleased no one except, perhaps, myself.

Textual notes follow the introductory comments preceding each document. Reference notes are found at the end of the book preceding the bibliography.

Some acknowledgments and I am done. Since the inception of this project I have worked closely with Katherine F. Pantzer, who shared with me the worksheets of the revised STC and sent air letters, when necessary, to direct me to copies of certain editions and states. The tasks of reading and editing were undertaken mostly at the Bodleian Library where D. H. Merry verified many of my conjectures and more importantly remained always the encouraging and interested friend, and David Vaisey occasionally assisted me in reading various Elizabethan manuscripts. Paul Morgan led me to scattered copies of particular STC books in the Oxford college libraries; and the librarians at Queens, Corpus Christi, and Brasenose Colleges were most congenial. Ronald Tandy, of the Bodleian map room, shared his immense knowledge with me. Patricia Brown, Michael Bull, Colin Harris, and W. G. Harris patiently fetched numbers of books daily, handled xeroxing and microfilming, and found secure places of storage. The staffs of other central places of investigation over the past three years—the British Museum and the City and County Public Records Offices, London—were cheerful, efficient, and knowledgeable. While I was working at the Widener Library, Harvard, Wallace T. MacCaffrey provided suggestions which helped me to deal with unusually stubborn allusions. As always, Betty C. Hunt was generous with her time and knowledge.

My work has been financed in part by two Morse Research Fellowships awarded by Yale University and by a Faculty Growth Grant awarded by the University of Massachusetts. For three years four successive research assistants—Emanuel White, William G. Harney, Stephen L. O'Brien, and Jamie LeBlanc—checked and rechecked my collations and a number of my notes. Mary Jo Lynch did research which verified and supplemented my own. Senior fellowships from the Huntington Library in 1973 and the Folger Shakespeare Library in 1974 enabled me to accomplish final checking and revision; Dr. Robert Wark of the Huntington Art Gallery and Jean Preston, Curator of manuscripts at the Huntington, and Mary Robertson, Manuscripts Division, Huntington, provided helpful suggestions. William Ingoldstoy, Jr. Research Associate, Huntington, assisted with the illustrations and captions. Mrs. Joy Sylvester prepared the Index.

I ought also to thank Eggs and Poultry, an aging but indespensible Austin van, which transported me valiantly to a number of copies of STC books, manuscripts, and county and parish records; and the couple to whom the book is dedicated, for listening to me talk about it so frequently and for so long a time.

Finally, I want to take a leaf from Bacon's *Of the advancement and proficence of learning* (1640 edition)—the errata leaf, to be exact: "Textual Errors (Courteous Reader) is a work of time that hath taken wing. The more faults thou findest, the larger field is presented to thy humanity to practice in. Be indulgent in thy censure."

A.F.K.

Amherst, Massachusetts
June, 1974

BOOKS BY ARTHUR F. KINNEY
Elizabethan Backgrounds
Markets of Bawdrie: The Dramatic Criticism
    of Stephen Gosson
Titled Elizabethans: A Directory of Elizabethan
    State and Church Officers and Knights, with
    Peers of England, Scotland, and Ireland,
    1558-1603
Rogues, Vagabonds, and Sturdy Beggars
H.R.'s *Mythomytes*

Elizabethan Backgrounds

Proclamation
of Accession (1558)

       Just two or three hours after Mary Tudor's death on November 17, 1558, Nicholas Heath, her lord chancellor and archbishop of York, told a joint session of Parliament, "God this present morning hath called to His mercy our late Sovereign Lady, Queen Mary; which hap, as it is most heavy and grievous unto us, so have we no less cause another way to rejoice with praise to Almighty God, for that he hath left unto us a true, lawful and right inheritress to the Crown . . . which is the Lady Elizabeth . . . of whose most lawful right and title . . . we need not to doubt." These words were delivered by a staunch Catholic; but if he had misgivings over Elizabeth's religion, he did not reveal them. From the assembly the Lords proceeded first to the door of Westminster Hall, where Elizabeth was publicly proclaimed Queen, and then continued on to Cheapside Cross where, jostled in a crowded market square, they stood solemnly alongside Lord Mayor Thomas Leigh and his aldermen, resplendent in their scarlet robes of office. The proclamation reprinted here was again read to the great joy of the crowd.

       Elizabeth herself was not present. She was anxious about the reception of the announcement and she preferred to stay secure in the country at Hatfield House. She knew, of course, that she was the champion of the Protestants, but she did not know the comparative strength of the Catholics and she was apprehensive. After all, Mary Tudor had found it almost unbearably difficult to consider a Protestant succeeding her—even her own half-sister— and as late as March 1558 this ill woman was "thinking myself to be with child," so hopeful was she to insure the ideological and religious revolution her reign had brought about. Not until October 28, in fact, when she knew she was mortally ill, did she add a codicil referring to her "next heir and successor by the laws and statute of this realm"; and not until November 6, 1558, did she allow her Privy Council to send Elizabeth a message reporting that the Queen was content to have Lady Elizabeth succeed her. So Elizabeth remained at Hatfield, prepared for the worst, even appointing Thomas Markham, head of a band of 300 footmen at Berwick, to solicit troops in her behalf. She was also eager the following day, November 18, to accept the advice of her devoted servant Sir Nicholas Throckmorton. He urged her to retain Mary's Privy Councillors through the period of transition, pointing out that she would be well advised to make new appointments slowly so that neither "the old or new should wholly understand what you mean."

None of this anxiety could be conveyed by the proclamation of accession, of course, but it is perhaps not so routine as it first appears. The central appeal here, for example, to Elizabeth's claim to the throne as "the onely right heyre by bludde and lawfull succession," provides in concise and therefore powerful language her case against all Catholics who would wish to find her illegitimate. Moreover, this proclamation quite deliberately gives Elizabeth Tudor the title of "defendour of the fayth," a title earned for the Tudors by Henry VIII, while neglecting to assign it—again deliberately—to Mary. This is a clear indication that Elizabeth's government would be Protestant and provides the basis for the warning that occurs rather suddenly in the second paragraph, telling people "to kepe themselves in our peax." In both what it says and what it implies, then, this proclamation—despite its brevity—is not merely a formal state document, but a carefully worded political act.

TEXTUAL NOTES
[For explanation notes for this selection see page 361]

Proclamation of Accession

Reference. STC 7886-7887[1]; Steele, I, 493-494.[2]

Editions. The proclamation issued on Elizabeth's accession as Queen of England is extant in two editions printed by Richard Jugge. An unusually high frequency of changes in spelling and punctuation distinguishes the two typesettings. The proclamation is undated.

Collation. 1°; single broadsheet (folio).

Description of Contents. Heading, text, and colophon in blackletter; end matter in roman. Ornamental capital *E*.

License. No entry in the *Stationers' Register*.

Base-Copy Text. Bodleian Arch. G.c.6.(f. 1). Copy of second edition consulted: Queens College (Oxford) Sel. b. 320.

Textual Variants. No substantial variants; 77 incidental variants.

Emendations. None.

By the Quene's Majestie

LIZABETH BY THE GRACE of God Quene of Englande, Fraunce and Ireland, defendour of the fayth, &c. Because it hath pleased almightie God by calling to his mercie out of this mortall life to our greate grief our derest suster of noble memorie *Mary* late Quene of England, Fraunce and Ireland (Whose soule God have) to dispose and bestowe uppon us as the onely right heyre by bludde and lawfull succession the crowne of the foresayed kingdomes of England, Fraunce and Ireland, with all maner titles and rightes therunto in any wise apperteyning: We do publishe and give knowledge by this our Proclamacion to all maner peple being naturall subjectes of every the sayd kingdomes, that from the beginning of the .xvii. daye of this moneth of November, at whiche tyme our sayd derest suster departed from this mortall life, they be discharged of all bondes and duties of subjection towardes our sayd suster, and be from the same tyme in nature and lawe bounde only to us as to their only Soveraigne Lady and Quene: Wherwith we do by this our Proclamacion streightly chardge and allye them to us, promising on our parte no lesse love and care towards their preservacion, then hath been in any of our progenitours, and not doubting on their parte but they will observe the dyeuty whiche belongeth to naturall, good and true loving subjectes.

AND further we streightly charge and commaund, all maner our sayd subjectes of every degree, to kepe themselves in our peax, and not to attempt uppon anny pretence the breache, alteration or chaunge of any ordre or usage presently establyshed within this our Realme, uppon payn of our indignacion and the perilles and punishment which therto in anywise may belong.

God save the Quene.

Imprynted at London by Rychard Jugge Printer unto
the Quene's highnes.
Cum privilegio ad imprimendum solum.

The Quene's Majestie's
Passage (1559)

Shortly after she was named Queen, Elizabeth remarked that she wished "to do some act that would make her fame
spread abroad in her lifetime, and after, occasion memorial for ever."
To some extent, she succeeded in this as early as her unusually lavish
recognition-procession, which made its stately way through the streets
of London on January 14, 1559, the day before her coronation. For
this she had little or no precedent. The chronicler Edward Hall tells
us that Henry VIII and Catherine of Aragon rode through the city
with a splendid retinue while his freemen, organized by guilds, lined
the streets; Edward VI added for entertainment a foreign tight-rope
walker who descended from a church steeple. Only Mary Tudor had
had pageants—and God's plenty, according to the city's historian,
John Stow: a show at Fenchurch, erected by the Genoese; at the cor-
ner of Gracechurch Street, erected by Easterlings; at the upper end of
Grace Street, set up by Florentines; at the fountain in Cheap Street;
and by the little conduit in Cheap next to Paul's. The Florentines'
display consisted of four pictures overseen by an angel dressed in
green who pretended to blow a trumpet as Queen Mary passed; at the
pageant near Paul's, the City Recorder made a brief oration and the
city chamberlain presented the new Queen with a purse of cloth of
gold containing one thousand gold marks, a tradition Elizabeth would
continue (C3 below). At Cornhill and at Cheap Street, fountains ran
red with wine. In St. Paul's Churchyard the epigrammatist and play-
wright John Heywood sat under a vine and made his oration in both
Latin and English; and Peter, a Dutchman, emulated the earlier tight-
rope display. Final pageants were played against the Dean of Paul's
gate and at the Fleet Street conduit.

To Mary's series of formal entertainments, Elizabeth added the
shaping force of state propaganda. She could do this partly because
her very presence commanded admiration and wonder. On the Thursday before her processional, January 12, she made a spectacular journey down the Thames—compared by an Italian observer to Ascension

Day at Venice, her retinue was so grand—and went directly to the
Tower of London to prepare for her Saturday celebration. On the
morning of January 14, it snowed lightly; but long before two—when
her passage was scheduled to begin—her people lined the entire way.
In the processional the Queen, attired in royal robes of cloth of gold
and wearing her princess's crown, was carried on a litter and accompanied by one thousand people on horseback. Before her went her
household staff; lesser officers of state; the bench of bishops and temporal peers; foreign ambassadors; the king of arms; Arundel, as lord
steward, bearing the sword of state; Norfolk, as earl marshal; and
Oxford, as high constable. Elizabeth's litter was open, trimmed to
the ground with gold brocade, and borne by two mules which were
also covered with brocade. She was followed by Dudley, as master of
the horse, leading a spare mount; 39 ladies of honor, 24 on palfreys
and the rest in three chariots; wives and daughters of the chief peers;
henchmen; and royal guards. All about there were footmen in crimson
velvet jerkins with gilt silver and, on back and front, a white and red
rose with the letters E. R. She had made her point: there could not
have been greater splendor.

Yet meaning was conveyed in such majesty; the procession was a
political affair. Tableaux, interpreted in Latin speeches and boys'
recitals of rather stiff translations, insisted on Elizabeth's pure
English heritage. The live icons promoted her rightful claim to the
throne (A4-A4v) as an emblem of unity (A4v) and her support of a
divine Protestant authority, as the tablets of beatitudes suggest (C1-C2):
in both "a quene of worthy fame" (C1v) even before she was crowned.
She was also represented repeatedly as the champion of truth (C4-C4v;
E2), omitting any reference to Mary Tudor. Unhesitatingly *"Pure
Religion, Love of subjectes, Wisedome and Justice"* are here all rendered synonymous (B3v). The past—the War of the Roses suggested
at Gracechurch Street (A4-A4v) and Mary's *Ruinosa Respublica* displayed at Cheapside (C4)—results here in the new Queen herself and
her *Respublica bene instituta* (C4). Like Deborah, "judge and restorer
of the house of Israel" (D3v), she defeats the forces of darkness; and
like Deborah she promises to judge rightly "till fourty yeres were
past" (D3v), a close prophecy. This is because, as the second pageant
makes clear, her rule is grounded firmly in *Pure Religion.*

The proud count de Feria, come from Spain to marry a lady in
Mary's court, had visited Elizabeth at Hatfield on November 10, and
noted then, "She is very attached to the people and very confident
that they take her part, which is true." Elizabeth's responses gathered
up in the terminal comments of the pamphlet here reflect this basic
attitude of hers, but the author turns them, like the pageant, into
symbols which fuse with the entire day's presentations. The women
with nosegays, the sprig of rosemary (for remembrance: Elizabeth's
treatment of the gift corresponds neatly with that of the woman who

gave it), the joke about Henry VIII all are elevated to metaphors. The actual detail of the day—the dazzling color of flying banners, flags, and uniforms are given little attention (C3), and the noise, the confusion, and the milling crowds are not really mentioned at all. Rather, there is the grim note (in a day of celebration) about the city's poor. But all is finally subordinated to the Queen's devotion which, mirrored in the people's reverence for her, as God's anointed, becomes the structural motif of this carefully constructed work: even the narrative is abrogated so as to conclude with the Queen in prayer.

It is true that this pamphlet was for sale in Paul's Churchyard only ten days after the event, but it is nonetheless a painstaking effort. Besides theme and image it attempts something else. In its formulaic language, its patterned descriptions of the pageants and the audience's reaction, and its stylized presentation of events generally, it adopts the tone, style, and shape of the English chronicle. The author may have been George Ferrers (see textual note, below), but—whoever he was—he deliberately elevated one observer's report into a formal document of historical record.

TEXTUAL NOTES

[For explanation notes for this selection see page 361]

The Quene's Majestie's Passage
   Reference. STC 7590-7592.
   Authorship and Editions. The detailed description and record of Queen Elizabeth's journey through London on route to her coronation at Westminster has been attributed by Neville Williams in *Elizabeth: Queen of England* (London, 1967) to George Ferrers (p. 58), one of the participants. The account is extant in three early editions, two of them in 1558, the third following her reign in 1604. The first two editions are often confused, since the same date (January 23, 1558) appears in the colophon of both (E4v). Indeed, the distinction was not known—and only one edition was recorded—as late as 1890 for Quaritch's American Exhibition as noted by James Osborn in his textual introduction to the Yale edition (see listing below), p. 17. Further confusion may be caused by the fact that both editions collate precisely the same—quartos of five sheets each gathered and signed as A through E—and employ the same ornamental pieces for the title-page and the same ornamental initial on A2. In fact, the inner forme of sheet C was not reset for the second edition (although the

running-head for C2 and the signature, mistakenly C3 in the first
edition, were corrected): as with the pamphlet on the Low Countries
(see blow, p. 188) it is probable that the printers deliberately distributed the type and reset it for a job which required more copies
than they were willing to print from one typesetting. (This conclusion
differs from Osborn, pp. 21-22, who argues that the pamphlet was
more popular than Tottel anticipated; this is often advanced, but in
this instance dismisses what I feel is an obvious piece of propaganda
sanctioned if not directed by the Queen.)

Despite appearances it is not difficult to distinguish the two typesettings, either by the title-pages, which differ remarkably in early
wording of the title (Osborn argues, p. 22, that the revision was to aid
sales he has already stated to have exceeded expectations) and in the
listing of the causes of a ruinous commonwealth as they appeared in
one pageant (D1-D1v), four causes being given on D1 of Q1, all nine
listed on D1 in Q2. But these are exceptions, for Q2 is a line-for-line,
page-for-page reprint of Q1. Indeed, *than=* deliberately fills out a line
in Q2 (A2) and "and priuate comfort of y partie" of Q1 becomes
"& priuate comfort of the partie" in Q2 (A2v in both) to keep the lines
and pages identical. Such copying is nearly always faithful, but there
are exceptions—on A3 and A3v, where the setting of Q2 is page-for-
page but not line-for-line; on B1-B3 where the number of lines varies;
and on D1-D2 and D3-D3v. Given such similarity it is easy to demonstrate that Q2 was set from Q1 and not from manuscript.

It is also possible that there was authorial intervention, for amidst
the customarily large number of incidental variants of spelling and
punctuation (for the most part evenly spread, although gathering D
has remarkably fewer incidental variants throughout), there are substantial variants on A1, B1v, B2, B2v, B3, B4v (in the Latin), C4v, D1,
D1v, D3, D4, E2, and E3, with Q2 in all cases providing a superior
reading (see the listing below). The dropping of a line on B1v in Q2
clearly indicates which quarto must be Q1; and the varying number
of lines on various pages of Q2 so as to retain a line-for-line resetting
of Q1 provides corroborating evidence. The change on B3 ("vnder
their state" becomes "vnder their feete") suggests further that the
author had close knowledge of the Queen's processional, possibly
through observation, but more likely through the actual texts (for
he could not, after all, remember the exact wording of the signs and
speeches without them). The care taken in proofing is suggested by
such a change as "maister Parrat" to "Sir Iohn Parrat" on C4v (Parrat
had been made a Knight of the Bath in King Edward VI's reign) and
by "The" to "Thys" (D4). One superior reading ("shooting" becomes
"shoutyng") in Q2 is the only hint of oral transmission for Q1 of
those parts of the manuscript not given in plans and texts of particular
pageants. Q2 also cleans up an obvious typographical error on B3
("certaiue" becomes "certayne") but is inferior at one point on C4v

("this rocke" to "his rocke"). In each instance of differentiation, the superior reading is followed in the present text. The full listing of emendations of Q1 is given below.

The third quarto (STC 7592) dated 1604 is an obviously later reprinting from Q2. Undoubtedly published for commercial purposes by Joan Millington (whose name appears on the title-page), the work is retitled "The Royall Passage / of her Maiesty from the Tower of Lon- / don, to her Palace of White-Hall, with all the Speaches and / Deuices, both of the Pageants and otherwise, / together with her Maiesties seuerall Answers, / and most pleasing Speaches to them all" (A1). Printed in a smaller point size of black-letter so as to be completed on four sheets (in quarto), the pamphlet is made more attractive with a lovely illustration of an angel of annunciation on the title-page and by setting off, with separate headings, the Queen's speech and prayer (appearing on C3v and E4 of Q1) as well as the child's oration (D1v of Q1). Although Q3 follows the wording of Q2 carefully, it changes much of the spelling and punctuation (and is actually easier to follow) and in one instance—with the lines "Pure religiō, . . . write, *Pure*" on B3v of Q1—drops a line of type.

Pollard apparently lists a quarto no longer extant in an introduction to a reissue of Arber's *Garner* in 1903 (see below); he talks of a Q "printed by S. S. for John Bury" (p. xxix n.1), but does not elaborate. This would supply a textual link to Q3, however, since "S. S." also served as Joan Millington's printer (Q3, A1).

Subsequent Editions. There have been five subsequent editions of this text. John Nicholas reprinted it from Q2 in his *Progresses and Public Processions of Queen Elizabeth* (London, 1823), I, 38-60; he is not aware of Q1, but he does make note of Q3 (p. 38). Edward Arber reprinted the text in his *English Garner* (Birmingham, 1882), IV, 217-247, in a modernized text with notes in brackets but without commentary, reissued in *Tudor Tracts* with an introduction by A. F. Pollard (Westminster, 1903), pp. 365-395. In both, the base-text is a pirated copy, for it follows the reading of Q2 on A1 and B1v (omitting the dropped phrase) but "shooting" of Q1 on E2; perhaps the copy consulted was the one in the Guildhall Library mentioned by Professor Osborn (p. 18). The Yale Elizabethan Club has published a facsimile of Q1 and established its authenticity (New Haven, 1960); this is the fifth subsequent printing of the work: Holinshed also reprints it, IV, X3v-Z4v (pp. 158-176).

Collation. 4°; A-E⁴. A1, title-page; A1v, blank; A2-E4v, text.

Description of Contents. Title-page: mixture of roman and italic types within border illustration; text in black-letter with title and Latin passages in italics. Ornamental initial on A2. Colophon, E4v. No head-pieces or tail-pieces. Unpaginated. Running-head reads "The receiuing" and "of the Quenes maiestie." in italics on verso and recto pages respectively. No marginal notes.

License. To Richard Tottel without precise date (*SR* ed. Arber, I, 96).

Base Copy-Text for this Edition. Yale copy of Q1 privately owned by the Elizabethan Club of Yale University. This copy is unique and is erroneously considered Q2 (and listed as STC 7591) by the Old STC. A pirated copy with sheet E of Q1 (used by Arber; see above) is at the Guildhall Library, London.

Title-page in Full. "THE QVENES / *maiesties passage through the* / *citie of London to westmin-* / *ster the daye before her* / *corona-cion.* / Anno. 1558. / *Cum priuilegio*"

Substantial Variants. (a) Between Q1 and Q2, listed as Q1]Q2: (A1) *THE QUENE'S* / *Maiestie's passage through*] THE PASSAGE/ *of our most drad Soueraigne Lady* / *Quene Elyzabeth through* (B1v) which so was, and euery personage appointed](phrase omitted) (B2v) *hostibus placet.*]*hostibus patet.* (B3) other vyces]their contrarie vyces vices vnder their seate]vyces vnder their feete (B4v)*Effigies sanctae*] *Effigiam sancttae* (C4v)this rocke]his rocke by maister Parrat] by Sir John Parrat (D1) [causes are in different ordering, with fewer on D1 in Q1] (D1v) vertues to the suppression] vertue to the suppression (D3) curious, artificiall maner was] curious and artificiall maner, was (D4) The ground] Thys ground (E2) shooting and crieng] shoutyng and crying *Quum primam*]*Cum primam* (E3) al natural Englishmen]all Englishemen (b) Between Q1 and Q3, listed as Q1]Q3; copy of third edition used=Bodleian Wood 537(1): (title-page) as given above]The Royall Passage/of her Maiesty from the Tower of Lon-/ *don, to her Palace of White-hall, with all the Speaches and* / Deuices, both of the Pageants and otherwise, / *together with her Maiesties seuerall Answers,* / and most pleasing Speaches to / them all. / [illustration] / Imprinted at London by S. S. for Ione Millington, and are / to be sold at her shop vnder S. Peters Church in / Corne-hill. 1604. (A2) *The Receuing of the Quenes maiestie.*] *The receiuing of the Queenes Maiesty into the City of London.* (A2v) she ledeth] she leades partie]parties (B1v) her, which so was, and euery personage appointed, and what]her, and what By ring of mariage]By Ring in Mariage (B2) concerning vnite.]concerning vnitie. (B2v)*hostibus placet.*]*hostibus patet.* (B3) came to it.]came vnto it: chaire a seate royall]chayre or seate royall (B3v) *Pure religiō, Loue of subiectes, Wisedome and Iustice,* which did treade their contrarie vices vnder their feete, that is to write, *Pure*]*Pure* (B4) rightwisenes]righteousnes (B4v)*Effigies*]*Effigiem* effrenes,]effraenos, (C1v)made to his]made to the (C2v)tofore the little conduit,]before the little conduit, (C3v) these. I]these. *The Queenes Speach.* I (C4)commonweale.]commonwealth. (a common distinction here) and in Latine]and Latine (C4v) maister Parrat]Sir Iohn Parrat (D1)english vpon]englished vpon (D1v)toward Paules]towardes Paules foloweth. *Philosophus*]followeth: *The Oration. Philosophus* (D4)The ground]This ground (D4v) pray and criue vnto]pray vnto (E2)*potēs, quum*]*potens, Cum* (E3)al

natural Englishmen]all Englishmen   (E3v)so her harkening]so in her
harkening   (E4)in their seate]in their seats   glorie issueth,]glory en-
sueth: and sayd. O Lord,]and sayd: *The Queenes Prayer. O Lord,*
(E4v)Imprinted at London in fletestrete within Temple barre. at the
signe of the hand and starre, by Richard Tottill, the .xxiii. day of
Ianuary.]*FINIS.*[illustration]

Emendations of the First Edition for This Text. Listed as Q1]
emended text. (Note: "common weale] commonweale" has been used
throughout this text.)   (A2)thother syde]the other syde   her selfe]
herselfe   nolesse]no lesse   (A2v)in dede]indede   excading]exceding
thenemie]the enemie   (A3)ioyoussye]joyousslye   thesame.]the same.
(poem flush left)](poem slightly indented)   Welcowe to]Welcome
to   God   the]God   thee   (A4)thone]the   one   thother,]the   other,
wyfe daughter]wyfe, daughter   that thone]that the one   and thother
which]and the other which   (A4v)with thother,]with the other,
theight]the eight   theyght,]the eyght,   thestate]the estate   thother
prynces were.]the other prynces were.   (B1v)skace]skarce   abouenamed:]above named: abouenamed to open]above named to open
(poem set flush left)](poem indented)   Elsabeth]Elisabeth   sit]sit.
(B2)concerning   vnite.]concerning unitie.   (B2v)*pngnant diuitius*]
pugnant   diuitius Dissidentes]Discidentes   sulditorum]subditorum
ben theoccasion of]ben the occasion of   (B3)expounde thesame,]
expounde the same,   was exteuded]was extended   certaiue]certaine
thoneside]the one side   (B3v)   (poem flush left)](poem indented)
(B4)while follie]While follie   that good]That good   (B4v)*Effigies*]
Effigiam relligine]relligione   fast in thesame]fast in the same   (C1)
thone syde]the one syde   to thother,]to the other,   thother tofore]
the other tofore Ladie Q uene Elizabeth]Ladie Quene Elizabeth (C1v)
theyght blessinges]the eyght blessinges   [C2]on thother syde]on the
other   syde   Chepe   syde.]Chepesyde.   (C2v)neare   vnto   thesame]
neare unto the same   pageaunt But]pageaunt. But   thaldermen]
the aldermen   (C3v)your selues]yourselves,   before   thesame]before
the same   in thesame]in the same   thesame pageaunt]the same
pageaunt   thesame tree]the same tree   (C4v)vppon thesame]uppon
the same   on thesame was erected]on the same was erected   vppon
thesame tree]uppon the same tree   C4v)thesame pageant.]the same
pageant.   (D1)maiestrats]majestrats.   (D1v)in subiectes]in subjectes.
cōmon weale]commonweale.   church-yard]churchyard.   (D2v)*Elizabeth Regni*]*Elizabeth Regni* (but correction precludes line from scan-
ning properly)   receiued thesame.]received the same.   (D3)consider
thesame,]consider the same,   (D3v)this sort.]this sort,   (D4)of thospi-
tall]of the hospitall   (D4v)delared]declared   wasthe euerlasting]was
theeverlasting   wherein thesame]wherein the same   (E1)theffect of al]
the effect of al   (E1v)graund father]graundfather   (E2)the strong]
thee strong to heauen warde]to heavenwarde   (E2v)of it selfe beautifyed it selfe,]of itselfe beautifyed itselfe,   shewed her selfe]shewed her-

selfe   prince   lyke]princelyke   (E3)confirme   thesame,]confirme   the
same,   expressed thesame.]expressed the same.   Henry theight.]Henry
the eight.   thesame.]the same.   (E3v)to their, so]to their so   pronounced thesame.]pronounced the same. (no paragraph)](paragraph
begun with "What more")   (E4)her selfe prepared]herselfe prepared
bownd her selfe]bownd herselfe   she her selfe]she herselfe shew her
selfe]shew herselfe   other. two]other. Two   (E4v)for euer.]forever.

The Quene's Majestie's passage
through the citie of London to westminster
the daye before her coronacion

 PON SATURDAY, which was the xiiii. day of Jan-
uarie in the yere of our Lord God .1558. about .ii. of
the clocke at after noone, the most noble, and christian princesse, our moste dradde soveraigne Ladie
Elizabeth by the grace of god Queen of England,
Fraunce and Ireland, defendour of the faythe &c.
marched from the towre to passe through the citie of London towarde
Westminster, richely furnished, and most honorablye accompanied, as
wel with gentlemen, Barons, and other the nobilitie of thys realme, as
also with a notable trayne of goodly and beawtiful ladies, richely appoynted. And entring the citie was of the people received merveylous
entierly, as appeared by the assemblie, prayers, wisshes, welcomminges,
cryes, tender woordes, and all other signes, whiche argue a wonderfull
earnest love of most obedient subjectes towarde theyr soveraygne. And
on the other syde her grace by holding up her handes, and merie
countenaunce to such as stoode farre of, and most tender and gentle
language to those that stode nigh to her grace, did declare herselfe
no lesse thankefullye to receive her people's good wille, than they
lovingly offred it unto her. To all that wished her grace wel, she gave
heartie thankes, and to suche as bade God save her grace, she sayd
agayn god save them all, and thanked them with all her heart. So that
on eyther syde ther was nothing but gladnes, nothing but prayer, [A2v]
nothing but comfort. The Quene's majestie rejoysed merveylouslye
to see, that, so excedingly shewed toward her grace, which all good
princes have ever desyred, I meane so earnest love of subjectes, so
evidently declared even to her grace's own persone being caried in

the middest of them. The people again wer wonderfully ravished with
the loving answers and gestures of their princesse, like to the which
they had before tryed at her first coming to the towre from Hatfield.
This her grace's loving behaviour preconceived in the people's heades
upon these consideracions was then throughly confirmed, and in dede
emplanted a woonderfull hope in them touching her woorthie
government in the rest of her reygne. For in all her passage she did
not only shew her most gracious love toward the people in generall,
but also privately if the baser personages had either offred her grace
any flowres or such like as a significacion of their good will, or moved
to her any sute, she most gently, to the common rejoysing of all the
lookers on, and private comfort of the partie, staid her chariot, and
heard theyr requestes. So that if a man should say well, he could not
better tearme the citie of London that time, than a stage wherin was
shewed the wonderfull spectacle, of a noble hearted princesse toward
her most loving people, and the people's exceding comfort in beholding so worthy a soveraign, and hearing so princelike a voice which
could not but have set the enemie on fyre, since the vertue is in the
enemie alway commended, much more could not [A3] but enflame her
naturall, obedient, and most lovyng people, whose weale leaneth onely
uppon her grace, and her governement. Thus therefore the queene's
majestie passed from the Towre tyll she came to Fanchurche, the
people on eche syde joyousslye beholding the viewe of so gracious a
Ladie their quene, and her grace no lesse gladlye notyng and obser-
vynge the same. Nere unto Fanchurch was erected a scaffold richely
furnished, wheron stode a noyes of instrumentes, and a child in costly
apparel, which was appointed to welcome the quene's majestie in the
hole citie's behalfe. Against which place when her grace came, of her
own wille she commaunded the chariot to be staide, and that the noyes
might be appeased till the child had uttered his welcomming oration,
which he spake in English meter as here foloweth.

O pereles soveraygne quene, behold what this thy town
Hath thee presented with at thy fyrst entraunce here:
Behold with how riche hope she ledeth thee to thy crown
Beholde with what two gyftes she comforteth thy chere.

The first is blessing tonges, which many a welcome say
Which pray thou maist do wel, which praise the to the skie
Which wish to the long lyfe, which blesse this happy day
Which to thy kingdome heapes, all that in tonges can lye.

The second is true hertes, which love thee from their roote
Whose sute is tryumphe now, and ruleth all the game.
Which faithfulnes have wonne, and al untruthe driven out,
Which skip for joy, when as they heare thy happy name.

Welcome therfore O quene, as much as hert can thinke,
Welcome agayn O quene, as much as tong can tell:
Welcome to joyous tonges, and hertes that wil not shrink,
God thee preserve we praye, and wishe thee ever well.   [A3v]

At which wordes of the last line the hole peple gave a great shout,
wishing with one assent as the childe had said. And the quene's majestie thanked most hartely both the citie for this her gentle receiving at
the first, and also the peple for confirming the same. Here was noted
in the Quene's majestie's countenance, during the time that the childe
spake, besides a perpetual attentiveness in her face, a mervelous
change in looke, as the childe's wordes touched either her person or
the people's tonges and hertes. So that she with rejoysing visage did
evidently declare that the woordes tooke no lesse place in her mynde,
than they were moste heartelye pronounced by the chylde, as from all
the heartes of her most heartie citizeins. The same verses wer fastned
up in a table upon the scaffolde, and the latine therof likewise in
latine verses in another table as hereafter enseweth.

Vrbs tua quae ingressu dederit tibi munera primo,
  O Regina parem non habitura, vide.
Ad diadema tuum, te spe quám diuite mittat,
  Quae duo laetitae det tibi dona, vide.
Munus habes primum, linguas bona multa precantes,
  Quae te quum laudant, tum pia vota sonant,
Foelicemque diem hunc dicunt, tibi secula longa
  Optant, et quicquid denique lingua potest.
Altera dona feres, vera, et tui amantia corda,   [A4]
  Quorum gens ludum iam regit vna tuum:

In quibus est infracta fides, falsumque perosa,
  Quaequm tuo audito nomine laeta salit
Grata venis igitur, quantum cor concipit ullum,
  Quantum lingua potest dicere, grata venis.
Cordibus infractis, linguisque per omnia laetis
  Grata venis: saluam te velit esse deus.

Now when the childe had pronounced his oration, and the Quene's highnes so thankefully had received it, she marched forwarde towarde gracious streate, where at the upper ende, before the sygne of the Egle, the citie had erected a gorgeous and sumptuous arke as here foloweth.

A stage was made whiche extended from the one syde of the streate to the other, rychelye vawted with batlementes conteining three portes, and over the middlemost was avaunced .iii. severall stages in degrees. Upon the lowest stage was made one seate royall, wherin wer placed two personages representing kynge Henrie the seventh and Elizabeth hys wyfe, daughter of king Edward the fourth, eyther of these two princes sitting under one cloth of estate in their seates, no otherwyse divyded, but that the one of them which was king Henrie the seventh proceding out of the house of Lancastre, was enclosed in a read rose, and the other which was Queene Elizabeth being heire to the house of Yorke enclosed with [A4v] a whyte rose, eche of them royallie crowned, and decently apparailled as apperteineth to princes, with Sceptours in their handes, and one vawt surmounting their heades, wherin aptlie wer placed two tables, eche conteining the tytle of those two princes. And these personages wer so set, that the one of them joyned handes with the other, with the ring of matrimonie perceived on the finger. Out of the which two roses sprang two braunches gathered into one, which wer directed upward to the second stage or degree, wherin was placed one, representing the valiant and noble prynce king Henrie the eight which sprong out of the former stocke, crowned with a crowne imperiall, and by him sate one representing the right worthie ladie quene Anne, wife to the said king Henrie the eyght, and mother to our most soveraign ladie quene Elizabeth that now is, both apparelled with Sceptours and diademes, and other furniture due to the estate of a king and quene and ii. tables surmounting their heades, wherein were written their names and tytles. From their seate also proceaded upwardes one braunche directed to the third and uppermost stage or degree, wherin lykewyse was planted a seate royall, in the whiche was sette one representynge the Quene's most excellent majestie Elizabeth nowe our most dradde soveraygne Ladie, crowned and apparelled as the other prynces were. Oute of the forepart of thys pageaunt was made a standyng for a chylde, whiche at the quene's majestie's comyng declared unto her the hole meaning of the said pageaunt. The two sydes of the [Bl] same were filled with loude noyses of musicke. And all emptie places thereof were furnished with sentences concerning unitie. And the hole pageant garnished with redde roses and white and in the forefront of the same pageant in a faire wreathe was written the name, and title of the same, which was *The uniting of the two houses of Lancastre and Yorke*. This pageant was grounded upon the Queene's majestie's name. For like as the long warre betwene the two houses of Yorke and Lancastre then ended, when Elizabeth doughter to Edwarde the fourthe matched in mariage wyth Henry the seventhe heyre to the howse of Launcaster: so synce that the Queene's majestie's name was Elizabeth, and forsomuch as she is the onelye heire of Henrie the eyght, which came of bothe the houses as the knitting up of concorde, it was devised that like as Elizabeth was the first occasion of concorde, so she another Elizabeth might maintaine the same among her subjectes, so that unitie was the ende wherat the whole devise shotte, as the Queene's majestie's names moved the firste grounde. This pageant now against the Quene's majestie's comming was addressed with children representing the forenamed personages, with all furniture dew unto the setting forthe of such a matter well ment, as the argument declared, costly and sumptuouslye set forthe, as the beholders can beare witnes. Now the Queene's ma- [Blv] jestye drewe nere unto the sayde pageant, and forsomuch as the noyse was great by reason of the prease of people, so that she could skarce heare the childe which did interprete the saide pageant, and her chariot was passed so farre forward that she could not well view the personages representing the kinges and Queenes above named: she required to have the matter opened unto her, which so was, and every personage appointed, and what they signified, with the ende of unitie and ground of her name, according as is before expressed. For the sight wherof, her grace caused her chariot to be removed back, and yet hardly coulde she see, because the children were set somewhat with the farthest in. But after that her grace had understode the meaning therof, she thanked the citie, praised the fairenes

of the worke, and promised, that she would doe her whole endevour
for the continuall preservacion of concorde, as the pageant did em-
porte. The childe appointed in the standing above named to open the
meaning of the said pageant, spake these wordes unto her grace.

The two princes that sit under one cloth of state,
The man in the red rose, the woman in the white:
Henry the .vii. And Queene Elizabeth his mate,
By ryng of mariage as man and wife unite.

Both heires to both their bloodes, to Lancastre the king
The Queene to Yorke, in one the two houses did knit,
Of whom as heire to both, Henry the eyght did spring,
In whose seat his true heire thou quene Elisabeth dost sit. [B2]

Therfore as civill warre, and shede of blood did cease
When these two houses were united into one
So now that jarre shall stint, and quietnes encrease,
We trust, O noble Queene, thou wilt be cause alone.

The which also were written in laten verses, and bothe drawen in
two tables uppon the forefront of the sayde pageant as hereafter
foloweth.

Hii quos iungit idem solium quos annulus idem:
Haec albente nitens, ille rubente Rosa:
Septimus Henricus Rex, Regina Elizabetha,
Scilicet Haeredes gentis vterque suae:
Haec Eboracensis, Lancastrius ille dederunt
Connubio, e geminis quo foret vna domus
Excipit hos haeres Henricus copula regum
Octauus, magni Regis imago potens
Regibus hinc succedis auis, Regique parenti
Patris iusta haeres Elizabetha tui.

Sentences placed therin concerning unitie.

Nullae concordes animos vires domant.
Qui iuncti terrent, deiuncti timent. [B2v]

Discordes animi soluunt, concordes ligant.
Augentur parua pace, magna bello cadunt.
Coniunctae manus fortius tollunt onus.
Regno pro menibus aeneis ciuium concordia.
Qui diu pugnant diutius lugent.
Discidentes principes subditorum lues.
Princeps ad pacem natus non ad arma datur
Filia concordiae copia, neptis quies.
Dissentiens respublica hostibus placet.
Qui idem tenent, diutius tenent.
Regnum diuisum facile dissoluitur.
Ciuitas concors armis frustra tentatur.
Omnium gentium consensus firmat fidem. &c.

These verses and other pretie sentences were drawen in voide places of this pageant, all tending to one ende that quietnes might be mainteined, and all dissention displaced, and that by the Queene's majestie, heire to agrement, and agreing in name with her, which tofore had joyned those houses, which had ben the occasion of much debate and civill warre within this realme, as maye apeare to soche, as will search cronicles, but be not to be touched in this treatise onely declaring her grace's passage through the citie, and what provision the citie made therfore. And ere the Quene's majestie came within hearing of this pageant, she sent certaine as also at all the other pageants [B3] to require the people to be silent for her majestie was disposed to heare all that shold be said unto her.

When the Queene's majestie had hearde the childe's oracion, and understode the meaning of the pageant at large, she marched forward toward Cornehill, alway received with like rejoising of the people, and there as her grace passed by the conduit which was curiouslye trimmed against that time with riche banners adourned, and a noyse of loude instrumentes upon the top therof, she espied the seconde pageant, and because shee feared for the people's noyse, that she should not here the child which did expounde the same, she enquired what that pageant was ere that she came to it. And there understode, that there was a childe representing her majestie's person, placed in a seate of governement, supported by certaine vertues, which suppressed other vices under their seate, and so forthe, as in the description of the said pageant shall hereafter apeare.

This pageant standing in the nether ende of Cornehill was extended from the one side of the strete to the other, and in the same
pageant was devised three gates all open, and over the middle parte
therof was erected one chaire a seate royall with clothe of estate to the
same apperteyning wherein was placed a childe representing the
Queene's highnesse with consideracion had for place convenient for a
table which conteined her name and title. And in a comelie wreathe
artifi- [B3v] cially and wel devised with perfite sight and understanding to the people. In the front of the same pageant was written the
name and title therof, which is *The seate of worthie governance,*
which seate was made in such artificiall maner, as to the apperance
of the lookers on, the foreparte semed to have no staie, and therfore of
force was stayed by lively personages, which personages were in numbre foure, standing and staieng the forefront of the same seate royal,
eche having his face to the Quene and people, wherof every one had a
table to expresse their effectes, which are vertues, namelie *Pure religion, Love of subjectes, Wisedome and Justice,* which did treade their
contrarie vices under their feete, that is to witte, *Pure religion,* did
treade uppon *Superstition,* and *Ignoraunce, Love of subjectes,* did
treade upon *Rebellion* and *Insolencie, Wisedome* did treade upon
follie and *vaine glorie, Justice* did treade upon *Adulacion* and *Briberie.* Eche of these personages according to their proper names and
properties, had not onlie their names in plaine and perfit writing set
upon their breastes easelie to be read of all, but also every of them
was aptelie and properlie apparelled, so that his apparell and name
did agre to expresse the same person, that in title he represented.
Thys part of the pageant was thus appointed and furnished. The two
sides over the two side portes had in them placed a noyse of instrumentes, which immediatlie, after the childe's speache gave an heavenly
melodie. Upon the top or [B4] uppermost part of the said pageant,
stoode the armes of England roially portratured with the proper
beastes to upholde the same. One representing the Quene's highnes
sate in this seate crowned with an Imperiall crowne, and before her
seate, was a convenient place appointed for one childe which did
interpret and applie the said pageant as hereafter shalbe declared.
Every voide place was furnished with proper sentences commending
the seate supported by vertues, and defacing the vices, to the utter
extirpation of rebellion, and to everlasting continuance of quietnes
and peace. The Queene's majestie approching nighe unto thys pageant

thus bewtified and furnished in all pointes, caused her charyot to be
drawen nyghe thereunto, that her grace myght heare the childe's
oration whych was thys.

While that religion true, shall ignorance suppresse
And with her weightie foote, breake superstitions heade
While love of subjectes, shall rebellion distresse
And with zeale to the prince, insolencie down treade.

While justice, can flattering tonges and briberie deface
While follie and vaine glory to wisedome yelde their handes
So long shal government, not swarve from her right race
But wrong decayeth still, and rightwisenes up standes.

Now all thy subjectes' hertes, O prince of perles fame
Do trust these vertues shall maintein up they throne,
And vice be kept down still, the wicked put to shame
That good with good may joy, and naught with naught may mone. [B4v]

Which verses were painted upon the right side of the same pageant,
and the latin therof on the left side in another table, which were these.

Quae subnixa alte solio regina superbo est,
  Effigiam sanctae principis alma refert,
Quam ciuilis amor fulcit, sapientia firmat,
  Iusticia illustrat, Relligioque beat.
Vana superstitio et crassae ignorantia frontis
  Pressae sub pura relligione iacent.
Regis amor domat effraenes, animosque rebelles
  Iustus adulantes, Doniuorosque terit.
Cum regit imperium sapiens, sine luce sedebunt
  Stultitia, atque huius numen inanis honor.

Beside these verses there were placed in every voide rome of the
pageant both in English and laten such sentences as advaunced the
seate of governaunce upholden by vertue. The grounde of this pageant,
was that like as by vertues (which doe aboundantly appere in her
grace) the Queene's majestie was established in the seate of governement: so she should syt fast in the same so long as she embraced vertue

and helde vice under foote. For if vice once gotte up the head, it woulde put the seate of governement in perill of falling. The Queene's majestie when she had heard the childe and understode the pageant at full, gave [C1] the citie also thankes there, and most graciouslie promised her good endevour for the maintenance of the sayde vertues, and suppression of vyces, and so marched on till she came against the great conduit in chepe, which was bewtifyed with pictures and sentences accordingly agaynst her grace's coming thither.

Against Soper lane's ende was extended from the one syde of the streate to the other, a pageant which had three gates all open. Over the middlemoste wherof wer erected three severall stages, whereon sate eight children as hereafter foloweth. On the uppermost one childe, on the middle three, on the lowest, iiii, eche having the proper name of the blessing, that they did represent, writen in a table and placed above their heades. In the forefront of this pageant before the children which did represent the blessinges, was a convenient standing cast out for a chylde to stande, which did expound the said pageaunt unto the quene's majestie, as was done in the other tofore. Everie of these children wer appointed and apparelled according unto the blessing which he did represent. And on the forepart of the said pageant was written in fayre letters the name of the said pageant in this maner folowing.

The eight beatitudes expressed in the .v. chapter of the gospel of S. Mathew, applyed to our soveraigne Ladie Quene Elizabeth.

Over the two side portes was placed a noyes of instrumentes. And all voide places in the pageant [C1v] wer furnished with pretty sayinges, commending and touching the meaning of the said pageant, which was the promises and blessinges of almightie god made to his people. Before that the quene's highnes came unto this pageant, she required the matter somewhat to be opened unto her, that her grace might the better understand, what should afterward by the child be sayd unto her. Which so was, that the citie had there erected the pageant with .viii. children, representing the eyght blessinges touched in the .v. Chapiter of S. Mathew. Wherof, every one upon just consideracions was applyed unto her highnes, and that the people therby put her grace in mind, that as her good doinges before had geven just occasion, why that these blessinges might fall upon her, that so if her grace did continue in her goodnes as she had entred, she shoulde hope for the fruit of these promises due unto them, that doe exercise themselves in the blessinges, whiche her grace heard merveilous graciously, and required that the chariot myght be removed towardes the pageaunt, that she might perceyve the chylde's woordes, which were these, the Quene's majestie geving most attentive eare, and requiring that the people's noyse might be stayde.

Thou hast been .viii. times blest, o quene of worthy fame
By mekenes of thy spirite, when care did thee besette
By mourning in thy griefe, by mildnes in thy blame
By hunger and by thyrst, and justice couldst none gette.

By mercy shewed, not felt, by cleanes of thyne harte
By seking peace alwayes, by persecucion wrong.
Therfore trust thou in god, since he hath helpt thy smart
That as his promis is, so he will make thee strong. [C2]

When these woordes were spoken, all the people wished, that as the child had spoken, so god woulde strengthen her grace against all her adversaries, whom the Quene's majestie did most gently thanke for their so loving wishe. These verses wer painted on the left syde of the said pageant, and other in laten on the other syde, which wer these.

Qui lugent hilares fient, qui mitia gestant
   Pectora, multa soli iugera culta metent
Iustitiam esuriens sitiensue replebitur, ipsum.
   Fas homini puro corde videre deum
Quem alterius miseret dominus miserebitur huius,
   Pacificus quisquis, filius ille Dei est.
Propter iustitiam quisquis patietur habetque
   Demissam mentem, caelica regna capit.
Huic hominum generi terram, mare, sidera vouit
   Omnipotens, horum quisque beatus erit.

Besides these, every voide place in the pageant was furnished with sentences touching the matter and ground of the said pageant. When all that was to be said in this pageant was ended, the Quene's majestie passed on forward in Chepesyde.

At the standarde in Cheape which was dressed fayre agaynste the tyme, was placed a noyse of Trumpettes, with banners and other furniture. The Crosse lykewyse was also made fayre and [C2v] well trymmed.

And neare unto the same, uppon the porche of Saint Peter's church dore, stode the waites of the citie, which did geve a pleasant noyse with theyr instrumentes as the Quene's majestie did passe by, which on everie syde cast her countenaunce, and wished well to all her most loving people. Sone after that her grace passed the crosse, she had espyed the pageant erected at the litle conduit in cheape, and incontinent required to know what it might signifye. And it was tolde her grace, that there was placed Tyme. Tyme? sayth she, and Tyme hath brought me hether. And so furth the hole matter was opened to her grace as hereafter shalbe declared in the descripcion of the pageaunt. But in the openyng, when her grace understoode that the Byble in Englishe shoulde be delivered unto her by Truth, whiche was therein represented by a childe: she thanked the citie for that gift, and sayd that she would oftentimes reade over that booke, commaunding sir John Parrat, one of the knightes which helde up her canapy, to goe before and to receive the booke. But learning that it should be delivered unto her grace downe by a silken lace, she caused him to staye, and so passed forward till she came agaynste the aldermen in the hyghe ende of Chepe tofore the little conduite, where the companies of the citie ended, which beganne at Fanchurch, and stoode alonge the streates one by another enclosed with rayles, hanged with clothes, and themselves well apparelled with many ryche [C3] furres and theyr livery whodes upon theyr shoulders in comely and semely maner, having before them sondry persones well apparelled in silkes and chaines of golde, as wyflers and garders of the said companies, beside a numbre of riche hangynges, aswell of Tapistrie, Arras, clothes of golde, silver, velvet, damaske, Sattyn, and other silkes plentifully hanged all the way as the Quene's highnes passed from the Towre through the citie. Out at the windowes and penthouses of everie house, did hang a number of ryche and costlye banners and streamers tyll her grace came to the upper ende of Cheape. And there, by appointment, the right worshipfull maister Ranulph Cholmley, Recorder of the citie, presented to the Quene's majestie a purse of crimosin sattin richly wrought with gold, wherin the citie gave unto the Quene's majestie a thousand markes in gold, as maister Recorder did declare brieflye unto the Quene's majestie, whose wordes tended to this ende, that the Lord maior, hys brethren, and comminaltie of the citie, to declare their gladnes and good wille towardes the Quene's majestie, did present her grace with that gold, desyeing her grace to

continue their good and gracious Quene, and not to esteme the value
of the gift, but the mynd of the gevers. The Quene's majestie with both
her handes tooke the purse, and aunswered to him againe merveilous
pithilie, and so pithilie that the standers by, as they embraced entierly
her gracious aunswer, so they mer- [C3v] vailed at the cowching therof, which was in wordes truely reported these. I thanke my lord maior,
his brethren, and you all. And wheras your request is that I should
continue your good ladie and quene, be ye ensured, that I wil be as
good unto you, as ever quene was to her people. No wille in me can
lacke, neither doe I trust shall ther lacke any power. And perswade
yourselves, that for the safetie and quietnes of you all, I will not spare,
if nede be to spend my blood, God thanke you all. Whiche aunswere
of so noble an hearted pryncesse, if it moved a mervaylous showte and
rejoysing, it is nothyng to be mervayled at, since both the heartines
thereof was so woonderfull, and the woordes so joyntly knytte. When
her grace hadde thus aunswered the Recorder, she marched toward
the little conduit, where was erected a pageaunt with square propor-
cion, standynge directlye before the same conduite, with battlementes
accordynglye. And in the same pageaunt was advaunced two hylles
or mountaynes of convenient heyghte. The one of them beyng on the
North syde of the same pageaunt, was made cragged, barreyn, and
stonye, in the whiche was erected one tree, artificiallye made, all
withered and deadde, with braunches accordinglye. And under the
same tree at the foote thereof, sate one in homely and rude apparell
crokedlye, and in mournyng maner, havynge over hys headde in a
table, written in Laten and Englyshe, hys name, whiche was *Ruinosa
Respublica*, A decay- [C4] ed common weale. And uppon the same
withered tree were fixed certayne Tables, wherein were written proper
sentences, expressing the causes of the decaye of a commonweale. The
other hylle on the South syde was made fayre, freshe, grene, and
beawtifull, the grounde thereof full of flowres and beawtie, and on
the same was erected also one tree very freshe and fayre, under the
whiche, stoode uprighte one freshe personage well apparaylled and
appoynted, whose name also was written bothe in Englishe and in
Laten, which was, *Respublica bene instituta*. A florishyng commonweale. And uppon the same tree also, were fixed certayne Tables conteyning sentences, which expressed the causes of a flourishing commonweale. In the middle betwene the sayde hylles, was made artificiallye
one hollowe place or cave, with doore and locke enclosed, oute of the

whiche, a lyttle before the Queene's hyghnes commynge thither,
issued one personage whose name was *Tyme*, apparaylled as an olde
man with a Sythe in his hande, havynge wynges artificiallye made,
leadinge a personage of lesser stature then himselfe, whiche was fynely
and well apparaylled, all cladde in whyte silke, and directlye over
her head was set her name and tytle in latin and Englyshe, *Temporis
filia*, the daughter of Tyme. Which two so appoynted, went forwarde,
toward the South syde of the pageant. And on her brest was written
her propre name, which was [C4v] *Veritas.* Trueth who helde a booke
in her hande upon the which was written, *Verbum veritatis*, the
woorde of trueth. And out of the South syde of the pageaunt was
cast a standynge for a chylde which should enterpret the same pageant.
Against whom, when the Quene's majestie came: he spake unto her
grace these woordes.

This olde man with the sythe, old father tyme they call,
And her his daughter Truth, whiche holdeth yonder boke
Whom he out of this rocke hath brought furth to us all
From whence this many yeres she durst not once out loke.

The ruthfull wight that sitteth under the barren tree,
Resembleth to us the fourme, when common weales decay
But when they be in state tryumphant, you may see
By him in freshe attyre that sitteth under the baye.

Now since that Time again his daughter truth hath brought,
We trust O worthy quene, thou wilt this truth embrace.
And since thou understandst the good estate and nought
We trust welth thou wilt plant, and barrennes displace.

But for to heale the sore, and cure that is not seene,
Which thing the boke of truth doth teache in writing plain:
She doth present to thee the same, O worthy Queene,
For that, that wordes do flye, but wryting doth remayn.

When the childe had thus ended his speache, he reached hys boke
towardes the Quene's majestie, which a little before, Trueth had let
downe unto him from the hill, whiche by maister Parrat was received,
and delivered unto the Quene. But she as soone as she had received

the booke, kyssed it, and with both her handes help up the same, and
so laid it upon her brest, with great thankes to the ci-[D1] tie therfore.
And so went forward towards Paule's churchyarde. The former matter
which was rehersed unto the Queene's majestie was written in two
tables, on either side the pageant eight verses, and in the middest,
these in laten.

Ille, vides falcem laeua qui sustinet vncam,
  Tempus is est, cui stat filia vera comes
Hanc pater exesa deductam rupe reponit
  In lucem, quam non viderat ante diu
Qui sedet a laeua cultu male tristis inepto
  Quem duris crescens cautibus orbis obit
Nos monet effigie, qua sit respublica quando
  Corruit, at contra quando beata viget.
Ille docet iuuenis forma spectandus amictu
  Scitus, et aeterna laurea fronde virens.

The sentences written in latin and englishe upon both the trees,
declaring the causes of both estates, were these.

Causes of a ruinous commonweale are these.

Want of the feare of god.	*Blindnes of guides.*
Disobedience to rulers.	*Briberie in majestrats.* [D1v]
Rebellion in subjectes.	*Unmercifullnes in rulers.*
Civill disagrement.	*Unthankfulnes in subjectes.*
Flattring of princes.	

Causes of a florishing commonweale.

Feare of god.	*Obedient subjectes.*
A wise prince.	*Lovers of the commonweale.*
Learned rulers.	*Vertue rewarded.*
Obedience to officers.	*Vice chastened.*

The mater of this pageant dependeth of them that went before. For as
the first declared her grace to come out of the house of unitie, the
second that she is placed in the seate of government staied with vertues to the suppression of vice, and thefore in the third the eight blessinges of almighty god might well be applied unto her: so this fourth

now is, to put her grace in remembrance of the state of the commonweale, which Time with Truth his doughter doth revele, which Truth
also her grace hath received, and therfore cannot but be merciful and
careful for the good government therof. From thence the Quene's
majesty passed toward Paule's churchyard. And when she came over
against Paule's scole, a childe appointed by the scolemaster therof
pronounced a certein oracion in latin, and certain verses, which also
wer there written as foloweth.

*Philosophus ille diuinus Plato inter multa preclare ac sapienter
dicta, hoc posteris proditum reliquit, Rempub: illam, faelicissimam
fore, cui princeps sophiae studiosa, virtutibusque ornata contigerit.
Quem [D2] si vere dixisse censeamus (vt quidem verissme) cur non
terra Britannica plauderet? cur non populus gaudium atque laetitiam
agitaret? immo, cur non hunc diem albo (quod aiunt) lapillo notaret?
quo princeps talis nobis adest, qualem priores non viderunt, qualem-
que posteritas haud facile cernere poterit, dotibus quum animi, tum
corporis undique faecilissima. Casti quidem corporis dotes ita apertae
sunt, vt oratione non egeant. Animi vero tot tantaeque, vt ne verbis
quidem exprimi possint. Haec nempe Regibus summis orta, morum
atque animi nobilitate genus exuperat. Huius pectus Cristi religionis
amore flagrat. Haec gentem Britannicam virtutibus illustrabit, clipeo-
que iustitiae teget. Haec literis graecis et latinis eximia, ingenioque
prepollens est. Hac imperante pietas vigebit, Anglia florebit, aurea
secula redibunt. Vos igitur Angli tot commoda accepturi Elizabetham
Reginam nostram celeberrimam ab ipso Christo huibus regni imperio
destinatam, honore debito prosequimini. Huius imperiis animo liben-
tissimo subditiestote, vosque tali principe dignos prebete. Et quoniam
pueri non viribus sed precibus officium prestare possunt, nos Alumni
huius scholae ab ipso Coleto olim Templi Paulini Decano, extructae,
teneras palmas ad caelum tendentes Christum Opt: Maxi: precaturi
sumus vt tuam celsitudinem annos Nestoreos summo cum honore
Anglis imperitare faciat, matremque pignoribus charis beatam reddat.
Amen. [D2v]*

*Anglia nunc tandem plaudas, laetare, re sulta,
  Presto iam vita est, praesidiumque tibi
En tua spes venit tua gloria, lux, decus omne
Venit iam solidam quae tibi prestat opem.*

Succurretque tuis rebus quae pessum abiere.
  Perdita quae fuerant haec reparare volet
Omnia florebunt, redeunt nunc aurea secla.
  In melius surgent quae cecidere bona.
Debes ergo illi totam te reddere fidam
  Cuius in accessu commoda tot capies.
Salue igitur dicas, imo de pectore summo.
  Elizabetha Regni non dubitanda salus,
Virgo venit, veniatque optes comitata deinceps.
  Pignoribus charis, laeta parens veniat
Hoc deus omnipotens ex alto donet olympo
  Qui caelum et terram condidit atque regit.

Which the Queene's majestie most attentively harkened unto. And
when the childe had pronounced he did kisse the oration which he
had there faire written in paper, and delivered it unto the Quene's
majestie, which most gently received the same. And when the Quene's
majestie had heard all that was there offred to be spoken, then her
grace marched toward Ludgate where she was received with a noyse
of instrumentes, the forefront of the gate being finelie trimmed up
against her majestie's comming. [D3] From thence by the way as she
went down toward fletebridge, one aboute her grace noted the citie's
charge, that there was no coast spared. Her grace answered that she
did well consider the same, and that it should be remembred. An
honorable answere, worthie a noble prince, which may comfort all
her subjectes, considering there can be no point of gentlenes, or obedient love shewed towarde her grace, which she doth not most tender-
lie accept, and graciously waye. In this maner, the people on either
side rejoysing, her grace went forwarde, towarde the conduite in
Fleetestrete, where was the fift and laste pageant erected in forme
folowing. From the conduit which was bewtified with painting, unto
the Northside of the strete, was erected a stage embattelled with foure
towres and in the same a square platte rising with degrees, and upon
the uppermost degree was placed a chaire, or seate roiall, and behinde
the same seate in curious, artificiall maner was erected a tre of reasonable height and so farre advaunced above the seate as it did well and
semely shadow the same, without endomaging the sight of any part
of the pageant, and the same tree was bewtified with leaves as grene
as arte could devise, being of a convenient greatnes and conteining

therupon the fruite of the date, and on the top of the same tree in a table was set the name therof which was *A Palme tree*, and in the aforesaid seate or chaire was placed a semelie and mete personage [D3v] richlie apparelled in parliament robes, with a sceptre in her hand, as a Quene, crowned with an open crowne, whose name and title was in a table fixed over her head, in this sort. *Debora the judge and restorer of the house of Israel. Judic.4.* and the other degrees on eyther side were furnished wyth vi. personages, two representing the nobilitie, two the clergie, and two the comminaltie. And before these personages was written in a table *Debora with her estates, consulting for the good government of Israel.* At the feete of these and the lowest part of the pageant was ordeined a convenient rome for a childe to open the meaning of the pageant. When the Queene's majestie drew nere unto this pageant, and perceived, as in the other, the childe readie to speake, her grace required silence, and commaunded her chariot to be removed nigher, that she might plainlie heare the childe speake, which said as hereafter foloweth.

Jaben of Canaan king had long by force of armes
Opprest the Isralites, which for god's people went
But god minding at last for to redresse their harmes,
The worthy Debora as judge among them sent.

In war she, through god's aide, did put her foes to flight,
And with the dint of sworde the bande of bondage brast.
In peace she, through god's aide, did alway mainteine right
And judged Israell till fourty yeres were past.

A worthie president, O worthie Queene, thou hast,
A worthie woman judge, a woman sent for staie.
And that the like to us endure alway thou maist
Thy loving subjectes wil with true hearts and tonges praie. [D4]

Which verses were written upon the pageant, and the same in latin also.

Quando dei populum Canaan, rex pressit Iaben,
  Mittitur a magno Debora magna deo:
Quae populum eriperet, sanctum seruaret Iudan,
  Milite quae patrio frangeret hostis opes.
Haec domino mandante deo lectissima fecit
  Faemina, et aduersos contudit ense viros
Haec quater denos populum correxerat annos
  Iudicio, bello strenua, pace grauis.
Sic, O sic populum belloque et pace guberna,
  Debora sis Anglis Elizabetha tuis.

The voide places of the pageant were filled with pretie sentences concerning the same matter. The ground of this last pageant was, that forsomuch as the next pageant before had set before her grace's eyes the florishing and desolate states of a commonweale, she might by this be put in remembrance to consult for the worthie government of her people, considering god oftimes sent women nobly to rule among men, as Debora which governed Israell in peace the space of xl. yeres: and that it behoveth both men and women so ruling to use advise of good counsell. When the Queen's majestie had passed this pageant, she marched towarde Temple barre. But at S. Dunstone's church where the children of the hospitall wer appointed to stande with their governours, her grace perceiving [D4v] a childe offred to make an oracion unto her, staied her chariot, and did cast up her eyes to heaven, as who shoulde saye, I here see this mercifull worke towarde the poore whom I must in the middest of my royaltie nedes remembre, and so turned her face towarde the childe, which in latin pronounced an oracion to this effecte, that after the Queene's highnes had passed through the citie and had sene so sumpteous, rich, and notable spectacles of the citiezens which declared their most hartye receyving and joyous welcomming of her grace into the same: thys one spectacle yet rested and remained, which was the everlasting spectacle of mercy unto the poore members of allmighty God, furthered by that famous and most noble prince king Henry the eyght, her grace's father, erected by the citie of London, and advaunced by the most godly verteous and gracious prince king Edwarde the .vi. her grace's dere and loving brother doubting nothing of the mercy of the Queene's most gracious clemencie by the which they may not onely be releved and helped, but also stayed and defended, and therfore incessauntly they would pray and crie unto almighty god for the long life and raigne of her highnes with most prosperous victory against her enemies.

The childe after he had ended his oracion, kissed the paper wherin the same was written, and reached it to the Queene's majestie which received it [E1] graciouslye both with woordes and countenance, declaring her gracious mynde toward their reliefe. From thence her grace came to Temple barre, whiche was dressed finely with the two ymages of Gotmagot the Albione, and Corineus the Briton, two gyantes bigge in stature furnished accordingly, which held in their handes even above the gate, a table, wherin was writen in laten verses, the effect of al the pageantes which the citie before had erected, which verses wer these.

Ecce sub aspectu iam contemplaberis vno
   O princeps populi sola columna tui.
Quicquid in immensa passim perspexeris vrbe
   Quae cepere omnes vnus hic arcus habet.
Primus te solio regni donauit auiti,
   Haeres quippe tui vera parentis eras.
Suppressis vitiis, domina virtute, Secundus
   Firmauit sedem regia virgo tuam.
Tertius ex omni posuit te parte beatam
   Si, qua caepisti pergere velle, velis.
Quarto quid verum, respublica lapsa quid esset
   Quae florens staret te docuere tui.
Quinto magna loco monuit te Debora, missam
   Caelitus in regni gaudia longa tui.
Perge ergo regina, tuae spes vnica gentis,
   Haec postrema vrbis suscipe vota tuae. [E1v]
Viue diu, regnaque diu, virtutibus orna
   Rem patriam, et populi spem tucare tui.
Sic o sic petitur caelum Sic itur in astra
   Hoc virtutis opus, caetera mortis erunt.

Which verses wer also written in Englishe meter in a lesse table as herafter foloweth.

Behold here in one view, thou mayst see all that plaine
O princesse to this thy people the onely staye:
What echewhere thou hast seen in this wide town, again
This one arche whatsoever the rest conteynd, doth say.

The first arche as true heyre unto thy father dere,
Did set thee in the throne where thy graundfather satte,
The second dyd confyrme thy seate as princesse here,
Vertues now bearyng swaye, and vices bet down flatte.

The third, if that thou wouldest goe on as thou began,
Declared thee to be blessed on every side,
The fourth did open Trueth, and also taught thee whan
The commonweale stoode well, and when it did thence slide.

The fifth as Debora declared thee to be sent
From heaven, a long comfort to us thy subjectes all,
Therfore goe on O Queene, on whom our hope is bent,
And take with thee this wishe of thy towne as finall,

Live long, and as long raigne, adourning thy countrie,
With vertues, and maintain thy peoples' hope of thee,
For thus, thus heaven is won, thus must they pearce the skye,
This is by vertue wrought, all other must nedes dye.

On the Southside was appointed by the citie a noyse of singing children, and one child richely attyred as a Poet, which gave the quene's majestie her farewel in the name of the hole citie, by these wordes.

As at thine entraunce first, O prince of high renowne, [E2]
Thou wast presented with tonges and heartes for thy fayre,
So now sith thou must nedes depart out of this towne
This citie sendeth thee firme hope and earnest praier.,

For all men hope in thee, that all vertues shall reygne,
For all men hope that thou, none errour wilt support,
For all men hope that thou wilt trueth restore agayne,
And mend that is amisse, to all good menne's comfort.

And for this hope they pray, thou mayst continue long,
Our Quene amongst us here, all vice for to supplant,
And for this hope they pray that God may make thee strong
As by his grace puissant, so in his trueth constant.

Farewell O worthy Quene, and as our hope is sure,
That into errours place, thou wilt now trueth restore,
So trust we that thou wilt our soveraigne Quene endure,
And loving Lady stand, from hencefurth evermore.

While these wordes were in saieng, and certeine wishes therein
repeted for maintenaunce of truthe and rooting out of errour she now
and then helde up her handes to heavenwarde and willed the people
to say .Amen.

When the childe had ended, she sayd, be ye well assured, I will
stande your good quene. At which saieng her grace departed forth
through temple barre towarde Westminster with no lesse shooting
and crieng of the people, then she entred the citie with a noyse of
ordinance which the towre shot of at her grace's entraunce first into
towre streat.

The childe's saieng was also in latin verses written in a table which
was hanged up there.

O Regina potens, quum primam vrbem ingredereris
    Dona tibi, linguas fidaque corda dedit [E2v]
Discedenti etiam tibi nunc duo munera mittit.
    Omnia plena spei, votaque plena precum.
Quippe tuis spes est, in te quod prouida virtus
    Rexerit, errori nec locus vllus erit.
Quippe tuis spes est, quod tu verum omne reduces
    Solatura bonas, dum mala tollis, opes.
Hac spe freti orant, longum vt Regina gubernes,
    Et regni excindas crimina cuncta tui.
Hac spe freti orant, diuina vt gratia fortem,
    Et verae fidei te velit esse basin.
Iam Regina vale, et sicut nos spes tenet vna,
    Quod vero inducto, perditus error erit.
Sic quoque speramus quod eris Regina benigna
    Nobis per regni tempora longa tui.

Thus the Queene's hyghnesse passed through the citie, whiche without anye forreyne persone, of itselfe beautifyed itselfe, and received her grace at all places as hath been before mencioned, with most tender obedience and love, due to so gracious a quene and soveraigne ladie. And her grace likewise of her syde in all her grace's passage shewed herselfe generallye an ymage of a woorthie Ladie and Governour, but privately these especiall poyntes were noted in her grace, as signes of a most princelyke courage, whereby her loving subjectes maye ground a sure hope for the rest of her gracious doinges herafter. [E3]

Certain notes of the quene's majestie's great mercie, clemencie, and wisdom used in this passage

Aboute the nether ende of Cornehill towarde Cheape, one of the knightes about her grace had espyed an auncient citizen, which wepte, and turned his head backe, and therwith said this gentleman, yonder is an Alderman (for so he tearmed hym) which wepeth and turneth his face backeward. How may it be interpreted that he so doth, for sorowe, or for gladnes? The quene's majestie hearde him, and said, I warrant you it is for gladnes. A gracious interpretation of a noble courage, which wold turne the doutefull to the best. And yet it was well known that as her grace did confirme the same, the partie's cheare was moved for very pure gladnes for the sight of her majestie's person, at the beholding wherof, he tooke such comfort that with teares he expressed the same.

In Cheapeside her grace smyled, and being therof demaunded the cause, answered, for that she had heard one say, Remember old king Henry the eight. A naturall child, which at the verie remembraunce of her father's name toke so great a joy, that all men may well thinke, that as she rejoysed at his name whom this realme doth holde of so woorthie memorie: so in her doinges she will resemble the same.

When the citie's charge withoute parcialitie, and onely the citie was mencioned unto her grace, she sayd it shoulde not be forgotten. Which saying might move al natural Englishmen hertely to shew [E3v] due obedience and entiernes to their so good a Queene which will in no point forget anie parcell of duetie lovinglie shewed unto her.

The answere which her grace made unto maister Recorder of London, as the hearers know it to be true, and with melting heartes herd the same: so may the reader therof conceive what kinde of stomacke and courage pronounced the same.

What more famous thing doe we reade in auncient histories of olde time, then that mightye princes have gentlie received presentes offered them by base and low personages. If that be to be wondered at (as it is passingly) let me se any writer that in any one prince's life is able to recount so manie presidentes of this vertue, as her grace shewed in that one passage through the citie. How many nosegaies did her grace receive at poore women's handes? how ofttimes staied she her chariot, when she saw any simple body offer to speake to her grace? A branche of Rosemarie given to her grace with a supplication by a poore woman about fleetebridge, was sene in her chariot till her grace came to westminster, not without the mervaillous wondring of such as knew the presenter and noted the Queene's most gracious receiving and keping the same.

What hope the poore and nedie may looke for at her grace's hande, she as in all her journey continuallie, so her harkening to the poore children of Christe's hospitall with eyes cast up into heaven, did fullie declare, as that neither the welthier es- [E4] tate stande without consideracion had to the povertie, neither the povertie be dewlie considered, unles they were remembred, as commended to us by godde's owne mouth.

As at her first enterance she as it were declared, herselfe prepared to passe through a citie that most entierlie loved her, so she at her last departing, as it were bownd herselfe by promes to continue good ladie and governor unto that citie which by outward declaracion did open their love, to their so loving and noble prince in such wise, as she herselfe wonderyd therat.

But because princes be set in their seate by god's appointing and therfore they must first and chieflie tender the glory of him, from whom their glorie issueth, it is to be noted in her grace, that forsomuch as god hath so wonderfullie placed her in the seate of government over this realme, she in all doinges doth shew herselfe most mindfull of his goodnes and mercie shewed unto her, and amongest all other. Two principall sygnes thereof were noted in this passage. First in the Towre, where her grace before she entred her chariot, lifted up her eyes to heaven and sayd.

O Lord, almighty and everlasting God, I geve thee most heartie thankes that thou hast been so mercifull unto me as to spare me to beholde this joyfull daye. And I acknowledge that thou hast dealt as wonderfully and as mercifully with me, as thou didst [E4v] with thy true and faithfull servant Daniel thy prophete whom thou deliveredst out of the denne from the crueltie of the gredy and rageing Lyons: even so was I overwhelmed, and only by thee delivered. To thee therfore only be thankes, honor, and prayse, forever. Amen.

The second was the receiving of the Bible at the little conduit in cheape. For when her grace had learned that the bible in English should there be offered, she thanked the citie therefore, promysed the reading therof most diligentlie, and incontinent commaunded, that it shoulde be brought. At the receit wherof, how reverently did she with both her handes take it, kisse it, and lay it upon her brest? to the great comfort of the lookers on. God will undoubtedly preserve so worthy a prince, which at hys honor so reverently taketh her beginning. For this saying is true, and written in the boke of Truth. He that first seketh the kingdome of God, shall have all other thinges cast unto him.

Now therfore all English hertes, and her naturall people must nedes praise God's mercie which hath sent them so woorthie a prince, and pray for her grace's long continuance amongest us.

Imprinted at London in fletestrete within Templebarre. At the signe of the hand and starre, by Richard Tottill, the .xxiii. day of January.

Proclamation for Peace
between England, France, and Scotland (1559)

Black has commented (p. 35) that "Elizabeth . . . made her first experiments in foreign policy with a boldness that hardly corresponded with her slender resources." There is no clearer evidence than this proclamation. After the loss of Calais, which England had held for 200 years, she seemed to be in no bargaining position. This was verified when it was reported to her that a French diplomat refused to negotiate the Câteau-Cambrésis treaty with her in advance of the signing on March 22, 1559, because he could not be certain she was the rightful Queen. The Frenchman's candidate for the English throne was Mary Stuart, then Queen of Scotland and, through her marriage to Francis II, a member of the French royal house of Guise. Even if Mary were not to seek a peaceful Franco-Scottish-English kingdom, as leader of the countries either side of Elizabeth she could remain a strong threat, closing her pincers whenever she wished.

Such a situation ought to have appeared hopeless to Elizabeth. France had been angry for some time, ever since Mary Tudor had committed England to Spain in the Valois-Habsburg conflict; and the Scots had disliked England since Henry VIII had tried much too early and aggressively to force a marriage between his son and Mary Stuart: and there was nothing Elizabeth could do to remedy either situation. It was, in fact, aggravated when King Henry II of France sought, and on February 16 won, a papal document from Pope Paul IV—the bull *Cum ex apostalatus*—opposing rulers who were like Elizabeth heretics to the Roman faith. Nor did Spain remain friendly for long; Philip, tiring of Elizabeth's refusal to marry him, was about to propose to Elizabeth Valois, thus sealing Câteau-Cambrésis with a firm Franco-Spanish alliance.

Although this proclamation is the first in Elizabeth's life-long offensive for peace, it is also her hasty attempt to prevent a further build-up of united enemy forces. The language is typically Elizabeth's, for under the rubrics of harmony and peace she seeks to guarantee support from France and Scotland without making any firm commitments herself. It is also typical in its Elizabethan strategy: by avoiding mention of Spain, Elizabeth is here seeking to drive a wedge between Philip and the leaders of France and Scotland. The deliberately vague rhetoric thus supports this basic tactic of the *realpolitik*: that to conquer one must first divide, then woo, the enemy.

TEXTUAL NOTES
[For explanatory notes for this selection see page 364.]

Proclamation for Peace between England, France, and Scotland
  Reference. STC 7892-7893; Steele, I, 504-505.
  Editions. Elizabeth's proclamation for peace between England, France, and Scotland exists in two editions made distinct by a high frequency of incidental variants in spelling and punctuation and by the omission of the date line (reading "Anno. M. D. LIX.") in the second edition. Both were issued by Richard Jugge as printer to the Queen on April 7, 1559.
  Collation. 1°; single broadsheet (folio).
  Description of Contents. Heading and text are in black-letter; the phrase "GOD save the Queene" is in italics; the colophon in black-letter and italics; the final Latin phrase in italics. Lovely ornamental capital T picturing a gathering of scholars.
  License. No entry in the *Stationers' Register*.
  Base-Copy Text. Queens College (Oxford) Sel.b.230. Copy of second edition consulted: Bodleian Arch.G.c.6.(f. 7).
  Textual Variants. First edition omits phrase *"in Poules* Churche-yard," and "Anno. M. D. LIX." In addition, there are 69 incidental variants.
  Emendations. contynewe for euer]contynewe forever   thother par-ty,]the other party,   estate so euer]estate soever

By the Quene

HE QUENE'S MAJESTIE considerynge, howe necessarye it is and pleasynge to almyghtye god, to have concorde and peace wyth all prynces, and speciallye with suche as be hir neighbours: And findinge not onely hir realmes and dominions lefte to hir in hostilytie and warre after the deceasse of hir deare sister the late Quene, with the realmes of Fraunce and Scotlande, but also an honorable occasion offred of treatie of peace with both the said Realmes: hath therfore upon good advise, removed al ennimitie, and hath upon most godly, honorable and profitable considerations (upon the second of thys moneth) passed, concluded and agreed, a good, perfect, sincere and perpetual amitie, ·peace, intelligence, confederacion and union, to remayne and contynewe forever betwene hir moste excellent majestie, hir heires and Successors on the one partie: and the ryght high and mightye Prince Henrye the Frenche kinge on the other party, their realmes, Countries, Cities, townes, landes, dominions, terrytoryes, segnories, castles, vassalles and subjectes, by land, sea, and fresh water, and elsewhere. And the like peace also betwene hir sayd majestie and the king and Quene, Dolphines of Scotlande, and their Realmes and countries. By the which peace it is provided, that al hostility and warre shal cease on eyther partie, and that the sayd Prynces, their Subjectes and vassalles, shall lyve together in peace, amitye, intelligence and frendshippe: And that all thynges be used and exercised as freely and lyberallye, as they have done in anye former tyme of peace, had betwene the sayd Realmes and dominions.

ALL which premisses hir majestie hath thought mete to notifie to al maner hir Subjectes of what estate soever the same be, that they and everye of them, observe all that hereto belongeth: as the like is at the Citie of Paris in Fraunce and on the french part publyshed and noti-fyed.

YEVEN at the palace of Westminster the seventh of Aprill the first yeare of the raigne of our soveraigne lady Elizabeth by the grace of god Quene of Englande, Fraunce and Ireland, defender of the faith, &c.

GOD save the Quene.

Imprinted at London by Rycharde Jugge and
John Cawood printers unto the
Quene's majestie.
Cum priuilego Regiae Maiestatis.

Homily on Obedience (1559)

Along with proclamations, homilies were a fundamental method for promoting state propaganda; and the Elizabethan churchgoer was constantly enjoined to civil obedience with no thought that his parish priest's message was unusual or inappropriate. This is indicated in the preface to *Certaine Sermons or Homilies* which "AS it was published in the *yere* 1562" argues that "Considering how necessary it is, that the word of GOD, which is the onely food of the soule, and that most excellent light that we must walke by, in this our most dangerous pilgrimage, should at all convenient times be preached unto the people, that thereby they may both learne their duety towards God, their Prince, and their neighbors, according to the mind of the holy Ghost expressed in the Scriptures." The state acknowledged "that all they which are appointed Ministers, have not the gift of preaching sufficiently to instruct the people, which is committed unto them, whereof great inconveniences might rise, and ignorance still be maintayned, if some honest remedy be not speedily found and provided" and so it set about to print official homilies for all the parishes: ministers, "her Majesty commandeth, and all other having spirituall cure, every Sunday and Holyday in the yeere, at the ministring of the holy Communion, or there be no Communion ministred that day, yet after the Gospel and Creede, in such order and place as is appointed in the Booke of Common Prayers, to reade and declare to their Parishoners plainely and distinctly one of the sayd *Homilies*, in such order as they stand in the Booke, . . . And when the foresayd Book of *Homilies* is read over, her Majesties pleasure is, that the same be repeated and read againe, in such like sort as was before prescribed" (π 4-A1). The state's control was therefore pervasive and universal. Ministers were licensed and the test was rigid. Councillors often exercised their personal choice of preachers on occasion and through the Bishop of London they controlled Paul's Cross, a popular outside pulpit in the yard of St. Paul's Cathedral where crowds gathered daily and Sunday, the Hyde Park of sixteenth century London. In this the

Queen's rule was much like Edward's; as early as 1548 Burghley was ordering Gardiner to preach from notes he and other Privy Councillors had prepared in defense of the young King's religious policies, and as late as 1601 William Barlow tells us that "On the Sabbath after [Essex's] insurrection [February 15]" he and his fellow preachers, "being commanded by authority, did in our several courses describe the nature and ugliness of rebellion."

The "homily on obedience" which follows is one of twelve homilies in the first book of *Certayne Sermons* of 1559 and later (see textual notes, pp. 48-49). Together these dozen sermons provide a singular systematic philosophy. The collection begins with a homily preaching that the Scriptures alone provide the way to salvation; continues by citing simple paradigms for the religious virtues of faith, hope, and charity—as the long anecdote of David below (S3-T1)—and concludes by denouncing the Roman church: its reliance on works which are ancillary to faith; its complicated formulae for salvation which defiantly oppose the simple commandments of Christ; and its specious claims to a presumed authority in theological and ecclesiastical matters. All three functions—the statement of faith, the citing of models for behavior, and the attack on Rome—are encapsulated in the central homily here. Indeed, the "homily on obedience" is perhaps the chief repository of commonplace Elizabethan thought and belief.

The Elizabethan congregations, who attended church regularly by command or habit, were repeatedly asked to provide a bifocal judgment of their own lives: they were to see their lives as sufficient preparation for Heaven, but they were also to judge their daily actions in their civil and earthly state. For them this was not a double focus, however, since they saw all actions as related to one another. Through an elaborate set of correspondences the Queen was transformed into God's vicar, and through her so was the parish priest, and so were parents with their children. The world was for them God's symbology, and all events were most profoundly seen as living emblems of religious significance. Their world was entirely anagogical; they inherited from the medieval church the implicit belief that their lives were allegorical journeys constantly on view and undergoing judgment by God, their Queen, and their fellow citizens. That Dante's world was born anew in Spenser's elaborately allegorical *Faerie Queene* or in a sermon transforming Essex's uprising into a morality play of good and evil was directly the result of this entrenched perspective.

Assuming that all creation is a single fabric, woven with purpose and beauty by a single artist, it is not difficult to understand, for example, *A philosophicall discourse, Entituled, The Anatomie of the minde* by T. R. [Thomas Rogers] first printed in 1576. Rogers comments that God "constituted, ordeined, and set earthly princes over perticular kingdomes, and dominions in earth, both for the avoyding of al confusion which else would be in the world, if it should be without governours, and for the great quiet and benefits of earthly men their subjects, and also that the princes themselves, in authoritie, power, wisedome, providence, and righteousnesse in governement of people and Countreis committed to theyr charge, should resemble his heavenly governance, as the majestie of heavenlye thinges may [by] the basenesse of earthly things be shadowed and resembled" (L16v-L17).

Since in God's orderly Heaven every man had his place, in the corresponding earthly world, each man had his place, too. But on earth, each man could choose his place. Each citizen could be like Christ, if he wished—long the basic doctrine of the church—but he was also potentially David, Abishai, and even Lucifer. Thus T. R. adds that "For as long as in this first kingdome the subjects continued in due obedience to God their king, so long did god imbrace all hys subjects wyth his love, favour, and grace, which to injoy, is perfect felicitie, whereby it is evident, that obedience is the principall vertue of all vertues, & indeed the very roote of all vertues, and the cause of all felicitie" (L14v). On the other hand, rebellion—following Lucifer's model as anti-Christ, rather than the model of Christ Himself— was clearly a sin. No man had the right or capacity to judge rulers; his singular duty was one of obedience. It is important to recognize that this obedience was neither surrender nor impotence, but a loving submission to a higher force which is God. Tyranny was a misconception, a sign of man's inability to know God's purpose: there was, from the Elizabethan point of view, no possibility of tyranny by a rightful monarch (for he was chosen by God as His vicar), but only a less successful and complete understanding of how the ruler, as God's vicar, was working out God's purpose. So "a rebell is worse than the worst prince, and rebellion worsse then the worst governement of the woorst Prince that hitherto hath beene" (L18). Religious and political heresy were synonymous.

For Elizabethans, man's security and contentment rested in his wholehearted acceptance of due order and degree; and they were especially fond of alluding to this. Each man had justifiable pride in his instinctual apprehension of his unique position in God's fabric. Thomas Elyot in his exceedingly popular *Boke Named the Governour* (1534; 1565; 1580) invited his readers to "Beholde also the order, that god hath put generally in all his creatures, begynnynge at the mooste inferiour or base, and assendynge upwarde: he made not onely herbes to garnishe the erthe, but also trees of a more eminent stature, than herbes: and yet in the one and the other, be degrees of qualities, some pleasante to behold, some delycate or good in taste, other holsome and medycinable, some commodyous and necessarie. Semblably in byrdes, beastis, and fysshes, some be good for the sustinance of man: some beare thynges profytable to sondry uses: other be apte to occupation and laboure: in dyverse is strengthe and fiersenes onely: in many is both strengthe and commoditie: some other serve for plesure: none of them hath all these qualities: fewe have the more parte or many, specially beautie, strengthe, and profytte" (A3-A3v). For Elyot as for all sixteenth century England, man was highest in this chain of existence, for he has understanding, "wherby he doth approche moste nyghe unto the similitude of god, whiche understandynge is the pryncipall parte of the soule" (A4). And Elyot's admonition against tearing this fabric is as pointed as T. R.'s: "Above over, take awaye Order from all thynges, what shulde than remayne? Certes nothynge finally, excepte somme man wolde imagine eftsones, *Chaos* . . . Also here there is any lacke of order, nedes must be perpetuall conflycte" (A2v). Pointedly enough the Queen—in 1569, upon the heels of the Northern Uprising—added the last homily, dealing with rebellion.

Each of these sermons preaches against self-interest, from lechery and drunkenness to conspiracies against state law. There is little theology and surprisingly little Scriptural reference; rather, examples are often drawn from daily life and the simple pure language is reminiscent of Hugh Latimer, without his metaphors. The diction is energetic and lucid. Community is the first value from which all thought and illustration are derived; for behind the community, distinct if undeveloped, is an Augustinian sense of a heavenly community directly analogous to their own earthly one. In his preface to *A Sermon Of Repentence* (1583), Arthur Dent is representative in commenting that "I seeke especially the salvation of the simple and ignorant: and therefore stoope downe to their reach and capacitie."

The direct source of the "homily on obedience" is William Tyndale's *The Obedience of a Christen Man* (1535), a book which served as the basis for all the homilies. Tyndale's central position is found in the passage from Romans 13—"Let every soule submit him selfe to the auctoritie of hyer power"—quoted below (S3). Like Paul, Tyndale and the anonymous author of this homily see the ruler as raised outside human law by God because he is God's viceregent or vicar. In the passage in which Christ talks of rendering unto Caesar what is his, God himself advocated civil order, law, and obedience: and this crucial link between the sacred and secular is the nexus from which Elizabeth's church seeks scriptural authority for the ends of state. Obedience to the state is a joyful and active willing of good conscience. Even in times of persecution God is believed to be testing man's faith; thus rebellion is never countenanced while obedience is always a holy act. Tyndale, like the writer of our homily here, also draws on David and Saul; on Korah, Dathan, and Abiram. Christ's suffering under Pilate is likewise exemplary. That this view is basic is demonstrated by the fact that both Archbishop Thomas Cranmer in *A Sermon concerning the Time of Rebellion* delivered between July 31 and August 27, 1549, and John Cheke in his tract on government, *The Hurt of Sedicion howe Greveous it is to a Commune Welth*, turned to it.

The writer of the "homily on obedience" chooses for his structure the common triunity of the medieval sermon, emphasizing the three-in-one nature of God and truth: here in theory, illustration, and interpretation and application. The parts are joined in their emphasis on order through community and the evil of individualism. For him these motifs are given a Hobbesian turn, warning against chaos as the alternative—much as Elyot had—and developing the sense of universal chaos as stemming from individual chaos, especially that initiated by the Bishop of Rome. There is little tendency here to argument; rather, the author is concerned with weaving his own many-colored fabric of thought which reflects (for the most part) the harmony and beauty he advocates. Yet he is also imaginative: while he dismisses the Marian worship of Catholicism, he pictures here a new Mary, the obedient if suffering mother of the Christ child born in a stable. Thus the author's own contribution to symbology falls on a human act, a central theological moment caught in simple and common terms, modulating his statement from an attack on Rome to a moment of gratitude, and, finally, to a prayer of concern that magistrates, like Mary, will receive in their labor other blessings of God. The thought in the "homily on obedience" is hardly original—save for the use made of Mary, there is not an idea in it that was not centuries old and widely used—but the expression here is the work of an unknown artist whose clarity and simplicity of style helped to shape the King James translation of the Bible and, through that, much of the best of our own English prose.

TEXTUAL NOTES
[For explanatory notes for this selection see page 364.]

Homily on Obedience
    References. STC 13648-13658.
    Authorship and Editions. The "exhortation, concerning good order and obedience, to rulers and Magistrates," known popularly as the "homily on obedience," was printed anonymously by Elizabeth first in 1559. This text essentially follows the one printed in *Certayne sermons or homilies* of 1547 written, we know now, by Bishop Bonner, Thomas Cranmer, John Harpsfield, and Thomas Becon; substantial variants between the two editions are set out fully below. The book contained, under both Edward and Elizabeth, twelve sermons to be read aloud in all English churches on every Sunday and Holy Day.

The original work of 1547 was sponsored by Cranmer, who wrote three of the homilies (on salvation, on true and lively faith, and on good works); and the volume was printed by the royal printer, Richard Grafton. *Certayne sermons* was later suppressed by Mary Tudor, who substituted a book of thirteen homilies of her own. In April 1559, only a few months after Elizabeth's accession, her Parliament passed the Act of Uniformity, establishing the Protestant Church of England and requiring the use of Cranmer's Book of Common Prayer. A rubric of the Communion Service found there required in turn the use of homilies; and the first of many Elizabethan editions, upon which the present text is based, was rapidly printed and circulated.

This first Elizabethan edition was not based on any of Grafton's copies, but rather on an edition of a later and less authoritative printer (perhaps on Whitchurch's edition of 1549), and all available evidence indicates the printer did not follow his copy-text verbatim. Instead changes were rendered which, while not changing doctrine, did tend to make matters clearer by substituting simple words and English words for those of Latin origin. We can probably date the first Elizabethan edition before the end of April 1559, when Edwin Sandys, afterwards Archbishop of York, wrote Matthew Parker, then still at Cambridge, that "Mr. Lever" had already "wisely put such a scruple in the Queen's head that she would not take [Henry VIII's] title of supreme head" in the Bill of Supremacy then passing through Parliament (*Correspondence of Archbishop Parker*, ed. Parker Society, p. 66), because "supreme head" appears in the first edition of 1559 (sig. Q1) and is changed in all subsequent editions to "governor." This is, however, the only significant variant in all the Elizabethan printings.

The first book of homilies—including the homily on obedience—went through eleven Elizabethan editions in all. Despite the lack of significant textual changes, an enormous number of incidental variants—sometimes the spelling of nearly every word—distinguish these editions of 1559, 1560, 1562, 1563, 1569 (two editions), 1574, 1576, 1582, 1587, and 1595. But this number of homilies was felt even in Edward's time to be insufficient and in 1563 Elizabeth had printed a second collection, eight editions of which appeared in the first year alone. It was apparently so much a concern of the Queen's that she revised it in publication as an "uncorrected copy" at the British Museum seems to indicate. The first and second book of homilies were never printed together, however, until King James's splendid folio in sixes in 1623 (the "homily of obedience" appearing on F5-G3 [pp. 69-77]). A facsimile edition of F1623 has recently been edited by Mary Ellen Rickey and Thomas B. Stroup and published by Scholars' Facsimiles and Reprints (Gainesville, Florida, 1968). The best scholarly edition of both books of homilies is still that of John Griffiths (Oxford, 1859); there the "homily of obedience" is on pp. 105-117.

The work has long been considered as central to English thought and has been frequently reprinted. Line-for-line reprintings of James's F1623 were issued in 1633 (two editions), 1635 (in another issue of F1623), 1640 (when the "homily of obedience" was moved to G4-H2 [pp. 69-77]); 1673 (I3v-K3 [pp. 62-69]); 1676 (following F1673); and twice—in two editions—in 1683 (I3v-K3v [pp. 62-70]) in an altogether new setting, being printed in Oxford rather than London. These folios are of varying quality, but most of them are quite fine; they all include the preface of 1562. A distinctly inferior duodecimo edition of both books was published as a single volume in 1687.

In the eighteenth century, a handsome folio of the two books of homilies was published in London in 1713 and again in 1726, following the editions of the previous century; the "homily on obedience" appeared on I1v-K1, pp. 60-67. A large folio (in twos) of both books of *Certain Sermons* somewhat different in appearance was issued in 1757, "Published by Authority," according to the title-page, "for the Use of Churches and Private Families." The "homily on obedience," in modern spelling and punctuation, is on R1v-T1, pp. 66-73 [BM 479.f.15]. Another edition of both books, "The Third Edition," according to the title-page, was published as a quarto in 1758; the "homily on obedience" is now modernized in spelling and punctuation on N3-04, pp. 101-111 [BM 4455.d.19(1-2)]. In Liverpool an edition of all the homilies was published with the royal arms on the title-page in 1799; a somewhat less expensive work in setting and paper, the "homily on obedience" is here modernized save for the long *s* and is reprinted without notes or commentary on W2v-Z1v, pp. 84-94. The book is collated as a folio, although quarto in size [BM 3405.cc.6]. The first extant edition of the homilies as tracts appeared in Guildford in 1799; only a handful were selected from Book I of *Certain Sermons* and abbreviated; the "homily on obedience" is not among them [BM 4454.de.6].

In the nineteenth century the Clarendon Press issued the "homily on obedience" in eight separate editions of Books I and II of the *Sermons or Homilies* (as the collection came to be known), in 1802, 1810, 1814, 1816, 1822, 1832, 1840 (to which were added the Constitutions and Canons Ecclesiastical), and 1844. The first three of these are identical line-for-line, the homily appearing on G4-M1, pp. 87-97, but the type has been reset (see the marginal note as variant, G7v, p. 94, e.g.). The 1822 (and subsequent) editions cite variants of four early editions; two Edwardian, the Elizabethan edition of 1562 (called text C); and James's edition of 1623. These editions all contain both books, but the Clarendon Press also published an edition of Book I separately, with variants based on MSS corrections and additional collations by Peter Elmsley, D.D. (Oxford, n.d.; Bodleian Clar. Press 1.b.56); these additions were incorporated in the Clarendon editions of 1832 and later. There were at least nine other nineteenth-century editions of

Books I and II of *Sermons or Homilies*: in Manchester in 1811 (with brief notes and with the Thirty-Nine Articles of the Church appended); in London in 1839 by the SPCK (with the original marginal notes); in Cambridge (by the University) in 1850 (with collations of Q1547, Q1563, Q1582, Q1587, Q1595, and F1623) along with a copy [M] of the "Homily against wilful Rebellion," first published separately and with a splendid index of subjects and textual allusions (the homily of Q1563 serves as base-text here); and in London in 1852, again by SPCK. *Certain Sermons or Homilies* was also published in Philadelphia with the addition of "The Constitutions and Canons of the Church of England, Set Forth A.D. 1603. With An Appendix, Containing the Articles of Religion, Constitution and Canons of the Protestant Episcopal Church in the United States of America" (1844). This in reality is the fifth Clarendon edition [BM 4455.d.6.]. Two editions (presumably nineteenth century) are undated. One [BM 4452.cc.13] prints only Book I with the "homily on obedience" on pp. 166-129 in a thoroughly modernized text. A final, large, and sumptuous publication in a part series by the Prayer-Book and Homily Society is that of *Sermons or Homilies* appearing in 1833, an oversize quarto (on inexpensive paper); the "Exhortation to Obedience" is still tenth, and is found on K4v-L4v, pp. 72-80.

The "homily on obedience" was also issued (without date) in nineteenth-century tracts series: probably by the Bristol Church of England Tract Society in an incomplete holding at the Bodleian [?about 1825] and in two editions of the separate work (1815, 1816) and in collections (1817 [pp. 95-117] and 1822 [pp. 102-115]) in the British Museum (Bodleian G. Pamph. 1656[8]; also BM 4452. bbb.27[1-2]). Finally, there is a tract of the homily printed for the Prayer-book and Homily Society for the United Church of England and Ireland (#10), probably 1840-1850 (Bodleian 992.e.13). There were also several nineteenth-century translations (see BM Catalogue, 64, col. 2732).

Collation. [First Elizabethan edition of *Certayne Sermons appoynted by the Quenes Maiestie*] 4°; A-Aa⁴;π². Al, title-page; Alv, contents; A2-A3, preface; A3v-Aa4v, text;πl, colophon, πlv,π2, blank. "An exhortation, concerning good order and obedience to rulers and Magistrates," is on R4-T3v.

Description of Contents. Title-page and contents in black-letter and italics; text of preface in black-letter with italics heading; texts of sermons in black-letter with black-letter headings. Ornamental border on title-page; ornamental initials on Alv, A2, A3v, B2, Cl, C3v, D2v, D4v, E3v, F2v, Gl, G4v, H2v, H4v, I4, L2v, Ml, M4, N3, P2, Ql, Q3v, R4, S2, Tlv, T4, U3, X2v, Y3, Z2, Aalv, Aa4v. No head-pieces or tailpieces. Running-head for each homily in italics. No pagination. Marginal notes throughout.

"*Homily on obedience,*" R4-T3v. Heading and text in black-letter. Running-heads in italics: "The first [or i.] parte of the Sermon." R4v,

S1v; "The .ii. parte of the Sermon." on S2v, S3v, S4v; "The .iii. parte of the Sermon." on T1v, T2v, T3v; "Of Obedience [.]" on all recto pages. Ornamental initial *A*, R4. Marginal notes in black-letter as follows: "Prou, 8." "Sap, 6," "Sap, 9," (S1); "Deut. 33" "Rom, 13" (S1v); "Ihō. 19," (S2v); "I, Pet, 2" "I, Pet, 2" "I, Pet, 2" "I, Re, 18 19. & 20." (S3); "Obiection." "Answer" (S4); "Psa, lxxx and 8," "2, Reg, I" (S4v); "Actes, 5" (T1); "2 Re. 18" "Eccle, I0" (T1v); "Mat, 17" "Luke, 2," "2, Pet, 2" (T2v); "I, Pet, 2" "Rom, 13" "Matt, 22." "Rom, 13" "I, Tim, 2" (T3); "Iudith 5" (T3v).

License. No entry in the *Stationers' Register*.

Base-Copy Text. Bodleian 1 b. 194. Copies of other editions consulted: STC 13649, BM c.25 $\frac{h12}{1\text{-}8}$; STC 13650, BM 695.a.21; STC 13651, BM c.25.e.8; STC 13652, Bodleian 1.d.305; STC 13653, Hn 20325; STC 13654, Bodleian 4°.N.28 Jur.; STC13655, Hn 61532; STC 13656, Bodleian Antiq.d.E.$\frac{1582}{1}$; STC 13657, Bodleian Mason G46; STC 13658, Bodleian 4° F 40(1)Th.

Title-page in Full. [within two rules within flowered border within two rules] *Certayne Sermons appoynted by / the Queenes Maiestie, /* [in black-letter] to be declared and read, / [in black-letter] by all Persons, Vycars, and / [in black-letter] Curates, euery Sonday and / [in black-letter] holy daye, in theyr Churches: / [in black-letter] And by her Graces aduyse / [in black-letter] perused & ouersene, for / [in black-letter] the better vnderstand- / [in black-letter] dyng of the simple people. / [in black-letter] Newly Imprynted in partes, / [in black-letter] accordyng as is menci=/ [in black-letter] oned in the booke [in black-letter] of Commune / [in black-letter] prayers. / (:) / [in black-letter] Anno.M.D.L ix. / *Cum priuilegio Regia / Maiestatis.* / [Cut into the bottom border is a circle in which is set *R.I.* for the printer Richard Jugge and a border reading DESVPER OMNIA]

Substantial Variants. (a)Between first Elizabethan edition and first Edwardian edition (STC 13639), thus first Elizabethan]first Edwardian:

(R4)distincte or seuerall]distincte   assigned and appoynted]assygned   kepe themselves in theyr]kepe them in their   (R4v)indure or laste] endure such estates]suche states   Lady Quene Elizabeth,]Lord kyng Edward the Sixth   beautiful order and goodly,]beautiful order, other godly orders]other their Godly orders   quenes majestie, supreme]kynges majestie, supreme   (S1)her honorable]his honorable   infallible and vndeceuable word]infallible worde   other supreme and higher officers]other their officers   apply and geue]applie   (S1v) committed or whom to gouerne they are charged of god.]committed. We rede(no paragraph)]WE rede(new paragraph)   vnto the]to the   punish, or maye]punishe, may   dere and chosen]dere and elect   Thus s. Paule(no paragraph)]Thus sainct Paul(new paragraph)   withstandeth]resisteth   withstandeth]resisteth   resiste   or   are   against,]

resiste, (S2)chosen]elect S. Chrisostom]Chrisost. high powers]
higher powers which he sette]to menne being constitute (space
before second part of sermon)](no space)FOrasmuch as God . . .
sake(on S2v)](passage omitted) (S2v)let al]let vs all resist or stand
against]resiste withstandeth]resisteth withstandeth, withstandeth]
resisteth, resisteth (S3)And therfore(new paragraph)]And therfore
(no paragraph) withstand]resiste withstande]resiste (S3v)with-
stode]resisted mortal or deadlye]mortall Insomuch(new paragraph)]
In so muche (no paragraph) And that Dauyd(new paragraph)]And
that Dauid(no paragraph) (S4)descende or go downe]descende Here
(no paragraph)]HERE(new paragraph) withstand]resiste withstand]
resiste once lay]once to lay reserved and kept]reserved (S4v)with-
stand]resiste regiment coercion and punishment]regimente and coercion deadly]mortal immediatly and forthwith]immediatly testified and witnessed]testified (T1)resistence or withstanding,]resistence,
withstande]resiste repugned]repyned (T1v)(space before third
part of sermon)](no space) YE . . . men](passage omitted) the
most detestable]that most detestable condingly or woorthelye]
condingly (T2)nor speake]or speche shall bewray]shal she bewray
Therefore let vs all(no paragraph)]LET vs al therfore(new paragraph)
resisteth or withstandeth]resisteth resisteth or withstandeth]re-
sisteth pretensed or coloured]pretensed And(no paragraph)]AND
(new paragraph) teacheth]teache agreable]agreably ye thei . . .
prince]immunities, privileges, exemptions, and disobedience (T2v)
remission and forgeveness]remission (passage omitted)]Our savior
Christ refused the office of a worldly Iudge, & so he dyd the office of a
worldly Kyng: Commaūding his disciples, and al that beleue in him,
that they should not contēde for superioritie, nether for worldly domi-
niō in this worlde. For ambicion and pryde is detestable in al christian
persones of euery degre. And the Apostles in that place, do not represent the persones of Bisshoppes, and Priestes onely, but also (as auncient authores do write) they represent the persones of Kynges &
Princes: Whose worldly rule and gouernaūce, they then ambiciously
desired. So that in that place Christ teacheth also christen Emperours,
Kynges and Princes, that they shoulde not rule their subiectes by will,
& to their awne commoditie, and pleasure onely: But that they shoulde
gouerne their subiectes, by good and Godly lawes. They shoulde not
make thēselfes so to be lordes ouer the people, to do with them and
their goodes what they list, and to make what lawes they list, without
drede of God and of his lawes, without consideracion of their honor &
office, wherūto God hath called them, (as Heathen Kynges and Princes do) but to thynke them selfes to be Gods officers, ordeined by God
to be his ministres unto y people, for their saluaciō, common quyetnes
& wealth: to punyshe malefactors, to defende innocentes, and to
cherishe well doers. yourselues or be subiect]your selues the praise]

laude　(T3)That is]This is all of them]al them　accepted or alowable]
accepted　(T3v)Quene]Kynge　the　worlde]this　worlde　euerlastyng
blesse]eternall blisse
(In addition, there are 2,438 incidental changes in spelling and punctuation.)

(b)Between first Elizabethan edition and second Elizabethan edition
[STC 13649; BM c.25. $\frac{h.12}{1-8}$ (1560)], thus first Elizabethan]second Eli-
zabethan:
(S2)euen in conscience]euen conscyence　(T1v)the most]that most
(T2v)vnto]to　(T3)your supreme]as supreme　(T3v)and punyshment]
of punishment
(In addition, there are 795 incidental changes in spelling and punc-
tuation.)

(c)Between first Elizabethan edition and third Elizabethan edition
[STC 13650; BM 695.a.21 (1562)], thus first Elizabethan]third Elizabethan:

(S1)head]gouerner　is this]in this　(S2)thys]the　(S2v)let al]let vs
al　(S3)For]First　(S3v)diligent]diligence　Insomuch(new　paragraph)]In so much (no paragraph)　caue]cause　(S4)Here is(no paragraph)　[Here is(new paragraph)　yet]yf　(S4v)regiment coercion
regiment, correction　(T1)Other (no paragraph)]Other (new paragraph)　were]where　(T1v)And(no paragraph)]And(new paragraph)
the　most]that　most　and　anointed]annointed　(T2)agreable]agre-
ablye　(T3)That]This　all of them]all them　(T3v)of our]on oure
blesse]blisse
(In addition, there are 1,377 incidental changes in spelling and punctuation.)

(d)Between first Elizabethan edition and fourth Elizabethan edition
[STC 13651; BM c.25.e.8 (1563)], thus first Elizabethan]fourth Elizabethan:
(S1)head]gouerner　Here(new　paragraph)]Here(no　paragraph)　is
this]in thys　(S1v)the dere]that dere　receiue to themselues]receiue
themselues　(S2)thys]the　(S2v)let al]let vs all　that it is]that is　the
powers]that powers　the contrary]that contary　(S3)And　therfore
(new paragraph)And therefore(no paragraph)　then it is]then is it
godly]goodly　hys owne wordes]hys wordes　(S3v)Insomuch(new
paragraph)]In so muche (no paragraph)　And that Dauyd (new paragraph)]And that Dauid (no paragraph)　by the plaine]by plaine
as　it　is]as is　(S4v)regiment coercion]regiment, correction　(T2)
agreable]agreably　(T3) that shall]that ye shall　all of them]al them
(In addition, there are 1,015 incidental changes in spelling and punctuation.)

(e)Between first Elizabethan edition and fifth Elizabethan edition
[STC 13652; Bodleian 1.d.305 (1569)], thus first Elizabethan]fifth
Elizabethan:

(R4)all in good]in all good   (S1)head]gouernour   and next]and the
next   Here(new   paragraph)]Here(no   paragraph)   (S1v)the   dere]
that dere   receiue to themselues]receyue themselues   of the power]
of that power   (S2)(second part of sermon continues on same page)]
(second part begins new page)   thys]the   (S2v)godlye]goodly   let al]
let vs all   of the powers]of that powers   (S3)And therfore(new paragraph)]And therefore(no paragraph)   then, it is]then, is it   hys owne
wordes]his wordes   (S3v)neuer withstode]neyther withstoode   Insomuch   (new   paragraph)]In so muche(no paragraph)   And   that
Dauyd(new paragraph)]And that Dauid(no paragraph)   as it is]as is
S4v).ii.   examples[two examples   regiment coercion]regiment, correction   he had killed]he killed   of his back]off his back   thine own]
thy   owne   (T1)other   waies]otherwise   (T1v)the   most]that   moste
(T2)agreable]agreably   (T3)all of them]all them   (T3v)bothe to oure]
both in our   blesse]blisse
(In addition, there are 1,133 incidental changes in spelling and punctuation.)

(f)Between first Elizabethan edition and sixth Elizabethan edition
[STC 13653; Hn 20025 (1569)], thus first Elizabethan]sixth Elizabethan:
(R4)distincte or]distinct and   all in good]in all good   (R4v)goodly]
godly (S1)head]gouernour   and next]and the next   Here(new paragraph)]Here(no paragraph)   officers]offices   diligently taught]taught
diligently   (S1v)and iudges]iudges   the dere]that deare   of the pow-
er]of that power   (S2)(second part of sermon on the same page)]
(second part of sermon begins on new page)   thys]the   (S2v)godlye]
goodly   let al]let vs all   (S3)And   therfor   (new   paragraph)]and
therefore(no paragraph)   it is]is it   hys owne wordes]his woordes
suffereth]endureth   suffereth]suffer   (S3v)ncucr   withstode]neyther
withstoode   mortal or]mortall and   Insomuch(new   paragraph)]In-
somuch(no paragraph)   in battaile perish]perish in battayle   And
that Dauyd(new paragraph)] And that Dauid (no paragraph)   by
the plaine]by playne   as it is]as is   (S4v).ii. examples]two examples
regiment coercion]regiment, correction   he had killed]he kylled
(T1)other waies]otherwise   or rebellious]and rebellious   (T1v)(third
part of sermon on same page)](third part of sermon on new page)
the   most]that   most   (T2)a   byrde]the   byrde   agreable]agreably
(T2v)that same]at the same   yourselues or]your selues and   or vnto]
and vnto   (T3)That is]This is   all of them]all them   (T3v)of our
side]on our side   blesse]blisse
(In addition, there are 1, 398 incidental changes in spelling and punctuation.)

(g)Between first Elizabethan edition and seventh Elizabethan edition [STC 13654; Bodleian 4°N.28Jur (1574)], thus first Elizabethan]
seventh Elizabethan:
(R4)distincte or seuerall]distinct and seuerall   all in good]in all good

(R4v)with godly]with a godly goodly]godly (S1)head]gouernour and next]and the next Here let(new paragraph)]Heere let(no paragraph) officers]offices diligently taught]taught diligently (S1v) and iudges]iudges the dere]that dere of the power]of that power (S2)(second part of sermon on the same page)](second part of sermon on a new page) thys]the (S2v)godlye]goodly let al]let vs all (S3) And therfore(new paragraph)]and therefore(no paragraph) it is] is it hys owne wordes]his woordes suffereth]endureth suffereth] suffer (S3v)his life]this life neuer withstode]neyther withstoode mortal or]mortall and Insomuch(new paragraph)]Insomuche(no paragraph) in battaile perish]perishe in batayle And that Dauyd (new paragraph)]And that Dauid(no paragraph)by the plaine]by playne as it is]as is (S4v).ii. examples]two examples regiment coercion]regiment, correction he had killed]he kylled (T1)other waies]otherwise or rebellious]and rebellious (T1v)(third part of sermon is on the same page)](third part of sermon is on a new page) the most]that most (T2)a byrde]the byrde agreable]agreably (T2v) that same]at the same in the stable]in a stable yourselues or]your selues, and or vnto]and vnto (T3)That is]This is all of them]al them (T3v)clemencye, zeale]clemencie, and zeale and for]for of our side:]on our syde, blesse]blisse
(In addition, there are 1,368 incidental changes in spelling and punctuation.)

(h)Between first Elizabethan edition and eighth Elizabethan edition [STC 13655; Hn 61532 (1576)], thus first Elizabethan]eighth Elizabethan:

(R4)distincte or seuerall]distinct and seueral all in good]in all good (R4v)with godly]with a godly goodly]godly (S1)head]gouernour and next]and the next of this]for this Here(new paragraph)] Here(no paragraph) officers]offices diligently taught]taught diligently (S1v)and iudges]Iudges the dere]that deare against]against it of the power]of that power (S2)(second part of sermon on the same page)](second part of sermon on a new page) seconde].ii. thys] the (S2v)godlye[goodly let al[let vs all (S3)And therfore(new paragraph)]and therefore(no paragraph) it is]is it hys owne wordes] his woordes suffereth]endureth suffereth]suffer (S3v)neue withstode]neyther withstoode mortal or]mortall and Insomuch(new paragraph)]Insomuche(no paragraph) in battaile perish]perishe in battaile And that Dauyd(new paragraph)]And that Dauid(no paragraph) by the plaine]by playne as it is]as is (S4v).ii. examples] two examples regiment coercion]regiment, correction he had killed] he kylled (T1)other waies]otherwise or rebellious]and rebellious (T1v)(third part of sermon is on the same page)](new part of sermon is on a new page) the most]that most (T2)a byrde]the byrde agreable]agreablie (T2v)that same]at the same the stable]a stable yourselues or]yourselues and or vnto]and vnto (T3)That is]This is all

of them]all them (T3v)zeale]and zeale and for]for of our side]on
our syde the worlde]this worlde blesse]blisse
(In addition, there are 1,448 incidental changes in spelling and punctuation.)

(i)Between first Elizabethan edition and ninth Elizabethan edition
(STC 13656; Bodleian Antiq.d.E. $\frac{1582}{1}$ (1582)], thus first Eliza-
bethan]ninth Elizabethan:
(R4)distincte or seuerall]distinct and seuerall all in good]in all
good in theyr order]in order (R4v)with godly]with a godly good-
ly]godly (S1)head]gouernour and next]and the next Here(new
paragraph)]Here(no paragraph) officers]offices deligently taught]
taught diligently (S1v)and iudges]Iudges the dere]that deare (S1v)
against]against it of the power]of that power (S2)vs al learne]vs
learne thys]the (S2v)godlye]goodly let al]let vs al (S3)and ther-
fore(new paragraph)]and therefore(no paragraph) by force to with-
stand]to withstande S. Peter]Peter hys owne wordes]his wordes
suffereth]endureth suffereth]suffer (S3v)neuer withstode]neyther
withstoode mortal or]mortall and Insomuch(new paragraph)]Inso-
much(no paragraph) in battaile perish]perish in battaile And that
Dauyd(new paragraph)]And that Dauid(no paragraph) by the
plaine]by plaine as it is]as is (S4v).ii. examples]two examples
regiment coercion]regiment, correction (T1)other waies]other wise
or rebellious]and rebellious (T1v)rebell]or rebell at the length]
at length the most]that most agreable]agreably (T2v)that same]
at the same the stable]a stable yourselues or]your selues and or
vnto]and vnto (T3)That is]This is all of them]al them (T3v)
zeale]and zeale and for]for faithfully]most faithfully most faith-
full]Kings we shall]shall wee of our side]on our side the worlde]
this worlde blesse]blisse
(In addition, there are 1,429 incidental changes in spelling and punctuation.)

(j)Between first Elizabethan edition and tenth Elizabethan edition
[STC 13657; Bodleian Mason G46 (1587)], thus first Elizabethan]
tenth Elizabethan:
(R4)distincte or seuerall]distinct and seuerall all in good]in all good
in theyr order]in order (R4v)and common wealthes]common-weales
with godly]with a godly goodly]godly (S1)head]gouernour and
next]and the next Here (new paragraph)]Here (no paragraph) of-
ficers]offices power is geuen]power giuen diligently taught]taught
diligently (S1v)and iudges]Iudges the dere]that deare against]
against it of the power]of that power (S2)vs al learne]vs learne
thys]the (S2v)godlye]goodly let al]let vs all resist or]resist and
(S3)And therfore(new paragraph)]and therefore (no paragraph) by
force to withstand]to withstand suffereth]endureth suffereth]suffer
(S3v)neuer withstode]neyther withstoode mortal or]mortall and In-
somuch(new paragraph)]Insomuch(no paragraph) in battaile per-

ish]perishe in battail And that Dauyd(new paragraph)]And that Dauid
(no paragraph) by the plaine]by playne as it is]as is (S4v).ii. ex-
amples]two examples S. Dauid]Dauid regiment coercion]regiment,
correction (T1)other waies]other wise traitors]traiterous or rebel-
lious]and rebellious (T1v)rebell]or rebell (T1v) at the length]at
length the most]that most a byrde]the byrde agreable]agreably
(T2v) that same]at the same the stable]a stable yourselues or]your-
selues and or vnto]and vnto (T3)he sayth]saith he That is]This
is S. Paule]Paul all of them]them all (T3v)zeale]and zeale and
for]for faithfully]most faithfully most faithfull kings]Kings we
shall]shall wee of our side]on our side the worlde]this worlde
blesse]blisse
(In addition, there are 1,449 incidental changes in spelling and punctuation.)

(k)Between first Elizabethan edition and eleventh Elizabethan edition [STC 13658; Bodleian 4°F 40(1)Th. (1595)], thus first Elizabethan]
eleventh Elizabethan:
(R4)distincte or seuerall]distinct and seuerall all in good]in all good
in theyr order]in order (R4v)most dere]deare with godly]with a
godly goodly]godly (S1)head]gouernesse and next]and the next
Here(new paragraph)] Here(no paragraph) officers]offices power
is geuen]power giuen diligently taught]taught diligently (S1v)and
iudges]Iudges the dere]that deare against]against it of the power]
of that power (S2)vs al learne]vs learne sette]sent thys]the (S2v)
godlye]goodly let al]let vs all resist or stand]resist and stand (S3)
And therfore(new paragraph)]And therefore(no paragraph) by force
to withstand]to withstand suffereth]endureth suffereth]suffer S.
Dauid]Dauid neuer withstode]neither withstod mortal or]mortall
and (S3v)Insomuch(new paragraph)]Insomuch(no paragraph) in
battaile perish]perish in battel And that Dauyd(new paragraph)]
And that Dauid(no paragraph) by the plaine]by plaine as it is]as
is (S4v).ii. examples]two examples S. Dauid]Dauid regiment coer-
cion]regiment, correction (T1)other waies]other wise traitors]trai-
terous or rebellious]and rebellious (T1v)in this]of this rebell]or
rebell at the length]at length the most]that most (T2)a byrde]the
bird agreable]agreably that same]at the same the stable]a stable
yourselues or]yourselues and or vnto]and vnto (T3)he sayth]saith
he That is]This is S. Paule]Paul all of them]them al (T3v)gods
proteccion]protection zeale]and zeale and for]for faithfully]most
faithfully most faithfull kings]Kings we shall]shall we of our
side]on our side the worlde]this worlde blesse]blisse
(In addition, there are 1,367 incidental changes in spelling and punctuation.)

Emendations. Listed as first Elizabeth edition]emended text. (R4)
earth]earth, manne hym selfe]manne hymselfe laye menne]laye-
menne (R4v)euery one]everyone common wealth]commonwealth

rulers, magistrates]rulers, magistrates, hygh way]hyghway soules bodies]soules, bodies common wealthes.]commonwealthes. (S1) spoken to kynges.]spoken to kynges, th infallible]the infallible (S1v)Ro.]Romans: (S2)preiste,]prieste, S. Chriso.)]S. Chrisostom) liue tenauntes]liuetenauntes Sermon.]Sermon common wethes,] commonwelthes, (S2v)death it selfe]death itselfe crucifye the]crucifye thee loce the?]loce thee? geuen the]geven thee (S3)greife,] griefe, wrōfullye]wrongfullye (S3v)In so much,]Insomuch, seing] seeing And that](new paragraph) Also an other]Also another (S4) sure for euer.]sure forever. vice gerent]vicegerent office]office's iudgment]judgment. (S4v)an other notable]another notable witnessed agaist]witnessed against (T1)the graunting]thee graunting to do any thing.]to do anything, (T1v)common weale,]commonweale, (T2)common welth]commonwelth (T2v)conscience]conscience's submit your selues]submit yourselves chiefe]chiefe them selfes,]themselfes. submit your selfes]submit yourselfes (T3)your selfes frō]yourselfes from your selfes vnto]yourselfes unto conscience]conscience's epistle.]epistle: (T3v)and cheifely,]and chiefely, common wealth.]commonwealth. pray for our selues,]pray for ourselves, euer lastyng]everlasting

An exhortation, concerning good order and obedience, to rulers and Magistrates

LMIGHTYE GOD hath created and appoynted all thinges, in heaven, earth and waters, in a mooste excellente and perfecte order. In heaven, he hath appoynted distincte or severall orders and states of Archaungelies and Aungelles. In earth he hath assigned and appoynted kynges, prynces, with other governoures under them, all in good and necessarye order. The water above is kepte and raygneth downe in due time and season. The Sunne, Moone, Sterres, Raynebowe, Thundre, Lightnynge, Cloudes, and all byrdes of the ayre, do kepe theyr order. The earth, Trees, Sedes, Plantes, Herbes, Corne, grasse, and all maner of beastes, kepe themselves in theyr order. All the partes of the whole yeare, as Winter, Sommer, Monethes, Nyghtes and Dayes, contynue in theyr ordre. All kyndes of fyshes in the Sea, ryvers, and Waters, with all fountaynes, Sprynges, yea, the seas themselves, keepe theyr comelye course and order. And manne hymselfe also hath all his partes, both within and wythoute, as soule, hearte, mynde, memorye, understandynge, reason, speache, with all and synguler corporall members of hys bodye, in a profitable, necessarye, and pleasaunte ordre. Everye degre of people in theyr vocation, callyng, and office hath appointed to them, theyr duety and ordre. Some are in hyghe degree, some in lowe, some kynges and prynces, some inferiors and subjectes, priestes, and layemenne, Maysters and Servauntes, Fathers [R4v] and chyldren, husbandes and wives, riche and poore, and everyone have nede of other: so that in all thynges is to be lauded and praysed the goodly order of god, wythoute the whiche, no house, no citie, no commonwealth can continue and indure or laste. For where there is no ryght ordre, there reigneth all abuse,

carnal libertie, enormitie, synne, and Babilonical confusyon. Take
away kinges, princes, rulers, magistrates, judges, and such estates of
god's order, no man shall ryde or go by the hyghway unrobbed, no
man shall slepe in his owne house or bed unkylled, no man shal kepe
his wyfe, children and possessions in quietnes: all thinges shalbe
common, and there must nedes folowe all myschief and utter destruction both of soules, bodies, goodes and commonwealthes. But blessed
be God that we in this realme of Englande fele not the horrible calamities, miseries, and wretchednes, whiche al thei undoubtedly fele and
suffer, that lacke this godly order, And praised be god that we know
the great excellent benefyt of god shewed towardes us in this behalfe.
God hath sent us his hygh gyft, oure moost dere soveraygne Lady
Quene Elizabeth, with godly, wyse and honorable counsayle, with
other superyors and inferiors in a beautiful order and goodly. Wherfore let us subjectes do our bounden duties, gevyng harty thankes to
god, and praying for the preservation of this godly order. Let us al
obey even from the botome of oure heartes, all theyr godly procedinges,
lawes, statutes, proclamations, and injuctions, wyth all other godly
orders. Let us consider the scripturs of the holy goste, whiche perswade and commaund us al obediently to be subjecte: fyrst and chieflye,
to the [S1] quene's majestie, supreme head, over al, and next, to her
honorable counsaile, and to al other noble men, magistrates and officers, whiche by God's goodnes be placed and ordered: for almighty
god is the only authour and provider of this forenamed state and
ordre, as it is written of God, in the booke of the Proverbes: through
me kinges do raygne: throughe me counsaylours make just lawes:
through me do prynces beare rule, and all judges of the earth execut
judgment, I am loving to them that love me.

Here let us marke well and remembre, that the high power and
auctoritie of kinges, with their makyng of lawes, judgementes, and
officers, are the ordinaunces, not of man but of god, and therfore is
this word (through me) soo manye times repeted. Here is also well to
bee considered and remembred, that thys good ordre is appoynted
of god's wisedom, favour, and love, specially for them that love god,
and therfore he saith I love them that love me. Also in the boke of
wisedom we may evidently learne, that a kinge's power, authoritie
and strength, is a great benefyte of god geven of his great mercye, to
the comfort of our great misery. For thus we reade there spoken to
kynges, Heare O ye kinges and understand: learne ye that be judges

of the endes of the earth: geve eare, ye that rule the multitudes: for the power is geven you of the lord and the strength from the highest. Let us learne also here by the infallible and undecevable word of god that kings and other supreme and higher officers, are ordeined of god, who is most highest, and therfore they ar here diligently taught to apply and geve themselves, to knowledg and wisedome, necessary for the ordring of god's people, to [S1v] their governaunce committed or whom to governe they ar charged of god. And they be here also taught by almighty god, that they should reknowledge themselves, to have all their power and strength, not from Rome, but immediatly of god most highest. We rede in the boke of Deuteronomi that al punishment perteineth to god by this sentence: Vengeaunce is mine and I wyll rewarde. But this sentence we must understand, to perteine also unto the magistrates, which do exercise godde's roume in judgment and punyshing by good and godly lawes, here in erth. And the places of scripture which seme to remove from emong al christian men, judgment, punishment, or killing, ought to be understand, that no man (of his own private aucthoritie) may be judge over other, may punish, or maye kil. But we must refer al judgement to god, to kings and rulers, and judges under them, which be god's offycers to execute justice, and by plain woordes of scrypture, have their auctoritie and use of the sweord, graunted from god, as we are taught by S. Paule the dere and chosen Apostle of our savior Christe, whom we ought diligently to obey, even as we would obey our saviour Chryst if he wer present. Thus .s. Paule writeth to the Romans: Let every soule submit himselfe unto the auctoritie of the higher powers: for ther is no power but of god: the powers that be, be ordeined of god, whosoever therfore withstandeth the power, withstandeth the ordinaunce of god, but they that resiste or are against, shal receive to themselves damnacion, for rulers ar not feareful to them that do good, but to them that do evil. Wilt thou be without feare of the power? Doo well then, and soo shalte thou be praysed of the same, [S2] for he is the minister of God, for thy welthe. But and if thou doe that which is evil, then feare, for he beareth not the sweorde for naughte, for he is the minyster of God, to take vengeaunce on hym that doeth evill. Wherefore ye muste nedes obey, not onelye for feare of vengeaunce, but also because of conscyence: and even for this cause paye ye tribute, for they are God's ministers, serving for the same purpose.

Heare lette us al learne of S. Paule the chosen vessell of god, that al persons having soules (he excepteth none, nor exempteth none, neither prieste, Apostle, nor prophet, saith S. Chrisostom) do owe of bounden duetie and even in conscience, obedience, submission and subjeccion, too the high powers, whiche be sette in auctoritie by god, forasmuch as they be god's liuetenauntes, God's presidentes, God's officers, God's commissioners, god's judges, ordeyned of God hymself, of whom onely they have al their power, and all their auctoritie. And the same .S. Paule threatneth no lesse pain then everlasting damnacion, to al disobedient persones, to al resisters against this general and common auctoritie, forasmuch as they resist not manne but god: not man's devise and invension, but god's wisedome, god's ordre, power and auctorytie.

The seconde part of the Sermon of Obedyence.

FOrasmuch as God hath created and dysposed all thinges in a comelye ordre, wee have bene taught in the first parte of thys sermon, concerning good ordre and obedience, that we also ought in all commonwelthes, to observe [S2v] and kepe a dewe ordre, and to be obedient to the powers, their ordinaunces and lawes, and that all rulers are appointed of god, for a godlye ordre to bee kept in the worlde. And also howe the Magistrates oughte to learne howe to rule and governe according to god's lawes. And that al subjectes are bounden to obey them as god's ministers: yea althoughe they be evil, not only for feare, but also for conscience's sake. And here (good people) let al marke diligently, that it is not lawful for inferiours and subjectes, in any case to resist or stand against the superior powers: for s. Paule's words be plain, that whosoever withstandeth, shal get to themselves damnacion: for whosoever withstandeth withstandeth the ordinaunce of god. Our saviour Christ himself and his Apostles, received many and diverse injuries of the unfaithefull and wicked menne in aucthoritie: yet we never reade, that they, or any of them, caused any sedition or rebellion against autoritie. We reade oft, that they paciently suffered all troubles, vexations, slaunders, pangues and paines, and death itselfe obedientlye, without tumulte or resystence. They commytted theyr cause to hym that judgeth righteouslye, and prayed for their enemies heartely and earnestlye. They knewe that the auctoritie

of the powers, was god's ordinaunce, and therefore both in their wordes
and dedes, they taughte ever obedience to it, and never taughte nor
dyd the contrary. The wicked judge Pilate said to Chryste: knowest
thou not that I have power to crucifye thee and have power also to
loce thee? Jesus aunswered: Thou couldest have no power at all
againste me, except it were geven thee from above. Wherby Chryste [S3]
taught us plainly, that even the wicked rulers have their power and
aucthoritie from God.

And therfore it is not lawfull for their subjectes, by force to withstand them, although they abuse their power, much lesse then, it is
lawful for subjectes to withstande their godly and christian princes,
which doo not abuse their aucthoritie, but use the same to god's
glory, and to the profitte and commoditie of God's people. The holy
Apostle s. Peter, commaundeth servauntes to be obedient to their
maisters, not onely if they be good and gentle, but also if they be evill
and frowarde: affirming that the vocation and calling of god's people,
is to be pacient, and of the sufferinge syde. And there he bringeth in
the pacience of our savior Christ to perswade obedience to governors,
yea althoughe they be wicked and wrong doers. But let us nowe heare
.s. Peter himself speake, for hys owne wordes certyfye best our conscience. Thus he uttereth them in his first Epystle: Servauntes obeye
your Maistres with feare, not onely if they be good and jentle, but
also if they be frowarde: For it is thankewoorthy, if a manne for
conscience towarde god, suffereth griefe, and suffereth wronge un-
deserved: for what praise is it, when ye be beaten for your faultes, yf
ye take it paciently? but when ye do well, if you then suffer wrong
and take it paciently, then is there cause to have thanke of god, for
hereunto verelye were ye called. For so did Christ suffer for us, leav-
inge us an example, that we should folowe his steppes. Al these be
the very wordes of .s. Peter. S. David also teacheth us a good lesson
in this behalfe, who was manye times most cruelly and wrongfullye
persecuted of kynge [S3v] Saule, and manye times also put in jeoper-
dye and daunger of his life by kinge Saule and his people: yet he
never withstode, neither used any force or violence against king
Saule his mortal or deadlye enemye, but did ever to his liege lord and
master kinge Saule, most true, most diligent, and most faithful service.

Insomuch, that when the lord god had geven kynge Saule into
Davide's handes in hys owne cave, he woulde not hurte him, when he

might without al bodely peril easely have slaine him, no, he would not suffer any of his servauntes, once to laye their handes upon king Saul, but prayed to god in this wise: lord kepe me from doing that thing unto my maister, the lorde's anointed: kepe me that I laye not my hande upon him, seeing he is the anointed of the lord: for as truly as the lorde liveth (except the lorde smyte hym, or except his day come, or that he goo down to war and in battaile perish) the lorde be mercyfull unto me, that I lay not my hande upon the lorde's anoynted.

And that Davyd might have killed his enemy king Saule, it is evidently proved, in the first boke of the kinges, both by the cuttinge of the lappe of Saule's garment, and also by the plaine confessyon of kynge Saule. Also another time (as it is mencioned in the same booke) when the most umercifull, and mooste unkind king Saule did persecute pore Davyd, god dyd againe geve kinge Saule into Davyde's handes, by castinge of kynge Saule and hys whole armye, into a deade sleepe: so that Davyd and one Abisay with him, came in the nighte into Saule's hoste, where Saul lay sleepinge, and his speare stacke in the grounde at his heade. Then said Abisai unto [S4] Davyd: god hath delivered thine enemye into thy handes at this time, now therefore let me smite hym once with my speare to the earth, and I wil not smyte him againe the second time: meaning therby to have killed him with one stroke, and to have made him sure forever. And David aunswered and said to Abisai: destroy him not, for who can laye his handes on the lorde's anointed and be giltles? And David said furthermore: as sure as the lorde liveth, the Lorde shall smite hym, or his daye shall come to dy, or he shall descende or go doune into batall, and there peryshe. The lord kepe me from laying my handes upon the lorde's anointed. But take thou nowe the speare that is at his head, and the cruse of water, and let us go: and so he did. Here is evidently proved, that we maye not withstand nor in any wayes hurt an anoynted king, whiche is god's liuetenaunt, vicegerent, and highest mynister in that countrye where he is kinge. But peradventure, some here would say that David in hys owne defence might have killed king Saule lawefullye, and with a safe conscience. But holy Davyd did knowe that he might in no wise withstand, hurt, or kyl hys soveraigne lorde and king: he did knowe, that he was but king Saule's subjecte, though he wer in gret favor with god, and his enemy king Saule out of god's favor. Therefore, though he wer never

so much provoked, yet he refused utterly to hurte the lorde's anoynted.
He durst not for offending god and his owne conscience, (although
he had occasion and oportunytie) once lay his handes upon god's
high officer the kynge, whom he did know to be a person reserved
and kept (for his office's sake) onely to god's punishment and judgment. [S4v] Therfore he praieth so oft, and so earnestly, that he lay
not his handes upon the lorde's annointed. And by these .ii. examples
.s. David (being named in scripture a man after god's own heart)
geveth a generall rule and lesson to al subjectes in the world, not to
withstand their liege lord and king, not to take a swearde by their
private aucthoritie against their king, god's anoynted, who only
beareth the sworde by god's auctoritie for the maintenance of the
good, and for the punyshment of the evill: who onely by god's lawe,
hath the use of the sweard at his commaundement and also hath al
power, jurisdiccion, regiment coercion and punishment, as supreme
governour of al his realmes and dominyons, and that even by the aucthoritie of god, and by god's ordinaunces. Yet another notable story
and doctrine is in the seconde booke of the kinges, that maketh also
for this purpose. When an Amalechite, by kinge Saule's own consent
and commaundement, had killed king Saule, he went to Davyd, sup-
posyng to have hadde greate thanke for his message, that he had
killed David's deadly enemye, and therefore he made gret hast to tel
to David the chaunce: bringing with him king Saul's Crowne that
was upon his head, and his bracelet that was upon his arme, to perswade hys tydinges to be true. But godly David was so far from re-
joysynge at these news, that immediatly and forthwith he rent his
clothes of his back, he mourned and wept and said to the messenger:
how is it that thou wast not afraid to lay thy hands on the lord's
anointed to destroy him? And by and by David made one of his servauntes to kil the messenger, saying: thy bloud be on thine own head
for thy own mouth hath testified and witnessed against [T1] thee
graunting that thou hast slaine the lorde's anoynted. These examples
being so manifest and evydent, it is an intolerable ignoraunce, mad-
nes, and wickednes, for subjectes to make any murmuring, rebellyon,
resistence or withstanding, commocion, or insurrection against there
most dere and most dreade soveraygne Lorde and king, ordeined and
appoynted of Godde's goodnes, for their commoditie, peace and quyetnes. Yet let us beleve undoubtedly, (good christian peple) that we
maye not obey kynges, Magystrates, or any other, (though they be

our owne fathers) yf they woulde commaund us to do anything, contrary to god's commaundementes. In such a case, we ought to say with the Apostles: we must rather obey God then man. But nevertheles in that case, wee may not in any wise withstande violently, or rebel against rulers, or make any insurrection, sedicion, or tumultes, either by force of armes, (or other waies) against the annointed of the lord, or any of his appointed officers. But we must in such case, pacientlye suffer all wronges and injuries, referring the judgment of oure cause onelye to god: Let us feare the terrible punishment of almightie God, against traitors, or rebellious persons, by the example of Chore, Dathan, and Abiron, which repugned and grudged agaynst god's Magistrates, and officers, and therfore the earth opened, and swallowed them up alyve. Other for their wicked murmurynge and rebellion, were by a sodaine fire sent of god, utterlye consumed. Other for their frowarde behavyoure to their rulers and governers, God's ministers, were sodainelye strycken, with a foule leprosye. Other were stinged to death with wonderfull strange firie [T1v] serpentes. Other were sore plagued, soo that there was killed in one day, the numbre of fourtene thousand and seven hundred, for rebellion against them, whom god had appointed to be in authoritie. Absalon also, rebelling agaynste his father kyng David, was punished with a straunge and notable deathe.

The third parte of the Sermon of Obedyence.

YE have hard before in this sermon of good ordre and obedience, manifestly proved both by scryptures and examples, that all subjectes are bounden to obey theyr magistrates, and for noo cause to resyst or withstande, rebell, or make anye sedicion agaynste them, yea although they be wicked men. And let noo man thinke that he can escape unpunyshed, that committeth treason, conspiracie, or rebellyon, agaynste his soveraigne Lord the king, thoughe he commyt the same never so secretlye, either in thought, worde or dede: never so privelye, in his prievy chambre, by himselfe, or openly communicating, and consultyng with other. For treason wil not be hid: treason wil out at the length. God wil have the most destestable vyce, both opened and punished, for that it is so directelye against his ordeynaunce, and agaynst his high pryncipal judge, and anointed in earth. The violence and injury, that is committed against aucthoritie, is committed agaynst

God, the commonweale, and the whole realme, which god wil have
knowen, and condingly or woorthelye punyshed, one waye or other.
For it is notably wrytten of the wise man in Scripture, in the booke
called Ecclesiastes: wishe the kynge no evyll in thy [T2] thought, nor
speake no hurt of him in thy privy chambre: for a byrde of the ayre
shal betraye thy voice, and with her fethers, shall bewray thy woordes.
These lessons and examples are written for our learnyng. Therefore
let us al feare the most detestable vice of rebellion, ever knowing and
remembring, that he that resisteth or withstandeth common auctoritie,
resisteth or withstandeth god and his ordinaunce, as it may be proved
by many other mo places of holye Scrypture. And here let us take hede
that we understand not these or such other like places (which so
streightly commaund Obedience to superiours, and so straightly
punisheth rebellion, and disobedience to the same) to be meant in
any condition of the pretensed or couloured power of the Bishop of
Rome. For truly the scripture of god alloweth no such usurped power,
ful of enormities, abusions, and blasphemies. But the true meaning of
these, and suche places, be to extoll and set forth godde's true ordy-
naunce, and the aucthoritie of god's annoited kinges, and of their
officers appointed under them. And concerning the usurped power
of the Bishop of Rome, which he most wrongfully challengeth, as
the successor of Chryst and Peter: we may easily perceive how fals,
feined, and forged it is, not onely in that it hath no sufficient ground
in holy scrypture, but also by the fruites and doctrin therof. For our
saviour Christ, and S. Peter, teacheth most earnestly and agreable
obedience to kynges, as to the chiefe, and supreme rulers in this
worlde, nexte under god: but the bishop of Rome teacheth ye thei
that ar under him, ar free from al burdens and charges of the common-
welth and obedience towardes their prince, most clearly against
Christe's doctrine and S. Peter's. He ought, therefore [T2v] rather
to be called Antichrist, and the successour of the Scribes and Pharisies,
then Christe's vicar, or S. Peter's successour: seing, that not only in
this pointe, but also in other waighty matters of Christian religion, in
matters of remission and forgevenes of sinnes, and of salvation, he
teacheth so directly against, both s. Peter and against our saviour
Christ: who not onely taught obedience to kinges, but also practised
obedience in theyr conversacion and living. For we read, that they both
paied tribute to the king. And also we read, that the holy virgin Mary,
mother to our saviour Christ, and Joseph, who was taken for his

father, at the Emperour's commaundement, went to the citie of David, named Bethleem, to be taxed emong other, and to declare their obedience to the magistrates, for god's ordinaunce's sake. And here let us not forgette the blessed virgyn Marie's obedience: for although she was highlye in god's favour, and Christe's naturall mother, and was also great with childe that same time, and so nighe her travaile, that she was delivered in her journey: yet she gladly without any excuse or grudging (for conscience's sake) did take that cold and foule winter journey, beyng in the meane season so pore, that she lay in the stable, and there she was delivered of Chryste. And according to the same, lo how .s. Peter agreeth, writinge by expresse wordes, in his first Epistle: submit yourselves or be subject (saieth he) unto kinges, as unto the chiefe heades, or unto rulers, as unto them that ar sent of him, for the punishment of evyll doers, and for the praise of them that do well, for so is the will of God. I nede not to expound these wordes, they be so plaine of themselfes. S. Peter doth not say: submit yourselfes [T3] unto me, as supreme head of the Church: neither he sayth, submit yourselves from time to time, to my successors in Rome: but he saieth, submit yourselfes unto your kinge, your supreme head, and unto those that he appointeth in aucthoritie under him. For that ye shall so shewe your obedience, it is the wyll of God. God will that you be in subjection to your head and king. That is god's ordinaunce, god's commaundement, and god's holy wil, that the whole body of every realme, and al the membres and partes of the same, shalbe subject to their heade, their king, and that (as S. Peter writeth) for the lorde's sake: and (as S. Paule writeth) for conscience's sake, and not for feare onely. Thus we learne by the worde of god, to yelde to our kyng, that is dewe to our king, that is honor, obedience, paimentes of dewe taxes, customes, trybutes, subsedies, love and feare. Thus we knowe partly our bounden dueties to common aucthoritie, nowe let us learne to accomplishe the same. And let us most instauntly and heartily praye to God, the onely authour of all aucthoritie, for all of them that be in aucthoritie, accordyng as S. Paule willeth, writing thus to Timothie, in his fyrst epistle: I exhorte therefore, that above all thinges, prayers, supplycations, intercessions, and geving of thankes be done for all men: for kinges, and for al that be in aucthorytie, that we maye live a quiete and a peaceable lyfe, with all godlines and honestie: for that is good, and accepted or alowable in the sight of god our savioure. Here saint Paule maketh an earnest, and an especiall exhortacion, concerning gevyng of thankes, and prayer for kinges and rulers, saying: above all thynges, as hee [T3v] might say, in any wise principally and chiefely, let prayer be made for kynges. Let us heartely thanke God for his great and excellent benefite and provydence, concerning the state of kinges. Let us pray for them, that thei maye have god's favoure, and god's proteccion. Let us pray, that they maye ever in al thinges have God before their eies. Let us praye, that they may have wisedom, strength, justice, clemencye, zeale to god's glorye, to god's veritie, to Chrystyan soules, and to the commonwealth. Let us praye, that they maye ryghtly use theyr sweorde and aucthoritie, for the maintenaunce and defence of the catholique fayth conteyned in holye Scripture, and of theyr good and honest subjectes, and for the feare and punyshment of the evyll, and vitious people. Let us praye, that they maye faithfully folowe the most faithfull kings and Capitaynes in the Byble, David, Ezechias, Josias, and Moses, with suche other. And let us praye for ourselves, that we may live godlye, in holy and chrystian conversation: so we shall have God of our side: And then let us not feare what man can doo against us. So we shall live in true obedience, bothe to oure most mercifull kyng in heaven, and to oure mooste Christian Quene in earth: so shall we please GOD and have the exceding benefite, peace of conscyence, rest and quietnes here in the worlde, and after thys life, we shal enjoye a better lyfe, rest, peace, and the everlastyng blesse of heaven, which he graunt us all that was obedient for us al, even to the death of the crosse Jesus Chryst: to whom with the father and the holy ghost, be all honour and glorye, both nowe and ever. Amen.

Declaration to Aid France (1562)

Elizabeth sought slowly to consolidate power; and her exceptional intervention in the French civil war of 1562-1563, formally announced and justified in the following declaration, was an unfortunate and premature decision. The Queen thought that she could fortify the French Protestant (Huguenot) cause signalled by her own church by entering the conflict on the side of Catherine de Medici, regent then for her second son, Charles IX. At the same time, Elizabeth hoped to embarrass and defeat the French Catholic Guises, forever precluding their alliance with their niece Mary Stuart in a Franco-Scottish pact which could seriously threaten England.

It is true that at the time France was in serious enough straits and that Catherine could use what help she could get. When Henry II died in 1559, the actual annual income of his country was five million livres; and every centime of that was needed to pay on the national debt, by then carrying an interest of twelve to sixteen percent. The fiscal difficulties led to financial and political malfeasance. The French King was free to tax whatever he chose; and his main source of revenue, the *taille,* had risen steadily while peasants fled their lands and merchants balked. The French government responded by selling offices at its disposal and creating more: the result was that the King surrendered any control over his own administrative and judicial bureaucracy. Economic collapse heralded political chaos: courtiers sold influence, judges sold justice, bureaucrats sold favors; and all servants thought of their jobs as sinecures or commodities rather than public trusts.

The French nobility exacerbated the situation by developing strong factions and wrestling for total power while the weakened government sought stubbornly and vainly to oblige, supplicate, and compromise them. Three of the factions were important. The proudest—insatiably so, since they traced their ancestry from St. Louis and Charlemagne— were the Guises. In 1562 this dynasty was led by two brothers, the prelate Charles, cardinal of Lorraine, dominant at the court of Henry

II and ripe with papal aspirations; and the soldier Francis, duke of Guise, a magnificent warrior whose direct action and capacity for discipline won the respect of Catholics and court alike. The second faction was that of the Bourbons, again with twin leadership— "Weathercock Anthony," who was as uncertain as his nickname suggests but whose strongly assertive Calvinistic wife wished always to convert him; and his younger brother, Louis Prince of Condé, a belligerent, penurious, hunchbacked young man whose hatred of the Guises forced him into the Calvinist camp where he united the forces of baronial gangs and religious discontents. The final faction—the Montmorencys—were the aristocrats, servants to the Crown: Anne, Duke of Montmorency, Constable of France; his son Francis, Marshal of the Kingdom, Governor of Paris, and Lieutenant-General of Ile-de-France; another son, Henry Damville, Governor and uncrowned king of Languedoc; and Gaspard de Coligny, his nephew, Admiral of France. This final house was split religiously: the Constable was a staunch Catholic, the Admiral as strongly Protestant. Indeed, Coligny was so successful in his tactless, blunt, Bible-quoting way that he served as the national hero for Protestant hagiographies. It was little matter to him that he also became the national villain when he sold LeHavre [Newhaven] to the English for 6,000 men and 1,000 crowns, for he intended himself to be the champion of the enlightened Protestant understanding of God.

Reconciling such factional strife was more than Catherine could handle, although she thought she could if only she cajoled, gossiped, and proposed marriage in her family as often as Elizabeth used such ploys. She had a family, after all, and a number of sons, but to her misfortune she lacked Elizabeth's youth (Elizabeth was now 28, Catherine 41), her good looks, and her birth. The painter Vasari once said of Catherine, "Her charm cannot be painted or I would have preserved its memory with my brushes"—and indeed, the Medici mother was not beautiful, for she was large, with bulging eyes, heavy lips, greasy skin, and a sharp nose. She shared Elizabeth's passion for intrigue and ceremony but she was too sanguine about her own ability and she overlooked the fact that, Italian-born, she was for the French both a foreigner and a plebeian. It is not strange that she lacked Elizabeth's magic in attracting her people through heartfelt patriotism and love such as Elizabeth commanded.

Extreme Protestant activity in France began with the government's release of all Huguenots from jail in February 1561: by April they were holding services before audiences of 600 and attracting students from Geneva; on June 5 they ignored an order to decorate their houses for Corpus Christi; in August they held their first funeral; in September they won control over the government elections; and in October they required Protestant and Catholic services in all town churches. Open conflict finally erupted in Castres during December. The Catholic Friar Claude d'Oraison was preaching when a Protestant in his congregation called him a liar and Catholic members ejected him. That evening Calvinists took up arms, seized the friar, and threw him out of the district. On January 1, 1562, they formally abolished Catholicism, and when in February they discovered a Trinitarian monk celebrating a secret mass, they dressed him in sacredotal robes, placed him backwards on a donkey, and paraded him through the streets of the town. He was subsequently put in a chair, shaved, offered the host, and asked if he were ready to die for his "idolatry." But he was not; and only his robes were burned.

The Guises pleaded with Catherine for retaliation, but her conciliations only increased their fury while it annoyed—even as it encouraged—the Protestants. Forced to answer for themselves, the Catholics, under the Duke of Guise, discovered on the Duke's lands on March 1 a band of some 500 Protestants holding service. The soldiers and worshippers exchanged insults, and then blows leading to bloodshed. Guise himself was hit on the nose by a rock. Seeing this, his men slaughtered as many as 125 Protestants and wounded another hundred: the Massacre of Vassy. As soon as report of this reached Paris, Condé called his troops to arms; and the French religious wars had begun. The siege that followed was brutal and bloody. Wholesale attacks and executions were common, and Blaise de Montluc, Governor of Guyenne, hanged every Huguenot he could: "one man hanged," he said, "is a better example than a hundred killed." Towns were pillaged, the countryside ravaged.

Elizabeth's entry into this conflict is stated in clear and forceful language in the declaration below; and there is no reason to doubt the case she sets out here. She was distressed by the cruelty of the Guises; and she saw her own role as peacemaker both with Mary Stuart, a Guise by marriage, and with France, by repeated embassies to the Continent. Thus her "reasonable, evident, urgent, and necessary Considerations" (p. 181) are real enough; they are, moreover, deeply grounded in her belief, epitomized in the preceding homily, in the sanctity of royalty now quite overthrown. She was firmly opposed to the Guises' attempt "to subvert the whole Profession of true Religion through *Christendome* by Force, without Mercy" (p. 180) and she thought that her own action, which both justified religion and peace on the one hand and traditional rule on the other "by saving of *Chrystien* Bloud, shal wel please Almyghtie God" (p. 181). She was fearful as well that Spain would seal its new-found alliance with France in the Treaty of Câteau-Cambrésis by entering on behalf of the Guises, a fear she could not afford to make public here. Partly on this account, partly because she would not go so far as to proclaim herself the world champion of Protestantism, Cecil had much difficulty in drafting this declaration: there are at least three versions extant where he tried to work it out. But the sincerity of the argument is ample and evident; only the matter of Brittany may not have been so important as the text says.

Of all threats, perhaps Elizabeth felt closest to the potential loss of Calais, for she knew how important it had been in 1558 and how helpful her ability to forge terms under which she might salvage it were for her in 1559. Beyond the loss, if the French Guises should unite with Mary Stuart in Scotland, she would be caught in a pincers movement. She was therefore susceptible to the unfounded sentiments of her resident ambassador in Paris, Sir Nicholas Throckmorton. Throckmorton had written to Cecil on April 17, 1562, that "Our friends, the Protestants, must be handled and dandled" but, if Spain intervened "for their defence, or for desire or revenge or affection to the Queen, [Catherine] might be moved to give [Elizabeth] possession of Calais, Dieppe, or Newhaven, perhaps all three" in order to keep the throne. In September Elizabeth was further persuaded by Coligny and Condé at the Treaty of Hampton Court to intervene with money and troops, for in return she would receive Calais as a permanent port after the rebellion had been put down, and gain LeHavre at once as a temporary "security." The French Calvinists wished to win their country over to the Kingdom of God; in the process Elizabeth seemed guaranteed Calais as well as a partitioning of her ancient enemy. But as the following statement makes painstakingly clear, we still do best to see this action on Elizabeth's part as primarily defensive. She was, in the last analysis, after all the tedious theorizing and careful construction of events, unwilling to surrender her role of international and internal peacemaker, even for the Kingdom of God.

TEXTUAL NOTES

[For explanatory notes for this selection see page 365.]

Declaration to Aid France
  Reference. STC 9187 (in Latin).
  Authorship and Editions. Like all state papers, the declaration by the Queen is anonymous, although Cecil composed three drafts for it (see *Calendar of State Papers, Foreign,* 1562, 325). It was published in Latin and French. No English copy now exists and there is no way of telling the number of editions through which it went; the only available copy of the text in English known to be extant—and hence the source of the text printed here—is that which appeared in the first edition of *The Harleian Miscellany* (London, 1745), III, 177-181, with some annotations. This text was reprinted with minor alterations in typography, spelling, and punctuation in the second edition

of *The Harleian Miscellany,* ed. William Oldys and Thomas Park (London, 1809), III, 185-190, with the same annotations, preceded by a cheaper impression (but actually another edition, being another setting of type) with similar modifications in *The Harleian Miscellany,* ed. J. Malham (London, 1808), I, 374-379.

Collation. 4°; a note in *The Harleian Miscellany,* III, 177, tells us the book was thirteen pages in black-letter.

Description of Contents. Little is known; see *Collation* above.

License. No entry in the *Stationers' Register*; Hn. Q of Latin text printed by R. Wolfe.

Base-Copy Text. That of *The Harleian Miscellany* (London, 1745), III, 178-181.

Title-page in Full. [from *The Harleian Miscellany*] A Declaration of the Quenes Maiestie, *Elizabeth,* by the Grace / of God, Quene of *England, Fraunce,* and *Irelande,* Defen- / dor of the Fayth, &c. Conteyning the Causes which haue / constrayned her to arme certeine of her Subiectes, for De- / fence both of her owne Estate, and of the moste Christian / Kyng, *Charles the Nynth,* her good Brother, and his Sub- / iectes. *Septemb.* 1562. Imprinted at *London,* in *Powles* / *Churchyarde,* by *Rycharde Iugge* and *Iohn Cawood,* Printers / to the Quenes Maiestie. *Cum Priuilegio Ragiae Maiestatis.* / In *Quarto,* containing thirteen Pages, black Letter.

Substantial Variants. None.

Emendations. (178)Defence of her self,]Defence of herselfe, both to her selfe]both to herselfe (179)no o her cause]no other cause (180) often tymes]oftentymes (181)nearest to her selfe,]nearest to herselfe, Defence of her selfe,]Defence of herselfe, in the meane Time,]in the meaneTime, any Thyng,]anyThyng, Libertie to hym selfe,] Libertie to hymselfe, content them selues]content themselves

A Declaration of the Quene's Majestie, Elizabeth, . . . Conteyning the Causes which have constrayned her to arme certeine of her Subjectes

LTHOUGH THE MYSERABLE and afflicted Estate of the Realme of *Fraunce* is to be lamented of all *Chrystien* Princes and Nacions, and requyrethe som good Remedie, not only for Preservation of the Kyng there, with the Quene his Mother, and the Subjectes of that Realme from Danger and Ruyne; but also for the Staye of the reste of *Christendome* in Peace, and to be free from the lyke Cyvyle Warre, into the whiche, as it appeareth by these straunge Dealinges in the sayde Realme, it is meant the same shall fall; yet there is no Prince, that hath more juste Cause to have Regarde herunto, nor that hath more indifferently and earnestly intended the Recovery of Quietnesse and Accorde therin, than the Quene's Majestie of this Realme of *Englande,* both by her owne gracious Disposition, and by Advyse of her Councell. For, as the Matter is nowe playnly discovered to the Worlde, and as her Majestie hath proved the same sufficientlye by her owne late Experience, she is not only touched, as other Princes ought to be, with great Compassion and Commiseration for the unnaturall Abusyng of the *French* Kyng, her good Brother, by certen of his Subjectes, the Daunger of his Person and his Bloud, the lamentable and barbarous Destruction, Havocke, and Spoyle of so manye *Chrystien* innocente People beyonde all Measure: But her Majestie also evidently seeth before her Eyes, that, yf some good Remedye be not, by God's Goodnesse, provided in Season, the very Fyre, that is nowe kindeled and dispersed there, is purposelye ment and intended to be conveyed and blowen over to inflame this her Crowne and her Realme. Whiche great Peryll, although it be so playnly sene to all wyse and provident Men, both at Home and Abrode, that they can

not mislyke her Care and Providence to remedye the same in Tyme; yet hath her Majestie thought not unmeete to notifie some Parte of her Dealynges herin, so as it shall well appeare howe sincerely her Majestie hath both hytherto proceaded with her Neyghbours, and how playnly and uprightly she is determined to continue.

Fyrst, It hath ben well sene to the Worlde, howe well disposed her Majestie was, even at the Beginning of her Raigne, to the Restitucion of Peace to *Christendome,* that, for Love therof, was contented to forbeare for certein Yeres the Restitucion of a Portion of her auncient Dominion, when all other Parties to the same Peace, with whom, and by whose Alliaunce her Crowne susteyned Losse, were immediatly restored to the most Parte of their owne in Possession: And yet it can not be forgotten, within howe short a Space, or rather no Space after, and by whom, and upon howe greate, evidente, and juste Causes (aswell by Meanes of Force and Armes first taken, as by other open Attemptes agaynst her Majestie) she was constrained to prepare like Armies of Defence only, even for her whole Crowne and Kingdome, and joyntly therwith for the Safetie of her nexte Neyghbours from a playne Tirrannye. And also howe sincerely her Majestie proceaded therin, *firste,* by sundry Requestes and Meanes made to forbeare theyr Attemptes; *next,* by open Declaration of her Intent to be onely for Defence of herselfe, and by the whole Handelyng of the Matter; and, *lastly,* by the Event and Issue of the Cause all the Worlde hath clerely understande.

After which daungerous Troubles pacified, the Quene of *Scottes,* at her Returne to her Countreye, felyng the greate Commoditie herof folowyng, both to herselfe and her Realme, and understandyng the sincere Dealyng of the Quene's Majestie in all her former Actions, dyd by divers Meanes geve Signification to her Majestie, of a greate Desire to enter with her into a strayghter Kynde of Amitie: Wherunto her Majestie, being of her owne Nature much enclined, redely accorded. And howe farre and prosperously they both proceded therin by many and sundry mutuall Offices of Frendshippe, aswel the good Wyl shewed by her Majestie to the Quene of *Scottes'* [179] Uncles, the *Guyses,* and to all her Frendes and Ministers passyng and repassyng through this her Realme; as also the Accorde of the Enterview intended betwixt them both, this last Sommer, hath well declared.

But, in the Middest of these her Majestie's quiet and peacyble Determinations, she hath ben, to her great Griefe, utterly disapoynted;

and constrayned, for her owne Interest, to attende and intermedle in
the Pacification of these great Troubles in *Fraunce* neare to her
Realme, the same beyng styrred up by suche, as both were her laste
manifest greate Enemies, and have also (they know howe) continued
the Cause of Mistrust tyl this Day, by manifest Argumentes of Injustice, which her Majestie is content to conceale, for the great Affection
that she beareth to the *Scottyshe* Quene. *Fyrste,* Her Majestie at the
Beginning, doubting, by the Encrease of these *Frenche* Troubles, that
not onely that Realme should fall into Daunger of Ruyne by Division,
as it nowe is; but also that the reste of *Christendome,* and specially
her owne Realme, both for the Nearenesse thereto, and for the Respectes of them which were the principall Aucthours and Parties in
these Troubles, shoulde be also disturbed and brought to Daunger;
used all the Meanes that might be, by Messages, by Solicitations, by
Advyse, yea, by a speciall Ambassade of a Person of good Credite, to
have some Mediation made betwixt these Parties beyng at Controversie. But suche was the Policie and Violence of the one Partie in hastye
Proceadyng, even at the Firste, as no Mediation coulde be harde of, or
allowed. And yet coulde not her Majestie discontinue her good Intent,
but, seyng the Cruelties encrease, the Bloudsheddyng and Murders
continue; yea, which was most peryllous, the yonge Kyng, and the
Quene his Mother, being sodeynlye assayled, and founde without
Force, were directed and drawen altogether, by the verye Aucthours
of the Troubles, to suffer theyr Name and Aucthoritie to be abused,
even to the Kyllynge of the Kynge's owne unarmed innocente People,
the Spoylyng of his ryche Townes, the Breakyng of his best advysed
Edictes, the Persecutyng of his owne Bloud and his Nobilitie, the
Destroying of his faithfull approved Servauntes, with many suche
other Heapes of Mischiefes; and all these for no other Cause, but for
the particuler Appetites of some, and to breake with Violence the
Ordinaunces of the Realme, specyallye those which were lately devysed by the long and great Councell of the Realme, both for Quietnesse in Matters of Religion, and for the Reliefe of the Kynge's Estate
divers Wayes.

And, *Finally,* her Majestie understandyng very certeinly of an open
Destruction and Subvertion there, put already in Ure, and lykewyse
intended against all States and Persons professyng the Gospell Abroade,
her Majestie thought it very nedefull to thynke of some other Meanes
of more Efficacie to induce the Aucthours of those Troubles to geve

Eare to some reasonable Mocions of Accorde, and not to adventure the Ruyne of a Realme for theyr particuler Appetites; and therefore determined to sende a solempne Ambassade of a certeine Numbre of Personages of her Councell, being of great Aucthoritie, Experience, and Indifferencie, to repayre into *Fraunce*, to assay howe some Staye myght be reasonably devysed for these Extremities, by preservyng of both Partes indifferently, to the Service of the Kyng theyr Soveraigne, according to theyr Estates of Byrth and Callyng.

But thys Maner of Proceadyng also could no wyse be lyked nor allowed, nether coulde Answere be hadde hereunto from the good yonge Kyng, nor the timerous Quene his good Mother, without the onely Direction of that Part, which both began and continued the Troubles from the Begynnyng.

And whylest her Majestie was thus well occupyed, meanyng principallye the Weale and Honour of the Kyng, her good Brother; and, *secondly*, well towardes both the Parties beyng at Devision, without the Prejudice of eyther; a playne contrary Course and Proceadyng was used agaynst her Majestie, by the [180] whiche was made manifest what was further ment and intended by them that had so oftentymes refused to heare her Majestie speake for Mediation and Accorde. All her Majestie's Subjectes and Marchauntes, aswell of her Cities of *London* and *Excester*, as of other Porte Townes in the *West* Partes of the Realme, beyng at that very Tyme in divers Partes of the Countrey of *Bryttayne*, resortyng thyther onely for Trade of Marchaundizes, and ready to returne to theyr owne Portes, were in the same Tyme apprehended, spoyled, miserably imprisoned; yea, such, as sought to defend themselves, cruelly kylled, theyr Shyppes taken, theyr Goodes and Marchaundize seased, and nothyng sayde nor devysed to charge them, but onely furiouslye callyng them al *Hugenotz*: A Word, though very strange and folyshe to many of the honest Marchauntes and poore Maryners, yet fully sufficient to declare from whence these Commaundementes came, and what their Intent is to prosecute, when theyr Tyme shall serve them. Neither were these Spoyles small or few, but in Value and Numbre greate and many; neither done by private Furye, but by publique Officers, who were also mainteined by Governours of the Countreys; yea, none of her Majestie's Subjectes were there spared, that coulde be taken, though some escaped with great Hazarde. Well; herof Complaint was made, where it ought to be, but therin hath ben as small Regard had, as was before for Robbyng of her Majestie's owne Messengers with her Letters from her Embassadour, and yet the Fact unpunyshed, without any Satisfaction for the same: Wherin her Majestie surely noteth and pitieth the Lacke, rather of Aucthoritie, then of good Wyll, in the Kyng, or the Quene his Mother, or the Kyng of *Navarre* his Lieuetenaunt; but seethe manifestly, by this, and by al other Proceadinges, in what harde Tearmes the Estate of the yong Kyng is set, that can neither be permitted to preserve his owne People and Servauntes, his owne Lawes and Ordinaunces, neither to aunswere to other Princes and People, in Fourme of Justice, that which he ought to do.

Upon these, and other former daungerous Enterprises agaynste her Majestie and her Crowne, may it well appeare, to all Persons of indifferent Judgement, howe these violent Proceadynges in *Fraunce*, conducted at this Tyme by the Duke of *Guyse* and his Adherentes, do touch the Quene's Majestie much nearer for her State and Realme, then anye other Prince of *Christendome*. Wherfore, seyng the Aucthoritie of the King, and the Quene his Mother, with theyr quiet good Councellours, can not at this Tyme have Place to direct theyr Affayres, neyther towardes theyr owne People, nor towardes theyr Neyghbours; neither can any Mediation, sought by her Majestie, for Concorde, be allowed; but, contrarywise, the tender Persons of the King, and the Quene his Mother, be manifestlye abused, and daungerouslye caried about, for the particuler Pleasures onely of a fewe Persons, and specially those of *Guyse,* to waste the Kinge's Countreys, to sacke and spoyle his ryche and greate Townes, to kyll and murder the Multitude of his good and true Subjectes: And, seyng also the Quarrell manifestly publyshed, and prosecuted, both by Wrytyng and otherwyse, by them, is to subvert the whole Profession of true Religion through *Christendome* by Force, without Mercy, and thereby to stirre up a Civile blouddy lamentable Warre in all *Christendome*. Lastly, seyng they, whiche be the Aucthours and Mainteyners of all these Divisions, are well knowen to the Worlde to be the same that, when Tyme served them, bent theyr whole Endevours to offend and diminishe the Crowne and Dignitie of this Realme of *Englande*: and of late Tyme, for the Exaltation of theyr particuler House, devysed unjustly to assayle the whole Crowne of *Englande* by sundrye Wayes; though, by God's Goodnes, theyr Practises and Counsels turned, for that Tyme, to theyr owne Confusion, as, by the same Goodnes, they shall at all Tymes hereafter.

Howe may her Majestie, without Note of manifest Unkyndnes to her deare yonge Brother and Confederat; of Unmercifulnes to her next Neighbours, his Subjectes; of Uncarefulnes to the common Quiet of *Christendome*; [181] and, lastly, whiche is nearest to herselfe, of mere Negligence to the Suertie of her owne Estate, her Countrey, and People, suffer these fewe troublesome Men, *firste*, to destroye and shedde the Bloud of a Number of *Chrystien* People, whose Bloud, by Nearnesse of Place to her Majestie's Realme, may be stopped, or some wyse saved: *Nexte*, to surprise and take such Townes and Havens, whereby theyr former long intended and manyfest Practises agaynst the Crowne of this Realme may be most easyly for them, and daungerously for this Realme, put in Ure and Execution. Wherfore, for these reasonable, evident, urgent, and necessary Considerations, and not without the lamentable and continuall Request of the *Frenche* Kynge's Subjectes, her Majestie's nexte Neyghbours, crying to her Majestie onelye for Defence of themselves, their Portes, and Townes, from Tiranny and Subvertion, duryng this theyr Kinge's Minoritie, or, at the least, duryng this his Unhabilitie to pacifie these Troubles; her Majestie hath put certayne Numbres of her Subjectes in Order, both by Sea and Land, to save some Parte of her good Brother's innocent People from this Tiranny, Slaughter, and Ruyne; and to preserve some speciall Townes and Portes of Importaunce for the Kyng, her good Brother, that they come not into the Possession of them; who, yf they hadde them, myght more easely therby prosecute theyr old particuler Practises against this Realme, as in Tymes lately paste they dyd manifestly attempte; wherby of Necessitie they muste nedes endaunger the Perpetuitie of the Peace betwixt the *Frenche* Kyng and her Majestie, and so, consequentlye, though agaynste the Meanyng of the Kyng, deprive her Majestie of her good Ryght to her Towne of *Callyce*, and the Membres thereof, wherof it behoveth her Majestie, as Thinges be handled, to have good Regarde. And in this Sort her Majestie doubteth not, but the Sinceritie of her Doynges, tendyng onely to procure *Chrystien* Quietnes, by saving of *Chrystien* Bloud, shal wel please Almyghtie God; content the Kyng her good Brother, when he shal be in Estate and Libertie, to ponder the same indifferentlye; and serve also for the juste and naturall Defence of herselfe, her People, and Countreys; and, *finallye*, by God's Grace, shal establyshe the Continuaunce of some more assured Peace and Concorde betwixt both theyr Majesties and Countreys, so as eyther of them quietly enjoy and rule theyr own. And,

in the meaneTime, her Majestie assureth the sayde Kyng, the Quene
his Mother, the Kyng of *Navare,* and al his good Councellours and
Subjectes, that, whatsoever anye malicious or miscontented Person
shall sinisterly report of her Intent and Doynges, her Majestie meaneth
nothing herin, but sincerely, and as the Necessitie of the Time and
Cause requireth, without Usurpyng anyThing, or Doyng Wrong or
Violence towardes any the *French* Kynge's Subjectes; protesting before God and all the Worlde, that her Meanyng is for a necessary
Defence onely of the true and good Subjectes of the *Frenche* Kyng,
whiche otherwyse apparantly, in this troublesome Tyme, shoulde be
violentlye kylled or destroyed: And so, consequentlye, her Majestie
intendeth, by al Maner of Meanes possible, to kepe and continue good
Peace with the sayde Kyng and all his Countreys, and to neglect no
reasonable Meanes, that may procure Libertie to hymselfe, and Quietnesse betwixt his Subjectes; which then shall suceede, when it shall
please Almyghtye God to geve to the first and chiefe Aucthours of
these Troubles Grace to content themselves with theyr owne Estates,
and to lyve within the Compasse of theyr Degrees, lyke quiet Subjectes, and Favourers of the common Peace and Tranquillitie of
Christendome: A Matter more necessarye at this Tyme to be sought for,
rather by Conjunction of *Christen* Princes and States in Unitie of
Mynde, and Love of Peace and Concorde, then in this Sorte by Sworde
and Fyre, by private Devises and secrete Factions to stirre a Devision
and Civile Warre in *Christendome,* under the Cloke and Pretence of
Religion.

Proclamation against Hostilities
to the French (1564)

Elizabeth's reaction to the Protestant uprising in France in 1562 was markedly different from her response to the Scots uprising in 1559—and so were the results. In 1559 she had been most cautious. She had neither sided openly with the Scots rebels—lest she risk retaliation from the Guises in France or Philip in Spain—nor had she refused the rebels aid, since her own Protestant rule was more akin to what they wished than what Mary Stuart might offer them, especially if she were in league with the French. But Elizabeth's support had been modest; as Cecil had predicted, it came in three stages: "first with promises, next with money, and last with arms." She did not commit troops in quantity until the French defeat was assured.

But in 1562 she listened less to Cecil and more to Throckmorton, whose own Calvinistic zeal colored his reports and led to unfounded optimism. He gave exaggerated accounts of Protestant strength from Paris, and he was supported by the Queen's favorite, Robert Dudley, who had for some time been seeking Protestant alliances and an expansionist policy in sharp contrast with Elizabeth's policy of moderation. Dudley was, according to MacCaffrey (p. 126) "the moving spirit in this whole enterprise."* In contrast, Cecil seems to have been relatively quiet. He wrote only one policy paper, unusually unproductive for him, which stressed the fearful results attending a Guisian victory, foremost among them French alliance with Scotland and Spain. Elizabeth did more than listen to poor advice. She also named Dudley's elder brother, the earl of Warwick, an unseasoned gentleman volunteer, to command the new English garrison at LeHavre [Newhaven]. Warwick himself turned to Protestant zealots, and put on his war council Thomas Wood, a Marian exile, as clerk, and Wood's brother-in-law William Whittingham, another member of Knox's circle, as chaplain. Robert Dudley, meanwhile, supported the war effort by forming a coalition in England between the religious expansionists and those who wanted to reform the English church along more Genevan lines.

The decisive battle of this French civil war was at Rouen; but by then Elizabeth was wary enough to commit few troops. Rouen fell to the Catholics as did Dieppe; and suddenly the English garrison at Le Havre was confined by hostile forces. Under Catherine de Medici's leadership, the French factions—with the assassination of the duke of Guise, the battlefield death of Anthony of Navarre, and the capture of both Condé and the Constable—entered a negotiated settlement, combined forces, and marched on the English. Elizabeth now had no hope of victory but she had invested too much in lives and money to withdraw without a fight and she rationalized holding her ground, hoping that she could trade Le Havre for Calais. In no way was she lucky. She had provided insufficient funds for fortifications at Le Havre and the battle was miserably one-sided. The French advanced steadily with 40,000 men and 40 cannon. Bad weather prevented the shipping of reinforcements to the English. Plague broke out at Le Havre, killing a number of English soldiers and they returned, ill and broken, bringing the epidemic with them. So Elizabeth lost Le Havre and sued for peace.

Clearly the English Queen had acted impetuously; clearly this was a blunder of the first order. She submitted to humiliating terms. She tried her best to prevent a second embarrassment atop the first: she threatened to ban French wines, to starve the French of English coal, to harrass their fishing, even to raid their coast, but she could not bluff them into the restoration of Calais. Her invasion had forfeited the port according to the terms she herself had agreed to in the 1559 Treaty of Câteau-Cambrésis.

The only thing Elizabeth could now do was to gather whatever shreds of internal morale remained; and she set Cecil to writing the following proclamation in the hopes of promoting peace while shoring up any direct admission of grave loss. Her stress was necessarily on peace and "mutuall entercourse and trade of marchaundize, as becommeth good neyghbours and freendes"; and there is a gentle acknowledgment that the French allowed the defeated soldiers freedom to return home, that "none of [Elizabeth's] Subjectes shalbe impeched or molested." But the grim insistence here as well on "no impediment" is tonally distinct and equally important. She could risk this much, for France was still suffering from her management of a pastiche of religious and factional sentiments at home. England had lost her continental foothold, it was true, but she was in no danger of further loss: she had spent some lives, money, and arms, though not much; and her international position was neither much strengthened nor much harmed. The language of the following proclamation, then, is noticeably subdued, a fine example of Cecil's ability to speak vaguely and tactfully about defeat even as he could speak boldly and openly of success: a skill in which he came closest to the Queen and an ability which they both fostered. With it they attempt in this document to

regain the Queen's posture as a harbinger of peace and, in a moment
of loss, to reassert the stability of her government at home as well as
abroad.

Textual Notes

[For explanatory notes for the selection see page 366.]

Proclamation against Hostilities to the French

Reference. STC 7973; Steele, I, 595.

Editions. The Queen's brief proclamation regarding hostilities of
the English to the French was issued in a single edition printed by
the Queen's printer, Richard Jugge, on April 20, 1564. It was written
by William Cecil, principal secretary.

Collation. 1°; single broadsheet (folio).

Description of Contents. Heading and text in black-letter; end
phrase "God saue the Quene" in italics; colophon in black-letter;
formulary "Cum priuilegio Regiae Maiestatis" in italics. Large ornamental initial *T*.

License. No entry in the *Stationers' Register.*

Base-Copy text. Bodleian Arch.G.c.6.(f.81).

Emendations. disarmyng them selues]disarmyng themselves

By the Quene

HE QUENE'S MOST excellent Majestie, wylleth all persons to understande, that lyke as for maintenaunce of her Realme, and the tytles and ryghtes therof, she hath continued in warre hytherto with the French Kyng: So nowe upon honorable and reasonable conditions, accorded the .xi. of this moneth, by treatie betwixt her Ambassadours, and the sayde Frenche Kynge's, Her Majestie hath also, to the honour of God, to the weale of her Realme, and preservation of all her tytles and ryghtes thereto belongyng, assented to a perfect, good, and honorable peace, with the sayde Frenche kyng. And therefore her Majestie strayghtly chargeth and commaundeth all maner of persons of her obeysaunce, to forbeare all hostilitie agaynste the Subjectes of the sayde Frenche Kyng her good brother, by disarmyng themselves and theyr shippes, and to lyve in good peace with them, by mutuall entercourse and trade of marchaundize, as becommeth good neyghbours and freendes.

And for that no impediment shoulde aryse to the entercourse, by reason of private offences committed by any of her Majestie's Subjectes, agaynst the Frenche Kynge's, by Lande or by Sea in this laste warre, or in the doubtfull tymes before the same warre publyshed: Her Majestie letteth all her Subjectes to understande, that it is accorded betwixt her and her good brother the sayde Frenche Kyng, that none of her Subjectes shalbe impeched or molested, for the takyng, spoylyng, or deteynyng of any ships, armure, marchaundize, victuall, or any other kynde of goodes belongyng to the Frenche, from the first of September, in the yere of our Lorde God a thousande fyve hundred threescore two, untyll the tyme of the publication hereof, which is appoynted to be by the .xxiii. of this present moneth of Apryll.

Geven at Wyndsor the twentith day of Apryll, the sixth yere of her Majestie's raigne. 1564.

God save the Quene.
Imprinted by Richard Jugge and John Cawood, Printers to
the Quene's Majestie.
Cum privilegio Regiae Maiestatis.

Proclamation against the Traffic
in Spanish Countries (1568)

This proclamation first appears, like the declaration to aid France, to be an open and detailed explanation of Elizabeth's actions. It is not. Rather, it is a deliberate act of state propaganda masking the Queen's true purposes—to gain necessary money and to weaken Philip's position in the Netherlands—and cloaking a sharp change in foreign policy. This document is historically significant since it illustrates what will be her major tactic in international affairs: to insinuate power without committing it, to induce acts of provocation which reward with maximal benefits while costing minimal commitments.

At the time this proclamation was issued, the Netherlands was especially difficult for Philip to handle: independent merchants had given way in the streets of Brussels, Amsterdam, and Antwerp to strident Calvinists. His choice appeared to be one of prosperity with Protestantism (now that he had inherited the rule of the seventeen provinces from his father, Charles V) or discontent and perhaps rebellion with enforced Catholicism. The Dutch states were still loosely tied together in allegiance to Habsburg rule, but part of them were industrial, part commercial; part spoke Dutch, part French; and none of them was congenitally Spanish in outlook and custom. Yet the largest trading center in Europe was Antwerp and the best university next to Paris was Louvain: the Netherlands were a prize from which Philip sought much profit.

Unfortunately, Philip's hand was forced and in 1566 a group in the Spanish council of State headed by Ruy Gomez, prince of Eboli, Margaret of Parma, Pope Pius V and Cardinal Granvelle combined to persuade him to conciliatory policies through religious toleration. In August of that year a Calvinist minority, thus encouraged, led the Netherlands to violence and even religious hysteria. Over 400 churches and monasteries were looted, tombs were broken open, icons smashed, and gold taken from the altar of Antwerp Cathedral. Monks and nuns were beaten; Catholic homes were sacked; and the revolution spread rapidly. Now his religious duty and his sense of empire both demanded of Philip instant and complete repression and in the summer of 1567, considering his "duty as a Christian prince," he dispatched the Duke of Alba and 10,000 veteran soldiers to Brussels. Both the commander and his troops hated the bourgeoise laxity of the Dutch: "I have tamed men of iron," Alba bragged, "and shall I not be able to tame these men of butter?" Within a year his chief accomplishment was to fix in the Dutch an abiding hatred of Spain.

Alba's repressive acts—enforced law, special courts of inquisition, crushing taxes—disturbed Elizabeth, especially since his forces were so close to her own coasts. It was in this season of tension that Philip sent to Alba a large consignment of funds on a ship bound for Brussels. The money, newly minted, had been loaned by bankers in Genoa; but the sailors, unwilling to carry their precious cargo past the Dutch Sea Beggars—Dutch pirates who supported the Protestant cause—in the Narrow Seas, sought relief and protection in the English ports of Cornwall and Devon. This much is clear. What follows is not. The English claimed that on November 29 the Spanish ambassador to London, Don Guerau de Spes, sought protection for the ships to proceed and Elizabeth granted it, offering him both land and sea routes. According to her, he chose the sea, but when she offered him Admiral Winter, who was intending to sail to France, he asked that the gold be brought ashore for a time since that searoute was unsafe. The Spanish version held the English sailors at Southampton intimidated Spanish sailors into bringing the money ashore. At any rate, once the cargo had been unloaded, de Spes grew suspicious, and urged the eager Alba, on December 21, to make reprisals on English goods in the Low Countries; on December 29, de Spes won an audience with the Queen in which he told her that the money did not belong to the Spanish, but was borrowed. She replied that merchants in Antwerp had already reported this to her, and she would tell de Spes what she determined to do with the Italian coinage in four or five days. On December 30, hearing of Alba's actions, she declared the Spanish in bad faith and so took the money as her own.

At least two people seemed to help her engineer this open act of piracy in her own waters. The first proponent was William Hawkins of Plymouth, the brother of John Hawkins, who had heard early in December of his brother's misfortune in San Juan de Ulloa where Spanish treachery had robbed him of his treasure, killed most of his men, and destroyed most of his fleet. William now sought reprisal of his own. The other proponent was Cecil who, in drawing up one of his detailed "white papers" for the Queen, painted a gloomy picture. Spain, he noted, freed now from Moorish uprisings, had turned her attention on the Netherlands while in France the Huguenot cause appeared doomed. With England the only remaining Protestant power of consequence, he predicted that France and Spain—with or without the final conquest of the Netherlands—would unite in an attack on England unless the English did something to disperse and weaken the threat. Surely Cecil's notion that they spur unrest to preclude invasion appealed to the Queen's temperament.

Other factors also persuaded Elizabeth. Members of her Privy Council—Leicester, Clinton, Bacon, and Knollys among them—supported her since they, too, saw the general cause of the Protestant faith imperilled. Condé was again in arms but in short supply of money; Chatillon had come to London in September requesting support. Egmond and Horn had been executed in the previous summer in the Netherlands; Count Louis of Nassau had been defeated decisively in Jemmingen in July. One could hardly disagree with Louis's cry of dismay for "God [to] have mercy on His poor and weak flock who are ready to be devoured in all places."

Thus Cecil and Elizabeth saw the treasure ship as a remarkable opportunity. On balance the decision was not incautious. For markets, the Queen could always turn to Emden or Hamburg without much if any loss; and the Spanish conquest of the Low Countries was still too indecisive for them to risk invading another country. Much of this kind of thinking is contained between the lines and in the mixture of tones in the following document. As a whole, it is carefully and conscientiously constructed. The relative length and the stockpiling of details repeatedly emphasize the malice of the Spanish while assigning patience and moderation to Elizabeth. The opposition is arranged through a distorting selection of facts—no mention is made of England's piracy against Spain on the high seas, for example, or trading agreements she had bent to her will, or her support of the Dutch Beggars and her harboring of them—and it is carried through in carefully calculated postures of dismay and justifiable anger: Elizabeth pretends to see this new-born, as "A matter very straunge, and theretofore in no tyme used betwixt the Crowne of Englande and the house of Burgondy, without some manner of former conference precedyng" but displays outward common sense and caution lest "any spoyle, waste, or damage be done to their goodes and merchaundizes." In drawing on the precedent of peaceful negotiations in the past while listing the Spanish acts of aggression of the present, she registers a quiet but prevailing horror which evokes sympathy for her own position, however misrepresented it actually is here.

History proved her, in this instance, correct. On January 6 Cecil wrote Sir Henry Sidney in Ireland, "Every day will teach another what is to be done. In London all merchants of the King of Spain are in great perplexity, the richest taken to guard and the others expecting no favour." The blame had been openly fixed on Alba, to de Spes's discredit, and the success of this insinuation of the initiative was assured when Alba's own ambassador d'Assonleville arrived in London to open talks on a settlement. Elizabeth now became remarkably vague and indecisive, dragging on the talks until any danger passed away. In the end, she proved to have been clear on only one thing, in fact. She kept the money.

TEXTUAL NOTES

For explanatory notes for the selection see page 366.]

Proclamation against Traffic in Spanish Countries

Reference. STC 8008; Steele, I, 632.

Editions. The proclamation of Elizabeth concerned with Spanish trade is extant in a single edition printed by the royal printer, Richard Jugge, on January 6, 1568.

Collation. 1°; three broadsheets (folio), unnumbered.

Description of Contents. Heading in roman and black-letter; text in black-letter (first line only in italics); "God saue the Queene." in roman; colophon in roman and italics; formulary "Cum priuilegio Regia Maiestatis." in italics. Large ornamental initial *T* (with picture of animals).

License. Not registered in the *Stationers' Register.*

Base-Copy Text. Bodleian Arch.G.c.6.(ff. 116-118). [Slash marks indicate change of sheet.]

Emendations.   of the Princes them selues]of the Princes themselves kyng hym selfe]kyng hymselfe   meane tyme,]meantyme,   foorth commyng and aunswerable.]foorthcommyng and aunswerable,   asalso] as also   to be foorth commyng,]to be foorthcommyng,   aswell for] as well for   to be foorth commyng, and suffer]to be foorthcommyng, and suffer   meane tyme,]meanetyme,   in the meane tyme hauyng] in the meanetyme havyng   same xxix.]same .xxix.   to possesse any thyng]to possesse anythyng

By the Queene

A proclamation to admonishe all persons to forbeare traffique in the king of Spayne's countreys, with other advertisementes for aunsweryng of a generall arrest made in the lowe countreys by the Duke of Alva.

 *HE QUEENE'S MAJESTIE lately understandyng, that by a sodaine commaun*dement of the Duke of Alva, as governour in the low countreys belonging to her majestie's good brother the kyng of Spayne, al maner her marchaunts and other her subjectes inhabytyng in the towne of Andwerpe, were arrested and put under garde of certaine companies of souldiours, and their goodes and marchaundizes also seased, about the xxix. of the last moneth of December, and since that time the like arrest is made generally in the sayde low countreys: A matter very straunge, and heretofore in no tyme used betwixt the Crowne of Englande and the house of Burgondy, without some maner of former conference precedyng, and intelligence had of the myndes and intentions of the Princes themselves on both sydes. Whereupon her majestie hath thought good, to geve warnyng to all her subjectes that have any cause to traffique in any of the countreys of the saide kyng, that they shal forbeare the same, untyll further knowledge may appeare of the mynde of the sayde kyng hymselfe howe he shall alowe hereof: whiche beyng knowen to her majestie, shalbe notified to her sayde subjectes. And in the meanetyme, her majestie wylleth and commaundeth all maner her officers, of all townes, burghes, cities, portes, and all other landyng places within any of her dominions, that they do cause all and every person

borne under any part of the obedience of the sayd kyng of Spayne, or
lyvyng in his countreys and professyng obedience to the sayd kyng,
and their goodes, marchaundizes, shippes, and vessels, to be arrested
and stayed, to be foorthcommyng and aunswerable, aswell for the
indemnitie of her majestie's subjectes alredy, without any just cause
deteyned, as for other necessarie consequencies: and that also in all
townes, havens, and dwellyng places, where any marchauntes borne
or professyng the obedience of the sayde kyng, shalbe founde to be
suspected for convertyng or conveying of their goodes, by any maner
of fraude or colour of bargayne, from the arrest and seasure therof:
there the principall officers of that towne or place, with assistaunce of
others Justices of peace, shal proceede to the inquisition therof by all
maner good meanes, and shal commit to warde aswell the parties, of
what nation soever they be, that have or shalbe privie or aydyng to
any fraudulent colouryng, except they shall first confesse the same,
as also the others that have so coloured the same, and the goodes to be
also put in safetie. And yet because her majestie hath no other meanyng herein, but to have the persons of the sayde kynge's subjectes
and their goodes put in safetie by this arrest, for the preservation of
her owne good subjectes and their goodes, and to be respondent for
such other disordered actions as may ensue of these so straunge and
hasty attemptes: she wylleth and chargeth all maner her officers,
ministers, and subjectes, that no violence be used to the hurt of the
persons of any of the sayde kynge's subjectes by reason of this arrest,
without they shall by manifest wylfull resistaunce provoke the same,
neither that any spoyle, waste, or damage be done to their goodes and
marchaundizes, but only to cause them to be put in good garde and
safetie. And yf any of the sayde kynge's subjectes shall chalenge to be
exempted out of this arrest by reason they be denizens, her majestie
in dede having no meaning to impeach them therof, and yet for the
tyme not knowyng howe in lyke cases her subjectes beyng naturalized
in the sayde kynge's countreys, are or shalbe used: is pleased that the
sayde persons beyng in deede denizens, shall but fynde sufficient
suerties to be foorthcommyng, with their goodes: and yf they so wyll
not, then they shalbe committed to the custody and garde of some
other Englyshe marchauntes, and due inventories taken of their
goodes, untyll knowledge may be had howe her majestie's subjectes
be or shalbe used on the other part. And consideryng also her majestie
understandeth that a number of artificers and other sortes of people,

have since the begynnyng of the late inwarde troubles in the lowe
countreys, resorted hyther into her realme for avoydyng of the sayde
troubles, as well for their consciences, as for the daungers that properly
folowe such civile troubles: her wyll and pleasure is, that in all places
where suche shalbe founde to be (beyng of honest and quiet conversation) and except they shalbe participant to the colouryng of other
marchauntes' goodes, the same shall not be molested eyther in their
persons or goodes, otherwyse then where to the officers of the place it
shall so seeme nedefull, and there they shall geve bondes one for another to be foorthcommyng, and suffer inventories to be made of their
goodes.

Furthermore her majestie hearing by report, that the arrest of her
subjectes on the other side the seas, shoulde be upon a pretence, for
staying of one shippe and three or foure small barkes, lately come into
certayne her portes of her Realme, wherein certayne money was: hath
thought good briefely to notifie the circumstaunce of that pretence,
wherby may be seene manifestly, that the same is gathered without
just cause, and the devisers and promoters of the same, whosoever
they were, to have proceeded unorderly and unadvisedly. Her majestie was first infourmed by her officers in certaine her portes in the
West countrey of this Realme, that three or foure small barkes, called
Zabras, were come out of Spayne into certayne portes there, having in
them a quantitie of money belonging to sundry marchauntes of Italie
and the lowe countreys, and that divers shippes of Fraunce in warlike
maner were upon the same coastes, attending to surprise the sayde
Spanishe vessels and treasure, if they shoulde passe to the seas, and
that it was also to be feared, that they woulde enter into the very portes,
and take them away by force. Whereupon her majestie did sende
straite commaundement by speciall letters, to all the portes in those
West partes, that the marchauntes and owners of those vessels shoulde
have knowledge thereof, and that they and all other the kyng of
Spayne's subjectes, should be assisted and defended against the attemptes of the Frenche, by all meanes possible. After which done, the
Spanishe ambassadour here now resident, made like request to have
newe order for mayntenaunce and assistaunce of the sayde vessels
and treasure against the sayd Frenche, whiche was also graunted to
hym, and severall letters pattentes to that effect were delivered to his
owne messengers. And a whyle after this, he requiring of the Queene's
Majestie, to understande her pleasure, whether she woulde be content

that the owners and conducters of the sayde treasure might be eyther conducted by sea or by lande to Dover, pretending the money to appertayne to the kyng his maister: her majestie graunted to him, that whiche soever of these two wayes he would desire, shoulde be foorthwith directed for hym, whereof he thanked her majestie, saying that he woulde stay untyll he might sende into the lowe countreys, and have worde from the Duke of Alva, whiche of those two wayes he woulde have it transported. In the meanetyme, her majestie was infourmed that the Frenche had secretely in the night entred into one of her havens in the West, where the sayde treasure was, and had attempted the surprise thereof, but were onlye repulsed by suche force as her majestie's officers had in redinesse for that purpose: a matter notorious to all the partes where the sayde shippes were assaulted, and well reported also to the ambassadour. Whereupon, considering howe doubtfull and therewith chargeable a matter it was, from tyme to tyme to preserve the same lying abrode in the havens: it was thought best even for the honour of the Realme, that the sayde treasure shoulde be taken on lande, and there safely preserved in the sight and presence of them that had the charge thereof, without touching or withdrawing any part of the same. And being then certaynely knowen to belong unto marchauntes, it was also thought, after the due preservation thereof from the perill of the seas, not an unreasonable motion, nor against the honorable usage of princes in their owne dominions, to treate with the owners with their good contentation, and not otherwyse, to borowe it or some part therof, upon lyke good assuraunce and conditions, as her majestie hath oftentymes borowed of other marchauntes, subjectes to the sayde kyng in his owne lowe countreys, and as other princes have done lately in the very lyke cases. The lyke maner was used towardes a ship lying neare Southampton laden with wolles, and wherin also treasure was, and in apparaunt daunger of Frenchmen hovering upon that coast, who had made great offers to the officers there, onlye to withdrawe their defence: for whiche purpose, her majestie sent her captayne of the Isle of Wight for securitie, to have the same likewise preserved from the Frenche, and to be taken on lande: as if it had not ben, the Frenche had taken it within foure and twentie houres after, whiche also was knowen to belong unto marchauntes, and so is to be notoriously proved. And before the sayde captayne had taken care to see the same preserved, it is knowen what summes of money were offred to hym, to have only left the ship wherin the woolles were, after the money taken on land, remayning to be undefended: which the sayd captayne woulde not suffer, but armed certayne souldiers to very great charges by sea, whiche presently yet do continue to garde the sayde ship. And during this time, whylest this was in ordering, the Spanishe ambassadour came to her majestie about the .xxix. of December, bryngyng with hym from the Duke of Alva a short letter, only of credence, and therupon required, that the vessels and money stayed in the portes might be put to libertie, as belonging to the kyng his maister. To whom her majestie aunswered, that she had in her doynges (if it were the kynge's) shewed hym great pleasure to save it from the Frenche, shewing hym therin some particularities of the diligence of her officers, but she was infourmed that it belonged to marchauntes, and herein within foure or five dayes she shoulde understande/more therof, and assured hym on her honor, that nothyng shoulde be herein done, that in reason shoulde miscontent the kyng her good brother, as he shoulde also knowe within foure or five dayes at his next commyng. And so he departed, not seemyng but to alowe of the aunswere. And her majestie in the meanetyme havyng accordyng to her expectation aunswere from the west countrey, whereupon she intended to have satisfied the ambassadour at his commyng (which she loked for accordyng to her appoyntment) not only for the delivery of the sayde shippes and treasure, for such portion as myght appeare to belong to the sayde kyng: but also to have perfourmed her first offer to have geven conduct for the same by lande or by sea. The first intelligence brought to her majestie (without any returne of the ambassadour) was, that all her subjectes, goodes, marchaundizes, and shippes, were arrested, taken, and kept at Andwerpe as prysoners, the very same present xxix. day that the ambassadour was with her meajestie, so as it falleth out to every man's understandyng, that howsoever her majestie had then satisfied the ambassadour the same xxix. day, all her subjectes and their goodes had ben neverthelesse arrested, as they were at Andwerpe the same day. Whereupon her majestie nowe leaveth it to the judgement of all the worlde, to consider not only whether such a pretence was sufficient to cause so sodaine, so violent, and so generall arrest to be made with force, in such maner, and at the tyme it was: but also in whom any default shalbe founde, whatsoever may folowe hereof, her majestie havyng had no intention to miscontent the kyng of Spayne, nor to possesse anythyng belongyng to his subjectes, otherwise then with their good wyll, upon juste, reasonable, and usuall conditions. And thus muche her majestie hath thought convenient to notifie to all persons, for testimonie of her sinceritie, and for maintenaunce of her actions, whatsoever they shalbe, wherunto she may by this meanes be provoked.

At Hampton Court the vi. of January, the xi. yere of her majestie's raigne, and the yere of our Lorde, *1568.*

God save the Queene.
Imprinted at London in Powles Churchyarde by Richard Jugge and
John Cawood, Printers to the Queene's Majestie.
Cum privilegio Regiae Maiestatis.

Proclamation against
the Earl of Northumberland
and His Accomplices in Rebellion (1569)

Thomas Percy, earl of Northumberland, and Charles Neville, earl of Westmoreland, were nobility of the relatively wild northern part of England, a reactionary district which due partly to its remoteness remained strongly Catholic for some years into Elizabeth's reign. Their region was still grounded in feudal law and organized by bands of families who sought their primary identity with a landed lord, not the Queen. The "olde good-wyll of the people, deepe-graftyd in their harts" caused them to pledge their allegiance to "their nobles and gentlemen"; together they shared a legacy of the Roman church, the poverty of a decaying pastoral area made desolate by frequent border raids, and temporary unemployment, especially in the West Riding, because of the embargo on the trade of woolen goods with the Low Countries. Since London was a hard week's ride for them and since they "knew no other Prince but a Percy" or a Neville or a Dacre, they ignored any commands from Westminster or Whitehall.

For some time Elizabeth had distrusted these independent border lords. She knew their loyalty to her religious settlement was suspect; and she had a premonition that they would defend Mary Stuart if given half a chance. So early in her reign she divided their forces the better to conquer them: she deprived Northumberland of the Wardenship of the Middle March, replacing him with the loyal Sir John Forster, Northumberland's particular enemy; and she put her cousin Lord Hunsdon, a southerner of certain loyalty, in charge of Berwick and the East Marches. Both appointments rankled. The lords sensed further reproof in their being systematically and pointedly neglected.

Their revenge took the form of rebellion; their plot stemmed from Norfolk's plan to free Mary Stuart and marry her, a plan approved by the Bishop of Ross; by the Spanish ambassador de Spes; and, they hoped, by the Spanish commander Alba who would furnish necessary troop support from the Low Countries. On Saturday, October 8, 1569, Norfolk was sent by Elizabeth to the Tower to be detained for questioning in connection with suspected treason; about that time, the earl of Sussex, the Queen's Lord Lieutenant of the North, heard rumors of a raid on Durham and the North Riding originally scheduled for October 6. Sussex summoned Northumberland and Westmoreland to York to answer to this charge and on Sunday, October 9, they appeared, denied the rumors, renewed their vow of fealty to Sussex, and promised to aid him in putting down any such rebellion. Even while the Lord Willoughby in Lincolnshire was alarmed by continued reports of an uprising which he quickly forwarded to London, Sussex was cheerfully reassured by the earls, and he urged the Queen that she delay any further investigation "until winter, when the nights are longer, the ways worse, and the waters bigger to stop their passage, if there shall be any stir." In his message he even proposed that he journey to London just after Hallowtide.

But the government refused to be so sanguine. They continued questioning Norfolk's associates. On October 17 the Privy Council issued orders for a "general state" of every shire—a report on the political and religious stability of each. On November 6 the Council required all Justices of the Peace and ex-Justices to take the Oath of Supremacy. The bench of every shire was required to send reports on defaulters to the Council. The Queen herself wrote Sussex again, this time commanding him to order both earls to attend her at court. At this point, not knowing what Norfolk had revealed, Westmoreland stiffened. "I dare not come where my enemies are," he declared, "without bringing such a force to protect me as might be misliked; therefore I think it better to stay at home and use myself as an obedient subject." Sussex was in turn remonstrative: both earls should be wary "of honey and deliver you poison" and urged them "stand, as noblemen, upon your honour and truth, for it will stand by you"; he told them the Council had ordered their appearance in London and he wrote the Council that he now feared a rebellion himself.

Sussex's messenger was still at Topcliffe, Northumberland's home, however, when around midnight on November 9 the peal of church-bells rung backwards signalled the uprising. Northumberland rode to Brancepeth where he joined a tactical session of Westmoreland; the Sheriff of Yorkshire, Richard Norton; and his sons, the Marken-fields. The men discussed each of the alternatives facing them: flight, a fight to the death, submission. Sussex's letter had forced them to choose now. In the end they were swayed by Norfolk's sister Jane, the Lady Westmoreland, who urged them forward: "We and our country were shamed for ever," she warned them, "that now in the end we should seek holes to creep into." Another session on strategy convinced the men that they should choose the matter of religion as their cause since it was the only grievance widespread enough to give them a substantial following. They armed themselves, placed Cru-saders crosses on their backs as their emblem, and went in solemn procession to Ripon Cathedral where they formally proclaimed their rebellion: "Forasmuch as divers evil-disposed persons about the Queen's Majesty have, by their subtle and crafty dealings to advance themselves, overcome in this our realm the true and Catholic religion towards God and by the same abused the Queen, disordered the realm and now lastly seek and procure the destruction of the nobility, we therefore have gathered ourselves together to resist by force, and the rather by the help of God and you good people, to see redress of those things amiss, with restoring of all ancient customs and liberties to God's Church and his whole realm." But there was no mention of the Queen of Scots.

On November 14 these poorly organized forces reached Durham where, joined by shepherds and farmers on foot and horse, carrying pikes and harquebus, they marched to songs of piety and defiance. It was a disappointingly small troop, if enthusiastic—only 2,500 men including those on horseback—but they stormed the cathedral at Durham, destroyed the communion table, trampled on the prayer books, and celebrated Mass. Some lay siege to Barnard's Castle, a royal stronghold, which capitulated almost at once; others captured a secondary seaport at Hartlepool—apparently not knowing that its harbor ran dry at low tide—to prepare for the landing of Alba's troops. By November 24 others were at Selby, within striking distance of Tutbury where they had heard Mary Stuart was imprisoned.

This was the moment of the following proclamation: perhaps the critical moment, since the rebellion had reached its zenith. For Elizabeth the situation looked grim indeed. She distrusted Sussex's loyalty and sent off a new army under Hunsdon. She removed Mary to Coventry. Since papists about her in London were certain that Alba would be there with Spanish troops by Candlemas, they told Elizabeth she would be forced to hear Mass said again in St. Paul's Cathedral by Easter. She urged full military action from the north, but Sussex staunchly refused to call out the militia for fear it would join the rebels.

Then, overnight, there was a sharp reversal. The rebel leadership was racked by cowardice, divided aims, mutual jealousies, and hesitation. On November 25, at Tadcaster, the earls gave up and returned home. Dacre, in London, had pledged his loyalty to the Queen and so his support from Carlisle for the rebels never materialized. The northern earls heard Mary Stuart was not at Tutbury after all. Alba's troops were nowhere in sight. Elizabeth, meantime, had called up trained bands from the midlands and southern counties and these, under firm leadership, forced a sudden retreat. Hunsdon's men blocked the way south and forces under lord Clinton and the earl of Warwick were starting out against them. As these troops all penetrated northwards, the rebel leaders fled over the border into Scotland.

There was a final battle: Dacre returned home where he decided to assist Lord Scrope in the West March in a private war. He seized Graystoke Castle and fortified Naworth with an army of border men. Elizabeth sent Hunsdon against him in February 1560 so as to eliminate all possibility of further civil war. The castle at Naworth was too strong and Hunsdon headed on for Scrope at Carlisle when he met Dacre and his men on the banks of the Gelt River four miles beyond the castle. Hunsdon defeated Dacre on February 19. Elizabeth was elated, and she sent him a warm letter. "I doubt much my Harry, whether that the victory were given me, more joyed me, or that you were by God appointed the instrument of my glory; and I assure you that for my country's good the first might suffice, but for my heart's contentation the second pleased me . . . . And that you may not think that you have done nothing for your profit, though you have done much for honour, I intend to make this journey somewhat to increase your livelihood, that you may not say to yourself, *peridtur quod factum est ingrato*. Your loving kinswoman, Elizabeth R."

In early spring Sussex did make his trip to London, though this time it was to clear his name. It was good he did so: for Elizabeth finally recognized that in holding out against the rebellion, this proponent of the Norfolk-Stuart marriage had actually discouraged a number of men who might have joined the rebels' forces. But Elizabeth was not finally content until she drove home the lesson of evil represented by rebellion. She executed upwards of 750 and she levied fines on all those who could pay them; and she forfeited to the crown the vast estates of Northumberland, Westmoreland, Dacre, the Nortons, Swinburne, and Tempest and gathered up other property most of which she then leased or granted to Hunsdon and his followers. She also tamed the Cliffords, earls of Cumberland, by bringing their son, the third earl, south to be reared as a ward to the Puritan earl of Bedford.

Given the tense moment at which the following proclamation was written, it seems remarkably distanced, astonishingly measured in its tone. It is also designedly vague; it can be seen now—though it could not have been then—as the cool complement to the ruthless deaths on the gallows that were to follow. In its insistence on the doctrines of obedience and right order, in its reiteration of the need for stability, and in its bold allegorical strokes—all rendering it similar to a homily—this proclamation, unlike the others, combines in interesting ways the generality of illustration with the forceful particularity of its lesson. It thus turns history into parable, event into sermon, a state report into state doctrine in linguistic strategies that make this particular document unique and continually fascinating.

TEXTUAL NOTES
[For explanatory notes for this selection see page 366.]

Proclamation against the Earl of Northumberland and His Accomplices in Rebellion

Reference. STC 8021; Steele, I, 645.

Editions. Queen Elizabeth's proclamation on the Northern Rebellion, printed by the royal printer Richard Jugge, was issued in a single edition on November 24, 1569.

Collation. 1°; two broadsheets (folio), unnumbered.

Description of Contents. Heading in roman; text in black-letter (with first line in italics); "God saue the Queene." in italics; colophon in roman and italics; formulary "Cum priuilegio Regiae Maiestatis." in roman. Ornamental capital *T* identical to that used for proclamation against Spanish trade (see above).

License. No entry in the *Stationers' Register.*

Base-Copy Text. Bodleian Arch.G.c.6.(ff. 130-131). [Slash marks indicate change of sheet.]

Emendations. protested them selues]protested themselves   some what further]somewhat further   which not withstandyng,]which notwithstandyng,   fortifying   them   selues]fortifying   themselves shew them selues]shew themselves   retayne them selues]retayne themselves   by them selues,]by themselves,   Maie sities raigne.]Majestie's raigne.

By the Queene

HE QUEENE'S MAJESTIE *was sundry wyse about the latter end of* this sommer infourmed of some secrete whysperynges in certaine places of Yorkshire, and the Bishopricke of Durham, that there was lyke to be shortly some assemblies of lewde people in those partes, tendyng to a rebellion: Wherof, because at the first the informations conteyned no evident or direct cause of proofe, therfore her Majestie had the lesse regarde therto, untyll upon certaine conventions and secrete meetynges of the Earles of Northumberlande and Westmerlande, with certaine persons of suspected behaviour, the former reportes were renewed, and thereof also the sayde two Earles were in vulgare speaches from place to place expressely noted to be the aucthors. Wherupon the Earle of Sussex, lorde President of Her Majestie's councell in those north partes, gave advertisement of the lyke bruites, addyng neverthelesse (to his knowledge) there was no other matter in deede but lewde rumours, sodaynly raysed, and sodaynly ended. Any yet shortly after he sent for the sayde two Earles, with whom he conferred of those rumours: Who as they coulde not denie but that they had hearde of such, yet (as it nowe afterwarde appeareth) falsely than dissemblyng, they protested themselves to be free from all such occasions, offeryng to spende their lyves agaynst any that shoulde breake the peace, and so much trusted by the sayde lorde President upon their othes, they were licenced not only to depart, but had power geven them to examine the causes of the sayde bruites. Neverthelesse, the fire of their treasons which they had covered was so great, as it dyd newly burst out mo flames. Wherupon her Majestie beyng always loth to enter into any open mistrust

of any of her nobilitie, and therfore in this case desirous rather to
have both the sayde Earles cleared from suche slaunders, and her
good people that lyved in feare of spoyle to be quieted: commaunded
the lord President to require the sayde two Earles in her Majestie's
name to repayre to her. Wherupon the sayde lord President (as it
seemed) havyng than discovered somewhat further of their evyll purposes, dyd only at the first wryte to them, to come to hym to consult
upon matters appertaynyng to that counsell, wherunto they made
delatorie and frivolous aunsweres: and so beyng once agayne more
earnestly required, they more flatly denyed. And last of all her Majestie sent her owne private letters of commaundement to them to repayre to her presence, all which notwithstandyng, they refused to
come: And havyng before the deliverie of her Majestie's letters to
them, assembled as great numbers as they coulde, (which were not
many, for that the honester sort dyd refuse them) they dyd enter into
an open and actuall rebellion, armyng and fortifying themselves
rebelliously in all warlyke maner, and have invaded houses and
Churches, and publisshed proclamations in their owne names, to
move her Majestie's subjectes to take their partes, as persons that
meane of their owne private aucthoritie to breake and subvert lawes,
threatnyng the people that yf they can not atchyve their purposes,
then straungers wyll enter the Realme to finishe the same: And with
this they adde, that they meane no hurt to her Majestie's person: a
pretence alwayes first publysshed by all traytors. And as for reformation of any great matter, it is evident they be as evyll chosen two persons (yf their qualities be well consydered) to have credite, as can be
in the whole Realme.

And nowe her Majestie manifestly perceaving in what sort these
two Earles beyng both in povertie, the one having but a very small
portion of that which his auncesters had and lost, and the other having
almost his whole patrimonie wasted, do go about through the perswasion of a number of desperate persons, associated as parasites
with them to satisfie their private lacke and ambition, whiche can
not be by them compassed, without covering at the first certaine high
treasons against the Queene's Majestie's person and the Realme, long
hydden by such as have hereto provoked them, with the cover of some
other pretended general enterprises: Hath thought good that all her
good loving subjectes should speedyly understande, how in this sort
the sayde two Earles, contrary to the naturall propertie of nobilitie,

(whiche is instituted to defende the prince beyng the head, and to preserve peace) have thus openly and traytorrously entred into the first rebellion and breache of the publique blessed peace of this Realme that hath happened (beyonde all former examples) during her Majestie's raigne, whiche nowe hath continued above eleven yeres, an act horrible against God the only gever of so long a peace, and ungratefull to their soveraine Lady, to whom they two particularly have heretofore made sundry professions of their fayth: and lastly, most unnaturall and pernitious to their native countrey that hath so long enjoyed peace, and nowe by their only mallice and ambition is to be troubled in that felicitie. And herewith also her majestie chargeth al her good subjectes, to employ their whole powers to the preservation of common peace, (which is the blessing of almightie God) and speedyly to apprehend and suppresse all maner of persons that shal by any deede or word shew themselves favourable to this rebellious enterprise of the sayde two Earles, or any their associates: who as her Majestie hath alredy wylled and commaunded to be by the foresayde Earle of Sussex, her liefetenaunt generall in the north, published rebelles and traytors against her crowne and dignitie: so doth her Majestie by these presentes, for avoyding of al pretences of ignoraunce, reiterate and eftsoones notifie the same to her whole Realme, with all their adherentes and favourers to be traytors, and so to be taken and used to all purposes, not doubting but this admonition and knowledge geven, shall suffise for all good subjectes to retayne themselves in their duties, and to be voyde from all seducing by these foresayde rebelles and traytors, or their adherentes and favourers, whatsoever their pretences shalbe made or published by themselves, or such as have not the grace of God to delight and live in peace, but to move uprores to make spoyle of the goodes and substaunces of all good people, the true proper fruites of all rebellions and treasons.

Geven at the Castell of Windsor the .xxiiii. day of November .1569. in the twelfth yere of her Majestie's raigne.

God save the Queene.
Imprinted at London in Powles Churchyarde by Richard Jugge
and John Cawood, Printers to the Queene's Majestie.
Cum privilegio Regiae Maiestatis.

The Offices of Excester
[Exeter] (1584)

Elizabethan Exeter had a population now estimated at 7500: it was sixth in the country in size (about equal to Gloucester and Coventry in the reign of Henry VIII) and as the leading city in the west country an important center for trade and government. But both in its local rule and in its relations to the Crown, Exeter was throughout the sixteenth century a remarkably conservative city, a fact reflected in the descriptions given in the pamphlet that follows. Nevertheless, so far as we can tell, the local government of Exeter was representative for Elizabeth's time.

Exeter rose to prominence in agriculture, mining, and wool chiefly because of a unique and ideal geography: the city was located on the wide estuary of the Exe near a main harbor looking out at France— from the Seine estuary around Breton to Bordeaux and then to Cadiz —and, making it superior to Plymouth and Dartmouth, joining through the north end of the Exe with the wide and productive valleys of the Exe, Culme, and Yeo rivers leading respectively to Riverton, Cullompton, and Crediton, all flourishing sixteenth century wool towns. Because of her centrality and prosperity, Exeter was also the shire town of one of the three most economically successful English counties in the sixteenth century. To add to such good fortune Exeter had for centuries been a cathedral city as well, the seat of the bishop for Devonshire and Cornwall. Thus as a center of secular government for the West she had the seat of the Justice of Assizes as well as the Admiralty Judge who held court; as a center of religious activity, she gained increasing prominence in the church and with Parliament.

Historically, Exeter was made a bishop's seat under Edward the Confessor; she received her first royal charter as a city from Henry II. In the early thirteenth century she had her first mayor; he was soon assisted by four stewards, two of whom seem to have been the two reeves who had governed an earlier, more feudal society. A major change in local government, developing through the fourteenth and fifteenth centuries, was the emergence of the council, perhaps formed by merging the jury of presentment with an electoral group that chose local officers; in 1450 its composition was fixed at twenty-four members annually elected by a group of thirty-six. Not a democracy but an oligarchy, this local government was further strengthened in 1500 when the Twenty-Four ceased being elected and became a self-perpetuating body of wealthy and influential citizens bound together by ties of family and business. This change, and the annual election of a mayor by the city freemen from two candidates nominated by the Twenty-four, were fixed indelibly in 1509 when Henry VIII confirmed the municipal constitution. Jurisdiction did not cover all the territory within the city walls, however, for the lands of the Cathedral of St. Peter were exempt, as well as the lands of St. Stephen outside the city walls to the east.

In 1535 the mayor, recorder, and ex-mayors ranking as noblemen were made justices of the peace, and empowered to hear and determine felonies, trespasses, and misdemeanors. In 1537 Exeter became a county in itself and the mayor, recorder, and aldermen became justices of gaol delivery while the city added a sheriff to its list of officers. In 1549 a local rebellion over the new prayer book was successfully put down by the city magistrates who cared more for tradition and authority than religious disputes and Biblical interpretation, thus insuring order by their own inner harmony: nothing was allowed to break their unity as nothing was allowed which did not coincide with the actions of the King.

The national government did much to support the local authorities of Exeter. The Act of 1537 gave the local rulers membership in the privileged orders of society, local control over local affairs, and protection from the interventions of nobility by giving the city borough status and making them, relatively speaking, rulers unto themselves. Indeed, with this act local officials became so strong in obtaining influence in high quarters of the national government that they even took on a bishop as an opponent and won. Their economic basis was also guaranteed stability when in 1538 they obtained a charter to build a market for yarn and cloth, thus substantially aiding the goods and trade of the West country. In 1563 they began building a canal from the city to the sea as well.

The work which follows lists the traditional duties of each office and it is at once evident that on one hand the duties are traditional, while on the other hand they are loosely defined, with untidy boundaries of responsibility—or no boundaries at all. In fact, unity was maintained by a government of a single house, the select group of aldermen (also ex officio justices of the peace) and the council of the Twenty-Four. From this group were chosen the mayor, the sheriff, and the receiver. The chief executive officers were the recorder (alderman and justice ex officio), the town clerk, and the chamberlain. Less important was a group composed of the three city stewards, the stewards of the city manors of Awliscombe and Exe Island, the sword-bearer, the warden of Exe bridge, the warden of Magdalen alms-houses, and the lawyers of the common council. Least significant was a third body of town servants: the four serjeants, the constables, the warden of the shambles, the market man, the gate porters, the waits, the bullring man, the common plumber, and the bellman; dur-ing military emergencies there was also a city gunner and a muster master. In addition, Exeter had a mayor's chaplain (who drew city livery and a stipend, and usually assumed also the city living of St. Edmund on Exe bridge), a keeper of the cloth hall, and a supervisor of the canal. Under Elizabeth three or four of the justices were named deputy lieutenants (for the county of the city of Exeter, as the borough government was called); and her increased social legislation led as well to an overseer of the poor, a warden of the house of correction, and a keeper of the gaol. Almost all of these were appointed by the mayor and the Twenty-Four.

Election of the mayors was annual; on the Monday following Michaelmas, the Council met to name by ballot two of their own members who had served as mayor or receiver; and the two nominees were presented to the body of franchised freemen in the Guildhall for an election by acclamation. The new mayor and the Twenty-Four then chose the bailiffs (one of whom was the receiver and one of the Twenty-Four; three of whom did not need to be one of the Council and usually were not, the office serving as preliminary to election to the Council) and three serjeants (the new mayor alone selecting the fourth). The mayor and Council elected the sheriff by a separate pro-cess; only the wardens of Magdalen almshouses and of Exe bridge in addition served annual terms. Since final power always rested with the Twenty-Four—each of whom could take his turn as mayor—there was little or no friction; as in practice the mayor was the most active, the council had more power than labor.

The pathway to the mayoralty was routine: whether of the Twenty-Four or not, a candidate was elected steward (or bailiff), then sheriff, four or five years later receiver, and two years subsequently, mayor. Deviations from this pattern were rare. As for reelection, a law of 1564 ordered that due to the burden of the office, an eight-year interval was thought necessary; in practice, ten years intervened, although of 74 men holding the office between 1540 and 1640, 19 were reelected, seven served three terms, and one Hurst served five. Evidence indicates that the mayor drew up the agenda for Council meetings held about once a month. A majority of the Council could make anything de-batable. Customarily the Council meetings dealt with managing city property, regulations, ordinances, proclamations, military obli-gations, purchases of grain to provide against shortages, the management of city charities, the building of the city canal, and the appointment of city officers.

In addition, the mayor performed a number of other functions. He proclaimed his own regulations (in which he announced himself as the "Queen's Lieutenant in this city"), he was the local executor of the royal will as communicated by proclamations and royal letters, he was a justice of the peace and of gaol delivery ex officio, clerk of the market, escheator of the city, general warden of orphans, and general overseer of the poor: the description given below (Clv) hardly does him justice.

The agendas of Council meetings illustrate that the activities of the Twenty-Four centered chiefly on the economy; supervising minor offices and administering justice were generally carried out by other hands. But if the Council member escaped certain tasks, he did not evade financial obligation: election to this honorific and life-long office meant that upon accepting his position he provided the city a sum of twenty pounds for the period of one year. Often Council members had to advance money for the purchase of public grain and once they had to contribute to a repair of the city weir. They were repaid by the city in time, it is true, but with no interest. Thus there exist requests for resignation and some refusals of acceptance, but actual resignations, dismissals, or declinations of appointment are few—only 15 members were let go of the 163 serving between 1536 and 1603. Occasionally there were quarrels within the Council, but these must have been offset in some measure by the colorful Sabbath processions to divine services mentioned in the following document—where it comes to serve as thematic motif—as well as the feastday celebrations, and the honor which the office bestowed as well as its power and privileges.

After the mayor and Council, the eight aldermen (the city recorder made a ninth) were most important. Each was assigned to a quarter of the city where his main burden was to supervise law enforcers. The four stewards, elected annually, were next in authority, but they had more minor functions, the most important of which was to hold provost's court. The receiver-general was in charge of tax revenues and city bills which often put him out of pocket; given a salary of 39 shillings for the year, he often remained a creditor of the city for some time after serving his term.

Throughout the sixteenth century the expansion of the Council and the appointment of a special custodian of records other than than the chamberlain testify both to the increasing complexity and details of Council matters and to a new desire for a more tidy administration. The three major appointive officers involved with record-keeping were the town clerk (Richard and Edward Hert, father and son, filled the position from the time of Henry VIII to that of James I), the

chamberlain, and the recorder. During Elizabeth's rule, these special-
ists did much to order and record the town's legal proceedings and
legislative and economic activity more fully. Contrary to the following remarks, the freeman's only function was to elect the mayor: he
was the least significant man in such an oligarchic arrangement.

The man most responsible for the increasingly effective records of
Exeter in Elizabethan times was John Hooker (John Vowell), uncle
to Richard Hooker and author of the pamphlet on city officers which
follows. He was named the city's first chamberlain in September 1555.
As such he was to care for the orphan wards and assist in the administration of certain city properties; in addition he held the bailiwick
of St. Nicholas Fee and later that of Exe Island as well as the custody
of Duryard Wood: his fees totalled to more than nine pounds a year.
A fastidious antiquarian, Hooker was perhaps most valued as keeper
of the city records. He took enormous civic pride in Exeter. Though
he was an aristocrat by birth, he need not have been so indefatigable
an historian as he was: yet to him we owe most of our knowledge of
early Exeter. The work which follows, for example, incomplete and
selective as it is, goes far in naming and defining the sort of local
rule and justice which customarily flourished under Elizabeth I, and
here and there, in hints of illustration or traces of unconscious humor,
he brings to life a document which might in other hands—less fond
of Exeter than his own—have been far less appealing even in trying
to set forth simply an accurate record of routine administrative pro-
cedures.

TEXTUAL NOTES

[For explanatory notes for this selection see page 367.]

The Offices of Excester
  Reference. STC 24889.
  Authorship and Editions. John Hooker's (alias John Vowell's)
pamphlet on the duties of the officers of Exeter exists in a single edition rather unusually printed as a quarto in twos by Henry Denham
(1560-1589) in 1584. The work was licensed and issued with "Vowell's"
Catalog of the Bishops of Excester which collates as a separate work
(also a quarto in twos, A²-K²; K2 missing [probably blank]) and
having its own title-page. Both follow a lengthy and relatively useless
dedicatory epistle.

Collation. 4°; π²; A²-I². π2, title-page; π2v, crest; A1-B2, epistle dedicatory; B2v, crest; C1-I2, text; I2v, blank.

Description of Contents. Title-page in roman and italics with head-piece and design; epistle dedicatory in roman with roman and italics heading; text in black-letter with first paragraph of each section (appearing here as italics) in roman. Running-heads in roman for "The Epistle Dedicatory" (A1-B2); running-heads for text give name of office discussed in roman on that page. Unpaginated; no marginal notes. Tail-pieces on B2 and I2; decorative initials on A1, C1. Large script initials on C1v, D1, D1v, D2, D2v, E1v, E2v, F1, F2, G1, G1v, G2v, H1, H1v, H2, H2v, I1, I1v.

License. Entered to Henry Denham on Dec. 20, 1583 (*SR*, ed. Arber, II, 429).

Base-Copy Text. Bodeleian Gough Devon 34.

Title-page in Full. [Under line under decorative border] A Pamphlet of the / Offices, and duties of euerie parti- / *cular sworne Officer, of the Citie* / of Excester: / *Collected by* Iohn Vowell *alias* Hoker, / Gentleman & Chamberlaine / *of the same.* / *Numb.* 30. / VVho so euer sweareth an oth to bind him / selfe, he shall not breake his promise. / [woodcut border] / Imprinted at London by / *Henrie Denham.* / 1584.

Emendations. [Throughout, these emendations have been silently made: common wealth]commonwealth &]and xxiiij.]xxiiii. vij] vii. and possessive apostrophes have been added.] (C2)there vpon] thereupon C2v)hand seale]handseale (D1)veiwed]viewed night watches]nightwatches (D1v)in netorie]inventorie (D2)there vnto] thereunto (E1v)stranger, or new come]stranger, or newcome (E2v) well for anie thing]well for aniething (F1)specall]speciall (F2) Guild hall]Guildhall (F2v)any thing]anything (G1)dronkards] dronkards, holiedaies,]holie daies, (G1v)peutises]pentises (G2v) for euer]forever (H1v)of anie thing]of aniething (H2v)ante hew] anie hew (I1)*Bull ring]Bullring Bull ring]Bullring* meane time.] meanetime. (I1v)sufficienrlie]sufficientlie immediatlie]immediatelie sunne set]sunneset night watchers]nightwatchers foorth comming] foorthcomming

A Pamphlet of the Offices, and duties of everie particular sworne Officer, of the Citie of Excester

The office and duetie of a Freeman.

HE FREEMAN is the cheefest and principallest member of the commonwealth of the Citie: and as it were out of his loines doo proceed all such as be officers, and have any government or charge in the same. And albeit there be three degrees of freemen, yet they doo all enjoie the same and the like privileges; and none can use nor exercise any trade, art, calling, or office in the Citie, unlesse he be first sworne to the libertiee of the Citie. Manie are the points wherewith the freeman is charged, and is bound to observe; but the most speciall are these.

First he is to be true and faithfull to the Queene's Majestie, hir heires and successors, and under hir to be obedient to the Maior, bailife, and commonaltie.

Also he is to keepe the peace, and defend the liberties of the citie.

Also he is to come before the Maior and common counsell, whensoever he shall be thereunto required.

Also he shall not sue nor implead anie franchised man of the citie, but onelie in the courts of the citie, in all matters determinable in the same, except for lacke of justice.

Also he shall not be a reteiner, nor weare the cloth, liverie, badge, nor cognisance of anie person, being not a franchised person.

Also he is to be justifiable and guildhable to all scots and lots, taxes and tallages, and all other contributions.

Also he may not colour anie man's evill dooings, nor anie forrener's goods, whereby anie hurt or prejudice may turne to the Queene's Majestie, or to the magistrates and state of the citie.

Also he must come yearelie to the election of the Maior and officers, and then and there to give his voice, if he have no reasonable cause of absence.

Also he must be alwaies loiable, and of good behaviour, and no longer shall he be a franchised man than he is so, neither shall he enjoie the liberties of the citie than when he is resiant and dwelling within the same, or the franchises thereof. Sundrie other articles are incident to his charge, which partlie in the oth of a freeman, and partlie in the generall lieger of the citie are conteined. [Clv]

The office of the Maior of the citie of Excester.

The office of the Maior is the highest and cheefest in the citie, and is named in the Latine, Maior, *and in the Saxon Mayer, both which importe one, and the same thing; namelie one more excellent and above the rest. And as he is in authoritie above all others, so much the more is he in godliness, wisdom and knowledge to excell and exceede them. He is the eie and the head of the whole common-weale, and therefore must he see and understand all things incident and apperteining both to the common governement of the citie, and to the preservation of the publike state. His office consisteth in manie branches, of which some in particularitie are as followeth.*

FIrst he is not onelie to be godlie and religious in his owne person, but also to have care, that all others under his government be the like. If therefore there be anie inhabitant, that doo mainteine anie false religion or heresie, or doo not resort to his church, at or upon the sabaoth daies, he is to punish him, or to take order with him according to the lawes.

Also he is upon sundaies and holie daies, to send abroad his officers, to see if anie be sitting upon the stalles, walking the streates, or sitting in tavernes, or using anie gaming at the time of preaching and praiers: and to compell them either to go to the church, or commit them to ward, or to take further order with them, as shall be thought good.

Also he must upon the first fridaie after he hath taken his oth, cause to be proclamed his generall proclamation, for and concerning the government of the citie.

Also when anie proclamation is to be made for hir Majestie, or otherwise, it is to be doone in decent maner, namelie in the open market and assemblie of the people, the sword-bearer with the sword, and the sargeants with their maces, standing before him and his brethren.

Also he is with the bailiffes, upon everie mondaie through the whole yeare, to keepe the Queene's court, in the open Guildhall, and then and there, uprightlie to minister justice, and to give true judgements in all matters depending before them, and to see true records to be kept.

Also he is to see the peace and common tranquillitie to be kept and [C2] observed, and the offenders punished.

Also he and his officers is to attend weekelie the markets, for all maner corne and victuals, that the same be wholesome and good, and at reasonable prices.

Also that no victuals nor wares be forestalled, ingrossed, or regrated, contrarie to the lawes.

Also that he doo from time to time, as occasion shall serve, take the view and search of all maner of measures, weights, and vessels, whether they be according to the statute; and being defective to reforme the same.

Also upon everie mondaie to give to the bakers the assise of bread, and weekelie to examine and weigh their bread, whether the same be according to the assise given or not.

Also that he give to the brewers the assise of their drinke, and to set reasonable prices for and upon the same.

Also he shall command his stewards, constables, and other his officers to make search everie moneth once; in all and everie suspect place, for plaiers at games unlawfull, keepers of ill rule, nightwatchers, vagarant, naughtie, and suspect persons, and such strangers, as who cannot give account for their honest life, and them to commit to ward, to be kept or be punished, according to their offense, and by order of the lawes.

Also he shall take bonds and sufficient suerties of everie innekeeper, tipler, and for keeping of good rule in their houses.

Also he is yearelie to keepe lawe courts, and cause inquisition to be taken of all things concerning the state of the citie, and liberties of the same.

Also he is to see the nightwatches in the times appointed, to be kept.

Also he shall yearelie make his perambulations round about the citie, and about the limits and bounds of the same; and shall also cause the like perambulations to be made everie rogation weeke, about the limits and bounds of the countie.

Also he shall twise in the yeare at Michelmas and Easter, visit the almeshouses of the citie, and examine whether the same be ordered as it apperteineth.

Also he shall yearelie call to account all the collectors for the poore in everie parish, and to see that the poore be provided for, according to the statute.

Also the Maior being the eschetor of the citie, and warden in socage, [C2v] is from time to time to cause at everie mondai's court, present-ment to be made of the death of everie citizen and inhabitant, what heires and orphanes he left behind him, and that thereupon he doo take order for the preservation of the orphanes, and of all such goods and rents as doo growe unto them, as also not to admit anie person to the freedome of the citie, but that he be sworne unto the order of the orphanes.

Also he is at all time and times convenient, to call and assemble the common counsell of the xxiiii, unto the counsell chamber, when matter and occasion shall require; and then and there to determine what by their devise and counsell is to be determined.

Also he is then and there to see and command everie one of the said xxiiii, and all other persons, comming there, to behave and use them-selves modestlie, soberlie, and in all good maner: according to the orders of the said house: and whoso shall offend therein, to be pun-ished accordinglie.

Also he is to appoint six of the forsaid xxiiii, to be auditours as well of the account of the generall receiver, as of all other accounts, for and concerning anie of the citie's rents, receipts, or revenewes.

Also he may not be absent from out of the citie anie night, except it be for some necessarie and urgent cause; and in his absence he is to appoint his lieutenant in writing under his handseale.

Divers other things doo belong to his office, which more at large are to be seene in the great lieger booke.

The office of the Stewards.

THe Stewards are verie ancient officers of this citie, and were in the time of the Saxons, named in Latine Praepositi, *and in the Saxon tong* Portegreves, *that is to saie; The wise, grave governours of the citie or towne: after the conquest they were named* Praefecti, *which*

in the Normand and French toong, are called Provorstes: *the name of
the person is worne out, but the court of their jurisdiction reteineth
his former name, being called the provorst court; after this in respect
of the courts kept before them, they were called* Senescalli, *that is to
saie stewards; and not long after, bicause they or some one of them
was put in trust for collecting of the citie's revenewes, they were
called* Ballivi, *bailiffes. These two latter names are still reteined and*
[D1] *indifferently used at these presents. Their offices consist in manie
points, whereof some in particular as followeth.*

FIrst they al, or two at the least of them, are to be attendant, present
and sitting, as well with the Maior upon everie mondaie, in the court
of the Guildhall, as also in their own court, called the Provorst court,
which they may adjourne and keepe, from daie to daie, at their owne
will and pleasure.

Also they are to see true records to be kept, true justice to be ministred, and true judgements to be given in all causes, depending in
either of the courts before them.

Also they are to attend the Maior, at his going to the sermons at
S. Peter's, upon the sondaies at the forenoone, and at his going and
returning, at the Guildhall court, upon everie mondaie, and at the
markets and proclamations: and upon everie saturdaie, at the shambles, and at all other times, whensoever they shall be called and required.

Also forasmuch as they are clarkes of the market, they are to execute
and doo, what dooth apperteine to the clarke of the market, that is
to saie; That corne and victualles brought to the market, be good and
wholesome, and sold at prices reasonable. That no victualles or wares
brought to the citie, or in market, be forestalled, ingrossed, nor regrated. That all vessels, weights and measures, be viewed and searched,
and being found defective, to be redressed according to the lawes.
That bakers doo keepe their assise, and brewers doo sell according to
the price appointed unto them. With manie other articles belonging
to the clarke of the market.

Also that they doo monethlie, and as often as need shall require,
make search throughout the citie, for all lewed, idle, and vagarant persons, for all plaiers at unlawfull games, for nightwatchers, and suspected persons, and for all manner of misdemeanors, whatsoever.

Also that they doo see the peace and tranquillitie to be kept, and
that everie inhabitant have in readines, some sufficient weapon in his

house, for keeping of the same, and restraining of the disloiall and unrulie persons.

Also that they doo see and cause, all annoiances, which they know of themselves, or which be presented of others, to be remooved and amended.

Also that at all times, when nightwatches be appointed, they or some one of them, be at the Guildhall, and to give the charge to the [D1v] watchmen.

Also that they nor anie of them, be absent anie one night out of the citie, without licence of the Maior, and that at all times, two at the least, be still continuing within the citie. The residue of their charge, is conteined in the blacke lieger.

The office of the Receiver.

THe Receiver is alwaies one of the foure bailiffes, and hath the like and the same charge, as everie of them hath: but the office of the Receiver is particular to himselfe, and none is chosen thereunto, except he be one of the number of the common counsell, or xxiiii. And concerning this office, these are the things which are speciallie required of him.

FIrst that he doo collect and gather all such summe or summes of money, rents, revenewes, issues, and profits, belonging to the citie, as well ordinarie as extraordinarie, and incident unto his office and charge.

Also he is to disburse, defraie and paie, all such summe and summes of monie ordinarie and extraordinarie: for charges, expenses, fees, rents, annuities whatsoever, due and paiable by the chamber of the citie: so that in extraordinarie charges, he have a sufficient warrant for the same.

Also he is to have a speciall care to the edifices, howsings, buildings, walles, water conduicts, and all other works of the citie, and to see the same to be builded, repaired, and sustained, in all things needfull and necessarie, saving that in anie new worke, he shall not bestowe therein above fortie shillings, without the consent of the Maior and the xxiiii.

Also he shall attend or cause to be attended, all the labourers and workemen in all the citie's works, and so see them to be weekelie paid and satisfied of their wages, and thereof to keepe a true booke of accompt.

Also he shall receive into his custodie by inventorie all the powder, shot, ordinances, armour, and artillerie, and all other things belonging to the citie, and safelie and in good order to keepe the same, and at the yeare's end, to deliver the same up, or a just accompt thereof.

Also he shall keepe the keies of the counsell chamber, and keepe in [D2] safetie, the records, immunities, evidences, and all other things there kept, and to be kept, without disclosing of anie secrets thereof.

Also he shall, after the end of his yeare and office, yeeld, and deliver, and make a true and perfect accompt, before the auditors appointed, of all his receits, and paiments, and that the same be fullie concluded and determined, before the election of a new Maior and officers. And what he shall be found to owe upon his account, the same to be foorthwith paid.

Also he shall attend the common counsell, at all time and times, whensoever they shall assemble and meete, for, and about, anie of the citie's affaires, and not to be absent without some speciall cause.

The office of the Recorder.

THe Recorder is an officer of the best credit, and in cheefest place next to the Maior, and chosen thereunto for his wisedome, knowledge, and learning, that thereby the governement of the citie in ech degree and estate, should well and orderlie be directed. His name is derived out of the Latine toong, Recordator, which signifieth a rememberer, or adviser: that is to put everie man in remembrance of his dutie, both according to the course and order of the lawes, and according to the orders and customes of the citie, and to see all things in government, to be directed accordinglie. And bicause the use of his service was continuallie necessarie, therefore in times past he was ever resident and dwelling within the citie, or verie neere to it, whereby accesse at all times presentlie was had unto him, for his advise and counsell in all matters of weight. His office consisteth cheefelie in these points following.

FIrst he is to aide, attend and assist the Maior and bailiffes, in all their courts, and to direct the same according to the course and order of the lawes, and that justice be uprightlie ministred.

Also he is to see that the records of the court be made and entred truelie, and that they be safelie kept and preserved.

Also he is at the end of everie yeare, to see the records of the yeare past, and all rolles of accounts, to be brought into the counsell chamber of the citie, and there to be laid up in the treasurie and place appointed, safelie to be conserved. [D2v]

Also he is to attend the Maior and common counsell, from time to time, and at all times, whensover he shall be called: as also to be at the yearelie elections of the Maior and officers.

Also he is to attend and be, at everie quarter sessions, and gaole deliverie, if he have not some urgent and necessarie let, and that then he is to appoint some other wise and grave man in his stead.

Also he is to defend and mainteine the orphanes and the liberties, franchisies and privileges of the citie.

Sundrie other articles be incident to his charge, which more at large are conteined and set downe in the blacke booke or leiger.

The office of the xxiiii. of the common counsell, and of everie of them.

THe common counsell of the citie, named the xxiiii. is a selected and a chosen companie, of the most wise and gravest citizens of the citie, and who have beene tried, and borne the office of one of the baliffes of the same. They were sometimes xxxvi. in number, and of which the Maior then was none: but sithens, the kings of this realme have reduced them, to the number of xxiiii. and thereof the Maior is alwaies one. They have no authoritie nor jurisdiction in anie matters judiciall, be it civill or criminall, other than to advise, aide and assist the Maior and bailiffes: but they are to mainteine, devise, order, and establish all good acts, orders, and ordinances, as be most convenient and good, for the preservation of the bodie of the commonwealth, and of ancient customes, liberties and orders of the same, and of the rents and revenues of the citie. The particular and most speciall points incident to their charges and offices, are as followeth.

FIrst they are upon reasonable summons, to come and to appeare at the counsell chamber of the said citie, as well yerelie at the times appointed and accustomed, for the election of the Maior and officers, as at all other time and times, when they shall be summoned upon paine of such penalties, as by the orders of this citie are limitted, unlesse he have a lawfull cause of absence. [E1]

Also when they are assembled and come togither at the time appointed, they shall then and there take their proper place appointed,

and in all modestie, wisedome, and sobrietie, behave and use themselves, and not to depart from thence, during the times of their counsell and consultations, unlesse they be licensed, upon paine of the
penalties alreadie ordered, and assessed.

Also when anie matter is proposed, then everie one who is to speak
his mind, shall stand up, in all reverence and dutifull manner: and
then to speake, and declare his opinion uprightlie, without anie
maner of affection, and as shall be for the best behoofe of the commonwealth.

Also whatsoever shall be there concluded, and determined, they are
to see the same to be set downe, and registred, in their booke of acts,
and before their departure, to heare the same read openlie unto them.

Also they shall not discover, nor disclose anie of their secrets, or
counsels, to anie person or persons, to the hurt or prejudice of the
citie, upon the paines which be limitted: and as by the saied Maior,
and common counsell, shall be further ordered, and set downe.

Also they shall not let, set, demise, sell, nor alienate, anie parts of
the citie's lands, rents, revenewes, or other commodities, but to and
for the best advantage, benefit, and commoditie of the citie, and commonwealth of the same.

Also there shall no assemblie be made to passe, doo or conclude anie
thing, under the number of twelve persons at the least, and what shall
be agreed upon and concluded by the said whole assemblie, or the more
part of them being present, to be of effect; and for a perfect order.
Provided, that if in anie matter proposed, the voices be equall and of
like number, then the Maior shall give his double voice, and so the
matter to be determined.

Also none of xxiiii. shall misuse or misname one the other in
word or deed, upon paine of such penalties as be for such offenses
provided.

Also the said xxiiii. shall attend and accompany the Maior upon
the festivall daies, and upon the election daies, and to bring him home
to his house from S. Peter's, and from the guildhall.

Also they shall have a speciall care and regard to the preservation
of all the liberties, priviledges, and orders of the citie, and especiallie
to the charter of the orphanes, according to the statute and ordinance
therefore provided. [E1v]

Also they shall yearelie attend the Maior, for the viewing of the
limits, bounds, and walles of the citie.

The office of an Alderman.

THe Alderman, is a verie ancient officer, in all cities and townes, and in great estimation and credit, in the times of the Saxons and Brittons. They were alwaies the most ancient, grave, and wisest men, and thereof they looke their name, as who saith Elder men; not altogither in respect of age, but for their wisedome, gravitie, and good counsels: they have beene officers, in all the best commonwealths in all ages, as in Roome, where they were called Senators, in Athens, where they were called Areopagitae, and in Sparta, and there named Ephori, and so the like in all other good cities; their offices were rather inquisitive than judiciall, that is, to make inquirie and search, whether that all things were in good order, and what were the abuses to bee amended, which being knowne and understood, then by their advise and counsels, and according to the lawes, reformation insued. The order and maner of their inquisitions, is the like, or the same, as in times past was used in this citie, and at these presents is kept and observed in the citie of London, and there called by the name of the wardemote's inquest. The speciall points whereof be as followeth.

FIrst they are everie moneth, to make a search throughout their wards; and twise in the yeare, to make inquirie by the othes of a jewrie, whether that the peace be kept, and whether everie inhabitant have a club, sword, or some other sufficient weapon in readines, for keeping the peace, and also whether everie man be assistant, and in readines, to helpe and succour the officer therein.

Also whether anie stranger, or newcome, be received into anie house, and there harbored above a convenient time.

Also whether anie undertenants be admitted, without licence of the alderman of the quarter.

Also what journimen, and apprentises, everie artificer hath, and in what order.

Also whether there be anie outlawes, felons, riotars, barrators, [E2] night-watchers, bawdes, whoores, or anie misliving, or suspect persons in the warde.

Also whether the Maior's Proclamation be observed and kept.

Also whether anie person do breake anie the orders to be enquired by the clarkes of the market: that is, for forestalling, ingrossing and regrating: Whether victuals be good and whoalesome, and solde at prices reasonable: Whether vessels, weightes, and measures, be sealed, marked, and true.

Also whether the Bakers do keepe the assise appointed, and whether every one have his marke upon his bread.

Also whether anie hostler or Innekeeper do bake his bread within his house and sell it.

Also whether the brewers do brewe according to the Maior's price, and his vessels do conteine their just contentes, and be marked.

Also whether there be anie noisance or purpestures in the Citie, as by setting of pales, wales, stales, bulkes, porches, windowes, and such like, whereby any incroching is used: or anie timber, stones, doonghils, or heapes of durt, or any other thing be cast and laid in the streets to the letting or hindering of anie waie, or to the anoisance of anie person.

Also whether anie doo keepe slaughtering within the Citie, or doo keepe and feede anie hogges, duckes, or anie other filthie beast.

Also whether the streetes be kept cleane, and swept twise in the weeke at least.

Also whether anie house be ruinous, and stand dangerouslie, and whether anie chimney, oven, or fornance, or backes, or heathes for fire do stand dangerously and in perill of fire, and the same not presented by the scavenger.

Also whether there be crookes, ladders, and buckets in readines to serve if neede should be in perill of fire: and whether everie man have in a readines a vessell of water at his doore when anie house is adventured with fire, and not advertised by the scavengers.

Also whether anie leprosie or sicke person, vagabonds or beggers do go abroade a-begging within the Citie, other than such as be licenced, and be not brought to the cage or other prison.

Also whether everie officer do attend his office and do his dutie, and whether any do use any extortion, briberie, or anie inordinate meanes by waie of corruption. [E2v]

The office of the Chamberlaine.

THe Chamberlaine is an officer of a late erection, and was made and ordered by act of Parleament. His office chiefly and especiallie concerneth the orphanes, and then consequentlie in all things concerning the governement and the state of the commonwealth: and therefore it is verie requisite that he be wise, learned, and well acquainted in all the orders, ordinances, customes, and the whole estate of the commonwealth. *The chiefest points incident and apperteining to his office in particularitie are as followeth.*

FIrst he is to attend the Maior and common counsell at all times, being lawfullie summoned, and according to his knowledge to advise, instruct, and informe them in all things concerning the governement, usages, customes, liberties, and privileges of the Citie.

Also he if he be thereunto required, in the absence of the towne-clearke, shall sit downe and write all such actes, orders, and determinations, as by the Maior and common counsell shall be concluded and agreed upon.

Also he shall not discover nor open the secrets and counsels of the Maior and common counsell to the hurt of them, or of the commonwealth.

Also he shall see that all the records, charters, miniments, evidences, and other writings of the chamber shall be safely kept in the treasurie of the counsell chamber, and shall not deliver, carrie out, nor shew them, or anie of them out of that place, to any person or persons without the consent of the Maior, or some necessarie and urgent cause.

Also he shall be present and attendant at all and everie the Citie's audits, and all the accompts to be heard and passed before the auditors, he shall see and cause to be put up in the treasurie of the counsell chamber.

Also he shall from time to time survey and take the view of all the cities, manors, lordships, woods, lands, and housings, and to see that no part thereof be impaired, imbecilled, or lost, and the same or anie part being ruinous or in decaie, to be in time convenient repaired and amended.

Also he shall aide, helpe, and instruct the receiver, and all other officers in all things to their office apperteining, as well for aniething concerning the citie's works, as for the overseeing of the workemen, [F1] and providing all things necessarie for the same.

Also he shall have a speciall care to the defending and preservation of the commonwealth, and of all the priviledges of the same, and especiallie of the orders of the orphanes according to the charter, orders, and ordinances of the same.

The office of the Towneclarke.

THe Towneclarke was an officer even as old as the oldest, and in times past he was yearely chosen as other officers, and most common-lie he was one of the stewardes or bailiffes: of which number one was alwaies learned and of good experience and knowledge in the lawes, usages, customes, and orders of the citie: but in the ende for sundrie reasons and considerations, this office was altogether cast upon one man, who beeing once chosen, did continue therein so long and untill he died, or for some reasonable cause was remooved. The office is of great credite and importance, for he is not onlie to write and trulie to set downe both in records and in bookes what is done by the Maior and bailiffes in their courts, and by their offices, and by the com-mon counsell in their assemblies, but also to informe and instruct them what is to be done, and what everie of them ought to do: and there-fore his service is so requisite and necessarie, that he can at no time be absent, or elong himselfe from out of the citie without speciall license. The chiefest points of his office are these.*

FIrst he must be honest, wise, and learned, and well acquainted in the knowledge of the charters, records, customes, liberties and orders of the citie, which he shall defend.

Also he must attend the Maior and bailiffes at and in all their courts, and at and in doing their offices at all time and times, and is to instruct and informe them how they are to proceed in the execution thereof.

Also he may not lie out or be absent out of the citie anie one night, without speciall leave and licence.

Also he is to make true entries, and to keepe true records of all the whole processe of the Maior and bailiffes' courtes, and the same to engrosse weekelie in parchment, and at the yeare's end to deliver them into the treasurie. [Flv]

Also he is to attend the Maior and common counsell, and to give them his best advise in all their dooings, and whatsoever by them or the more part of them shall be determined, shall register and write in their booke of actes: these nor anie other the secrets of the citie shall he not disclose to the hurt or prejudice of them or of the citie.

Also he shall aide and assist, instruct and informe all and everie officer and officers for the true doing of their offices and duties.

Also he shall attend to keepe the audites of the citie, and all the accompts he shall ingrosse in parchment.

Also he must maintaine and defend all the liberties and priviledges of the citie, and the right of the orphanes to his uttermost.

Also he is to attend the markets and the waying of bread, suring of weights and measures, making of proclamations, and finally, whatsover else apperteineth to be done for and concerning the governement of the citie. Many other things are required to be done by him, and which are incident to his charge, and which are more at large set downe in the blacke booke.

The office of the Sergeants.

THe Sergeants are verie auncient officers, and had their beginning when the magistrate had. First they were called Subballiui bicause under the head bailiffs they were wont to collect and gather the issues of the citie, and to execute their precepts and commaundements: after this, they were called Ministricuriae, bicause their greatest service then was to attend the court, and to execute services thereunto apperteining. And lastly, they were and are yet called Seruientes ad clauam. And according to the speciall point of their service they take their severall names Sergeants at the mace: for that is chiefely required of them, to summon, attach, and arrest all such persons as against whome anie action or suite is commenced in anie of the courts within this citie, and by their mace which is their warrant, they are knowne to be the ministers to that end. They are also the generall servitures in all or the most part of all the affaires in the commonweale, and in whose services resteth the performance and execution of all things to be done, wherein, if they should be corrupted, slouthfull, carelesse, and negligent, then should all the travels of the magistrates, the governement of the commonwealth, and the execution of all lawes and orders be fru-[F2] strate and come to small effect. It is requisite therefore that they be of good name, credite, and honestie, voide and free from all corruption and briberie, and also diligent and carefull to execute and performe what to their offices apperteineth and belongeth. Many are the things and sundrie which are incident and apperteining to their ministeries and services, and all which were too long to be set downe in these presents, but of manie, these few heere following may suffice.

FIrst that they be men of honest fame and of good credit and behaviour, and sworne to the liberties of the citie, that they be loiall

and obedient to the magistrates and governors, and carefull to keepe
and mainteine the common peace and quietnesse, and readie to do and
performe all such things as to them shall be commanded and injoined
by the Maior and magistrates.

Also they must serve and attend the Maior at all time and times
convenient, namely, to bring him upon sundaies and festivall daies
to the churches at divine services and preachings: at the Guildhall upon
everie mondaie to and from the court: at the markets upon wednesdaies
and fridaies, and at the shambles upon saturdaies, at making of proclamations, &c.

Also some one of them by course is speciallie to attend the Maior
himselfe, and not to be absent from him nor his house.

Also they are to attend the bailiffes at the provorst court, and at the
markets, and in all things to be doone at their commandements.

Also they are to summon, attach, and arrest all and everie such person and persons as are to be summoned, attached, and arrested by
action or commandement, and all such as be so summoned, attached,
or arrested, to carrie and bring to the counter or place appointed for
ward, unlesse he or they do put in sufficient baile, if the matter be
baileable.

Also they shall impanell indifferent inquests betweene partie and
partie, and shall certifie the same to the court, before the same be returned.

Also they shall levie and execute all maner of distresses, condemna-
tions, judgements, and executions awarded in anie of the courts: they
shall likewise do and execute all maner of commandements and precepts of the Maior and common counsell, justices, and Aldermen.

Also they shall from time to time give summons to everie inhabi-
[F2v] tant for their watchmen and marketmen when their turne com-
meth.

Also they shall not take anie bribes, nor be corrupted to do anything
for and concerning the executing of their office.

Also they shall upon everie mondaie at the court present all breakers
of the peace, all maner of misdemeanors which they knowe to have
bene done the weeke before.

Also they, or one of them at the least, shall attend the auditors of the
citie, at the time when the audits shall be kept.

Also they shall not lie out of the citie anie one night without speciall
licence.

Also they shall not, so long as they shal be sergeants, weare the liverie, or serve anie man in anie office or otherwise.

Also they shall not discover nor disclose the counsels or secrets of the citie to anie person or persons, to the hurt of the citie.

Also what service soever is to be done concerning the citie and governement of the same, they are, and must be at all commandements, and in readines to execute the same.

Also they shall upon everie mondaie present the death of everie inhabitant of the citie, which leaveth anie heire or orphanes behind him.

The rest of their charge and offices are written in the blacke booke.

The office of the Constables.

THe office of a Constable is verie ancient, and in times past the chiefest within the realme for conservation of the peace, and thereof taketh his name Constabularius, quasicuncta stabiliens, *one that establisheth and setteth all things in peace, good order and quietnesse. What constables by law may do, and in times past were wont to do, it is needelesse now to set downe, because a great part of their office is shortned and committed by statute to the justices of the peace: and unto whome and to whose commendements they are now servitors and to attend, yet manie things are incident and belonging to their charge, of which, these which follow, are the chiefest to be kept by such as are within cities and townes.* [G1]

FIrst they must keepe, and see to be kept the Queene's peace, and the common tranquillitie of the citie and countie.

Also they must take and apprehend, all malefactors, peacebreakers, rowters, and rioters, all men going armed, or carieng any pistols, and wearing any privie coate, all traitours, felons, murtherers, and everie other person or persons, offending against the peace, and the crowne, and them to commit, and bring to the ward, to be safelie kept, untill he be brought before the Maior and Justices.

Also they are to take, and arest all such persons as live idelie, and suspiciouslie, night-watchers, dronkards, plaiers at unlawful games, roges, vagabonds, whores, and bawds, and all such as cannot give good account, how and in what vocation they doo live.

Also they are from time to time, to search, both by daie and by night, all suspected houses, and all innehouses, for all suspected persons, and strangers, and such as have lien above iii. daies and iii. nights, in any inne, or other house, having no sufficient businesse, or other cause so to doo, and them they are to commit and send to ward, there to remaine, untill they be further examined.

Also they are to search and view, whether everie inhabitant, and house-keeper, have in his house, and in readines, a club, or some sufficient weapon, for defense of himselfe, and for keeping of the peace.

Also they must upon Sundaies and holie daies, at the time of praiers and preachings, walke the streets, to see and search, whether anie person and persons, be sitting or standing idelie in the streets, or be at anie alehouse, or tipling house, or be at anie game or games, and without just cause be absent from the sermons, preachings, and praiers, and these either to commit to ward, or send to the church.

Also they are upon Sundaies and holidaies, upon the court daies, and quarter session daies, to attend the Maior, from thence to his house.

Also they are to attend the Maior and Justices, to doo and obeie their commandements, for all things concerning their offices, and by them to be doone.

Also they are upon everie Mondaie, to present the death of everie free citizen, for that weeke past, leaving anie heire or orphane behind him, or having any lands, or tenths, and who is his next heire.

Also they are to joine with the scavengers, and other expert men, whensoever anie question is betweene the Lord, and the tenant, or occupier of any house, for and concerning paiments, of rents, repara-[G1v] tions, ammisances, remooving of implements, &c.

Also to view and search, whether any brewer, baker, or other person, have their ovens, fornaces, chimneis, or backs, ruinous and in danger and perill of fire.

Finallie they are to attend in all matters touching the Queene's service, the keeping of the peace, the repressing of malefactors, and of the commendements of the Maior, the justices and the aldermen.

Also they are speciallie to attend the Maior, as well upon sundaies to and from S. Peter's at the sermons, as upon mondaies to and from the court of the Guildhall, as at all other times convenient and being thereunto required.

For other things concerning their offices, looke in the blacke booke.

The office of the Scavengers.

THe Scavingers are necessarie officers, and who cannot be wanting in anie well governed citie or towne; bicause by them and their service, all things noisome to the health of man, and hurtfull to the state of the bodie of the commonwealth, are advertised unto the magistrate, and so they be a meanes of the redresse thereof. And therefore they be called scavengers, as who saith, shewers or advertisers, for so the word soundeth. The speciallest points incident to their offices, are these.

FIrst they are to see the peace and common tranquillitie of the citie to be kept.

Item that the streetes be well paved, and meete for all passages of man, horse, and cart, and that they be weekelie swept and made cleane, and the sweeping carried awaie: and that none laie timber, stones, or anie like thing in the streets, but during the time of building.

Item that there be no slaughter of cattell or beast, kept within the walles: that no pigges or filthie beast be kept within the same: no doong hils, nor anie noisome thing kept, whereby the aire be corrupted, or the people annoied.

Item that there be no houses, pentises, chimneis, nor walles, nor anie other thing, hanging or standing dangerouslie, to the perill and danger of such as shall passe thereby. [G2]

Item that they doo make view and search, whether everie inhabitant, doo yearelie and from time to time, as occasion shall require, cleanse and sweep their chimnies, and that all ovens, fornaces, mantels, backes, and such like, be kept in such order, as thereby no perill of fire may happen.

Item that when anie house is adventured with fire, that then they do take order as well for voiding of the presse of people, as to see and to bring ladders, crookes, water, and all things necessarie in place for quenching of the fire.

Item that everie householder have at all time and times in the summer and hote and drie weather, a tub or some other vessell full of water in readines, at or neere their foredore, for the quenching of fire if anie house should happen to be adventured, and for cleansing of the streetes.

Item that the common conduites be cleane and orderlie kept, and the pipes which convaie the water from the spring to the said conduits be well repaired and mainteined from time to time, and that no private person do incroch the common commoditie of the waters therein for brewing, washing, or anie such like use, other than for dressing of their meates and such like.

Item that no maner of person do incroch anie part of the streetes or waies to his private use, nor do build nor set anie porch, boulke, stall, windowes, wall, chimneie, or anie other edifices upon the said streets or soile, or anie part thereof, before a composition be made with the Maior and common counsell.

Item that whensoever anie controversie doth happen betweene lord and tenant, for and concerning the orderly paiments of rents, or removing of implements, or other buildings, that they call unto them the constables and other expert artificers and men of knowledge, and then according to the truth and customs of the citie, to decide the same.

Item that they weekelie upon everie mondaie at the court do present all breaches of peace, misorders, and all other defaults appertaining to their office.

Item that they do upon everie sundaie, festivall daie, and mondaie, attend the Maior to and from his house to the court, and to the church at S. Peter's at the sermons.

Item that they be attendant to the Maior, bailiffes, and all other officers at all time and times whensoever they shall be required concerning anie service of the prince and commonwealth.

The rest of their charge is conteined in the blacke booke. [G2v]

The office of the Swordbearer.

THe office of the Swordbearer is of a late erection, and had his beginning when King Henry the vii. in the xiii. yeare of his reigne came to this citie for the resisting of Perkin Warbecke, at which time, for the good service of the Maior and citizens, he gave his owne sword from his waste unto the Maior, with the priviledge that the same and the hat of maintenance should forever at all times convenient be borne before him, and for the doing of this service, the swordbearer was then chosen, the points of whose office are these, and such like as followeth.

FIrst he is to attend the Maior for bearing the sword before him upon sundaies and festivall daies, when he goeth to S. Peter's to the sermons, upon mondaies and session daies when he goeth to the hall, and upon and at all other times and daies when anie proclamation shall be made, or he thereto required.

Also he shall attend the Maior at the markets, and at the waying of the assises of the bakers' bread, and all other like services.

Also he is to attend the Maior at his table, and at all other convenient times when he shall be thereunto required.

Also he shall keepe the common peace, apprehend malefactors, and preserve the state and priviledges of the citie as much as in him lieth.

Also he shall not discover nor disclose anie secrets or counsels of the citie to the prejudice of the same, nor consent to anie hurt to be done against the said citie or anie officer, but shall discover it to such officer or officers as it shall appertaine.

Also as being a sergeant at armes he shall attend the causes of the orphanes, as well at the court of the orphanes, as at all other times, and in all other things pertaining to the behoofe of orphanes, according to the orders of the same, that is to saie, he shall upon everie mondaie present the name of everie inhabitant of the citie dead, and leaving anie orphanes: he shall call for the testament and inventorie of everie such decessed man, he shall call the praisers appointed before the Alderman of the quarter to be sworne, he shall sequester the goods, and execute the writs of *Scire facias* and *fieri facias,* and all processe to him directed for the behoofe of the orphanes: he shall summon the courts for orphanes as to him shall be commanded. Sundrie like [H1] things are incident to his charge, and which at large are set downe in the booke of orders for orphanes.

The office of the wardens of the Magdalen and of the poore.

THese officers are of trust, and committed to such as should take a speciall care for the poore, as well for the good ordering of them in persons, as for the preservation of such lands and goods as are provided for their sustenance and maintenance.

FIrst therefore the warden of the Magdelen is to governe and to see to be governed all such Lazar people, as shall be received for sicke persons into the Magdelen house, according to the orders of the said house, and according to the direction of the Maior and common counsell.

Also that they be weekelie paide of such salaries and stipends as to them is and shall be assigned by the Maior and common counsell.

Also the wardens' proctor shall provide and see to be provided meate, drinke, washing, cleansing, and all other things necessarie for them.

Also the said warden shall see their church, houses, and buildings from time to time to be repaired.

Also he shall be carefull to save, keepe, and preserve the lands, rents and profits whatsoever, appointed and allowed for the maintenance of the said hospitall.

Also they shall not admit anie person or persons to be one of the said hospitall, without the consent of the Maior and common counsell, and that the same be a sicke person in the disease of the leprosie.

Also they shall not set, let, nor demise anie the lands belonging to the said hospitall, without the consent and agreement of the Maior and xxiiii.

Also they shall yearelie yeeld up and make a true accompt before the auditors of the citie of all their receipts and paiments, and upon the determination of the said accompt, shall discharge, paie, and satisfie what shall be found remaining in their hands, and to be due by them.

The like is required of everie warden of thè poore, and for everie almeshouse, and of everie collector for the same [H1v]

The office of the wardens of the bridges.

THe wardens of the bridges, commonlie called by the names of the wardens of Exbridge, are verie auncient officers, and of great credite, and in times past great circumspection was had in the choise of them, and for the most part they were most grave citizens. They were alwaies two in number, the one being the elder, and the other the yonger. The things which are incident to their offices, are as followeth.

FIrst they both jointly are to have the care to view and search from time to time the two bridges, which belong to the citie's reparations, as namely, Exbridge, and Cowleighbridge, and the banks next adjoining on everie side of Saint Leonard's weare, and what defaults soever they shall finde and see to be amended, or be advertised thereof by the Receiver or Chamberlaine of the citie, that they do cause the same to be repaired and amended.

The head warden is to collect, receive, and gather all the rents, revencwcs, profits and issues belonging to the bridges, and shall after the end of his yeare, at the time appointed, make a true and perfect account of all his receipts and paiments, before the auditors of the citie, asking no allowance, but as shall be just and true.

Also he shall procure and provide from time to time, by the advise and direction of the chamberlaine of the citie, all things meete and necessarie, as well for the reparations of the houses belonging to the bridge, as for the bridges themselves, and all things thereunto apperteining.

Also he shall provide and procure by the advise aforesaid, meete and convenient workemen and labourers, for and about all the aforesaid buildings and reparations, and to see them weekelie and from time to time to be paied for their salaries and wages.

Also he shall see and command the bridge called Exbridge, to be clensed and swept from time to time, and that no doonghils, nor heapes of durt doo lie upon the same.

Also the yoong warden, is to attend and take the oversight of the workemen, that they doo keepe their times and worke, and that nothing doo want them being necessarie.

Also he is to keepe account of the number of the workcmcn, and to see that there be no wast or spoile, either of the worke, or of aniething provided for the worke. [H2]

Also they are to attend the Maior upon sundaies and feastivall daies, to and from S. Peter's church, as other officers doo, and are bound to doo.

The office of the wardens of the Shambles.

THe office of the wardens of the Shambles, are verie ancient, and chosen yearelie by the Maior and common counsell, when other officers are, and their office is speciallie to attend all things as be necessarie, for and concerning flesh victuals, and the good ordering of the same, and of the Shambles. The speciall points are these.

FIrst they are upon everie saturdaie, except it be some holie daie, or festivall daie, at or about one of the clocke, in the afternoone, to come to the Maior's house, and to bring him to and from the shambles.

Also they are to see, then and at all other times, the shambles to be furnished with meate, good, wholsome, and sufficient for the citie.

Also that no slaughters be kept in anie place, within the walles of the citie.

Also that no pigs be nourished, nor doonghilles, nor anie corrupt thing breeding a corrupt aire, be kept within the walles of the citie.

Also that no bull unbaited, nor sow brenning, nor yew tupping, nor anie beast unseasonable be slaughtered, nor flesh blowen, foistered, salted, or unreasonable, be set to sale.

Also that no butcher doo ingrosse, forestale, nor regrate, anie victuals, nor doo sell the same, but at reasonable prices.

Also that everie butcher, upon everie market daie, doo bring with the carcase, the fell or skinne, of everie beast slaughtered.

Also that they doo attend upon everie sundaie, and festivall daies, the Maior to the church, and upon everie mondaie, to the guildhall court, as other officers are bound to doo, and that upon everie mondaie, at the court, they doo present all such faults, as have the weeke before beene committed, and ought to be presented.

Item that none of the butchers doo keepe anie market or open shop, upon the sundaies. [H2v]

The office and dutie of the Porters.

THe Porters, are officers of good trust, and unto whose credit is committed the safetie of the citie: for when everie man taketh his rest, and thinketh to be in safetie, it is their office, that the gates be not at commandement, of such as by whom their restes, and sleepes be disturbed, nor unquieted, by receiving any person or persons into the gates, nor in dooing of anie act, which may be hurtfull to the citie, or inhabitants of the same.

FIrst therefore, they must everie night, shut and make fast the citie's gates, at the times and hours appointed, and accustomed, that is, at ten of the clocke at night, in the summer, and at nine of the clocke in the winter, and likewise must open the said gates, at the times accustomed, that is, at foure of the clocke in the morning in the summer, and at five of the clocke in the winter.

Also in the times of warres, commotions, and rebellions, they are to deliver up the keies, into the custodie of the Maior.

Also at no time in the night, after the gates be shut, they shall suffer anie person, or persons, to come or go in and out, but such as they doo knowe to be honest, and of good credit, and conversation.

Also at all time and times, if anie post happen to come, they shall open the gates to receive him, and to bring him to the Maior, and to his lodging.

Also if anie hew and crie shall happen to be, they shall open the gates, to receive and followe the same.

Also if anie tumults, uprores, escapes of prisoners, fiering of houses, or anie such like things shall happen, they shall foorthwith, close and make fast the gates, and so keepe the same shut untill all be appeased, and order given for the opening of them.

Also they shall attend the Maior, upon everie sundaie, and festivall daies, to and from S. Peter's church, and upon everie mondaie, to the guildhall court, as other officers doo, and are bound to doo; and shall at the said court, present all bloudsheds, fraies, and breaches of the peace, and whatsoever else by them is and ought to be presented. [Il]

The office of the Bullring keeper, named commonlie the Maior of the Bull ring.

THe Maior of the Bullring, is an office of countenance, and appointed for the keeping of a good order in such things as be committed
to his trust and office.

FIrst when anie bull or beare baiting be appointed, he is first to make the Maior privie thereof, and no baiting to be used within the citie, but that the said Maior be present or give leave thereunto.

Also he shall see all things to be well and orderlie used at such pastimes.

Also he shall not see or suffer anie pigges, poulterie, or duckes, to rainge abroad the streetes.

Also upon everie market daie he shall not suffer anie horse to stand in the streetes in the market place, but shall cause them to be carried out of the market.

Also if anie straiers come, he shall cause them to be brought to the place of the high conduct upon the market daies, and there to be tied to the ring, and to be proclaimed in the market, and from market daie to market daie, during three markets, to keepe them in pound, or in some place safelie.

Also if the said beasts be chained and challenged, he shall upon proofe made before the Maior and bailiffes, redeliver to the owners, taking his fees, and for the reasonable keeping of such beasts in the meanetime.

Also if the said beasts, at or within three courts, be not challenged, then he shall bring them at the Guildhall, the next mondaie then following, and there to be praised.

Also he shall attend the Maior upon sundaies to the church, and upon mondaies to the court, as other officers doo, and ought to doo. [I1v]

The office of the VVatchemen and VVardens.

THe VVatchmen are officers of trust, for the safe custodie and preservation of the citie, as well in times of troubles and warres, as in the daies of peace, when ordinarie night watches by the lawes of the realme are kept.

FIrst the watchmen, are housholders, who by course are to watch themselves in person, or to appoint some meet and convenient persons in their place, and which are to be well and sufficientlie armed with harnesse and weapon.

Also they are to repaire in the summer in the evening, immediatlie upon the sunneset, unto the Guildhall, and there to take their oth, to heare their charge, and to receive their watchword.

Also they are then to depart hence in good order, and to go to everie of the gates, and to see them to be shut and made fast, and then to come all to Corfoixe or the great conduit: and there to divide themselves into their severall quarters, by order of such as be appointed captaines over them, and the same severall quarters they shall gard and keepe.

Also they shall all night be watchfull and walking abroad in their divisions, leaving alwaies someone at the least at the gate.

Also they shall view and looke whether all things be quiet and in good order, and if they find anie candlelight in anie house late and out of season, they shall cause the same to be put out, unlesse some cause be to the contrarie, and if they find anie fiers perillous, or houses adventured, they shall rowse and call up the scavengers and constables, and other the officers for quenching thereof.

Also if they find anie nightwatchers, plaiers, quarellers, dronkeards, suspect persons, whatsoever, they shall apprehend them, and bring them, either to the ward or to some convenient place, as where the parties may be foorthcomming before the magistrate the next morning.

Also if anie poste or stranger come, they shall receive him, if his arrant and comming be honest, and shall bring him to his lodging, or present him to the magistrate, according as his cause shall require. [I2]

Also they shall attend the Maior upon everie mondaie at the Guild-hall court, and then and there to present what faults have been doone and committed in the nights of their watches.

Also that in their watches they doo ball and kill all such dogges as they shall find balling or ranging in the streets, or lieng out of anie man's house.

There be other officers which are sworne also: as the justices of the peace, the shiriffes, the clarke of the peace, the undershiriffes, &c. But for so much as their offices are limited by statutes, and at large therein expressed, I will referre them to the same.

FINIS.

A discoverie of the treasons attempted by Francis Throckemorton (1584)

Predictably, the most detailed account of the "Throckmorton Plot"—and the only work distributed on the matter—is a government pamphlet of his treasonous activity circulated in England and abroad in June 1584, shortly before his execution. This report is clever propaganda, combining and eventually fusing an incomplete narrative with a didacticism that, in the opening pages, becomes a bit heavy-handed. The pamphlet, reprinted below, invites the reader, as a homily might, to maintain a double perspective—to observe and judge Throckmorton as both individual and symbol.

Francis Throckmorton was only an agent in a complex scheme, but he was well known enough in England. His general reputation was that of an outspoken Catholic. His father had sat in Parliament for Mary Tudor, but he had also managed to be knighted and appointed as a justice in Chester by Elizabeth. Francis's brother was an active Catholic on the continent. Francis, like mad John Somerville, attended Hart Hall, Oxford, before going down to London; after a short period there at the Inner Temple he departed for a grand tour of Europe. His travels seem to have been centered on educating himself to conspiracy. He was frequently in touch with Charles Arundel, Sir Francis Englefield, Charles Paget, and, through them, with other leaders among the English fugitives; and he became acquainted with active Jesuits and Spanish friars in Brussels, Madrid, Rome, Paris, and Eu, Normandy, where Guise had recently founded a seminary to train English and Irish exiles.

This journey was the turning point in Throckmorton's life. Then it was he must have learned of Guise's plan to enter England through Scotland; of his use of Lennox as his agent; of Lennox's fall and departure in December 1582; and of his death and the departure of Mainville, Guise's other agent in Scotland, in May 1583. He probably learned, too, of Guise's determination to continue plans of invasion and of his support from both Rome and Madrid. In response, Throckmorton offered his own information, for when Guise reformulated his

"Enterprise of England," Throckmorton became the English representative and he was asked to supply the names of good harbors and a listing of tides. He was in addition required to prepare a list of known Catholics and weaponry available should other Catholic forces land to capture England and seat the Queen of Scots on the throne at White-hall. So trusted was he, in fact, that he became advisor to the Spanish ambassador in London—for this was an international plot of no mean proportions—and acted as well as Mary Stuart's intermediary by keeping in touch with both Mendoza and the French embassy. He returned to England to perform all these tasks in April 1583.

The month following, one of Hunsdon's men, keeping watch along the border of Scotland, stopped a suspicious man who posed as a tooth-drawer, discovered he was a servant of Mendoza's, and learned he was carrying letters for Mary and Guise hidden behind a little looking-glass. This was the first indication the English government had of Guise's enterprise, but it was sufficient to cause Walsingham to set loose his system of spies. Soon the Jesuit Holt was taken at Leith with letters in cipher and admitted, after a tough cross-examination, that there was "a purpose in hand by the Pope and divers Catholics" to make war on England and reestablish Mary Stuart. Walsingham needed help with the cipher, and he obtained it from a man in the French embassy who called himself "Henry Fagot"; not long after, Fagot told Walsingham that Throckmorton came frequently to the French embassy, but always at night. Furthermore, "On the 29th of April Mr. Throgmorton visited the ambassador's house. He sent to the Queen of Scots some days ago fifteen hundred crowns of the sun, for which Monsieur the ambassador is security." Walsingham now trailed Throckmorton for more than five months, on into the autumn; and when he felt he had the proper opportunity to confront him—Popham says it was on November 4—he raided the rooms of the suspected spy at Paul's Wharf. Throckmorton ran upstairs, chewing and swallowing the letter he was in process of writing to Mary and, apparently, hiding a green velvet-covered casket of secret messages. But his efforts to seek help then and later, as the following narrative reveals, were fruitless.

The Elizabethan habit of thinking in symbols was encouraged by the government as well as by the church; and both interpreted events as archetypal. To find this in the following account is therefore understandable, but there is a considerable loss in hearing only part of the story. The references to Throckmorton's torture on the rack (A2v) are teasing in the extreme, and this understatement only hints at the tortures he underwent: on November 18, for example, Walsingham asked Thomas Wilkes to join the rackmaster Norton at the second torture set for November 19 commenting, "I have seen as resolute man as Throgmorton stoop, notwithstanding the great show he hath made of Roman resolution. I suppose the grief of the last torture will suffice without any extremity of racking to make him more conformable than he hath hitherto shown himself." Again, the whole situation provoked by Walsingham's espionage and his use of double-agents—perhaps Thomas Morgan and Charles Paget were among them, perhaps not—is suggested by the surveillance of Throckmorton (A1v), by the raid on his lodgings (A1v-A2v), by the search for secret letters and maps in hidden houses by night, and by the secret message, written with a coal, that Throckmorton tries to sneak to his solicitor.

Throckmorton's arrest and execution were Walsingham's first real clues to the plot—his network of agents was far from perfect—but here the recounting of this important trial (B3-B3v) is as obscure as the conditions of his imprisonment, and much of the testimony seems to have been an exchange of accusations and denial which led to further torture and extortion. None of this quite holds to Throckmorton's later sentiments when he remarks that he feels he has no extensive Catholic support, nor does the enterprise (C2-C2v) and that there is no man alive who could rescue Mary (C3). Nor does the substance of the pamphlet quite uphold Q. Z.'s comment that the "Queen's most happie Reigne" is a time of "the milde and temperate course" (A1). Admittedly, the pamphlet is framed by repentance, not punishment. Still the dominant motif—first beautifully under-narrated, then restored on C4v—is the image of the rack. In treating this as excruciating torture, as just punishment for heinous crimes, and, finally, as the only result of attempted treason, the didacticism remains as strong at the end of the pamphlet—though now more implicit—as it was in the opening blunt statements of Q. Z.

The "confession" and confessional statements which conclude this work are noticeably in the same style as Q. Z.'s earlier narrative; and like the double perspective in which the work is cast this "double voice" renders the reliability of the work suspect. That is primarily because the pamphlet was not conceived as a newspaper account, but as a newsmagazine interpretation in its theme of right obedience and right order juxtaposed to the increasing confusion, evil, and pain brought on by treachery and rebellion and the associated sins of pride and jealousy (A4; C3v).

TEXTUAL NOTES

[For explanatory notes for this selection see page 368.]

A discoverie of the treasons attempted by Francis Throckemorton
   Reference. STC 24050, 24051.
   Authorship and Editions. The anonymous account of Throckmorton's treason, published by the government, has come down in two sixteenth-century editions, the first in two issues; and in three later editions, one in the eighteenth, and two in the nineteenth, century. There were in addition two translations in the sixteenth century.
   All but one variant between the two issues of the first edition are incidentals; the one substantial variant—what]when on C2—produces an inferior reading in the second issue and is probably a printer's misreading. Changes were made in the preliminaries, the outer forme only of sheets A and B and the inner forme only of sheet C. The full table of variants between issues reads:

1st edition, 1st issue	*1st edition, 2nd issue*
π 2v vndutifully	vnduetifully
A1 verie lewde	very lewde
Francis Throckemorton lately	*Francis Throckmorton* lately
B4v *Royall hands.*	*Royall handes.*
C1v sayde submission,	sayd submission,
C2 *Morgan* (with	*Morgan,* with
intelligence was,	intelligence was (
what I thought	when I thought

Variants between the first and second editions are numerous; there are 262 changes in spelling, punctuation, and the changing of roman to italics typeface (or the reverse). The two substantial variants, probably printers' errors (the setting of the second edition is throughout inferior), are:

STC 24050	STC 24051
C1v former confessions,	former confession,
C2 eminent danger	imminent danger

   The second edition is a page-for-page resetting of the first and uses the spellings of the second issue except for *sayde submission* (C1v) and *what I thought* (C2) where it follows the first issue; there is no reason to suspect authorial intervention here either. The spelling and punctuation differences between the two editions are rather evenly scattered; the compositor(s) for the second edition consistently display(s) a preference for double *e* endings (*hee, bee*) and for *y* (*choyse, enterpryse*) and spells Throckmorton with a medial *e* throughout (*Throckemorton*). The proofing was not as well done for the second edition; hence *Reame.* for *Realme.* (A3v), *gtievous* for *grievous, haypie* for *happie* (C1) and *abid* for *abide* (C3).

Translations. A quarto in German was printed by Richard Schilders, from "Middelburgh," according to the title-page, on Feb. 25, 1585; a Latin translation was printed in octavo (presumably for distribution on the continent) in London in 1584.

Subsequent Editions. This account was later reprinted in *The Harleian Miscellany* (London, 1745), ed. Thomas Osborne, III, 182-193; in the second issue of that collection, ed. Thomas Park (London, 1809), III, 195-200; and in the third edition, called a cheap issue of the second edition, ed. J. Malham (London, 1808 [*sic*]), I, 522-537. In all three instances, the text is most similar to the second issue of the first edition, although the editors have made some changes in capitalization and punctuation.

Collation. 4°; π^2; A-C⁴. π1, title-page; π1v, blank; π2, preface; π2v, letter from a gentleman of Lion's Inn; A1-C4v, text.

Description of Contents. Title-page, mixture of roman and italic type with simple woodcut design; preface in roman type with heading in italics; letter in italics with heading in roman; text in roman with heading in roman. Decorative initials on π2; π2v; and A1; no head-pieces or tail-pieces. Running-head for text: *"A discouerie of Treason"* on each page. Unpaginated. Marginal notes on C1v only; they read "The declaration." and "William Ardington."

License. No certain entry in the *Stationers' Register,* but the sixpence fee paid by Christopher Barker on July 19, 1584 (*SR*, ed. Arber, II, 434) may refer to this pamphlet, for it does not give the work for which Barker is paying. It follows an entry on the same date in which Thomas Nelson paid eightpence for printing "twoo ballades th[e] one of *the traditor* [*sic*] *FFRAUNCIS THROKMORTON* th[e] other of *the sayles newe tantara.* The STC credits Barker with the printing. But Barker need not have paid a fee for an official publication; and this pamphlet has the earmarks of governmental approval and direction: the sparse design, the lack of identification. The presswork is unusually clean; this too is suggestive of Barker.

Base-Copy Text. Bodleian Malone 645(8). Copy consulted for variant issue of first edition: Bodleian Arch.A.f.79; copy consulted for second edition: Bodleian Wood 616(12).

Title-page in Full. A discouerie of the / *treasons practised and attempted a-* / gainst the Queenes Maiestie and / the Realme, by *Francis Throckemorton,* who / *was for the same arraigned and condemned* / in Guyld Hall, in the Citie of London, / *the one and twentie day of* / May last past. / 1584. / [ornamental woodcut of a flower, centered]

Emendations. [Throughout, *hand writing* has been silently changed to *handwriting.*] (A2v)any thing]anything   (B1)of him selfe]of himselfe   (B1v)country men]countreymen   associate him selfe]associate himselfe   (B2)Highnesse]Highnesse's   (B3)an   other   title]another title   (B4)grounding him selfe]grounding himselfe   (C1)my selfe]

myselfe common wealth,]commonwealth, (C1v)brother in Law,]
brother-in-Law, assoone]as soone (C3)before hande.]beforehande.
any thing)]anything) (C4) by my selfe,]by myselfe,

A discoverie of the treasons practised and attempted against the Queene's Majestie and the Realme, by Francis Throckemorton

To the Reader.

HERE IS in this short discourse delivered unto thee (gentle reader) a true report of the treasons and practises of *Francis Throckmorton,* and his complices against the Queene's Majestie and the Realme: which comming to my handes by chance from a gentleman, to whom it was sent into the Countrey, I have presumed to commit the same to the print, to the ende that such as in opinion and conceite are not satisfied, touching the matters proved against him, and the course of proceeding helde with him, might by the sight thereof (if trueth and reason may perswade them) bee resolved of all such doubtes and scruple as have risen by the variable reportes made of the qualitie of his offences, and the maner of dealing used towards him: for the better knowledge whereof, I referre thee to the declaration following, and so commit thee to God. [π 2v]

A letter sent from a gentleman of Lion's Inne to his friend, concerning *Francis Throckmorton,* who was arraigned and condemned of high Treason.

SYr, with my last letters of the first of June, I sent unto you in writing the arraignement of Francis Throckmorton, *penned by a*

gentleman of good skill and credite, being present at the same: and
because it hath seemed unto me that there is some scruple in your
conceite touching the sufficiencie of the evidence produced against
him, I have for your better satisfaction endevoured to attaine to more
particular knowledge thereof, and by the meanes of a secret friend,
there is come unto my hands, a verie perfect declaration, of the whole
proceedings helde by suche as were in commission for the examining
of him before his triall, containing the materiall pointes of the treasons
by him confessed, whereunto there is annexed a submission written
by Francis Throckmorton *to the Queene's Majestie, the fourth of*
June, whereby he acknowledgeth that he hath untruely and unduti-
fully denied his former confessions, and under his owne handwriting
hath eftsoones repeated and confessed the same confessions to be true
(some fewe things onely detracted, but of no moment:) which may in
mine opinion remoove all matter of doubt or scruple conceived by
you or by any other of his just condemnation. You know howe well I
have alwayes loved the man, and delighted to converse with him in
respect of the good partes wherewith he was indued, and of the pleas-
ant humour that for the most part did possesse him when hee came
in companie of friendes, yeelding at no time (to my seeing) any shew
or suspition, to have bene a dealer in matters of that qualitie: and
therefore I cannot but pitie his misfortune the more, wishing all men
to make profite of his fal, and to note, that miserie and calamitie of
this kinde, doeth for the most part followe such as forget God, to whose
protection I committe you. From Lyon's Inne, the 15 of June .1584.

Your assured friend. Q.Z. [A1]

A true and perfect declaration of the Treasons practised and
attempted by Francis Throckemorton, late of London, against
the Queene's Majestie and the Realme.

WHereas there have bene verie lewde and slaunderous bruites and
reportes given out, of the due and orderly proceedings held with
Francis Throckemorton lately arraigned and condemned of high
treason at the Guildhall in London the xxi. day of May last, whereby
such as are evill affected toward her Majestie, and the present governement, have indevoured falsely and injuriously to charge her Majestie
and her faithfull ministers with crueltie and injustice used against

the said *Throckemorton* by extorting from him by torture, such confessions as he hath made against himselfe, and by inforcing the same to make them lawful evidence to convict him of the treasons therein specified: Albeit her Majestie's subjects in general, calling to minde the milde and temperate course she hath helde all the time of her most happie Reigne, might rather impute her clemencie and lenitie used towards all sortes of offenders to a kinde of fault, then taxe her with the contrarie: yet such as allowe of practises and treasons against her Majestie, do alwayes interprete both of the one and of the other, according to the particular affections that doe possesse them, that is, to the worst. And forasmuch as the case of *Throckemorton* at this time hath bene subject to their sinister constructions, and considering that lies and false bruites cast abroad are most commonly beleeved, until they be controlled by [A1v] the trueth: it hath bene thought expedient in this short discourse to deliver unto your view and consideration, a true and perfect declaration of the treasons practised and attempted by the said *Throckemorton* against her Majestie and the Realme, by him confessed before his arraignement, whereby her Majestie was justly and in reason perswaded to put him to his triall. You shall likewise perceive what course hath bene helde with him by her Commissioners to bring him to confesse the trueth: with what impudencie and how falsely he hath denied his sayings and confessions: And lastly, how by a new submission and confession of his said treasons sithens his condemnation, he endevoureth to satisfie her Majestie, and to shew the reasons that mooved him to denie the first, which he affirmeth and confirmeth by the last: which may in reason satisfie, though not all, yet such as are not forestalled, or rather forepoysoned and infected with the lies and untruthes alreadie spred and delivered, in favour of the traitor and his treasons. You shall therefore understand, that the cause of his apprehension grewe first upon secret intelligence given to the Queene's Majestie, that he was a privie conveiour and receivour of letters to and from the Scottish Queene, upon which information neverthelesse divers moneths were suffered to passe on, before he was called to answere the matter, to the end there might some proofe more apparant be had to charge him therewith directly: which shortly after fell out, and thereupon there were sent unto his houses in London, and at Levsham in Kent, to search and apprehend him, certaine gentlemen of no meane credite and reputation: of whom, two were sent to his house by Poule's wharfe, where he was apprehended, and so by one of them convayed presently away, the other remaining in the chamber to make search for papers, writings, &c. which might give proofe of his suspected practises.

In that search, there were found the two papers contai- [A2] ning the names of certaine Catholique Noblemen and gentlemen, express-ing the Havens for landing of forraine forces, with other particulari-ties in the said papers mentioned, the one written in the Secretarie hand, (which he at the Barre confessed to be his owne handwriting) and the other in the Romane hand, which he denied to be his, and would not shewe how the same came unto his hands: howbeit in his examinations he hath confessed them both to be his owne hand-writing, and so they are in trueth. There were also found among other of his papers, twelve petidegrees of the discent of the Crowne of England, printed and published by the Bishop of Rosse, in the de-fence of the pretended title of the Scottish Queene his Mistresse, with certaine infamous libelles against her Majestie printed and published beyond the seas: which being found in the hands of a man so evill affected, comparing the same with his doings and practises against her Majestie, you wil judge the purpose wherefore he kept them.

Shortly after his apprehension, hee was examined by some of her Majestie's privie counsell, how he came by the said two papers of the Havens, and he most impudently denied with many protestations that he never sawe them, affirming they were none of his, but were foisted in (as he termed it) among his papers by the gentlemen that searched his house: Notwithstanding being more earnestly pressed to confesse the trueth, he sayd they had bene left (he knew not how) in his chamber by a man of his, who not long before was departed out of the Realme, named *Edward Rogers, alias Nuttebie*, by whome they were written. And to make this device to carie some colour of trueth, after his committing to the Tower, hee found the meanes to get three Cardes, on the backeside of which Cardes he wrote to his brother *George Throckmorton* to this effect: *I have bene examined by whom the two papers, conteining the names of certaine Noblemen and gentlemen, and of Havens &c. were written: and I have allea-* [A2v] *ged them to have bene written by Edward Nutteby my man, of whose handwriting you knowe them to be:* Meaning by this device to have had his brother confirme his falsehode. These Cardes were inter-cepted, and thereby the suspition before conceived of his practises increased, whereupon, as upon other just cause and matter against

him, having bin sundrie times brought before some of the principall
personages of her Majestie's most honorable privie counsell, and by
them with all industrie examined, and perswaded in very milde and
charitable maner, to confesse the trueth, promising to procure pardon
for him, in case he woulde bewray the depth of his practises: but no
persuasion prevailing, her Majestie thought it agreeable with good
pollicie, and the safetie of her Royal person and state, to commit him
over to the hands of some of her learned counsel and others her faithfull servants and ministers, with commission to them, to assay by
torture to drawe from him the trueth of the matters appearing so
waightie as to concerne the invading of the Realme, &c. These men
by vertue of that commission, proceeded with him, first as the counsell had formerly done by way of persuasion, to induce him to confesse:
but finding that course not to prevaile, they were constrained to commit him to such as are usually appointed in the Towre to handle the
Racke, by whom he was layd upon the same, and somewhat pinched,
although not much: for at the end of three daies following, he had
recovered himselfe, and was in as good plight as before the time of
his racking, which if it had then or any other time bene ministred unto
him with that violence that hee and his favourers have indevoured
slaunderously to give out, the signes thereof would have appeared
upon his limmes for manie yeeres. At this first time of torture, hee
would confesse nothing, but continued in his former obstinacie and
deniall of the trueth. The second time that hee was put to the Racke,
before hee was strayned up to any purpose, hee yeelded to confesse
anything [A3] hee knewe, in the matters objected against him: whereupon he was loosed, and then the Commissioners proceeded with him
according to such Interrogatories as had bene delivered unto them,
which for the more brevitie shall here bee omitted, the intent of this
declaration tending only to discover unto you the treasons and
treacherous dealings of the said *Francis Throckemorton* aswell before
as sithens his imprisonment, for your better knowledge of the man,
and manifestation of the due and just proceedings held with him by
her Majestie's Commissioners appointed to that service. And here you
are to note, that when hee was first pressed to discover by whome the
plottes of the Havens were sette downe, and to what purpose, he began
(without any further interrogation ministred) by way of an historicall
narration, to declare that at his being at Spaw in the Countrie of
Liege certaine yeres past, he entred into conference with one Jenney a

notorious knowen Traitor, touching the altering of the state of the
Realme here, and how the same might be attempted by forraine invasion, and to the like effect had sundrie conferences with *Sir Francis
Englefield* in the low Countreys, who daily solicited the Spanish
king in Spaine, and his Governours in the said Countreyes, to attempt the invading of the Realme, continued a course of practising
against her Majestie and the state, by letters betweene *Sir Francis Englefielde* and himselfe, untill within these two yeres last past, and that
he did from time to time acquaint *Sir John Throckemorton* his late
father with his traiterous practises, who (as he said) seeing no probabilitie of successe in them, dissuaded him from any further medling
with those practises.

He hath further confessed, that he used his Father's advise and
opinion in setting downe the names of the Catholique Noblemen
and Gentlemen, and did acquaint him with the description of the
Havens for the landing of forces, which he conceived and put in
writing onely by view of the Mappe, and not by particular sight or
survey of the [A3v] said Havens.

Item, he hath also confessed, that upon the intermission of writing
of letters, and the accustomed intelligences passed betweene *Sir Francis
Englefield* and him, he was made acquainted by his brother *Thomas
Throckemorton,* by letters and conference, and by *Thomas Morgan*
by letters (two of the principall confederates and workers of these
treasons residing in France) with a resolute determination agreed on
by the Scottish Queene and her confederats in France and in other
forreine partes, and also in Englande, for the invading of the Realme.

That the *Duke of Guyse* should be the principal leader and executer
of that invasion.

That the *pretention* (which shoulde be publiquely notified) should
be to deliver the Scottish Queene to libertie, and to procure even by
force from the Queene's Majestie, a tolerance in religion for the pretended Catholiques: But the *intention,* (the bottome whereof should
not at the first be made knowen to all men) shoulde be upon the
Queene's Majestie's resistance, to remoove her Majestie from her
Crowne and state.

That the *Duke of Guyse* had prepared the forces, but there wanted
two things, money, and the assistance of a convenient partie in England, to joyne with the forraine forces, and a third thing, how to set
the Scottish Queene at libertie without perill of her person.

For, the first thing wanting, *viz.* money, messengers were sent from forraine parts both to Rome and Spaine, and their returne daily expected to their liking: And the Spanish Ambassador to encourage the English to joyne both in purse and person, did give out, that the King his Master woulde not onely make some notable attempt against Englande, but also woulde beare halfe the charge of the enterprise. For the seconde thing, *viz.* the preparing of a sufficient partie in England, to receive and to joyne with the forraine forces, one especiall messenger was sent over [A4] into England in August last, under a counterfaite name from the confederates in France, to signifie the platte and preparation there, and to sollicite the same here.

That *Thomas Throckemorton* his brother made him privie to his negotiation at his last being here in England, and that thereupon *Francis Throckmorton* tooke upon him to be a follower and meane for the effectuating therof among the confederats in Englande, with the helpe of the Spanish Ambassadour, whom he instructed howe and with whome to deale for the preparing of a convenient partie heere within the Realme, for that himselfe woulde not be seene to be a sounder of men, lest hee might be discovered, and so endanger himselfe and the enterprise, knowing that the Ambassadour being a publique person, might safelie deale therein without perill.

That the *Duke of Guyse* and other heads of the enterprise had refused some landing places, and made speciall choise of Sussex, and about Arundel in Sussex, both for the neere cutte from the parts of Fraunce, where the *Duke* did or best could assemble his force, and for the oportunitie of assured persons to give assistance, &c.

That hee, taking upon him the pursuite of this course, shewed the whole plotte and devise of the havens for landing to the Spanish Ambassador, who did incourage him therein, he promising, that if hee might have respite untill the next spring, the same should be done more exactly.

That at the time of *Thomas Throckemorton's* being here, least the negotiation of the enterprise, by some casualtie might faile in the only hand of one man *Thomas Throckmorton*, there was also from the confederats sent over into Sussex, *Charles Paget*, under the name of *Mope, alias Spring*, and therof an advertisement covertly sent to *Thomas Throckmorton*, both that Thomas might understande it, and not be offended that another was joyned with him in his labour.

That the Spanish Ambassadour by advertisements from [A4v] the confederates, was made privie to this comming of *Charles Paget* under the name of *Mope*, and yet knowen to him to be *Charles Paget*.

That the said Ambassadour did according to his sayde advertisements, knowe and affirme that *Charles Paget* was come over to view the havens and Countrey for landing of such forraine forces about Arundell, and specially to sound and conferre with certaine principall persons for assistance.

The same Ambassadour also knewe and affirmed, that *Charles Paget* had accordingly done his message, and had spoken with some principall persons heere, according to his commission, and was returned.

Hee moreover confessed that there was a device betweene the Spanish Ambassadour and him, howe such principall Recusants here within the Realme as were in the Commission of the peace in sundrie Counties, might upon the first bruite of the landing of forraine forces, under colour and pretext of their authoritie and the defence of her Majestie, levie men, whome they might after joyne to the forraine forces, and convert them against her Majestie.

In these fewe articles is briefly comprised the whole effect of his confession made at large without any Interrogatorie particularly ministred, other than upon the two papers before mencioned, contayning the names of men and havens. And heere you are to note that at the time of his apprehension, there was no knowledge or doubt had of these treasons, or of his privitie unto them, but onely an information and suspition delivered and conceived of some practise betweene him and the Scottish Queene, as is before mentioned. For the discovering whereof, after he had bene sundrie times upon his alleagaunce commanded to declare his doings in conveying and receyving of letters to and from her, he did voluntarily confesse that hee had written divers letters unto her, and had conveyed many [B1] to and fro, betweene her and *Thomas Morgan* in France, by whose meanes he was first made knowen unto her, and that he had received as many letters from her. Hee also declared the effect of his letters to her, and of hers to him: which letters betwene them were alwaies written in Cipher, and the Cipher with the Nullities and markes for names of Princes and Counsailors, hee sent unto the Queene's Majestie written with his owne hand. Hee also delivered the names of some, by whom hee conveyed his letters to the Scottish Queene, as by one *Godfrey Fulgeam,* who fled the Realme immediatly upon *Throckemorton's* apprehension, and one other person, whom he described by his stature, shape, and apparell, and the man sithens apprehended and examined, hath confessed the same: the man's name is *William Ardington.*

The summe and effect of the most part of these confessions, although they were at the time of his arraignement opened and dilated by her Majestie's Sergeant, Atturney, and Sollicitor generall at the barre, and therefore seeme not needfull to be repeated heere, yet because the purpose of this discourse is to shew sufficient proofe, that the matters contained in his said confessions, are neither false nor fayned (as *Francis Throckmorton* most impudently affirmed at his triall, alleadging that they were meere inventions of himselfe by policie to avoyde the torture) they have bene here inserted, to the ende you may the better judge of the proofes, presumptions, and circumstances folowing, by comparing the matters with their accidents, and consequently see the falsehoode of the Traitor, the just and honourable proceedings of her Majestie, and the honest and loyall endevours of her Ministers imployed in the discovering of the treasons.

First, it is true and not denied by himselfe, that he was at Spawe about the time by him mencioned, and had conference with Jenney in that place, and with Sir *Francis Englefield* in Flaunders, and that he hath written letters [B1v] to Sir *Frauncis,* and received letters from him: for if he should denie the same, he were to be convinced by good proofe: for it hath bin noted in him by many of his countreymen English subjects, that both in those partes and in Fraunce, hee did continually associate himselfe with English Rebels and Fugitives. If then you consider with whom he hath conversed beyond the seas, and compare his religion with theirs, you wil judge of his conversation accordingly: and it is to be supposed, that those men, knowen to be continuall practisers against the Queene's Majestie and this Realme, from whence for their Treasons and unnaturall demeanures they are worthily banished, will not in their conventicles and meetings forget to bethinke them of their banishment, and howe they might be restored to their countrey, whereunto no desert in her Majestie's life time (which God long continue) can wel (without her Majestie's great mercie) restore them. Then I pray you what conferences might *M. Throckemorton* have with Sir *Francis Englefield,* with *Jenney,* with *Liggons,* with *Owen,* and with such like, who were his daily companions in Fraunce and in the Lowe countreis? He hath written letters to Sir *Frauncis Englefield*: to what purposes? he haunted continually two Ambassadors in London, by whose meanes he sent and received letters to and from beyond the seas daily. To whom, and from whom? even to and from *Thomas Morgan*, and *Thomas Throckemorton* at Paris, men knowen to her Majestie and her Counsell, to be notorious practisers, very inward with the Duke of Guyse, and contrivers of the Treasons and devises for the invasion intended: and for very certaine knowledge thereof, we neede not be beholding to *Frauncis Throckemorton* onely, (although he hath said much of them) but to others of better credite then himselfe.

That the Duke of Guyse did undertake the enterprise to invade the Realme with a forraine power, to be de- [B2] frayed by the Pope and King of Spaine (a part of *M. Throckemorton's* confession) and he in trueth the first discoverer thereof to her Majestie: if he will say that it was but invention, it will approve false. For sithens he discovered the same, there have bene divers advertisements thereof sent to her Majestie from forraine Princes her Highnesse's loving neighbours and Allies, as also by other good meanes and intelligences from her Ambassadours and servants residing in other Countries.

If he denie (as he hath done) that he never had knowledge of any such matter when he confessed the same, it hath no likelihood of trueth: for *Throckmorton* was never knowen to be a Prophet to fore-tell things *de futuro*.

He resorted often to the Spanish Ambassadour, at the least twice in a weeke when he was in London: this often repayre could not be to con-ferre with the Ambassadour for the exchange of money for his brother, as he pretended at his arraignment: there was some other cause. When he was apprehended, he had a Casket covered with greene velvet, very cunningly conveied out of his chamber by a maide servant of the house, taken up under a bed's side in his chamber (one of the gentle-men who were sent to apprehend him then being in the chamber and unknowing thereof) which Casket not long after his apprehension, was by one *John Meredith* a follower of *Frauncis Throckemorton*, conveyed to the handes of the Spanish Ambassadour: and why to him? If the matters therein might well have abidden the light, why shoulde not the Casket have bene kept still at home? and if not there, why not sent to some other place of safetie, as well as to the Spanish Am-bassadour? It is to be conceived, that this Casket was not conveyed thither without the direction of *Frauncis Throckmorton,* though caried by *Meredith,* who did well knowe of what moment the matters were that were within the Casket, and of what danger to *Throckemorton* if they had bene disclosed, and therefore [B2v] meant to bestowe them in a safe place where they could not readily be had (as he thought) and with a person not unacquainted with the qualitie of them. After the deliverie of the Casket, *Meredith* fledde: for in trueth he was privie to the Treasons, and a fellowe practiser in them: to whom *Frauncis Throckemorton,* being taken short at the time of his apprehension, and forced to runne up a staire to deface a letter which he was then in writing to the Scottish Queene in Cipher (as he hath confessed) being suddenly apprehended, and so forced to depart away presently out of his house, delivered privily into the hands of *Meredith,* either the Cipher by the which he was writing his letter to the Scottish Queene, or a letter in Cipher by him written unto her: therefore he trusted *Meredith* as a man privie to his doings. You are also to understande, that *Throckemorton* was in very great feare of the discovering of this Casket after his apprehension: for remayning two or three daies prisoner in the house of one of the gentlemen that were sent to apprehend him, before he was committed to the Towre, he was permitted to talke with a Sollicitor of his Lawe causes, who brought him certaine bookes drawen, or other like papers written, which hee made showe to peruse, but that was not the matter why he sent for his Sollicitor: for in perusing the bookes, he conveyed into them a litle piece of paper, upon the which he had written with a cole, *I would faine knowe whether my Casket be safe,* or to the like effect. The Sollicitor departing from him, and resorting to *Throckemorton's* house not farre distant from the place where he remained prisoner, opening his papers, did shake out this piece of paper, which he tooke up and delivered to one of *Frauncis Throckmorton's* men, but the Casket was alreadie conveyed to the Spanish Ambassadour: whereby you will perceive what care he had of the Casket, and howe much it might import him to have the writings or matters within the same concealed. He being examined touching the [B3] Casket, and what was in the same, he denied at the first, that ever he had any such Casket, but finding afterwards that the Casket was discovered, he confessed the Casket, and saide there were certaine letters therein that came to his hands for the Scottish Queene from *Thomas Morgan* at Paris, and other letters and papers, but confessed not all, as it is supposed.

That *Charles Paget* came over into the Realme to evil purposes, as *Throckemorton* doth declare in his confession, could not be invented: for even at the same time that he mentioncth, *Paget* came over, in secrete and suspitious maner, staied not above xv. dayes, indevoured in a sort to finde the disposition of *William Shelley* Esquier, how hee might stand affected to give assistance to the treasons, although *Paget* discovered not directly his traiterous intents to *Shelley:* therefore all *Throckemorton's* confessions were not forged or invented.

But because the two papers produced at his arraignement, containing the description of the Havens for the commodious landing of forces, do most apparantly condemne him, and are a manifest argument of his privity to the whole treason, you may not forget that he acknowledged one of the papers written in the Secretarie hand, to have bene of his owne doing, but denyed the other written in the Romane hande: In the which under the title of Cheshire &c. is said, *Upon the landing of forraine Supplies, Chester shal be taken:* but what in your opinions might be understoode by that sentence, *Chester shalbe taken,* when you shal compare the paper in Secretarie hand with the other written in the Romane hande, intituled, *The Names of Noblemen and gentlemen in every Countie fitte to bee dealt withall in this matter.* (which in trueth were both one, although the Romane were somewhat more inlarged.) The question is to bee asked, *What matter?* The answere followeth necessarilie, *To assist the forraine forces that shall come to invade the Realme*: for that there is another title in that paper [B3v] over the names of the havens, &c. *Havens in every coast fitte for the landing of forces.* Now judge you, to what end these names of men and descriptions of Havens, their entries, *Capacities,* what windes bring unto them from Spaine, France and Flanders, were written and set downe by *Throckemorton*: the papers are both of his owne handwriting, and the Secretarie but a project or copie of the Romane.

Is it not likely thinke you, that he would acquaint the Spanish Ambassadour with these papers (as he hath confessed) when he made him partaker of the rest of his traiterous practises and devices as you have heard, and thought his Casket of treasons to be most safely committed to his hands? It may bee thought that there is no man of so simple understanding, that will judge to the contrarie, unlesse he be partially affected to excuse the treasons.

And now to shew unto you what mynd this man hath carried towards her Majestie, you are to be informed that *Francis Throcke-*

morton, after he had discovered to her Majestie his course of practising, repenting himselfe of his plaine dealing in the bewraying
thereof, sayd to some of the Commissioners upon occasion of speach,
I woulde I had bene hanged when I first opened my mouth to declare
any of the matters by me confessed. And being at other times sent
unto by her Majestie with offer of pardon, if he would disclose the
whole packe and complices of the treasons, hee used this argument to
perswade her Majestie that he had confessed all, saying that sithens
hee had alreadie brought himselfe by his confessions within the
danger of the lawes, to the utter ruyne of his house and familie, hee
wondered why there should be any conceite in her Majestie, that he
had not declared all. But to perswade such as were sent unto him for
these purposes, the rather to beleeve that hee could discover no more,
at one time hee used these speaches following with great vehemencie:
Nowe I have disclosed the secrets of her who was the deerest thing
unto me in [B4] *the worlde* (meaning the Scottish Queene) *and whome*
I thought no torment should have drawen me so much to have preju-
diced as I have done by my confessions, I see no cause why I should
spare any one, if I could say ought against him: and sith I have failed
of my faith towards her, I care not if I were hanged. And when hee
began first to confesse his treasons, which hee did most unwillingly,
after hee was entred into the declaration of them, before al the Commissioners, upon advisement, hee desired hee might deliver his knowledge but to one of them onely, whereunto they yeelded, and thereupon
removing aside from the place where hee sate by the Racke, hee used
this proverbe in Italian, *Chi a perso la fede, a perso l'honore,* that is,
He that hath falsed his faith, hath lost his reputation: Meaning thereby (as it may be conceived) that he had given his faith to bee a Traitor,
and not to reveile the treasons, and then began to confesse as you have
heard.

By this discourse, contayning the principal heads of his treasons,
and the proofes and circumstances of the same, you that are not transported with undutifull myndes and affections, will cleerely perceive
howe impudently and untruely he denyed at his arraignement the
trueth of his confessions, charging her Majestie with crueltie, and her
ministers with untruethes in their proceeding against him.

But the cause that moved him thereunto, was a vaine conceite he
had taken, that his case was cleere in lawe by the intermission of the
time betwene his confession made and his arraignement, grounding

himselfe upon a Statute of the 13. yere of her Majestie's Reigne, in the which there are certaine treasons specified and made of that nature, that no person shalbe arraigned for any of those offences committed within anie of the Queene's Majestie's dominions, unlesse the offendor be thereof indicted within six moneths next after the same offence committed, and shal not be arraigned for the same, unlesse the offence be proved by the testimonie and othe of two sufficient witnesses, or his voluntarie con- [B4v] fession without violence: wherein he was greatly deceived: For it was made manifest unto him by the L. chiefe Justice and other of the Judges in Commission at his trial, that his treasons were punishable by a Statute of xxv. Edw. 3. which admitted no such limitation of time or proofe.

Herein his skill failed him, and forgot the advice given unto him by some of the Commissioners, who (pitying his misfortune for sundrie good gifts of the minde appearing in him) assured him that there was no way so readie for him to redeeme his life, as by submission and acknowledging of his offence, which, for a time after he had confessed his treasons, he was contented to followe, and now eftsoones after his condemnation by a new submission to the Queene's Majestie the fourth of June hath resumed that course. The submission *verbatim* written with his owne hand, followeth.

To her most excellent Majestie, even to her *owne Royall hands.*

MOst excellent Prince, and my most gratious Soveraigne, sith to mee the most miserable of all your Majestie's poore distressed subjects, being justly condemned by the ordinarie and orderly course of your Majestie's Lawes, there resteth no further meane of defence but submission: vouchsafe, most excellent Prince, graciously to accept the same, which prostrate in all humilitie, I here present unto the hands of your most excellent Majestie, beseeching the same, that as Justice hath bene derived from your highnesse, as from the fountaine, to the triall of mine actions: so I may receive from the same spring some droppe of grace and mercie for the great and grievous offence whereof I rest by your Majestie's Lawes justly condemned: some part, I say, of that your accustomed gratious clemencie, whereof most your distressed subjects have tasted, and few bene deprived. And albeit the inconsiderate rashnesse of [C1] unbridled youth hath withdrawen me from that loyall respect, which nature and duetie bounde me to owe unto your Majestie, as to my lawfull and naturall dread soveraigne, and that the naturall care in me of the defence of my life mooved mee lately to the untrue and unduetifull gainsaying of some such pointes as had bene before by me in most humble sorte confessed: nevertheles, I most humblie beseech your most excellent Majestie, that in imitation of God, whose image (both in respect of the happie place you holde, as also in regarde of your singular wisedome and other the rare and singular vertues and perfections wherewith God and nature hath plentifully indewed you) you represent unto us here in earth, it may please your Majestie to commiserate the lamentable estate of me now the most miserable of all your Majestie's subjectes, and gratiously to graunt unto me remission and forgivenes, that not only doe most humblie confesse myselfe worthie of death, but also in shewe of my repentance and sorowfull afflicted minde, doe not crave at your Majestie's handes the prolonging of my life, if the same shall not stande with your gratious good pleasure, but rather desire the trebling of the torment justly by your Majestie's lawes imposed upon mee, if the same may bee any satisfaction to your Majestie for the haynous cryme wherof I remaine by your Majestie's lawes justly condemned, or any mitigation of your Majestie's indignation worthily conceived against me, that desire not to live without your favour, and dying will wish from my heart, that my ende may bee the beginning of your Majestie's securitie, and my death the preservation of your life, and the increase both to your Majestie, and to this your most flourishing commonwealth, of all the most happie blessings of almightie God.

> Your Majestie's most wofull subject
> in that he hath offended you.
> *Francis Throckemorton.* [C1v]

HE sent unto her Majestie together with the sayde submission, a declaration written likewise with his owne hand, contayning the effects of the most principall pointes of his treasons formerly confessed: retracting onely the accusation of his father, and some other particularities of no moment to cleare him of his treasons, the effect whereof followeth in his owne words, as he set them downe.

THe only cause why I coyned the practise first by me confessed, and unjustly touched my father, was, for that partly I conceived that the paper written so long sithens, could not now by lawe have touched me: but principally, for that I was willing thereby to colour the setting downe of those names and havens in Romane hand, which were written long after the time by me confessed upon occasion of conference betweene the Spanish Ambassadour and me of this later practise.

Mine intelligence with the Scottish Queene began a little before Christmas was two yeres: the Cipher I had from *Thomas Morgan* in Fraunce: the first letter I received by *Godfray Fulgeam,* by whom also came all such others as I after received for the most part, unlesse it were such as came to me by *F.A.* his hands, who as hee tolde mee, received them of the fellowe by me spoken of in my former confessions, whose name, I protest before God, I knowe not, nor whence he is. And for such letters as came unto mee in the absence of *Fulgeam,* they were inclosed under a coverture from *Fulgeam,* and were delivered me by the hands of *Robert Tunstead* his brother-in-Law, to whom I delivered such as I had for the Scottish Queene, covered with a direction to *Fulgeam,* and once I remember or twise I sent by one of my men called Butler, letters for the Scottish Queene to the house of the said *Tunstead,* neere Buckstones, covered with a direction to *Tunstead,* and under a letter to *Fulgeam.* In such letters as came to me from the Scottish Q. were inclosed letters to *F.A.* many times, and most [C2] times some for *Thomas Morgan.* Her letters to mee contayned, &c. But before I retourned mine answere to her, I understoode of the death of the *Duke of Lenox,* and withall heard from *Morgan* (with whom all mine intelligence was, for with my brother I never had any, other then that the matters by mee written to *Morgan,* were by him imparted to my brother most times) that by the perswasion of the Pope and the King of Spaine, the *Duke of Guyse* had yeelded to performe the journey in person: and that it was thought that the next way to attayne libertie for the Scottish Queene, and to reforme Scotlande, was to begin here in England, and therefore he desired to knowe from me, whether in mine opinion Catholiques woulde not backe any such force as should be sent, considering a demaunde of tolerance in religion for them, should insue the wel performing of the said enterprise, and what I thought the force would amount unto, both of horse and footemen, and where I thought to be the fittest landing. Mine answere was, that as then, I sawe no great probabilitie of the good success of such an enterprise, for that the Catholiques were timorous, dispersed, the matter perilous tò be communicated to many, without which I saw not how any estimate could be made of the forces: besides, that it was an eminent danger to the Scottish Queene, whereof I sawe no remedie.

I tooke notice of this matter in my next letters to the Scottish Queene, whose answere was, that shee lately heard of that determination, &c.

Upon my former answere to *Morgan,* he desired me, that I would conferre with the Spanish Ambassadour, to whom I should bee re-commended from thence: hereupon the said Ambassadour sent for me, and brake with me in this matter, assuring me that in his opinion he found it verie easie to make great alteration here with very little force, considering the disuse in men to warre, and troubles woulde so amase them (as he thought) that they woulde be as soone [C2v] overthrownen as assailed, and he could not thinke but in such a case Catholikes would shewe themselves, sith the purpose tended to the obteyning for them libertie of conscience: and therefore hee desired mee to ac-quaint him, what I thought men would doe in such a case, and where I thought the fittest landing, and what holdes in these partes were easiest to be surprised.

I answered him, that as it seemed, the enterprise stood upon great incertainties, if it depended of the knowledge of a certaine force to be found here, which no man could assure him of, unlesse he had sounded all the Catholikes, which was not possible without a manifest hazarde of the discoverie of the purpose: for as for any great person-age, I know no one to be drawen into this action, that could carie any more then his ordinarie retinew: the onely way in such a case was (I tolde him) for such as woulde bee drawen into this matter, and were of credite in their countreys, to levie forces under colour of the Prince's authoritie.

But for that these things depended upon uncertaine groundes, which was not fit to be used in so great an action, I said it was to be resolved, that the force to bee sent should be of that number, that what backing soever they should finde here, they might be able of themselves to encounter with any force that might be provided to be sent against them, and therefore they could not bee lesse then 15000. men. For the place of their landing, I said it depended much upon the force that should be sent: for if that were in great number, it mattered not where they landed: if in a small companie, then was it requisite that it shoulde be in the Countreys best affected, and furthest from her Majestie's principall forces, which I said to be in the North-ren parts on either side.

To the danger of the Scottish Queene by me objected, he said he knewe no remedie, unlesse she might be taken away by some 200. horse, which I tolde him I sawe [C3] not to be possible, for that I knewe not any gentleman in those partes (which were men, if any, to perfourme it) that I durst wish to bee made acquainted with the matter beforehande.

Finally, our conclusion was, that I should informe him of the Havens as particularly as I could: and within fewe dayes after, finding by him that the force intended hither, was farre inferiour to that I spake of, and that there was some different betweene the Pope and the king of Spaine for the charge, I tolde him that the surest course and of least danger were, to send a supplie into Scotland, where a small force would breede a great alteration, and things being there established by the good liking of the king, I thought it was in him by a continuall warre, and by incursions so to anoy this state, as her Majestie here should be forced to yeelde the libertie of the Scottish Queene, and what should thereupon have bene reasonably demaunded for the benefite of Catholikes here. And herein I said it would be a great furtherance, if at the same time some fewe were landed in Irelande, where, although they abide the same hazarde that the former forces sustained, yet would the charge be so great to her Majestie, and so great an occasion of dispersing of her forces, as a much lesse companie then was spoken of first by me, would (being landed here in a convenient place) shake the mindes of men generally, and be of force (if anything) to drawe them to shewe themselves, in the furtherance of the purpose.

He utterly rejected the purpose for Ireland, and disliked not the purpose for Scotlande: but still hee was in minde to have forces landed here, and therefore desired me verie earnestly to inquire particularly of the Havens on the side of Cumberland and Lancashire, and what men were dwelling there that were well affected in religion, and what places easie to be taken, and what apt for fortification. [C3v]

The next time that I went to the Spanish Ambassadour, he found himselfe agrieved that he understood matters were determined in France without his privitie: and told me that *Parsons* the Jesuite was gone to Rome, sent as he thought, to understand the Pope's minde.

Soone after came over my brother *Thomas*, to make an ende of our accompt, and to perswade me to come over, assuring mee that for ought he could see in likelihood, the enterprise was never like to take effect. In the time of his being heere, and while I entertained intelligence with the Scottish Queene concerning her libertie, the Spanish

Ambassadour sent for me, and tolde me of the comming over of *Mope* to view Sussex and the Havens, and as he thought, to taste the best of accompt there: whereat he seemed to bee agrieved, for that such matters had not bene left to him, beeing one that they in France made beleeve that they relyed upon principallie in this enterprise. Afterwardes, the Ambassadour tolde me, that it was *Charles Paget,* and that he was returned, but where he had bene hee knewe not, and at the same time I received a letter from *Morgan,* that it was *Paget*: but assuring me, and so willed me to assure the Ambassadour, that his comming was not to move any man, but onely to viewe the countrey, for that the mooving of any man was referred to him. I did so: and he intreated me to remember him for those foresaide names and Havens, saying that so it were done exactly by the Spring, it would suffice: for that sooner he saw no likelihoode of the execution of the enterprise.

My brother having made an ende of his accompt with me, retourned with this resolution betweene us, (I protest before God,) that if the enterprise succeeded not betweene this and the next Spring nowe past, that I woulde settle my things here and goe over. And for this cause, he being gone, I went downe into the countrey, both to sell and take order for my land in those partes, as also to fetch the [C4] draught of Gentlemen and Havens for the most part of England, which had bene set downe by me above two yeres since, and left behinde me at Feckenham in my Studie.

Not finding the draught at Feckenham, I returned to London, where I founde the note of names in Secretarie hande, which I caried to the Spanish Ambassadour, and there drewe that other in Romane hande in his Studie, putting downe *Chester* to be taken, in respect of the easinesse I thought, and the rather to give him incouragement in the matter. I left it with him, promising him that by the next spring I woulde perfect it, if I taried so long, making knowen unto him, that I was had in suspition. and my determination to be gone: but he pressed the contrarie of me, assuring me, that if the enterprise proceeded not, he would then also depart.

Whether Sir *Frauncis Englefielde* were a dealer in this practise or no, I know not: but sure I am (for so the Spanish Ambassadour tolde me) that Sir *Frauncis* had intelligence with the said Ambassadour all the time of his being here.

The Spanish Ambassadour tolde me that he heard the people of Northwales were generallie wel affected, and therefore he desired to have the havens of that countrie: I tolde him that hereafter I would helpe him thereunto, although no good might be expected there, for the reasons by me set downe in my first confession: and hereupon the day before mine apprehension, the Ambassadour sent me backe the said paper in Romane hand, desiring me to set downe the same at my leasure more exactly, which was the cause that it was not in my greene velvet Casket. The writings in my Casket were such as were by mee confessed, and came unto my hands as I have confessed.

I Most humbly beseeche her most excellent Majestie, that the extremitie which I have alreadie sustained, and the causes by me discovered, to the safetie of her Majestie and the state, not made knowen (as hath appeared) by any other meane then by myselfe, may crave at her handes, [C4v] the extending of her gratious commiseration towardes the relieving of the lamentable estate of me, her Majestie's poor distressed subject, and mine, if God for mine offences forbid not the same.

Nowe judge all yee, that be not perversly affected, whether *Throckemorton* be justly condemned, and whether his confessions (though as hee pretended, extorted from him by violence) be of force in Lawe against him: he hath conspired to overthrowe the state: to bring in strangers to invade the Realme: to remove her Majestie from her lawfull and naturall right and inheritance to the Crowne of England, and to place a stranger in her seate: but this last point, for placing of a stranger, will (perchaunce) be denyed: then note, that in the whole course of the practise, the greatest barre to the prosecution of the enterprise, was, they found no way how to put the Scottish Queene in safetie. Then, if these dangerous treasons be discovered by torture, (the onely meanes left unto Princes to discover treasons and attemptes against their States and Persons, where they finde apparant matter to induce suspition, as in the case of *Throckemorton,* upon sight of the plottes of havens &c.) may the Law touch the traitour or not? If any man holde this question negatively, hold him for a friend to traitours and treasons, and an enemie to the Queene's Majestie, whome God long preserve, and confound her enemies.

FINIS.

The Earle of Northumberland's Treasons (1585)

Two of the names Francis Throckmorton listed as potential supporters of a Guisian invasion of England were William Shelley of Michelgrove and Henry Percy, eighth earl of Northumberland, the brother of Thomas Percy, the seventh earl, who had rebelled in the north in 1569 and been executed in 1572. Henry Percy was implicated in the conspiracy a second time when, on December 23, 1583, he was mentioned by Charles Arundel, also suspected to be in league with Throckmorton, in an examination conducted over the Christmas holiday by two anxious members of the Queen's Privy Council, Mildmay and Hunsdon. Arundel admitted visiting Northumberland, but he insisted the earl "had no conference with him but of ordinarie matters," and nothing was done to either man at the time. Nearly a year later, however, in September 1584, the Scottish Jesuit William Creighton, on route to England, was intercepted by the Admiral of Zeeland on Walsingham's orders. As his ship was boarded, Father Creighton tore up a letter and threw the pieces overboard. Unfortunately, he threw them to windward; and the scraps were blown back on board. When William Waad, the clerk of the Privy Council, reassembled them, the names of Arundel and Northumberland reappeared. Both men were confined to the Tower.

Arundel died a natural death there a decade later; but on June 20, 1585, Northumberland was found dead by his own hand, shot through the heart. Immediately after the suicide, a pamphlet appeared in Cologne claiming that Northumberland—unlike Throckmorton and the other suspects and prisoners, a peer of the realm—had been executed by the English government; and the work, originally in Latin, was translated and distributed in French, German, English, Italian, and Spanish. Rumors circulated widely that the earl, "unjustly detained in prison without proofe or just cause of suspition of treason," as the author of the following account remarks on A2v, was killed by Christopher Hatton, a favorite of Elizabeth's soon to be appointed lord chancellor. To clear the government of any such imputations, the Queen called for an inquiry by the Star Chamber. The result of the hearing, probably directed as well by the Queen, is the following work, a work which claims for itself no more than it substantially records: "how haynous his [Northumberland's] offences were, fearing the justice and severitie of the Lawes, and so the ruyne and overthrowe of his house [. . . and . . .] the destruction of himselfe" (C3).

This selection is among the very best pieces of Elizabethan reportage. The introduction is pretentious, but the basic idea of it—that incredulity hinders the discovery of truth while falsehood wins only the imperfect eye and the corrupted heart—is a telling point, for it assigns similar charges to Northumberland and the author of the Cologne pamphlet as well as to those who were too quick to judge Elizabeth's government. The twin ideas conveyed—that faulty schemes and fears emerge from evil intentions and that evil is transformed to goodness only as a willful act of corroded judgment—are implicitly related in the subsequent testimony to all the principals: to Northumberland, Lord Paget, Charles Paget, William Shelley, Francis Throckmorton, and even the groom Jacques Pantins. Only those who *see* according to this account— Owen Hopton, the anxious bailiff, and the anonymous old man—are exonerated.

This report dovetails with the preceding one of the Throckmorton plot, for it fills in part of the background (B2-B3) and picks up the earlier motif of the Queen's mercy, seen here with Throckmorton but more especially with the connection of the Percy family to the earlier rising in the north (A2). Along with the carefully explored organity of this account, the author demonstrates a keen sense of drama. He catches up in permanent record the hurried whisperings in the park at Petworth (B4) and the sudden sense of disaster which invades the very chamber of Petworth House (C2); and the suspense he evokes just preceding the discovery of Northumberland's corpse is sharply and splendidly handled.

The anonymous author claims to draw from memory (D1), but he has a genuine delight in specific fact:the evidence of Northumberland's messages to Shelley as incontrovertible (C2v), the testimony of the earl's groom (C3), the gun placement and wound of Northumberland (D2), and the number of bullets discharged (D2v). Still there are critical boundaries to this interest. He claims to reproduce the atmosphere of the hearing in Star Chamber, but all his facts are placed in the series of testimonies presented by the Crown's witnesses. He seems, in fact, to lean not only on Socratic dialogue and reportage for his form but on the construction of a simple morality play. Here each character is introduced to speak at length in a monologue which implies his character while it puts forward a continuing narrative with intense feeling for occurrence and suspense. We can, therefore, excuse the author for his introduction in the end, partly because it is so penetrating and relevant, and partly because it like the occasional later observations—such as the negative support of suicide (D1v-D2) and the Queen's mercy as "the onely maintayner of his holy Gospel among us" (D3v)—never allows him to lose sight of the tense courtroom and the heightened drama, deeply perceived and exactingly conveyed.

TEXTUAL NOTES

[For explanatory notes for this selection see page 369.]

The Earle of Northumberland's Treasons
    Reference. STC 19617, 19617.5.
    Authorship and Issues. The anonymous account of Northumberland's treason and death was printed in one edition (STC 19617) with one variant state (STC 19617.5) in which 51 changes have been made in the outer forme only of each gathering. All changes but one (which makes the second issue superior; see *Variants* below) are incidentals of spelling, punctuation, and changes in typeface. Of the latter, the second issue changes proper names from italic type to roman type generally (but not always; cf. *Bernardino de Mendoza*, B3). Some peculiar spellings also appear first in the second issue, as *Threasurer* for *Treasurer* (A3) and *Eschequier* for *Eschequer* (C3); but that 19617 is the earlier setting is clearly indicated not only by the single substantive variant but by the correction of *Shellye's* to *Shelley's* (also C3) in 19617.5 as well. There is no indisputable evidence of two compositors (the one setting the outer forme alone making corrections) since the changes are not made consistently throughout *each* outer forme (cf. *Paget* on C1, e.g.). There is one instance—in the case of *Throckemorton* on B3—in which the correction also introduces a spelling variant: the dropping of the medial *e*, perhaps to maintain a consistency in spelling his name throughout the work.
    Subsequent Editions. Later editions of the text of the first issue appear in *Somers Tracts*, fourth collection (London, 1751), III,420-435, without notes or commentary and in *Somers Tracts*, ed. Scott (London, 1809), I,212-224.
    Collation] 4⁰; A-D⁴ (A4, D4 wanting). A1, title-page; A2-A3v, preface; B1-D3v, text. [A4,D4 probably blank.]
    Description of Contents. Title-page, mixture of roman and italics, with Barker's crest; preface, roman heading with text in italic (running-head: "To the Reader." in roman); text of pamphlet in roman (no running-head). Paginated (body of text=pp. 1-22). Decoration at bottom of A3v and top of B1 (p. 1). Decorated capital letters for preface (A2) and

text (B1; p. 1). Some marginal notes; they are: *Master Atturney generall* and *Middlesex* (B1), *Master Solicitour.* (C1v), and *Sir Owen Hopton Knight, Lieutenant of the Tower. 1585.* (C4).

License. No entry in the *Stationers' Register*, but the pamphlet was printed (apparently for the Queen) by her official printer, Christopher Barker (see crest, A1).

Base-Copy Text. Bodleian Vet.A1.e.30. Copy used for variant issue: Corpus Christi College (Oxford), LG 2.5.

Substantial Variant. (A2) great prioritie,[great puritee,

Title-page in Full. A true and sum- / *marie reporte of the declaration of* some part of the Earle of Nor- / thumberlands Treasons, deliuered publiquelie / *in the Court at the Starrechamber by the Lord Chauncel-* / lour and others of her Maiesties most Honourable priuie / Counsell, and Counsell learned, by her Maiesties spe- / cial commandement, together with the examina- / tions & depositions of sundrie persons touching / the maner of his most wicked & violent mur- / der committed vpon him selfe with his / owne hand, in the Towre of / London, the 20. day of / Iune. 1585. /[Barker's crest] / *In aedibus C. Barker.*

Emendations. (A2)prioritie]puritiee [superior reading taken from second issue](A2v) them selues]themselves　intermedled my selfe]intermedled myself　(B4v)goods by an other course]goods by another course　(C1)noble man]nobleman　(C3)Highnesse]Highnesse's　(C3v)in the after noone]in the afternoone　chamher,]chamber,　meane time] meanetime　(C4)bed side]bedside　(C4v)bed chamber]bedchamber　bed clothes,]bedclothes,　(D1)East smithfield]East Smithfield　(D2) ynche or there about:]ynche or thereabout:　(D2v)all the daye time] all the dayetime　(D3) shewed her selfe]shewed herselfe　noble men] noblemen　(D3v)her highnes]her highnes's　compassion of him selfe]compassion of himselfe

A true and summarie reporte
of the declaration of *some part of*
the Earle of Northumberland's Treasons

To the Reader.

*ALICE AMONG OTHER essentiall properties ap-
pertaining to her ouglie nature, hath this one not inferiour to the rest and the worst, Incredulitie, wherewith shee commonly possesseth the mindes and
affections of all those that are infected with her, so
blinding the eyes and judgement of the best and
clearest sighted, that they cannot see or perceive the bright beames
of the trueth, although the same be delivered with never so great
puritie, proofe, circumstance and probabilitie. It is said that no
trueth passeth abroade unaccompanied with her contrarie, and as
they goe, trueth is ever constrained to yeelde the precedence and pre-
heminence to her yoke fellowe falsehood, whose lodging is alwaies
first made and prepared without a harbenger in the corrupt nature
of mankinde, by whom shee is first receaved, entertained and har-
boured at all times: whereof in our daily experience there happen
many and dangerous demonstrations, especially in matters of the
highest moment, tending to excuse or accuse the actions of the greatest personages.*

*There was of late delivered in publique by persons of honour,
credit and reputation, a large declaration of certaine treasons practised by the late Earle of Northumberlande, of the maner of his
untimely death, being with his owne hande murdered in the Towre,
and of the causes that wrought him thereunto: the particularities
wherof are such and so many, as for the helpe of my memorie (comming then to the Starre chamber by occasion, and not looking for*

any such presence of the Nobilitie and privie Counsell as I founde
there at that time, and not looking for any such cause of that nature
to have bene handled there that day) I toke notes of the severall mat-
ters declared by the Lord Chancelour, M. Attorney, and Solicitour
General, the Lord chiefe Baron, and Master Vice- [A2v] *chamber-*
laine: for (as I remember) they spake in order as they are heere mar-
shalled, and therefore I place them in this sorte, and not according to
their precedence in dignitie.

Upon the hearing of the treasons with their prooves and circum-
stances, and the desperate maner of the Earle's destruction delivered
in that place, and by persons of that qualitie, I supposed no man to
have bene so voide of judgement or the use of common reason, that
would have doubted of any one point or particle thereof, untill it
was my chaunce (falling in companie with divers persons at sundrie
times, aswell about the citie of London as abroade) to heare many
men reporte variablie and corruptly of the maner and matter of this
publique declaration, possessing the mindes and opinions of the
people with manifest untruthes: as, that the Earle had bene unjustly
detained in prison without proofe or just cause of suspition of
treason: and, that he had bene murdered by devise and practise of
some great enemies, and not destroied by himselfe. These slaunderous
reports have ministred unto me this occasion to set forth unto thy
view and consideration (gentle Reader) this shorte collection of the
said treasons and murder, as neere unto the trueth as my notes taken
may lead and permitte me, with the view of some of the examinations
themselves concerning this cause for my better satisfaction sithens
obtained: which I have undertaken for two respectes: the one to con-
vince the false and malitious impressions and constructions received
and made of these actions, by such as are in heart enemies to the happie
estate of her Majestie's present governement: the other, because it may
bee thought necessarie for the preventing of a further contagion like
to grow (by this creeping infection) in the mindes of such as are apt
(though otherwise indifferent) in these and the like rumours, to re-
ceive the bad as the good, and they most in number. Wherin if I
have seemed more bolde then wise, or intermedled myselfe in matters
above my reache, and not appertaining unto me, I crave pardon where
it is to be asked, and committe myselfe [A3] *to thy friendly interpreta-*
tion to be made of my simple travell and duetifull meaning herein.

Upon the three and twentie daie of June last, assembled in the

Court of Starchamber, Sir Thomas Bromley *knight Lord Chancelor of England,* William *Lord Burleigh Lord Treasurer of England,* George *Earle of Shrewsberie Lord Marshall of England,* Henry *Earle of Derby,* Robert *Earle of Leicester,* Charles *Lord* Howard *of Effingham Lorde Chamberlaine,* Henry *Lord Hunsdon Lord Governour of Barwicke, Sir* Francis Knollis *Knight Treasurer, Sir* James Crofte *Knight Comptroller of her Majestie's houshold, Sir* Christopher Hatton *knight Vicechamberlaine to the Queen's Majestie, the Lord chiefe Justice of her Majestie's Benche, the Master of the Rolles, and the Lord chiefe Barron of the Eschequer, and others: the audience verie great of Knightes, Esquiers, and men of other qualitie, the Lorde Chauncelour began briefly and summarily to declare, that whereas* Henry *late Earle of Northumberlande, for divers notable treasons and practises by him taken in hand, to the danger not onely of her Majestie's Roiall person, but to the perill of the whole Realme, had bene long detained in prison, and looking into the guilt of his own conscience, and perceiving by such meanes of intelligence, as he by corrupting of his keepers and other like devises had obtained, that his treasons were by sundrie examinations and confessions discovered, grewe thereby into such a desperate estate, as that thereupon he had most wickedly destroied and murdered himselfe, which being made knowen to the Lords of her Majestie's privie Counsel, order was thereupon taken, and direction given to the Lord chiefe Justice of England, the master of the Rolles, and the Lorde chiefe Baron of the Eschequer, to examine the manner and circumstances of his death, which they with all good endevour and diligence had accordingly perfourmed. And least through the sinister meanes of such persons as bee evill affected to the present estate of her Majestie's governement,* [A3v] *some bad and untrue conceipts might bee had as well of the cause of the Earle's detainement, as of the maner of his death: it was therefore thought necessarie to have the trueth therof made knowen in that presence: and then hee required her Majestie's learned Counsell there present to deliver at large the particularities both of the treasons, and in what sort the Earle had murdered himselfe. Then began John Popham Esquier, her Majestie's Attorney Generall, as followeth.* [B1]

THE Earle of Northumberland about the time of the last rebellion in the North, in the xi. yeere of her Majestie's raigne (then called by the title of *Henrie Percie* Knight) had undertaken the conveying away of the Scottish Queene: for the which as appeareth by a Record of the fourtenth yeere of her Majestie's raigne, in the Court of her Majestie's Bench he was indicted, he confessed the offence, and put himselfe to her Majestie's mercie. At which time, upon his said confession, submission and faithfull promise of his duetie and allegiance to her Highnesse from thenceforth, the Queene's Majestie of her merciful nature was pleased not to looke into his offence with the extremitie of her Lawes, but dealt therein as by way of contempt onely, as may appeare by the Recorde: the effect whereof was then shewed in the Court, under the hande of one of the Clarkes of her Majestie's sayde Bench, *in haec verba.*

MEmorandum, that Henrie Percie *late in Tinmouth in the Countie of Northumberland knight, was indicted in the Terme of Easter, in the foureteenth* [B1v] *yeere of her Majestie's raigne, for that hee with divers others did conspire for the delivering of the Queene of Scottes out of the custodie of the Earle of Shreusburie: upon which indictment the same Henry Percie did confesse the offence, and did put himselfe to the Queene's mercie, and thereupon judgement was after given by the Court, that the sayde Henry shoulde pay to the Queene for a fine for his said offence, five thousand Markes, as appeareth by the Recorde thereof in Court.*

> *Per Micha. 14 & 15. Elizabethae Reginae, Rotulo quinto inter placista Reginae, Concordat Cum Recordo.*
>
> *Per Io. Iue.*

BY this Record it may appeare that the Earle had his hande in that Rebellion: but for a further proofe thereof, it is most manifestly discovered in a certaine tracte written by the Byshop of Rosse (wherein he sheweth how faithfully he behaved himselfe in the managing of those treasons, at and about the time of that Rebellion) that the said Earle was in effect as farre plunged into the same as the late Earle his brother, howsoever he wound himselfe out of the danger thereof at that time.

Notwithstanding these traiterous practises, the Queene's Majestie was contented to remitte all within a short time, and then accepted most

graciously of him both in honour and favour, though unworthily
bestowed upon him, for that he utterly forgetting those graces and
favours received at her Majestie's mercifull hands, with a gracelesse
resolution was contented to enter into a newe plotte now lately contrived, not onely for the delivering of the Scottish Queene, but for the
invading of the whole Realme, the overthrowe of the Governement,
aswell concerning the state of Religion, as otherwise, the danger of
her Majestie's sacred person, and advaun- [B2] cing of the said Scottish Queene to the Regall crowne and Scepter of this Realme, whereunto her Majestie is linealy and lawfully borne and descended, and
wherein God of his mercie continue her long, in happie state of
Government, to the increase of her owne glory, and the comfort of her
loving and obedient subjects.

Then did master Atturney enter into the particularities of the
treasons, leaving many partes thereof untouched, because the case
stood so as it was not then convenient to reveale them (as hee saide)
in respect that they touched some other persons undealt withal at that
time, shewing that *Throckmorton's* treasons were not olde, but fresh
in every man's memorie, and how farre foorth they reached unto the
Earle, he declared. And for that the treasons of *Throckmorton*
tended especially to the invading of the Realme with forreine forces,
the purpose of that invasion long before intended, is prooved by
sundry examinations and confessions taken here within the Realme,
aswell of her Majestie's owne subjects as others, by letters intercepted,
written from and to the conspirators abroade and at home, and by
other good advertisements and intelligences had from forreine partes
discovering the same. He declared that in a letter written from Doctor
Sanders to Doctor *Allen* out of Spaine, in the yeere 1577. it is set downe
among other things, that the state of Christendome stood upon the
stoute assayling of Englande.

That in a letter sent to the same *Allen* from Rome, touching
audience given by the Pope to the Ambassadours of certaine forraine
Princes, betweene the Pope and whom a league was agreed on against
the Queen's Majestie, there were inclosed certaine articles containing
in effecte, that the Realme shoulde be invaded with 20000. men at
the charge of the saide Pope and Princes, that her Majestie should be
deposed, and some English Catholique elected king. [B2v]

That it was confessed, that the comming over of so many Priests
into the Realme, was to winne great numbers to the Catholique

partie, to joyne (if opportunitie served) either with forraine invasion, or with tumult at home.

That at *Narbonne* in Province, there was met an Englishman, being the head preacher there, who gave intelligence to one of her Majestie's subjects, that the Realme should shortly be invaded by a forraine king, and the Popish religion restored: and saide further, that Priestes came into England and dispersed themselves in countreyes, to make their partie strong.

A message was sent in November 1581. to Doctor *Allen* from a subject of this Realme, by a Seminarie priest then returning beyond the Seas, that whereas he had received worde from *Allen* at Allhallowtide before, that men and all things were in a readines, if the place of landing might be knowen: that *Allen* should forthwith send worde whether things were in such readinesse or not: and if they were, he would then send him such perfect instructions as he could.

One *Payne* executed for treason, confessed that this Realme could not continue in the state wherein it was, for that the Pope had a speciall care thereof, and would in short time eyther by forren princes, or by some other meanes worke a change of things here.

From hence, Master Atturney fell into the Treasons confessed by *Francis Throckmorton*, shewing that the state of this Realme had bene often presented to the consideration of forraine prince, who after long hearkening to the motion, had resolved to yeelde what furtherance he might, and to give all aydes necessarie for the refourming of religion, so they might be backed by such as were well affected within this countrey.

That the Duke of *Guise* had solicited for two yeeres together the pope and other princes, to supply him [B3] with forces: but being crossed by the death of a great personage, it was nowe growen to this passe, if there coulde be a partie founde in England to joyne in that action, and convenient places and meanes for landing, and other things necessarie, there should be a supply for *Guise* of forraine strength.

Francis Throckmorton was recommended from beyond the sea to *Don Bernardino de Mendoza*, Ambassadour resident for the Spanish king here in England, who acquainted *Throckemorton* what plotte was layde for the enterprise of the Duke of *Guise*, and that he was willed to conferre with *Throckemorton* in the matter, who thereupon acquainted the saide Ambassadour with the plotte of the Havens, and with the Noblemen and gentlemen that he had set downe as fitte to be dealt withall in that cause.

Throckemorton saide, that the bottome of this enterprise (which was not to be knowen to many) was, that if a tolleration of religion might not be obtained without alteration of the governement, that then the government should be altered, and the Queene remooved.

That the Scottish Queene was made acquainted from the Duke of *Guise* with the intention to relieve her by these forces.

It was in debate betwene *Throckemorton* and the Spanish Ambassadour, how the Scottish Queene might be delivered, as by an enterprise to be made with a certaine number of horse: and it was tolde *Francis Throckmorton* by his brother *Thomas Throckmorton*, that it was a principall matter in debate beyond the seas, howe she might be delivered with safetie: the lacke of resolution wherein, was the principall stay of the execution of the attempt of invasion.

Mendoza told *Francis Throckmorton* about Bartholomewtide 1583. that one *Moape* was come into England to sound the Earle of Northumberland, and other [B3v] principall men in Sussex: and about the ende of September following, the same *Mendoza* tolde him, that *Moape* was *Charles Paget,* and that he came not onely to sound the men, but to viewe the places, the havens, the provisions and meanes, and neerenesse and commoditie of men's abidings that should joyne with the forraine forces.

It was devised, that such Noblemen and others as would be contented to assist the forraine forces (being Justices of peace and of credit in their countreyes) might by colour of their authoritie, levie men as for her Majestie's defence, and yet employ them to assist the forraine forces. The Lord *Paget* was made acquainted with this devise, and answered, that it was a good course, and that he had thought upon it before.

Mendoza tolde *Throckmorton,* that *Charles Paget* had bene in Sussex, and had spoken with those that were there, and that he came to move the Earle of Northumberland and others.

The night before *Throckmorton* was apprehended, he came to the Lord *Paget,* and desired him that he would not acquaint the Earle of Northumberland and certaine others (whom he named) with such matters as had passed betweene them two, touching the practise of this invasion: and the Lord *Paget* willed him to deale as wisely for his part as he would doe for himselfe, and all should be well: but (quoth the Lord *Paget*) the Earle of Northumberland knoweth you well enough.

It was once agreed among the confederates, that the Duke of Guise should land in Sussex, being over against Deipe and Normandie: which after was misliked, because those partes lay too neere to her Majestie's greatest force and store, and that the people thereabout for the most part were protestants.

Master Attorney shewed further, that in Sommer last, there was taken upon the seas, sayling towards Scotland, a Scottish Jesuite, about whom there was founde a dis- [B4] course written in Italian of a like enterprise to be attempted against England, which should have bene executed in September or October then last past: wherein assurance is made that the Earles of Northumberland and Westmerland, *Dacres* that is dead, whom they termed Lord *Dacres,* and of al the Catholique Lords and Gentlemen in the North parts (where the invasion should have bene attempted) setting it downe that is not saide by conjecture that these men are assured, but that it is certainely knowen that they will joyne with the forren forces. In the said discourse it is also affirmed that the priests dispersed in the Realme, can dispose of the other Catholiques of the Realme, as they shalbe ordered: and that the Pope's excommunication shoulde bee renewed and pronounced against her Majestie and all those that shall take her part: and that all such should bee holden Traitours that did not joyne with that armie by a daye.

When Master Attorney had thus prooved the purpose of invasion, he proceeded to the proofe of *Charles Paget's* comming over about the practise and prosecution of that enterprise. And first, that *Paget* came to Petworth in September 1583, was secretly received, and brought in the night late to the Earle of Northumberland into his gallerie at Petworth, by one of the Earle's servants: where the Earle and he had secret conference together by the space of a large houre: from thence *Paget* was likewise conveied backe into the Towne by the same servant, and there lodged all that night, and the next night following was convayed secretly to a lodge in the Earle's parke at Petworth, called Conigar Lodge, where he was kept with like secrecie by the space of eight daies or thereabouts, and the servant by whom *Paget* was thus convayed, was by the Earle enjoyned and commanded in no wise to discover *Paget's* being there.

The Earle of Northumberland, upon the arrivall of *Charles Paget,* sent for the Lord *Paget* with the privitie [B4v] of this servant, who was made beleeve that *Charles* came over to set things in order, and to passe certaine deedes and conveyances betweene the Lorde *Paget* and him. The Lorde *Paget* came to Petworth, stayed there two nights, lodged in the Earle's house, conferred with *Charles Paget,* and with the Earle together sundrie times.

The Earle after his apprehension, being at several times examined what causes or affaires had passed betweene the *Lord Paget* and *Charles* his brother, when they were together at Petworth, answered one while, that they passed certaine deedes and conveiaunces: and another while, that there was onely a will or Testament signed and sealed betweene them: he confessed that he set his hande to the will, but knewe not what the same contained: all which appeared to be false, for that it hath fallen out by occasion of seasure of the landes and goods of the Lord *Paget* (after his departure out of the Realme) that hee had disposed of his landes and goods by another course of assurance executed at London: and therefore their pretence of the passing of deedes and will at Petworth, was but a devise to shadowe their trayterous conspiracies. And for better proofe thereof, it was alleaged by Master Attorney, that *Charles Paget* retourning from Petworth to the house of one *William Davies,* neere to the place where *Paget* had landed in Sussex, and tooke shipping againe at his departure beyond the seas, sent to *William Shelley* Esquier, residing then at his house at Michelgrove, distant about a myle from the house of *William Davies,* to come unto him (who within fewe days before had beene at the lodge at Petworth with the said *Paget:*) and nowe at their meeting in a coppice neere to *Davies'* house, *Paget* entred into speeche and discourse with him of divers matters, and at the last among other things, hee began to be inquisitive of the strength and fortification of Portesmouth, and what forces and strength her Majestie had in the other partes [C1] Westwarde.

Paget brake out and declared unto him that forraine princes would seeke revenge against her Majestie of the wronges by her done unto them, and woulde take such time and opportunitie as might best serve them for that purpose, and said that those princes disdained to see the Scottish Queene so kept and used here as shee was, and would use al their forces for her deliverie: that the Duke of *Guise* would be a dealer therein, and that the Earle of Northumberland would be an assistant unto them, willing *Shelley* whatsoever should happen, to followe the Earle of Northumberland, affirming that there was not a nobleman in England of conduct and governement like to the saide Earle: saying further, that the Earle of Northumberland was affected to the Scottish Queene, and would doe what he could for her advauncement.

That the *Duke* of *Guise* had forces in a readines to be employed for the altering of the state of Religion here in England, and to set the Scottish Queene at libertie.

Shelley gathered by these and other speeches which passed betweene him and *Paget,* that *Paget* had delt with the Earle as a chiefe partie, and a man forwarde in these actions: and *Paget* confessed that hee came over to breake and deale in these matters.

Paget delivered further, that the Catholiques woulde all joyne for so good a purpose, for that it woulde bee a meanes to reforme Religion.

He said, the stirre should be in the North partes, because Sussex was not convenient, aswell for that there were no safe landing places, as for that it was so neere London, where the Queene's Majestie would be ready to resiste them, and that whensoever any stirre shoulde bee, the Earle of Northumberland would not stay in Sussex, but would into the North partes.

When Master Attorney generall had in this sorte laid downe the particularities of the treasons and traiterous [C1v] practises of the confederates for this purposed invasion, then *Thomas Edgerton* Esquier, her Majestie's Sollicitour, to proove the Earle guiltie of these treasons by the circumstaunces of his owne proceedings, shewed that the Earle knowing how farre himselfe was touched with the said treasons, and in what degree of danger he stood if they should have bene revealed, found his onely hope of safetie to consist in the cunning concealing of them, and therefore hee endevoured to cover them by all the possible meanes he could devise.

And first, by convaying away of the Lorde *Paget,* a man not onely privie to the practises and treasons handled by *Francis Throckemorton,* but also to the treasons of his brother *Charles,* wherein the Earle and the Lorde *Paget* were doubtles both confederates with *Charles,* made acquainted by him with the causes of his comming over, as principall men with whome hee delt in those matters at Petworth.

The occasion that provoked the Earle to convay away the Lord *Paget,* grew upon the apprehension of *Throckmorton,* who being committed to the Tower, and charged with high matters, was in case to be delt withall by way of extremitie to bee made to confesse the treasons charged upon him, in revealing whereof, *Charles Paget's* comming to Petworth, and the cause of his repaire thither could not be concealed.

No man at this time within the Realme could accuse the Earle of these confederacies but the Lord *Paget* only, who stood in danger to be discovered by *Francis Throckmorton*: the safetie therefore of the Earle rested altogether upon the Lord *Paget's* departing out of the Realme, which was procured by the Earle with so great expedition, as that *Throckemorton* being committed to the Towre about the seventh day of November, 1583. the Earle made meanes the twelfth day to have the Lorde *Paget* provided of shipping in all hast by *William Shelley,* [C2] wherein the Earle used such importunate intreatie, and sent so often to hasten the preparation of the shippe, that the same was provided and the Lord *Paget* embarqued by the xxiii. day of the same moneth following, or thereabout.

The departure of the Lord *Paget* soone after discovered, and howe, and by whom he was convayed away: Her Majestie upon good cause taking offence thereat, the Earle being then at London had notice thereof, and of the confessions of *Throckemorton* (who began to discover the treasons) came presently downe to Petworthe, sent immediatly for *William Shelley,* who comming to him to Petworth the next morning about dinner time, met the Earle in a dining parlour ready to go to his dinner; the Earle tooke *Shelley* aside into a chamber, and as a man greatly distracted and troubled in minde, entred into these speeches: *Alas I am a man cast away,* and *Shelley* demanding what hee meant by those speeches, the Earle answered, *The actions I have entred into, I feare, will be my utter undoing,* and thereupon desired *Shelley* to keepe his counsell, and to discover no more of him then he must needes.

The Earle moreover at this meeting intreated *William Shelley* to convey away all such as he knew to have bene employed and were privie of the Lord *Paget's* going away, and of *Charles Paget's* comming over, which was accordingly perfourmed by *Shelley*: and the Earle for his part, convayed away a principall man of his own, whom he had often used in messages into France, and had bene of truste appointed by the Earle, to attende on *Charles Paget,* all the time of his stay at *Connigar Lodge.*

Master *Sollicitour* pursuing the matters that made the Earle's practises and devises for the concealing of his treasons manifeste: declared further, that after the Earle and *Shelley* had obtained some libertie in the Tower after their first restrainte: the Earle found meanes to have [C2v] intelligence with *Shelley,* and was advertised from him of all that he had confessed in his first examinations taken before they were last restrained: sithens which time, the Earle by corrupting of his keeper hath practised to have continuall advertisements as before, aswell of things done within the Tower as abroade: insomuch as by his said keeper, hee had sent and convayed twelve severall letters out of the Tower within the space of nine or tenne weekes, and one of those on Sonday the xx. day of June in the morning, when hee murdered himselfe the night following.

By the same corruption of his keepers, hee sent also a message to *William Shelley* by a maide servant in the Tower, by the which he required him to stand to his first confessions, and to goe no further, for so it would be best for him, and he shoulde keepe himselfe out of daunger. Wherunto *Shelley* retourned answere by the same messenger, that he could holde out no longer, that he had concealed the matters as long as he coulde, and willed the Earle to consider that there was a great difference betweene the Earle's estate and his: for that the Earle in respect of his nobilitie was not in danger to be delt withal in such sorte as he the said *Shelley* was like to bee, being but a private gentleman, and therfore to be used with al extremitie to be made confesse the trueth: wherefore he advised the Earle to deale plainely, and to remember what speeches had passed at his house at Petworth, when *Charles Paget* came last thither.

James Price by the same corruption of the Earle's keeper came to *William Shelley* on the Friday or Saturday before Trinitie Sonday last, and tolde him that the Earle was verie desirous to understand how farre he had gone in his confessions: and at *Price's* instance, *Shelley* did set down in writing the effect of the said confessions, and sent the same to the said Earle, who upon the sight therof, preceiving the treasons revealed and discovered, [C3] and knowing thereby howe haynous his offences were, fearing the justice and severitie of the Lawes, and so the ruyne and overthrowe of his house, fel into desperation, and so to the destruction of himselfe: for confirmation whereof, it was confessed by one *Jaques Pantins,* a grome of the Earle's chamber, who had attended on the Earle in the Tower by the space of tenne

weekes before his death, that he had heard the Earle often saye, that
Master *Shelley* was no faithfull friend unto him, and that hee had
confessed such things as were sufficient to overthrowe them both: that
he was undone by *Shelley's* accusations, affirming that the Earle began to despaire of himselfe, often with teares lamenting his cause,
which the Earle said to proceede onely of the remembrance of his wife
and children, saying further, that such matters were laide to his charge,
that he expected no favour, but to be brought to his triall, and then hee
was but a lost man: repeating often that *Shelley* had undone him, and
still mistrusting his cause, wished for death.

Herewith, Master Sollicitour concluded, and then Syr *Roger Man-*
wood Knight, Lord chiefe Baron of her Majestie's Eschequer, entred
into the discription of the Earle's death, and in what sorte hee had
murdered himselfe: shewing first howe the same had bene found by a
very substantiall Jurie chosen among the best commoners of the Citie,
empanelled by the Crowner upon the viewe of the bodie, and diligent
enquirie by all due meanes had according to the lawe, and declared,
That upon the discoverie of the intelligence conveied betweene the
Earle and *Shelley,* it was thought necessarie for the benefit of her
majestie's service, by such of her Highnesse's most honourable privie
Counsell, as were appoynted Commissioners to examine the course
of these treasons, that *Jaques Pantins* attending upon the Earle,
and the Earle's corrupt keepers shoulde be remooved: whereupon
Thomas Bailiffe gentleman, sent to attend [C3v] on the Earle of
Northumberland, upon the removing of *Palmer* & *Jaques Patins* from
about the said Earle (who from the beginning of his last restraint
attended on him) for the reasons lastly before mentioned, was by the
Lieutenant of the Towre on the Sunday about two of the clocke in
the afternoone (being the xx. of June) shut up with the Earle, as
appoynted to remaine with him, and serve him in the prison for a
time, until *Palmer, Pantins,* and *Price,* then committed close prisoners,
might be examined how the Earle came by such intelligences as were
discovered to have passed betweene the Earle and *Shelley,* and betweene the Earle and others. *Bailiffe* served the Earle at his supper,
brought him to his bed about nine of the clocke, and after some services done by the Earle's commaundement, departed from the Earle
to an utter Chamber, where he lay part of that night: and being come
into his chamber, the Earle rose out of his bed and came to his chamber
dore, and bolted the same unto him in the inner side, saying to *Bai-*

liffe, he coulde not sleepe unlesse his dore were fast. About twelve of the clocke at midnight, *Bailiffe* being in a slumber, heard a great noyse, seeming unto him to be the falling of some dore, or rather a piece of the house: the noyse was so sudden and so great, that he started out of his bed, and crying unto the Earle with a loude voice, said, My Lord, knowe you what this is? the Earle not answering, *Bailiffe* cryed and knocked still at the Earle's dore, saying, My Lord, how doe you? but finding that the Earle made no answere, continued his crying and calling, untill an olde man that lay without, spake unto him, saying, Gentleman, shall I call the watch, seeing he will not speake? Yea, quoth *Bailiffe* for God's sake, Then did the old man rise, and called one of the watch, whom *Bailiffe* intreated with all possible speede to call master Lieutenant unto him. In the meane-time *Bailiffe* heard the Earle give a long and most grievous grone, and after that, gave a se- [C4] cond grone: and then the Lieutenant (being come) called to the Earle, who not answering, *Bailiffe* cried to the Lieutenant to breake open the Earle's chamber dore bolted unto him in the inner side, which was done, and then they found the Earle dead in his bed, and by his bedside a Dagge, wherewith he had killed himselfe.

Sir *Owen Hopton* knight, examined upon his othe, affirmed that on Sunday last at night, lesse then a quarter of an houre before one of the clocke after midnight, he was called up by the watche to come to the Earle of Northumberland, who had bene called unto by master *Bailiffe* his keeper, and would not speake (as the watche tolde him:) whereuppon the sayde Syr *Owen* wente presently to the Earle's lodging, opened the utter dores till hee came to the chamber where master *Bailiffe* lay, which was next to the Earle's bedde Chamber. *Bailiffe* said to this Examinate as he came in, that he was wakened with a noyse as it were of a dore or some great thing falling, and that he had called on the Earle, and coulde have no answere: And this Examinate going to the Earle's Chamber dore, finding the same bolted fast on the other side within the earle's lodging, so as he coulde not goe into the Earle, this Examinate called on the Earle, telling him the Lieutenant was there, and prayed his Lordship to open the dore: but this Examinate having no answere made unto him, and finding the dore fast bolted in the inner side of the Earle's Chamber with a strong iron bolte, so as they coulde not enter into the same out of the lodging where the said *Bailiffe* lay without breaking up the Chamber dore, caused the Warders which were with this Examinate, to thrust in their Holbardes, and to wrest the dore thereby, as much as they could, and withall to runne at the dore with their feete, and with violence to thrust it open, which they did accordingly. And when this Examinate came into the Chamber, in turning up the sheetes, he perceived them [C4v] to be bludded: and then searching further, founde the wound, which was very neere the pappe, not thinking at the first sight, but that it had bene done with a knife. This Examinate went thereupon presently to write to the Court, and tooke the warders into the vtter chamber, and left them there untill he returned, bolting the dore of the Earle's bedchamber on the outside: and as soone as this Examinate returned from writing of his Letter to the Court, he searched above the chamber, and found the Dagge in the floore, about three foote from the bedde, neere unto a table that had a greene cloth on it, which did somewhat shadowe the Dagge: and after, turning downe the bedclothes, founde the boxe in the which the powder and pellets were, on the bed under the Coverlet, and sayth, that the Chamber where the Earle laye, hath no other dore but that one dore which was broken open as aforesayde, save one dore that went into a privie, which hath no maner of passage out of it: and that the Earle's lodging chamber, and the entring to the privie, are both walled rounde about with a stone wall, and a bricke wall, and that there is no dore or passage out of or from the saide Earle's bed Chamber or privie, but that onely dore which was broken open by the appoyntment of this Examinate. The Warders that were with this Examinate at the entrie into the prison, and the breaking up of the Earle's chamber dore, and the doing of the other thinges aforesayde, were *Michaell Sibley, Anthony Davies, William Ryland* and *John Potter,* and one *John Pinner* this Examinate's servant was there also.

For the proofe and confirmation of these severall parts and poyntes of this deposition, *Sibley, Davies, Ryland, Potter* and *Pinner* were deposed, and they *viva voce* affirmed so much thereof to be true, as was reported by the examination of the Lieutenant, concerning the comming of the Lieutenant to the Earle's chamber, the breaking up of the dore being bolted with a strong bolte on [D1] the inner side, the finding of the Earle dead upon his bed, the Dagge lying on the ground, the powder and pellets in a boxe on the bed under the Coverlet, with the rest of the circumstances thereunto appertayning. They affirmed also, that there was but one doore in the Earle's chamber, saving the dore of the privie, which together with the chamber was strongly walled above with stone and bricke: and further (as I remember) the Lord chiefe Baron confirmed the same, having viewed the Chamber himselfe where the Earle lodged and was founde dead.

Jaques Pantins in his examination of the xxi. of June confesseth, that *James Price* delivered the Dagge to the Earle his master in this examinate's presence: whereupon he presently suspected that the Earle meant mischiefe to himselfe, and therefore did his indevour to perswade the Earle to send away the Dagge, and tolde the Earle that he knewe not how the Devil might tempt his Lordship, and that the Devill was great: but could by no meanes prevaile with the Earle in that behalfe: and saith moreover, that the Earle required him to hide the Dagge, and he thereupon hanged the same on a nayle within the Chimney in the Earle's bed Chamber, where the Earle thinking the same not to be sufficiently safe in that place, it was by the Earle's appointment taken from thence, and put into a slitte in the side of a mattresse that lay under the Earle's bedde, neere to the bed's head, and that the same Sunday morning that the Earle murdered himselfe at night, he sawe the Dagge lying under the Earle's bed's head. The Dagge was bought not many dayes before of one *Adrian Mulan* a Daggemaker, dwelling in East Smithfield, as by the said *Mulan* was testified *viva voce* upon his othe in the open Court at the time of the publique Declaration made of these matters in the Starrechamber.

All these particularities considered, with the depositi- [D1v] ons and proves of the witnesse concerning the Earle's death, first, how he came by the Dagge: secondly, howe long he had kept the same, and in what secret maner: thirdly, the Earle's bolting of his Chamber dore in the inside: fourthly, the blow of the Dagge: fiftly, the breaking up of the Earle's Chamber dore by the Lieutenant of the Towre: and lastly, the finding of the Earle dead as aforesayde: what is he so simple that will thinke or imagine, or so impudent and malicious that will avouch and reporte, that the Earle of Northumberland shoulde have bene murdered of purpose, by practise or devise of any person, affecting his destruction in that maner? If men consider the inconvenience happened thereby, as well in matter of State, as commoditie to the Queene's Majestie, lost by the prevention of his tryall: who can in reason conjecture the Earle to have bene murdered of pollicie or set purpose, as the evill affected seeme to conceave? If the Earle had lived to have received the Censure of the lawe for his offences, all lewde and frivolous objections had then bene answered, and all his goods, chattels and lands by his attaindure, had come unto her Majestie, and the Honour and State of his house and posteritie utterly overthrowen: the consideration and feare whereof appeareth without all doubt to have bene the principall and only cause that made him lay violent hands upon himselfe. If objections be made, that to murder him in that sort might be a satisfaction to his enemies, who could be pacified by no meanes but with his blood: that seemeth to be as improbable, for that it is commonly discerned in the corrupt nature of man, that when we are possessed with so profound a hatred, as to seeke the death of our enemie, we imagine and wish his destruction to be had with the greatest shame and infamie that can be devised: thinke you not then, that if the Earle of Northumberland had any such enemie that knewe the danger wherein he stood, and that his tryall and conviction [D2] by lawe, would drawe upon him the losse of his life, lands and goods, fame, honour, and the utter subversion of his house, and would be so kinde hearted unto him, as to helpe to take away his life onely, and save him all the rest? I suppose there is no man of judgement wil beleeve it.

But to returne to the maner of the Earle's death. It was declared by the Lord *Hunsdon,* and the Lorde *chiefe Baron,* that the Dagge wherewith the Earle murdered himselfe, was charged with three bullets, and so of necessitie with more then an ordinarie charge of powder, to force that waight of Bullet to worke their effect. The Earle lying upon his backe on the left side of his bedde, tooke the Dagge charged in his left hand (by all likelihoode) layde the mouth of the Dagge upon his left pappe (having first put aside his wastcoate) and his shirte being only betweene the Dagge and his body (which was burnt away the breadth of a large hand) discharged the same, wherewith was made a large wounde in his sayde pappe, his heart pearced and torne in divers lobes or pieces, three of his ribbes broken, the Chine bone of his backe cut almost in sunder, and under the poynt of the shoulder blade on the right side within the skinne, the three Bullets were founde by the Lord *Hunsdon,* which he caused the Surgion in his presence to cut out, lying al three close together within the breadth and compasse of an ynche or thereabout: the bullets were shewed by his Lordshippe at the time of the publication made in the Court at the Starrechamber.

And whereas it hath bene slanderously given out to the advantage of the Earle, as the reporters suppose, that he was imprisoned and kept in so straight, narrowe and close roome, with such penurie of ayre and breath, that thereby he grewe sickely and weary of his life, and that to have bene the cause chiefly why he murdered himself, (if it were so that hee died by the violence of his owne hand which they hardly beleeve:) to answere that pee- [D2v] vish and senseles slander, there was much spoken by the Lord chiefe Baron, who had viewed and caused very exactly to be measured the chambers and roomes within the prison where the Earle lay, being part of her Majestie's owne lodging in the Towre: the particular length and breadth of the said chambers and roomes, and the qualitie of the lightes and windowes, expressed by the saide Lord chiefe Baron, I can not repeate: but well I doe remember it was declared that all the dayetime the Earle had the libertie of five large chambers, and two long entries within the utter doore of his prison: three of which chambers, and one of the entries, lay upon two faire gardens within the Towre wall, and upon the Towre wharfe, with a pleasant prospect to the Thames, and to the Countrey, more then five miles beyond. The windowes were of a very large proportion, yeelding so much ayre and light as more cannot be desired in any house: Note therefore how malitiously those that favour Traitours and treasons, can deliver out these and the like slaunderous speeches, to the dishonour of her Majestie, noting her Counsailers and ministers with inhumanitie and uncharitable severitie, contrary to all trueth and honestie.

When the Lord chiefe Baron had finished this discourse of the maner of the Earle's death with the circumstances, and had satisfied the Court and auditorie concerning the qualitie of the prison where the Earle had remained, Sir *Christopher Hatton* Knight, her Majestie's vicechamberlaine, who (as it seemed) had bene specially employed by her Majestie among others of her privie Councell in the looking into and examining of the treasons aforesaide, aswell in the person of the Earle as of others, and at the time of the Earle's committement from his house in S. Martin's to the Towre of London, sent unto him from her Majestie to put the Earle in minde of her Majestie's manifold graces and favours in former times conferred upon him, proceeding from the Spring of her Majestie's Princely [D3] and bountifull nature, and not of his deservings, and to advise him to deliver the trueth of the matters so cleerely appearing against him, either by his letters privatly to her Majestie, or by speech to Master Vice-

chamberlaine, who signified also unto him, that if he would determine to take that course, he should not onely not bee committed to
the Towre, but shoulde finde grace and favour at her Majestie's hands
in the mittigation of such punishment as the Lawe might laye upon
him. And here Master Vicechamberlaine repeated at length the effect
of her Majestie's message at that time sent to the Earle, beginning
first with the remembrance of his practise undertaken for the convaying away of the Scottish Queene about the time of the last rebellion (as hath bene declared in the beginning of this tracte) and that
he confessing the offence being capitall, her Majestie nevertheles
was pleased to alter the course of his triall by the justice of her lawes,
and suffered the same to receave a slight and easie punishment by way
of *Mulcte* or fine of 5000. markes, whereof before this his imprisonment (as it is crediblie reported) there was not one peny paide, or his
land touched with any extent for the paiment thereof, which offence
was by her Majestie not onely most gratiously forgiven, but also most
Christianly forgotten, receiving him not long after to the place of
honour that his auncestours had enjoyed for many yeeres before him,
and gave him such entrance into her Princely favour and good opinion, that no man of his qualitie received greater coutenance and comfort at her Majestie's hands then he, insomuch that in all exercises of
recreation used by her Majestie, the Earle was alwayes called to be
one, and whensoever her Majestie shewed herselfe abroade in publique, she gave to him the honour of the best and highest services
about her person, more often then to all the noblemen of her Court.

But the remembrance of these most gratious and more [D3v] then
extraordinarie favours and benefites received, nor the hope given
unto him by Master *Vicechamberlaine* of her Majestie's disposition
of mercie towards him, nor the consideration of the depthe and waight
of his treasons against her Majestie, her Estate, her Crowne and
dignitie, with the danger thereby like to fall upon him by the course
of her highnes's Lawes, to the utter ruyne and subversion of him and
his house (standing now at her Majestie's mercie) could once moove
his heart to that naturall and dutifull care of her Majestie's safetie
that he ought to have borne towards her, and she most worthely had
merited at his hands, or any remorse or compassion of himselfe and
his posteritie: but resting upon termes of his innocencie, having as
you may perceive convayed away al those that he thought could or
would any waye accuse him, he made choise rather to goe to the

Towre, abide the hazard of her Majestie's high indignation, and the extremitie of the Law for his offences: a notable augure of his fall, and that God by his just judgement, had for his sinnes and ingratitude taken from him his Spirit of grace, and delivered him over to the enemie of his soule, who brought him to that most dreadful and horrible end, whereunto he is come: from the which, God of his mercie defend all Christian people, and preserve the Queene's Majestie from the Treasons of her Subjects, that shee may live in all happinesse, to see the ruine of her enemies abroade and at home, and that she and we her true and loving Subjectes, may be alwayes thankefull to God for all his blessings bestowed upon us by her the onely maintayner of his holy Gospel among us.

FINIS.

A Declaration of the Causes
to Give aide in the lowe Countries (1585)

By 1570 the seventeen industrial and commercial provinces composing the Netherlands were already outspokenly Protestant in many areas and increasingly critical of Spain. They had by then become important as the center of trade—Antwerp was the European center of banking and investment; Brussels was the center of lucrative tapestry manufacture; and the ports of Holland and Zeeland harbored between them some 5,000 ships, enough to monopolize sixteenth century sea trade. In 1566 the Low Countries had joined together to demand an abolition of the Spanish Inquisition, and since then the rule Philip had inherited from his father Charles V proved difficult even as he was made more clearly aware of how important it was to him financially.

Yet the Low Countries were loosely allied enough that had it not been for an emerging hero like William of Nassau, prince of Orange, whose sense of *realpolitik* went beyond the interests of a single province and even a single religious outlook, their force might never have amounted to much. In 1573 William wrote his brother, "I have only aspired for the freedom of the country both in matters of conscience and government. . . . Therefore, the only articles that I have to propose are that the exercise of the Reformed religion in accordance with God's Word should be permitted, and that the Republic's ancient privileges and liberty should be restored, which means that foreign, and especially Spanish, officials and soldiers should be withdrawn." In 1575—after five long months of pursuing peace with the Estates-General at the conference of Breda—Philip's Governor-General, Don Luis de Requesens, learned how widespread and how deep William's philosophical position was: the talks fell apart on the issue of religious toleration.

Requesens was succeeded by Alexander Farnese, prince of Parma, in 1578. This appointment was Philip's master stroke, for Parma was a man skilled in diplomacy and military maneuvers and his ability to attract admiration soon fostered enough Catholic hatred of the Calvinists to break the young back of Flemish unity. Parma's tactic was to drive a wide religious and linguistic wedge between the north and south—for the Protestant, Dutch, commercial north had little in common with the Catholic, French, industrial south. So clever were his strategies and so firm his victories that he soon appeared invincible; and to add to other troubles, William found that he could not himself keep the loyalty of the Calvinists who wished to gain control over the cities of the Netherlands for themselves only. In October of 1577 a revolution in Ghent gave the Calvinists control of that city; and the guilds set up the Council of Eighteen, a committee of defense. In Brussels, led by the burgomaster Jan van Hembyze, Calvinists who used Ghent as their model took over and set up another council. The Calvinist zealot Peter Dathenus emerged as a new leader, a rival to William, for southern social and political radicalism.

In self-protection, seven northern provinces now set up the Union of Utrecht, encouraged by William, and, at his instigation, agreed to ask the French Roman Catholic son of Catherine de Medici, the Duke of Alençon, to lead their forces. Alençon was hungry for prestige, and he offered to use his own men and money, and to listen closely to William who as a native of the Netherlands could not himself claim leadership without opening himself to charges of rebellion. Unfortunately, Alençon was not an especially good soldier and by 1583 he was dead in France with few if any significant victories to his credit. William now took control only to be assassinated on July 10, 1584, by Balthazar Gerard, a cabinetmaker's apprentice who wished to prove that he could kill a prince. All this must have been awesome fulfillment to Thomas Churchyard who had prophesied early in England in his *Lamentable, and pitifull Description, of the wofull warres in Flaunders, since the foure last yeares of the Emperor Charles the fifth his raigne* (1578), by a first-hand account, that "their Countrey stoode never free from troubles, nor their Townes, Fortes, and fortifications coulde any long whyle in quietnesse remayne" (C1).

Meantime, affairs were going well for Philip in the south. The Walloon Catholics had countered the Union of Utrecht with their own union, the Union of Arran; and Parma's victories were supported by internal feuding among the Protestants. Hembyze, the uncrowned king of Brussels, was discovered in secret negotiations with Parma and put to death by his own men in August 1584. By the end of that year Parma had regained Flanders and most of Brabant. Brussels fell to him in February 1585 and, following a long siege, Antwerp itself fell on August 17, 1585. The reaction to this triumph was electric: Philip II learned of it in the middle of the night, but he leaped from his bed and ran to the room of his daughter Isabella crying, "Antwerp is ours!" So delighted was he that he gave Parma as reward the long-desired fortress of Piacenza.

Ever since Throckmorton had confessed in the fall of 1583 that plans had been afoot for an international invasion of England, with land forces from the Netherlands, to unseat Elizabeth and crown Mary Stuart, England had been fearful of Spanish victories there. If the Netherlands ceased to worry Philip and if the French Guises were not contained by the Low Countries but instead found allies there, Elizabeth might easily be overcome by foreign forces. Moreover, she was, throughout the world now, recognized as the leader of the chief Protestant power. Most significantly to her, she had as much reverence as William the Silent for political and religious liberty. Her hesitation to support William when he was alive and to intervene in behalf of his forces now that his crucial leadership was no longer available seemed unworthy and futile to the war-faction of her Privy Council, led now by Leicester and Walsingham. England could not afford to remain apart from the life struggle of Protestantism. Neutrality was no longer possible: and if principle could not stir the Queen, perhaps self-interest could. To all the English councillors in 1584 and early 1585 disaster did not seem far off.

Elizabeth and Burghley had no other choice than surrender to the Leicester-Walsingham faction for a more active commitment of forces to the Protestant cause in the Low Countries. But the way was not especially difficult for the Queen even now, since her war-faction had for the past decade developed close personal relationships with William's men—such Protestants as Joachim Ortell and Paulus Buys —who had come to see England, rather than France, as their sole support in the quest for Dutch salvation. With these preliminary steps long since undertaken, Elizabeth received an embassy from the Low Countries in June of 1585; they offered her the sovereignty of the provinces in return for her critical support. She refused, for it was not her nature to make so bold a commitment; nor was she, personally, an expansionist. Neither did she wish to oppose so directly the King of Spain whom she still chose to recognize as titular head of the Netherlands if he would only agree to certain basic liberties. But she did agree to take the Dutch under her limited protection and—spurred on by the fall of Antwerp on August 17—she signed, on August 20, the Treaty of Nonsuch by which she provided an army of 5,000 men and 1,000 horse and a large sum of money in return for the ports of Flushing and Brill as "cautions."

So far-reaching a move and so drastic a change in foreign policy was undoubtedly difficult for Elizabeth, and the following declaration is an honest and frank statement in which she sets forth her reasons for taking the step she did. In this there is no reason to disbelieve her. Indeed, there is here, despite the firmness of the statement as a whole, an uneasiness about "forreners and strangers of strange blood, men more exercised in warres then in peaccable government, and some of them notably delighted in blood" (B1) and a sad resignation in the realization that "no hope of reliefe . . . , but rather an increase therof by dayly conquests of their townes and slaughter of their people" (C3-C3v) is the best she can now expect from Spain. Her purpose is not "ambition or malice" (C4), but the pursuit of religious and political freedom, "the honour of God, whome they [the Dutch] desire to serve sincerely as christian people according to his holy word, and to enjoye their ancient liberties for them and their posteritie, and so consequently to preserve and contynue the lawful and ancient commerce betwixt our people and those countries and ours" (C3v). Like William, Elizabeth held strongly to her belief in the liberty of conscience, the sanctity of traditional privileges and rights, and personal faith in an open society. Her own reasons for intervention, then, as listed here, are four: (1) to establish peace, (2) to insure security, (3) to continue commerce as she has known it, and (4) to express her compassion for the suffering of others—and she probably ranked them in this order.

The document is unusually long and complicated; and it betrays a defensiveness, as if the truth will not convince others of her reasons for joining the Dutch war against Spanish repression. Her history of the government of the Low Countries seems unnecessarily detailed; her argument, unnecessarily repetitive. But there is a surprising lack of rancor, and she has good words for Parma—nephew to Don John

—on C3v, as well as respect for the traditional rule of the Spanish king. She does not argue in terms of power but in terms of peace, compassion, and man's hunger for free choice.

The actual authorship seems, surprisingly in some ways, to have been jointly Burghley's and Walsingham's. A draft of the "Addition" in a clerical hand with the Cecil Papers at Hatfield shows Burghley's endorsement and Walsingham's revisions. Burghley himself had been at the task for a year; on October 12, 1584, he wrote of a book— *De Leone Beligico*—which he wished he had used as a model for discussing the past nobility of the Low Countries. In August a copy of the *Declaration* below was carried by an English agent to Parma. Still, the two Privy Councillors continued to labor over it; Walsingham wrote Burghley that autumn, on October 12, that he had composed an answer to an Italian pamphlet, that the Queen approved of his draft, and that he hoped Burghley would "make such corrections as he thought meet." "I think it most expedient," Walsingham continued, "that the [Dutch] commissioners here should be made acquainted with the Declaration before it be printed. It may be that there is somewhat contained therein that haply may more prejudice the cause than yield benefit in point of justification. The perusal thereof can no way hinder her Majesty's intent and therefore, in my poor opinion, your Lordship shall do well to acquaint them herewith." It was an important moment, when the conservative Burghley and the radical Walsingham joined forces, and both men seem to have been as careful as the Queen. Publication followed before the year was out—and her official printer Chistopher Barker printed the pamphlet in a number of translations. The rhetoric of propaganda seems missing in this document; and it is therefore important as a first-hand glimpse at the thought of the Queen and her Privy Council: a fresh revelation of Elizabeth and her leading statesmen in a moment of extreme crisis which they tried to meet with extreme caution and honesty.

TEXTUAL NOTES
[For explanatory notes for this selection see page 371.]

A Declaration of the Causes to Give aide in the lowe Countries
Reference. STC 9188-9193.
Authorship, Editions, and Issues. Elizabeth's official defense of her military support to the Low Countries is the joint work of William Cecil, lord Burghley, and Sir Francis Walsingham; although there is no draft of the work, the addition to it, revised by Walsingham and endorsed by Burghley, is among the Cecil papers (138/155) at Hatfield. Burghley's *Execution of Iustice in England for maintenaunce of publique and Christian peace* (1583), a work somewhat similar in style, is bound with the present work in the copy at the Bodleian (Crynes 829).

This pamphlet was issued in three editions, the second in two issues; and a number of mixed copies exist, strongly suggesting that the editions were all printed about the same time and gathered and bound indiscriminately at the print-shop; this is highly likely, since Elizabethan printers insisted on limiting to between 1,200 and 1,500 the number of copies from one setting of type before distributing the type and at once resetting it, so that they could benefit financially from a book that sold well. (See Fredson Bowers, *Principles of Bibliographical Description* [Princeton, 1949], p. 108.) Similar resettings probably occurred for the account of the Queen's processional (pp. 9-10) and the pamphlet on Mary Queen of Scotts (pp. 216-217).

Setting A, represented by Bodleian Crynes 829 (1), differs in 4 substantial variants and 82 incidental variants in spelling and punctuation from the second edition, setting B (represented by Bodleian Smith newsb. e. 7), although the outer formes of sheets B and C were not reset. Except for D1-D1v, setting B is a line-for-line resetting of A; the superior readings—"Forraines, A restitution" (C4) and perhaps "world):" (C2v)—suggest B is subsequent to A. There is one mixed copy at the Bodleian with a combination of setting B for sheets A, B, and C and of setting A for sheet D for the most part. Signature D3 exists in three settings, bound indiscriminately with settings A and B of the first three sheets; since printers insisted that some typesetting change demonstrate a resetting after a maximum number of copies, this page, with incidental changes, may be the index to the fact that the pamphlet went through three, not two, nearly simultaneous editions. In all instances sheet D (the appendix) is paginated separately and may have been written independently of and later than the main text.

There is a separate issue of setting B printed without the ornamental type after Barker's colophon on D3v (STC 9189); this follows setting B except for D3 which uses spellings of settings A and C (D3 alone in sheet D was not fully reset three times).

Translations. Customarily British policy dictated that a justification of official action such as this be widely distributed. Thus several translations have come down: a quarto in three sheets (A-C) was issued in French in Delft in 1585 (Bodleian G. Pamp. 1837 [9]); an octavo in two and a half sheets (A-B⁸; C⁴) was published in German in "Coelln" (?Cologne) in 1585; a quarto in Dutch by Richard Schilders, Middelburg in 1585 (BM C.33.b.24 [11]); and four translations in octavo issued by Barker himself—Italian in italics (8°; A-B⁸; C⁴), French (8°; A-B⁸; C⁴) and Latin (A-B⁸; C⁴) in roman, and Dutch (8°; in fours, A-E⁴) in black-letter (all Bodleian Wood 580).

Subsequent Editions. The work reappears in J. Morgan, *Phoenix Britannicus* (London, 1732), I, 300-309, without notes or commentary, following setting B; in the third collection of *Somers Tracts* (London, 1751), I, 99-111, also without notes, following setting A; and in Scott's later edition of the *Somers Tracts* (London, 1809), I, 410-419, with notes, also after setting A.

Collation. 4°; A-D⁴; A1, blank; A2, title-page; A2v, official crest; A3-C4v, text; D1-D3, appendix; D3v, colophon ["Imprinted at Lon-/don by Christopher Barker, Printer to the Queene of England/her most excellent Maiestie./1585. (design)]; D4-D4v, blank.

Description of Contents. Title-page, mixture of roman and italics, with illustration; A2v, crest is page-size; text in roman with roman and italics heading; appendix, roman with roman and italics heading. Paginated; text, pp. 1-20; appendix, pp. 1-5. Head-piece on D1; no tail-pieces. Decorative intitial *A* (similar but different) on A3, D1. No running-head. Many marginal notes in roman as follows: "Kinges and Princes Soueraignes, are to yeeld account of their actions onely to almighty God, the King of Kĩngs." (A3), "Naturall causes of the Ancient continual traffique betwixt the people of England and them of the lowe countries." (A3v); "Confederations both betwixt yᵉ Kings of England and Lordes of the low Countries, and also the subjects of both Countries." (A3v); "The people of both the Countries bound by speciall obligations enterchangeablie, for mutuall fauours & friẽdly offices." (A4); "Treaties of anciẽt time, betwixt the Kinges of England and the Dukes of Burgundie, for the commerce betwixt their Countries." (A4v); "Conuentions for yᵉ subiectes of either side, to shewe mutuall fauours one to the other." (A4v); "Spanyards and stangers lately appoynted gouerners in the lowe Countries, to the violation of the liberties of the Countrie." (B1); "The destruction of the Nobilitie, and the people of the Countries by the Spanish gouernment." (B1v); "The lamentable violent death of the Countie of Egmond, the glorie of those Countries." (B1v); "The riche townes and strengthes with yᵉ wealth/thereof possessed by the Spaniardes." (B1v-B2); "The French kings offers to haue aided & receiued to his subiection the oppressed people of the lowe Countries." (B2); "The Queene of Englandes continuall frendly aduices to the king of Spaine for restraining of the tyrannie of his gouernours." (B2v); "The Queene of Englandes meanes vsed to staie the States of the lowe countries from yeelding their subiection to any other forreine Prince." (B3); "The enterprise of the Spaniardes in Ireland sent by the king of Spayne and the Pope." (B3v); "The refusall of ye Queenes messenger, and her letters to the King of Spayne." (B4); "The iust causes of dismissing of Bernardin Mendoza out of England." (B4); "Barnardin [*sic*] Mendoza fauourably licensed to depart the Realme." (C1v); "The Queene of Englandes proceeding for the deliuerie of Scotland from the seruitude wherein the House of Guyse meant to haue brought it." (C2); "The Realme of Scotlande restored to the ancient freedome, and so possessed by the present King by the meanes onely of the Queene of England." (C2v); "The conclusion of the causes of sending of certaine companies of english souldiers to the defence of the oppressed people of the low countries, and to withstand the attemptes against this Realme." (C3); "English power sent onely to defende." (C3v); "Three special things reasonably desired by the Queene of England. 1. The end of wars with Restitutiō of the low Countries to their anciēt liberties. 2. Suretie from inuasiō of her owne Realme. 3. And renewing of the mutual Traffique betweene the Countries." (C4); "The causes of taking some Townes into her Maiesties custodie." (C4)

License. No entry in the *Stationers' Register.* Colophon states Christopher Barker as printer and 1585 as date (D3v).

Base-Copy Text. Bodleian Crynes 829 (1). Copy consulted for second edition: Bodleian Smith newsb.3.7. Copy consulted for third edition: BM C.33.b.8. Copy consulted for issue of second edition: Hn (on STC film 419). [The present text follows the first edition with three emendations from the second edition: "world:)] worlde):" (C2v); "Forraines with a] Forraines, A" (C4); "falsly] falsely" (D1v.]

Substantial Variants. [First edition, Crynes 829(1)=BM 154.g.16(2) precedes second edition, Bodleian Smith newsb.3.7.] Lorde: and that amongst]Lorde: yet (though amongst   Lord GOD hath]Lorde God hauing Maiestie; yet we] Maiestie) wee (all on A3)   Forraines, with a restitution] Forraines, A restitution (C4).

Title-page in Full./[within rule within rule within decorative border] A/ DECLARATION OF/THE CAVSES MOOVING/THE QVEENE OF ENGLAND/to giue aide to the Defence of/*the People afflicted and*/oppressed in the lowe/*Countries.*/ [design]/Imprinted at Lon-/don by Christopher Barker,/Printer to the Queenes most/ *excellent Maiestie.*/[Overall layout is similar and designs identical to the title-page of the following work on Mary Queen of Scots, pp. 213-236.]

Emendations. (B1v) And howe so euer in the] And howesoever in the   but for euer] but forever (B4) what danger our selfe,] what

danger ourselfe,   (C1v) messenger afore mēcioned,] messenger aforemencioned,   disposed our selues] disposed ourselves of our selfe]
of ourselfe   (C2) *French* men,] *French*men,   for our selues] for ourselves   (C2v) Noble men,] Noblemen,   (C4) to our selfe] to ourselfe
suretie for our selues] surety for ourselves   vpō the sea side] upon the
seaside   (D1) found our selfe] found ourselfe   (D1v) who euer carried
our selfe] whoever carried ourselfe   (D2) speache, done any thing]
speache, done anything   (D2v) our selfe,] ourselfe,   (D3) assuring our
selues,] assuring ourselves, my selfe,] myselfe,   (C2) milke maides]
milkemaides   (C2v) in stead of gratefulnes,] instead of gratefulnes,
my selfe] myselfe   (C3) Stafford Shire] StaffordShire   (C4) great
goodwils] great good wils   But for as much] But forasmuch   commō
wealth] commonwealth   (C4v) what euer] whatever   (D1) her selfe]
herselfe   (D2) suit of any one] suit of anyone   (D2v) any one] anyone   (D3) hostages: *for asmuch*] hostages: *forasmuch*   (D3v) *any*
thing] *anything*   (D4v) wyer drawers] wyerdrawers   (E1) my selfe]
myselfe   (E1v) to me in deede] to me indeede   my selfe,] myselfe,
(E2) my selfe] myselfe   for euer] forever   my selfe:] myselfe: (E2v) our
selues.] ourselves.   (E3) my selfe] myselfe   my selfe] myselfe   your
selues] yourselves.

A Declaration of the Causes Mooving the Queene of England to Give aide to the Defence of the People afflicted and *oppressed in the lowe* Countries.

LTHOUGH KINGES and Princes Soveraignes, owing their homage and service onely unto the Almightie God the king of al kings, are in that respect not bounde to yeeld account or render the reasons of their actions to any others but to God their only Soveraigne Lorde: and that amongst the most ancient and Christian Monarches the same Lorde GOD hath committed to us the Soveraignetie of this Realme of *Englande* and other our dominions, which wee holde immediatly of the same Almighty Lord, and so thereby accountable onely to his divine Majestie: yet we are notwithstanding this our prerogative at this time specially mooved, for divers reasons hereafter briefly remembred, to publish not onely to our owne naturall loving Subjectes, but also to all others our neighbours, specially to such Princes and States as are our Confederates, or have for their Subjectes cause of commerce with our Countreis and people, what our intention is at this time, [A3v] and upon what just and reasonable groundes we are mooved to give aid to our next Neighbours the naturall people of the lowe Countries, being by long warres and persecutions of strange Nations there, lamentablie afflicted, and in present danger to bee brought into a perpetuall servitude.

First it is to be understoode (which percase is not perfectly knowen to a great nomber of persons) that there hath beene, time out of minde,

even by the natural situation of those low Countreis and our Realme
of Englande, one directly opposite to the other, and by reason of the
ready crossing of the Seas, and multitude of large and commodious
Havens respectively on both sides, a continuall traffique and commerce
betwixt the people of Englande, and the Naturall people of these
lowe Countries, and so continued in all ancient times when the
several Provinces therof, as *Flanders, Holland,* and *Zeland,* and other
Countries to them adjoyning, were ruled and possessed by severall
Lordes, and not united together, as of late yeeres they have beene by
entermariages, and at length by concurrences of many and sundrie
titles have also beene reduced to be under the government of their
Lordes that succeeded to the Dukedome of *Burgundie,* wherby there
hath beene in former ages many speciall alliances and confederations,
not onely betwixt the Kinges of England our Progenitours and the
Lordes of the said countries of *Flanders,* [A4] *Holland, Zeland,* and
their adherentes: but also betwixt the very naturall subjectes of both
Countries, as the Prelates, Noblemen, Citizens, Burgesses, and other
Comminalties of the great Cities and porte Townes of either countrie
reciproquelie by speciall Obligations and Stipulations under their
Seales interchangeablie, for maintenance both of commerce and entercourse of Marchantes, and also of speciall mutuall amitie to bee
observed betwixt the people and inhabitants' of both parties as well
Ecclesiasticall as Secular: and very expresse provision in such
Treaties contened for mutuall favours, affections, and all other
friendly offices to bee used and prosecuted by the people of the one
Nation towardes the other. By which mutuall Bondes, there hath
continued perpetuall unions of the peoples' heartes together, and
so by way of continuall entercourses, from age to age the same mutuall
love hath bene inviolablie kept and exercised, as it had bene by the
worke of nature, and never utterly dissolved, nor yet for any long
time discontinued, howsoever the kinges, and the Lordes of the
countries sometimes (though very rarely) have bene at difference by
sinister meanes of some other Princes their Neighbours, envying the
felicitie of these two Countries.

And for maintenance and testimonie of these natural unions of the
peoples of these kingdoms and countries in perpetuall amitie, there
are [A4v] extant sundrie autentique Treaties and Transactions for
mutuall commerce, entercourse and straight amitie of ancient times:
as for example, some very solemnely accorded in the times of King

Henrie the sixth our progenitour, and *Philip* the second Duke of *Bugundie*, and inheritour to the Countie of *Flanders* by the Ladie *Margaret* his Grandmother, which was above one hundred and fortie yeeres past, and the same also renewed by the noble Duke *Charles* his sonne, Father to the King of *Spayne's* Grandmother, and husband to the Ladie *Margaret* sister to our great Grandfather King *Edward* the fourth: and after that, of newe oftentimes renewed by our most Noble and sage Grandfather King *Henrie* the seventh, and the Archduke *Philip* Grandfather to the King of *Spayne* now being: and in later times, often renewed betwixt our Father of Noble memorie King *Henrie* the eight, and *Charles* the fifth Emperour of *Almaigne*, Father also to the present King of *Spaine*.

In all which Treaties, Transactions, and Confederations of amitie and mutuall commerce, it was also at all times specially and principally contained in expresse wordes, by conventions, concordes and conclusions, that the naturall people and subjects of either side, should shewe mutuall favours and dueties one to the other, and should safely, freely and securely commerce together in every their countries, and so hath the same mutuall and naturall concourse and com- [B1] merce bene without interruption continued in many ages, farre above the like example of any other countries in Christendome, to the honour and strength of the Princes, and to the singular great benefite and enriching of their people, untill of late yeeres that the King of *Spayne* departing out of his lowe countries into *Spayne*, hath beene (as it is to be thought) counselled by his counsellers of *Spayne*, to appoynt *Spaniardes*, forreners and strangers of strange blood, men more exercised in warres then in peaceable government, and some of them notably delighted in blood, as hath appeared by their actions, to be the chiefest governours of all his sayde lowe countries, contrary to the ancient lawes and customes thereof, having great plentie of noble, valiant and faithfull persons naturally borne, and such as the Emperour *Charles*, and the King himselfe had to their great honours used in their service, able to have bene employed in the rule of those countries. But these *Spaniardes*, being meere strangers, having no naturall regarde in their governement to the maintenance of those countries and people in their ancient and natural maner of peaceable living, as the most noble and wise Emperour *Charles*, yea, and as his sonne king *Philip* himselfe had, whilest he remained in those countries, and used the counsels of the States and natural of the countries, not violating the ancient liberties of the countries: but contrarywise, these *Spaniardes* being exalted to absolute government, by ambition, and for private lucre have violently [B1v] broken the ancient lawes and liberties of all the countries, and in a tyrannous sort have banished, killed and destroyed without order of lawe within the space of a fewe monethes, many of the most ancient and principall persons of the naturall nobilitie that were most worthie of governement. And howesoever in the beginning of these cruell persecutions, the pretence thereof was for maintenance of the Romish religion, yet they spared not to deprive very many Catholiques and Ecclesiasticall persons of their franchises and priviledges: and of the chiefest that were executed of the Nobilitie, none was in the whole countrie more affected to that religion then was the noble and valiant Countie of *Egmond*, the very glorie of that countrie, who neither for his singular victories in the service of the king of *Spaine* can be forgotten in the true histories, nor yet for the crueltie used for his destruction, to bee but forever lamented in the heartes of the naturall people of that countrie. And furthermore, to bring these whole countries in servitude to *Spaine*, these forreine governours have by long intestine warre, with multitude of *Spaniardes*, and with some fewe *Italians* and *Almains*, made the greater part of the said countries (which with their riches by common estimation, answered the Emperour *Charles* equally to his *Indias*) in a maner desolate, and have also lamentably destroyed by sworde, famine, and other cruell maners of death, a great part of the naturall people, and nowe the rich townes and strong places [B2] being desolate of their naturall inhabitants, are held and kept chiefly with force by the *Spanyardes*.

All which pitifull miseries and horrible calamities of these most rich countries and people, are of all their neighboures at this day, even of such as in auncient tyme have bene at frequent discord with them, thorowe naturall compassion very greatly pitied, which appeared specially this present yeere, when the *Frenche* king pretended to have received them to his protection, had not (as the States of the countrey and their deputies were answered) that certayne untimely and unlooked for complottes of the house of *Guyse*, stirred and maintained by money out of *Spayne*, disturbed the good and generall peace of *Fraunce*, and thereby urged the king to forbeare from the resolution hee had made, not onely to ayde the oppressed people of the lowe countries against the *Spanyardes*, but also to have accepted them as his owne subjectes. But in verie trueth, howsoever they were pitied, and in a sort for a tyme comforted and kept in hope in *Fraunce* by the *Frenche* king, who also hath oftentymes earnestly solicited us as Queene of *Englande*, both by message and writing to bee carefull of their defence: yet in respect that they were otherwise more straightly knitte in auncient friendship to this realme then to any other countrie, wee are sure that they could bee pitied of none for this long tyme with more cause and griefe generally, then of our subjects [B2v] of this our realme of *England*, being their most ancient allies and familiar neighbours, and that in such maner, as this our realme of *England* and those countries have bene by common language of long time resembled and termed as man and wife. And for these urgent causes and many others, we have by many friendly messages and Ambassadours, by many letters and writings to the said king of *Spayne* our brother and allie, declared our compassion of this so evill and cruel usage of his naturall and loyall people by sundrie his martiall governoures and other his men of warre, all strangers to these his countries. And furthermore, as a good loving sister to him, and a natural good neighbour to his lowe countries and people, wee have often, and often againe most friendly warned him, that if hee did not otherwise by his wisedome and princely clemencie restraine the tyranny of his governours and crueltie of his men of warre, wee feared that the people of his countries shoulde bee forced for safetie of their lives, and for continuance of their native countrie in their former state of their liberties, to seeke the protection of some other forreyne Lord, or rather to yeelde themselves wholy to the soveraigntie of some mightie Prince, as by the ancient lawes of their countries, and by speciall priviledges graunted by some of the Lordes and Dukes of the countries to the people, they doe pretend and affirme, that in such cases of general injustice, and upon such [B3] violent breaking of their privileges they are free from their former homages, and at libertie to make choise of any other prince to bee their prince and Head. The proofe whereof, by examples past is to be seene and read in the ancient histories of divers alterations, of the lordes and ladies of the countries of *Brabant, Flanders, Holland,* and *Zeland,* and other countries to them united by the States and people of the countries, and that by some such alterations, as the stories doe testifie, *Philip* the Duke of *Burgundy* came to his tytle, from which the king of *Spayne's* interest is derived: but the further discussion hereof, we leave to the viewe of

the monuments and recordes of the countries. And now for the purposes to stay them from yeelding themselves in any like sort to the soveraigntie of any other strange Prince, certaine yeeres past, upon the
earnest request of sundrie of the greatest persons of degree in those
countries, and most obedient subjects to the King, such as were the
Duke of *Ascot*, and the Marques of *Havery* yet living, and of such
others as had principall offices in those countreis in the time of the
Emperour *Charles*, wee yeelded at their importunate requests, to
graunt them prests of money, onely to continue them as his subjects,
and to maintaine themselves in their just defence against the violence
and cruelties of the *Spaniards* their oppressours, thereby staying them
from yeelding their subjection to any other Prince from the said king
of *Spayne*: and during the [B3v] time of that our aide given to them,
and their stay in their obedience to the king of *Spaine*, wee did freely
acquainte the same king with our actions, and did still continue our
friendly advices to him, to move him to commaund his governours and
men of warre, not to use such insolent cruelties against his people, as
might make them to despayre of his favours, and seeke some other
Lorde.

And in these kinde of perswasions and actions wee continued many
yeeres, not onely for compassion of the miserable state of the countries, but of a naturall disposition to have the ancient conditions of
straight amitie and commerce for our kingdomes and people to continue with the States and the people of the saide Dukedome of
Burgundie and the appendants, and namely with our next neyghbours the countries of *Flanders, Holland* and *Zeland*. For wee did
manifestly see, if the nation of *Spayne* shoulde make a conquest of
those countries, as was and yet is apparantly intended, and plant
themselves there as they have done in *Naples* and other countries,
adding thereto the late examples of the violent hostile enterprise of a
power of *Spanyardes*, being sent within these fewe yeeres by the king
of *Spayne* and the *Pope* into our Realme of *Ireland*, with an intent
manifestly confessed by the captaines, that those nombers were sent
aforehand to sease upon some strength there, to the intent with other
greater forces to pursue a conquest [B4] thereof: wee did we say againe,
manifestly see in what danger ourselfe, our countries and people
might shortly bee, if in convenient time wee did not speedily otherwise
regard to prevent or stay the same. And yet notwithstanding our
sayde often requests and advises given to the King of *Spayne*, mani-

festly for his owne weale and honour, wee founde him by his counsell
of *Spayne* so unwilling in any sort to encline to our friendly counsell,
that his governours and chiefetaines in his lowe countries increased
their cruelties towards his owne afflicted people, and his officers in
Spayne offered dayly greater injuries to ours, resorting thither for
traffique: yea, they of his counsell in *Spayne*, woulde not permit our
expresse messenger with our letters to come to the King their master's
presence: a matter very strange, and against the lawe of nations.

And the cause of this our writing and sending to the King, proceeded of matter that was worthy to be knowen to the King, and not
unmeete nowe also to be declared to the worlde, to shewe both our
good disposition towardes the King in imparting to him our grieves,
and to let it appeare howe evill we have beene used by his ministers,
as in some part may appeare by this that followeth. Although wee
coulde not have these many yeeres past any of our servaunts whome
we sent at sundrie times as our Ambassadours to the King our good
brother as was meete, suffered to continue there without many injuries and [B4v] indignities offered to their families, and divers times
to their owne persons by the greatest of his Counsellours, so as they
were constrained to leave their places, and some expelled and in a sort
banished the Countrey, without cause given by them, or notified to
us: yet we, minding to continue very good friendship with the king,
as his good Sister, did of long time and many yeeres give favourable
allowance to all that came as his Ambassadours to us, saving onely
upon manifest daungerous practises attempted by two of them to
trouble our estate, whereof the one was *Girald Despes*, a very turbulent
spirited person, and altogether unskilfull and unapt to deale in
Princes' affaires being in amitie, as at his retourne into *Spayne* hee
was so there also reputed: The other and last was *Bernardin de
Mendoza*, one whome we did accept and use with great favour a long
time, as was manifestly seene in our Court, and we thinke cannot be
denied by himselfe, but yet of late yeeres (we know not by what direction) we found him to be a secret great favourer to sundrie our evill
disposed and seditious subjectes, not onely to such as lurked in our
Realme, but also to such as fled the same being notoriously condemned as open Rebelles and Traitours, with whome by his letters,
messages and secret counsels hee did in the ende devise howe with a
power of men, partly to come out of *Spayne*, partly out of the low
Countries, wherof hee gave them great comfort in the Kinge's [C]

name, an invasion might bee made into our Realme, setting downe in writing the manner howe the same should be done, with what numbers of men and shippes, and upon what coastes, portes and places of our Realme by special name, and who the persons should be in our Realme of no small account, that should favour this Invasion and take part with the Invadours, with many other circumstances declaring his full set purpose and labours taken, to trouble us and our Realme very dangerously, as hath beene most clearely proved and confessed by such as were in that confederacie with him, whereof some are fled and now do frequent his companie in *France*, and some were taken, who confessed at great length by writing the whole course herein helde by the saide Ambassadour as was manifestly of late time published to the worlde uppon *Francis Throgmorton's* a principall Traitour's examination. And when we found manifestly this Ambassadour so dangerous an instrument, or rather a Head to a rebellion and Invasion, and that for a yeere or more together hee never brought to us any letter from the King his Master, notwithstanding our often request made to him that hee woulde by some letter from the King to us, let it appeare that it was the King's will that he should deale with us in his Master's name in sundrie thinges that he propounded to us as his Ambassadour, which wee did judge to be contrary to the Kinge his Master's will: wee did finally [C1v] cause him to be charged with these dangerous practises, and made it patent to him how, and by whom, with many other circumstances we knew it, and therfore caused him in very gentle sort to be content within some resonable time to depart out of our realme, the rather for his own safety, as one in very deed mortally hated of our people: for the which, we graunted him favorable conduct, both to the sea and over the sea: and thereupon we did speedily send a servant of ours into *Spaine* with our letters to the king, only to certify him of this accident, and to make the whole matter apparant unto him: and this was the messenger aforemencioned, that might not be suffred to deliver our message or our letters to the king.

And beside these indignities, it is most manifest how his ministers also have both heretofore many times, and now lately practised here in *England* by meanes of certaine rebelles, to have procured sundry invasions of our Realme, by their forces out of *Spayne* and the low Countries: very hard recompences (we may say) for so many our good offices. Hereupon we hope no reasonable person can blame us, if we

have disposed ourselves to change this our former course, and more
carefully to look to the safety of ourselfe and our people: and finding
our owne dangers in deed very great and imminent, we have bene
the more urgently provoked to attempt and accelerate some good
remedy, for that besides many other advices given us both at home and
from abrode, in due time to withstand these dangers, we have found
the general disposition of al our own faithful people very ready in this
case, and [C2] earnest in offring to us both in Parliaments and otherwise, their services with their bodies and blood, and their aides with
their lands and goods, to withstand and prevent this present common
danger to our Realme and themselves, evidently seene and feared by
the subverting and rooting up of the ancient nation of these low
countries, and by planting the *Spanish* nation and men of warre,
enemies to our countries, there so nere unto us. And besides these occasions and considerations, we did also cal to our remembrance our
former fortunate proceeding by God's special favor, in the beginning
of our reigne, in remedying of a like mischief that was intended
against us in *Scotland* by certaine *French*men, who then were directed
only by the house of *Guise*, by colour of the mariage of their Neece
the Queene of *Scots* with the *Dolphin* of *France*, in like maner as the
offsprings of the said house have even now lately sought to attaine to
the like unordinate power in *France*: a matter of some consequence
for ourselves to consider, although we hope the king our good
brother professing sincere frendship towards us, as we professe the like
to him, will moderate this aspiring greatnes of that house, that neither
himselfe nor the Princes of his bloud be overruled, nor wee (minding
to continue perfect frendship with the king and his bloud) be by the
said house of *Guise* and their faction disquieted or disturbed in our
Countries. But nowe to returne to this like example of *Scotlande*
aforesaide, when the *French* had in like maner (as the *Spanyardes*
have nowe of long time attempted in the lowe Countries) [C2v]
sought by force to have subdued the people there, and brought them
into a servitude to the Crowne of *France*, and also by the ambitious
desires of the saide house of *Guise*, to have proceeded to a warre by
way of *Scotland*, for the conquest of our crowne for their Neece the
Queene of *Scottes* (a matter most manifest to the common knowledge
of the worlde): it pleased Almightie God, as it remaineth in good
memorie to our honour and comfort, to further our intention and
honourable and just actions at that time in such sort, as by our aiding

then of the nation of *Scotland* being sore oppressed with the *French*, and universally requiring our aide, wee procured to that Realme (though to our great cost) a full deliverance of the force of strangers and danger of servitude, and restored peace to the whole Countrie, which hath continued there ever since many yeeres, saving that at some time of parcialities of certaine of the Noblemen, as hath beene usuall in that Countrie, in the mynoritie of the yong King there hath risen some inward troubles, which for the most part we have in favour of the King and his Governours used meanes to pacifie: so as at this day such is the quietnes in *Scotland*, as the King our deare brother and cousin, by name, *James* the sixth, a Prince of great hope for many good Princely respectes, raigneth there in honour and love of his people, and in very good and perfect amitie with us and our Countrie. And so our actions [C3] at that time came to so good successe by the goodnes of God, as both our owne Realme, and that of *Scotland*, hath ever since remained in better amitie and peace then can bee remembred these manie hundred yeeres before, and yet nothing heereby done by us, nor any cause justly given, but that also the *French* kinges that have since succeeded, which have bene three in number, and all brethren, have made and concluded divers treaties for good peace with us, which presently continue in force on both parties, notwithstanding our foresaide actions attempted for remooving out of *Scotland* of the saide *French* forces, so transported by the onely direction of the house of *Guyse*.

And therefore, to conclude for the declaration of our present intention at this time, wee hope it shall of all persons abroad be well intepreted, as wee knowe it will be of such as are not ledde by parciallitie, that upon the often and continuall lamentable requests made to us by the universall States of the countries of *Holland, Zeland, Guelders* and other provinces with them united (beeing desperate of the king of *Spayne's* favours) for our succours to bee yeelded to them, onely for their defence against the *Spaniards* and other strangers, and therewith finding manifestlie by our often and importunate requests and advices given to the king of *Spaine*, no hope of reliefe of these their miseries, but rather an increase therof by dayly conquests of their townes [C3v] and slaughter of their people, (though in very trueth wee cannot impute the increase of any late cruelties to the person of him that now hath the tytle of generall governour, shewing his naturall disposition more inclynable to mercie and clemencie, then it seemeth hee can direct the heartes of the *Spaniardes* under him, that have bene so long trayned in shedding of blood under the former *Spanish* governours:) And joyning thereunto our owne danger at hand, by the overthrow and destruction of our neighbours, and accesse and planting of the great forces of the *Spanyards* so neere to our countries, with precedent arguments of many troublesome attemptes against our Realme: we did therfore by good advice and after long deliberation determine, to sende certaine companies of souldiers to ayde the naturall people of those countries, onely to defende them and their townes from sacking and desolation, and thereby to procure them safetie, to the honour of God, whome they desire to serve sincerely as christian people according to his holy word, and to enjoye their ancient liberties for them and their posteritie, and so consequently to preserve and contynue the lawful and ancient commerce betwixt our people and those countries and ours.

And so, we hope our intention herein, and our subsequent actions will be by God's favour both honorably and charitably interpreted of all persons (saving of the oppressors themselves, and their [C4] partizans) in that wee meane not heereby, either for ambition or malice, (the two rootes of al injustice) to make any particular profit hereof to ourselfe or to our people, onely desiring at this time to obtaine by God's favour for the countries, A deliverance of them from warre by the *Spaniardes* and Forraines, restitution of their ancient liberties and governement by some christian peace, And thereby, a suretie for ourselves and our realme to be free from invading neighbours, And our people to enjoy in those countries their lawful commerce and entercourse of friendship and marchandise, according to the ancient usage and treaties of entercourse, made betwixt our Progenitors and the Lordes and Earles of those countries, and betwixt our people and the people of those countries.

And though our further intention also is or may be to take into our garde, some fewe townes upon the seaside next opposite to our realme, which otherwise might be in danger to be taken by the strangers, enemies of the country: yet therein considering we have no meaning at this tyme to take and retaine the same to our owne proper use, we hope that al persons wil thinke it agreeable with good reason and princely policie, that we should have the gard and use of some such places for sure accesse and recesse of our people and soldiers in safety, and for furniture of them with victuals and other things requisite and neces-

sary, whilest it shall be needful for them to continue in those countries for [C4v] the aiding therof in these their great calamities,
miseries, and imminent daunger, and untill the countries may be
delivered of such strange forces as do now oppresse them, and recover
their ancient lawfull liberties and maner of government to live in
peace as they have heeretofore done, and doe nowe most earnestly in
lamentable manner desire to doe, which are the very onely true endes
of all our actions nowe intended, howsoever malitious tongues may
utter their cankred conceits to the contrary, as at this day the worlde
aboundeth with such blasphemous reportes in writings and infamous
libels, as in no age the Devill hath more abounded with notable
spirites replenished with all wickednesse to utter his rage against pro-
fessours of Christian Religion. But thereof we leave the revenge to
God the searcher of hearts, hoping that he beholding the sinceritie of
our heart, wil graunt good successe to our intentions, whereby a
Christian peace may ensue to his divine honour, and comfort to al
them that love peace truely, and wil seeke it sincerely. [D1]

AN ADDITION TO THE DECLARATION: TOUCHING THE
SLAUNders published of her *Majestie*.

AFter we had finished our declaration, there came to our hands a
Pamphlet written in *Italian*, printed at *Milan*, entituled *Nuouo
aduiso*, directed to the Archbishop of *Milan*, conteyning a report of
the expugnation of *Anwerpe* by the Prince of *Parma*: by the which we
found ourselfe most maliciously charged with two notable crimes, no
lesse hatefull to the worlde, then most repugnant and contrary to our
owne naturall inclination. The one, with ingratitude towards the
King of *Spaine*, who (as the authour saith) saved our life being justly
by sentence adjudged to death in our sister's time: The other, that
there were some persons procured to be corrupted with great promises,
and that with our intelligence as the reporter addeth in a parenthesis
in these wordes (*as it was said*) that the life of the Prince of Parma
should be taken away: and for the better prooving and countenancing
of this horrible lie, it is further added in the saide [D1v] Pamphlet,
that it pleased the Lorde God to discover this, and bring two of the
wicked persons to justice. Now, knowing howe men are maliciously
bent in this declining age of the world, both to judge, speake and

write maliciously, falsely and unreverently of Princes: and holding
nothing so deare unto us, as the conservation of our reputation and
honour to be blamelesse: we found it verie expedient, not to suffer two
such horrible imputations to passe under silence, least for lacke of
answere, it might argue a kinde of guiltinesse, and did therefore thinke,
that what might be alledged by us for our justification in that behalfe,
might most aptly be joyned unto this former Declaration nowe to be
published, to lay open before the worlde the maner and ground of our
proceeding in the causes of the lowe Countreyes.

And for answere of the first point wherewith wee are charged touching our ingratitude towardes the King of *Spaine*, as we do most willingly acknowledge that we were beholding unto him in the time of
our late sister, which we then did acknowledge very thankefully, and
have sought many wayes since in like sort to requite, as in our former
Declaration by our actions may appeare: so doe wee utterly denie as a
most manifest untrueth, that ever he was the cause of the saving of our
life as a person by course of Justice sentenced unto death, whoever
carried ourselfe towardes our said sister in duetifull sort, as our loyaltie was never called in question, much lesse any sentence [D2] of death
pronounced against us: a matter such, as in respect of the ordinarie
course of proceeding, as by processe in Lawe, by place of triall, by
the Judge that should pronounce such sentence, and other necessary
circumstances in like cases usuall, especially against one of our qualitie, as it coulde not but have bene publiquely knowen, if any such
thing had bene put in execution. This then being true, wee leave to
the worlde to judge howe maliciously and injuriously the author of the
saide Pamphlet dealeth with us, in charging us by so notable an
untrueth with a vice that of all others we doe most hate and abhorre.
And therefore by the manifest untrueth of this imputation, men not
transported with passion may easely discerne what untrueth is conteined in the second, by the which wee are charged to have bene acquainted with an intended attempt against the life of the said Prince:
a matter if any such thing should have bene by us intended, must have
proceeded either of a mislyking wee had of his person, or that the
prosecution of the warres in the lowe Countreyes was so committed
unto him, as no other might prosecute the same but he.

And first for his person, we could never learne that he hath at any
time, by acte or speache, done anything that might justly breede a
mislike in us towards him, much lesse a hatred against his person in

so high a degree, as to bee either privie or assenting to the taking
away of his life: Besides, he is one of whom we have ever had an
honourable [D2v] conceite, in respect of those singular rare partes
we alwaies have noted in him, which hath wonne unto him as great
reputation, as any man this day living carrieth of his degree and
qualitie: and so have we alwayes delivered out by speache unto the
world, when any occasion hath bene offered to make mention of him.
Nowe, touching the prosecution committed unto him of the warres in
the lowe Countreys, as all men of judgement knowe that the taking
away of his life carrieth no likelyhood that the same shall worke any
ende of the said prosecution: so is it manifestly knowen, that no man
hath dealt more honourablie then the saide Prince, either in duely
observing of his promise, or extending grace and mercie where merite
and deserte hath craved the same: and therefore no greater impietie by
any coulde bee wrought, nor nothing more prejudiciall to ourselfe,
(so long as the King shall continue the prosecution of the cause in
that forcible sort he now doeth) then to be an instrument to take him
away from thence by such violent meanes, that hath dealt in a more
honourable and gracious sort in the charge committed unto him, then
any other that hath ever gone before him, or is likely to succeede
after him.

Nowe therefore how unlikely it is, that we having neither cause to
mislike of his person, nor that the prosecution of the warres shoulde
cease by losse of him, should be either authour, or any way assenting
to so horrible a fact, wee referre to [D3] the judgement of such as looke
into causes, not with the eyes of their affection, but doe measure and
weigh things according to honour and reason. Besides, it is likely if it
had bene true that we had bene any way chargeable, (as the author
reporteth) the confessions of the parties executed, (importing such
matter, as by him is alledged) would have bene both produced and
published: for malice leaveth nothing unsearched, that may nourish
the venime of that humour.

The best course therefore that both we and all other Princes can
holde in this unfortunate age that overfloweth with nombers of
malignant spirits, is through the grace and goodnesse of Almightie
God, to direct our course in such sort, as they may rather shewe their
willes through malice, then with just cause by desert, to say ill, or deface Princes either by speach or writing: assuring ourselves, that besides the punishment that such wicked and infamous libellours shall

receive at the handes of the Almightie for depraving of Princes and lawfull Magistrates who are God's ministers, they both are and alwayes shall be thought by all good men, unworthie to live upon the face of the earth.

Given at Richmount the first of October, 1585.
and the 27. yeere of the reigne of our
Soveraigne Lady the Queene, to be published.

1. QUEEN ELIZABETH: THE "DARNLEY PORTRAIT" (oil painting by an unknown artist c. 1575). The "Darnley Portrait" (formerly in the possession of the Earls of Darnley) is a key portrait of Elizabeth for two reasons: (1) it is one of the first surviving large-scale portraits of her and (2) its formalized face mask provided the portrait pattern for the remainder of her reign. (*Reprinted by permission of the National Portrait Gallery, London*)

2. THE SECOND GREAT SEAL OF QUEEN ELIZABETH I. Affixed to a document of 1588 granting land to Henry Hastings, 20th Earl of Huntington, this second seal, conceived by Nicholas Hilliard, was in use between 1586 and 1603. It displays finer workmanship than the first seal. (*Reprinted with permission of the Henry E. Huntington Library and Art Gallery*)

3. ELIZABETH'S CORONATION PROCESSION. This contemporary pen-and-ink drawing of Queen Elizabeth's processional ride through London on her way to her coronation at Westminster Abbey was executed in 1558. (*Reproduced by permission of the British Library Board*)

4. THE QUEEN'S ROUTE TO HER CORONATION. The afternoon before Queen Elizabeth's coronation, January 14, 1558, the Queen processed from the City of London to the City of Westminster, a traditional practice of the Kings and Queens of England. On route she was greeted with a succession of orations, some of which were staged allegorical representations of what was expected of Elizabeth as the new head of church and state. These were called "pageants" and were spoken by children.

The processional began at (1)*the Tower of London*, where it was customary for the monarch to spend one or two nights before making the processional. The Queen received (2)*Fanchurch* her first formal greeting—an oration—from the City of London. The route up to this point is presumed. At the upper end of (3)*Gracious* (or *Gracechurch*) *Street* the first pageant was presented. At the "nether" or lower end of (4)*Cornhill*, the second pageant took place. The site of the third pageant was (5)*Soper Lane and Cheapside*. As the Queen passed down (6)*Cheapside*, she was presented (near the little Conduit) a thousand marks in gold by the Recorder of the City of London. This was the site of the fourth pageant. At (7)*St. Paul's Churchyard*, a child delivered an oration. At (8)*Ludgate* the Queen was greeted with a "noyse of instruments." The (9)*City wall* marks the bounds of London proper. It ran approximately as a semicircle from the Fleet ditch on the west to the Tower on the east. The Thames bounded the City on the south. The fifth and final pageant was presented at (10)the *Conduit in Fleet Street*. The meaning of the five allegorical pageants was written on (11)*Temple Bar*; here a farewell was sung to the Queen. (12)*London Bridge* was the only bridge spanning the Thames; it carried houses on its 20 arches. (*Reprinted with the permission of the Henry E. Huntington Library and Art Gallery*; route detail by Ward Ritchie)

5. QUEEN ELIZABETH ENTHRONED BEFORE PARLIAMENT. The Queen is seated under the canopy of state in this engraving while the members of the House of Lords are seated in the chamber and members of the House of Commons stand in the foreground at the bar. From Robert Glover, *Nobilitas Politica vel Civilis*. (*Reprinted with the permission of the Henry E. Huntington Library and Art Gallery*)

6. [top] WILLIAM CECIL, 1st BARON BURGHLEY (1520-1598) (oil painting attributed to Marcus Gheeraerts the Younger, after c. 1585). Burghley is wearing his robes as Knight of the Garter. About the time that this portrait was painted, Burghley was the Lord High Treasurer and Elizabeth's chief minister. (*Reprinted by permission of the National Portrait Gallery, London*)

7. [bottom] ROBERT DEVEREUX, 2nd EARL OF ESSEX (1566-1601) (miniature by Isaac Oliver, c. 1596). Essex, one of Elizabeth's favorites, was a politician, military commander, poet and patron of literature but he may be remembered best as the instigator of an improvident rebellion which resulted in his execution. (*Reprinted by permission of the National Portrait Gallery, London*)

8. A MAP OF LONDON AND WESTMINSTER IN 1563. Reproduced in Thomas Pennant, *Some Account of London* (1805). (Reprinted with the permission of the Henry E. Huntington Library and Art Gallery)

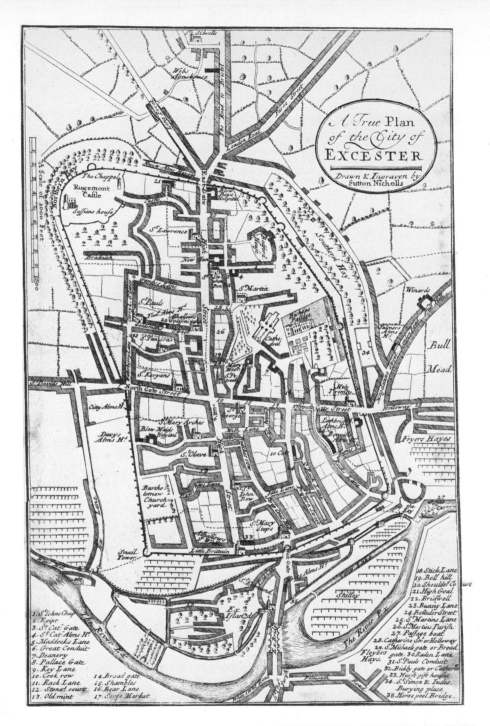

9. "A TRUE PLAN OF THE CITY OF EXCESTER" (EXETER) IN THE SIXTEENTH CENTURY. This nineteenth-century engraving by Sutton Nicholls is based on an Elizabethan map of Exeter and is Bodleian MS Top Devon b.6. (*Reprinted with permission of the Bodleian Library*)

11. [above] THE EXECUTION OF MARY STUART (MARY QUEEN OF SCOTS). This pen-and-ink sketch of the execution of Mary Stuart at Fotheringhay Castle on February 8, 1587, was probably drawn by a contemporary. Mary is shown on the raised execution block; she is surrounded on three sides by the lords of the realm who were commissioned to travel to Fotheringhay Castle to try her for treason against Elizabeth. (*Reproduced by permission of the British Library Board*)

---

10. [left] THE PROCESSION OF QUEEN ELIZABETH I (attributed to Robert Peake the Elder, c. 1600). Although this picture was originally thought to depict Queen Elizabeth in procession to Blackfriars to give thanks for the victory over the Spanish Armada, it now seems certain that she is in procession to celebrate the wedding of the Lady Anne Russell to Lord Herbert of Cherbury in June 1600. She is carried here in a litter borne by four gentlemen; the seven Knights of the Garter accompanying her have been identified from left to right as (i) Edmund Sheffield, 3rd Lord Sheffield and 1st Earl of Mulgrave; (ii) Charles Howard, Lord Howard of Effingham and Earl of Nottingham; (iii) George Clifford, 3rd Earl of Cumberland; (iv) Thomas Butler, 10th Earl of Ormonde; (v) unknown; (vi) Gilbert Talbot, 7th Earl of Shrewsbury; and (vii) Edward Somerset, 4th Earl of Worcester. The background to the painting is probably built up from Flemish architectural engravings. (*Reprinted with the permission of Mr. Simon Wingfield Digby. Sherborne Castle.*)

12. RESOLUTION TO PURSUE THE ARMADA. This document was drawn up by the English Council of War on August 1, 1588 and signed by a number of peers; Lord Admiral Howard's signature is first here and most prominent. The MS is at the British Museum. (*Reproduced by permission of the British Library Board*)

Charles (lord) Howard (of Effingham)   George (Earl of) Cumberland

(Lord) Thomas Howard   Edmund (Lord) Sheffield

Francis Drake   Edward Hoby

John Hawkins

Thomas Fenner

I Augusti Determyned by the consayle to returne from thwarte of the Frythe.

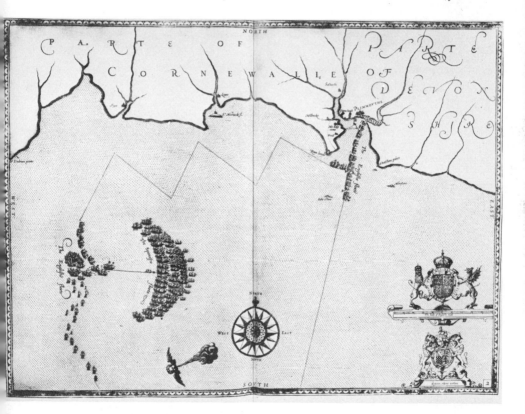

13. OPENING FORMATIONS DURING THE SPANISH ARMADA. This map shows the position of the English and Spanish fleets on July 31, 1588. Part of the English fleet has stayed at Plymouth harbor (top right) to protect the coast and the English Channel; the other part of the English fleet has apparently tacked west along the coast and proceeded south to take the weather-gauge west of the Spanish fleet; the westerly wind which is signified here placed greatest power behind the English ships allowing them to chase the Spanish inland from the ocean. The Spanish responded by taking a crescent formation, hoping to present a strong front to English forces farther up the Channel (where they expected the main concentration of enemy ships); it also allowed them to form wide points which, they hoped, could circle back around the English fleet catching them and surrounding them completely. (From Roxburghe Club 161; *reprinted with permission of the Bodleian Library*)

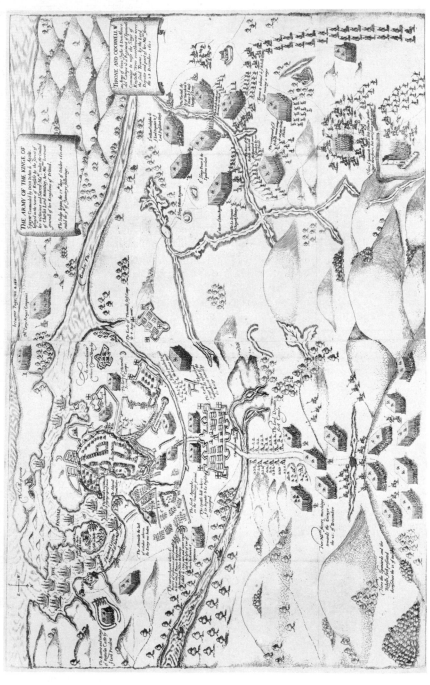

14. MAP ILLUSTRATING THE SIEGE OF KINSALE, 1601-02. A Spanish fleet of 33 ships and 4500 soldiers landed at Kinsale Bay, on the southern Irish coast, to aid the Irish in their religious and patriotic struggle against the English. The Spaniards, commanded by Don Juan d'Aquila, easily entered the town on September 23, 1601. The Spaniards were joined by Irish forces headed by Hugh O'Neill, Earl of Tyrone, and Hugh O'Donnel, Earl of Tyrconnell. The English, under Charles Brooke, Lord Mountjoy, defeated the combined Spanish and Irish troops, who capitulated to the English on January 2, 1602. This map shows the positions taken by the Spanish ("Enimies"), the Irish ("Rebells") and the English forces throughout the campaign. In Sir Thomas Stafford, *Pacata Hibernia* (London, 1633). (Reprinted with permission

15. THE AGING QUEEN (oil painting by Marcus Gheeraerts the Younger in 1608). This is one of the few extant portraits of the elderly Queen Elizabeth; it is often said that Gheeraerts waited for a period after the Queen's death in 1603 to paint this portrait since she had refused when alive to allow herself to be painted looking old. The portrait is in the Burghley House Collection. (*Photograph by the Courtauld Institute; reprinted with the permission of Burghley House*)

16. [top] QUEEN ELIZABETH'S FUNERAL PROCESSION. This portion of Queen Elizabeth's funeral roll shows her coffin covered with purple velvet. Six knights carry the canopy held over the coffin. The Queen was buried at Westminster Abbey. (*Reproduced by permission of the British Library Board*)

17. [bottom] THE QUEEN IN EFFIGY. This illustration is a portion of the engraved title to Samuel Purchas, *Hakluytus Posthumus or Purchas His Pilgrimes* (1625), Vol. I, showing Henry, Prince of Wales, mourning at the tomb of Queen Elizabeth in Westminster Abbey. (*Reprinted with permission of the Henry E. Huntington Library and Art Gallery*)

The Copie of a Letter
to the Earle of Leycester (1586)

"What will they not now say, when it shalbe spread,
That for the safety of her life, a Mayden Queene could be content
to spill the blood, even of her own kinsewoman?" (E1v): Elizabeth's
pointed and poignant question concerning the possible beheading of
Mary Stuart, Queen of Scots, lies at the heart of this tense and
dramatic pamphlet, registering in detail the anguishing stalemate
between the Queen, and her Privy Councillors and Parliament. This
official document of state propaganda was prepared by Burghley's
son Robert when he was 22. It transcribes two taut confrontations
between the Queen and delegations from Parliament and their pain-
ful but inescapable opposition. Elizabèth had urged the Bond and
Association to be enacted; she had declared a special trial of treason
to hear Mary far from her own presence; she had avoided the opening
sessions of Parliament. She could not, however, prevent the final
verdict against Mary.

These interchanges of woeful entreaty reprinted here did not occur
because Elizabeth had not sought other strategic avenues. She tried
to sound out both the Scottish and French delegations for a com-
promising solution in the fall of 1586. There were also reports that
Burghley had invited to dinner Archibald Douglas, James's quasi-
ambassador in London; he had also debated at some length with
Pomponne de Bellièvre—one of the French King Henry III's most
able counselors who had been sent to intervene for Mary—on points
of law with quotations from Cicero and from legal precedents. Elizabeth's secretary William Davison unburdened himself to Walsingham on October 29 of the Queen's numerous techniques and the
grave hesitations: she was cautious over James's reaction to his
mother's death; she worried about the French response; "Another
scruple was that yet the King of Spain, having a title, might affect
the kingdom for himself."

Clearly the scruples were genuine and the Queen's doubts manifest.
For Burghley the only solution lay in Parliament; earlier, on Septem-

ber 8, he had written to Walsingham, "We stick upon Parliament which her Majesty misliketh, but we do all persist to make the burden better borne and the world abroad better satisfied." The session that had been called in 1584 was still in being; but the Council persuaded Elizabeth to dissolve it on September 19 and call a new one with circular letters so that the personnel would be similar and informed of the delicate complications of this great issue of state. A writ was issued on September 15; the session was called on October 16; but the Queen, who had at first planned to come to Westminster from Lambeth to open the session as usual, went instead to Richmond; she would have no connection with a body summoned to pronounce the death sentence on a kinswoman and fellow sovereign.

Until December 2, when it was prorogued, Parliament talked of nothing else. In the joint opening session Lord Chancellor Sir Thomas Bromley told both houses of the extraordinary case of "great weight, great peril and dangerous consequence" which had brought them together; Sir Christopher Hatton opened the case; and then the aging Sir Ralph Sadler, Mary Stuart's former keeper, prayed to God to assist the Queen "to take away this most wicked and filthy woman." Sir Walter Mildmay, Chancellor of the Exchequer, pointed out to Commons that "neyther the feare of God, neyther respect to honor, neyther naturall affinity, nor infinite benefitts recyved, could stay her from continuall and malicious practices." Both houses prepared a petition to the Queen with their resolution for prompt execution of the Queen of Scots; and they asked to see her on November 12; apparently restless the night before she asked Burghley if she could see a copy of their petition.

There was some difficulty concerning the composition of the delegation to the Queen. Burghley wrote Davison on November 11, "Yesterday in the parliament chamber grew a question whether it were convenient for the two archbishops and four other bishops to accompany the Lords temporal in the petition to her Majesty for the execution of the Scottish Queen. Some scruple I had whether her Majesty would like it because in former times the bishops in parliament were wont to absent themselves. But yet I do not think [it] unlawful for them to be present and persuaders in such causes as the execution of the sentence tends to the state of the church as it does." He asked Davison to consult the Queen; on the following day, Burghley wrote Shrewsbury that the delegation to Richmond would be constituted "by 21 Lords temporal, 6 Lords spiritual and 40 of the Commons," but apparently Elizabeth changed her mind for the clergy did not go.

Below is Elizabeth's reply, which in manuscript was carefully worked over by the Queen herself before it was hastened to the printer in December (C1-D1); it is one of her most masterful pieces of prose. She takes the edge off Parliament's arguments by acknowledging the necessity of her own safety and that of her country (C2), Mary's position, sex, and kin relationship (C1v), and notes the fairness and propriety of Mary's trial (C3): still she remains the merciful Queen who cannot execute a fellow monarch. She hints to Parliament of the Bond of Association (C3v-C4), an obvious directive; and in testifying to her own ability for self-sacrifice (C2) criticizes Mary Stuart and justifies the act of regicide by others. Clearly the posture she wishes to present to the public—at the interview and again in this pamphlet—is one disclaiming all intentions and association with Mary Stuart's inevitable death, at the same time she makes evident her love of her people, her faith, and her country. But Parliament refused to take the hint; and on November 24 they returned to her virtually the same petition (D1v ff.). With contrary positions thus frozen, the Queen decided to prorogue Parliament until March 6 and told Burghley so; then after some reflection she changed her mind and adjourned Parliament for a week.

Burghley wasted no time; he set about at once preparing and engrossing a proclamation of Mary's sentence. Elizabeth thought the first version too brief and formal; she asked to have a propagandistic explanation added. On December 2 Parliament reconvened and the Lord Chancellor announced that Elizabeth was content to proclaim under the great seal of England the sentence they had advised. Parliament adjourned until February 15, giving Elizabeth time either to execute Mary or to dissolve Parliament. The sentence was issued two days later, on December 4, "with great port and stateliness" across all England; and the people of London responded with bonfires, bells, and the singing of Psalms "in every street and lane of the City."

Now all that was needed was a warrant for Mary's execution, yet again Elizabeth balked. She wrote a directive to Mary's keeper— Amyas Paulet—and was sharply rebuked. In no uncertain terms, he told her, "I am so unhappy to have lived to see this unhappy day in which I am required by direction from my most gracious sovereign to do an act which God and the law forbiddeth. . . . God forbid that I should make so foul a shipwreck of my conscience, or leave so great a blot on my poor posterity, to shed blood without law or warrant." Other tensions grew—many of them caused by rumors some of which were by January nationwide. Walsingham tells us that "False bruits were spread abroad that the Queen of Scots was broken out of prison; that the City of London was fired; that many thousand Spaniards were landed in Wales; that certain noblemen were fled; and such like. . . . The stir and confusion was great: such as I think happened not in England these hundred years past, for precepts and hue and cries ran from place to place, even from out of the north into these parts, and over all the west as far as Cornwall."

On February 1, 1587, the Queen sent for Davison. Fortified by the pressure of events and concerned herself about the effects of the rumors, she was now firmly resolved. She signed the warrant, ordered

Davison to afix the great seal, and sent him off. He sought Burghley's
support. The next day, the warrant having passed the seal, Elizabeth
inquired of his haste; and Davison, now worried that he alone might
be accused of the execution of the Queen of Scots's death, sought
Burghley's advice again. Hatton and Burghley called a meeting of the
Privy Council which jointly assumed the responsibility for Mary's
death, wrote the customary official letters to that effect, and sent the
warrant to Fotheringhay with Robert Beale. There in a private, not a
public, execution, Mary was beheaded on February 8.

Elizabeth's anger when she heard of Mary's death fell on Davison
and Burghley—but Walsingham, like Burghley, was tactfully away
from court and both escaped any reprimand. No doubt the anger was
genuine enough: the deed was sacrilegious, infamous—and irre-
vocable. The news must have seemed momentous to Elizabeth, after
all those years of tense waiting. But she had already prepared for
public response in the pamphlet of deliberate propaganda reprinted
here which, in December of 1586, had been widely circulated and distributed in a number of translations. Her markings, changes, and
deletions preserved in the Cotton Collection at the British Museum
[Faustina F. X, fol. 256] show that she revised cautiously and repeatedly over a period of time: she now had only to pursue the role of the
diligent and sorrowing Queen—the tragic heroine in a Greek play,
as Neale calls the exchange below, with Parliament chanting the
chorus—while remaining as divorced from the final act as possible.
This assumed posture of regal mourning, rooted in propaganda even
as it flourished from the soil of truth, was a dangerous, vulnerable
necessity attending to her *realpolitik*. Her rhetoric, never put to better
use or shaded in more successful manner, shows that even under
pressure Elizabeth's political instincts and her capacity for political
expression could do her well. With this document alone, Elizabeth
demonstrates her marked personal ability at accomplished rhetoric
even in an age which is characterized by literary mastery.

TEXTUAL NOTES
[For explanatory notes for this selection see page 374.]

The Copie of a Letter to the Earle of Leycester
  Reference. STC 6052, 6053.
  Authorship and States. This pamphlet, designed to cushion public
response to the act of executing royalty, was one of the most successful—and widespread—pieces of Elizabethan propaganda. The author-

ship was multiple. The pamphlet is signed R. C. (which the STC unaccountably assigned to Richard Crompton) for Robert Cecil (see the statement of Robert Beale in BM Additional MS 48027 [Yelverton 31], f. 396, and Cecil's own allusion in BM Cotton MS Faustina F. X, f. 256), but manuscript copies of the text prepared by Cecil for the printer (Lansdowne MS 94, ff. 84ff.) are corrected by the Queen herself. This would suggest that there had been no written copies of these speeches; so that there is reason to believe Cecil when he claims to have written down what he could remember (A3v *et passim.*), though the editorial results are finer and more carefully controlled than this off-hand remark wishes to convey. This accounts for all but the first interview which Cecil did not attend: that report may have come from still a third collaborator, Francis Alford, who was in attendance and whose manuscript "report" is now the only known copy (Inner Temple, Petyt MS 538/10, ff.6b-7). See Neale, *E & HP*, II, 129-130. The English version of the pamphlet has come down in two states, the second state resulting from two stop-press changes on A3:

Lord)hath]Lord (I haue

I had not,]I had, not

There is no apparent rationale to these changes, and it is rather likely, therefore, that they indicate a second edition (since Elizabethan printers refused to print more than a maximum number of copies without first distributing the type and resetting it so as to be paid in proper accord with the number of copies printed; see p. 193 above). No doubt a number of copies were printed and distributed broadly. There are no other variants.

Translations. Walsingham coordinated and directed a number of translations; there was one in Latin as well as one in German (possibly set by Christopher Barker, although the title-page reads "R. Schilders, Middleburgh") in 1587 and one in French the same year.

Subsequent Editions. The text was hastily included in Holinshed's *Chronicle* in January, Vol. III (pp. 1433-1538 are wanting and replaced by leaves 1433 and 1490; 1491 and 1536; 1537 and 1538). The entire work appears later in Volume I of the second collection of *Somers Tracts* (London, 1750), pp. 61-74, and again in Volume I of the second edition (London, 1809), ed. Scott, pp. 224-236; both follow the original typesetting. Elizabeth's speeches, fully modernized, are also reprinted in George P. Rice, Jr., *The Public Speaking of Queen Elizabeth* (New York, 1951; 1956), pp. 88-95; extracts are printed in Prothero, pp. 109-111.

Collation. 4°; A-E⁴. A1, blank; A1v, royal crest; A2, title-page; A2v, blank; A3-A4 (pp. 1-3), dedication; A4v, blank; B1-E3 (pp. 4-32), text; E3v, crest and colophon; E4-E4v, blank.

Description of Contents. Title-page roman and italics with illustration; dedication in roman with decorative head-piece and tail-piece; body of text in italic and roman; tail-piece B4v, C4v, D4, E3. The typesize on D1 is smaller, allowing the entire B gathering to contain the Lord Chancellor's first speech and Master Sergeant Puckering's speech and C gathering to contain the Queen's first response; this may have been done to allow for later changes in sheet C while sheet B was being set and run off. Decorative initials on A3, B1, B2v, C1, D1v, D2v, D4v. No running-head; marginal notes are as follows: "The danger of the ouerthrow of the true Religion." (B3) and "The perill of the state of the Realme" (B3v).

License. No entry in the *Stationers' Register,* but the pamphlet was printed by Christopher Barker, the Queen's printer (see colophon, E3v).

Base-Copy Text. Bodleian Crynes 829. Copy used for variant state [edition?]: Bodleian 4°B49(9)Jur.

Title-page in Full. /[within rule within rule within decorative border] THE / COPIE OF A LET- / TER TO THE RIGHT HO- / nourable the Earle of LEYCESTER, Lieute- / nant generall of all her Maiesties forces in the / *vnited Prouinces of the lowe Countreys, writ- / ten before, but deliuered at his re- / turne from thence: /* With a report of certeine petitions / and declarations made to the QVEENES / Maiestie at two seuerall times, from all the / Lordes and Commons lately assem- / bled in Parliament. / And her Maiesties answeres thereunto by her / *selfe deliuered, though not expressed by the repor- / ter with such grace and life, as the same /* were vttered by her Maiestie. / [design] /] Imprinted at London by Chri- / stopher Barker, Printer to the Queenes / most excellent Maiestie. / 1586.

Emendations. (B1)Highnes]Highnes's (B1v)xxiij.]xxiii. (B3) when so euer she may:]whensoever she may: (B3v)Noble men]Noblemen it selfe]itselfe (B4v)our selues]ourselves expectation]expectation. (C1)her selfe]herselfe xij.]xii. xxviij.]xviii. them selues]themselves (C1v)my selfe]myselfe xxviij.]xxviii. my selfe,]myselfe, (C2)milke maides]milkemaides (C2v)in stead of gratefulnes,]instead of gratefulnes, my selfe]myselfe (C3)Stafford Shire]StaffordShire (C4)great good-wils]great good wils But for as much]But forasmuch commo wealth] commonwealth (C4v)what euer]whatever (D1)her selfe]herselfe (D2) suit of any one]suit of anyone (D2v)any one]anyone (D3)hostages: *for asmuch*]hostages: *forasmuch* (D3v)*any thing*]*anything* (D4v)wyer drawers]wyerdrawers (E1)my selfe]myselfe (E1v)to me in deede]to me indeede my selfe,]myselfe, (E2)my selfe]myselfe for euer]forever my selfe:]myselfe: (E2v)our selues.]ourselves. (E3)my selfe]myselfe my selfe]myselfe your selues]yourselves

The Copie of a Letter
to the Right Honourable the Earle of *Leycester*

TO THE RIGHT HOnourable the Earle of
Leicester, &c.

LBEIT WITH EARNEST desire of my hart (right
honourable my very good Lord) hath alwayes
endevoured to do your Lordship some acceptable
service, for the honour you first vouchsafed me
from beyond my cradel, and after confirmed with the
favourable opinion wherewith you have alwayes
countenaunced me ever since, even thus farre onward on my daies,
which also together with my yeres hath increased faster then mine
abilitie to performe, being crossed in nothing more deepely, then
when I was letted by the overmuch tendring of me by my parents,
to attend your Lordship in your late voyage and honourable expedition into the Lowe Countries: yet have I bene ever since most studious
to observe and apprehende some good occasion, or fitte oportunitie, to
testifie the duetifull reverence I beare to your Lordship: wherein if
hitherto I have beene slacke in performance during your absence, it
hath proceeded of the care I had not to entertaine your Lordship with
matter either frivolous or vulgar: though thinges of that nature might
best become my condition, and well agree with my understanding.

In which cogitation it came to my minde, that the report of the
speaches delivered by the Queene's most ex- [A3v] cellent Majestie in
a late and weightie cause dealt in this Parliament, in answere to the
petitions presented to hir Majestie the 12. and 24. of November at
Richmond by the Lord Chauncelour and Speaker, respectively, in
the name and behalfe of both Estates, accompanied with divers of

either sort, would doubtlesse bee a thing to your L. most gratefull, as
one ever pleased justly to admire the rare perfections of her mind, and
approoved Judgement, wherewith, according to your Estate and place,
deservedly, your L. hath beene vsually acquainted: as also worthie of
eternal monument and everlasting memorie, for as much as on the
sodaine they were delivered by herselfe, for answere of a matter propounded, debated, resolved, and digested, with great labour and
premeditation, of the greatest, gravest, wisest, and most choise persons of the whole Realme. Whereof although I have but slenderly pur-
traied the lineaments, without expressing to life the external ornaments of her Royall speach, accompanied with all Princely and grace-
full accomplementes: yet doubt I not but your Lordship will easily
finde her inward vertues, whereof it is impossible for mee to make the
least adumbration.

And because in the dayly expectation of your Lordship's returne, I
rested uncertaine how these might come safely to your Lordship's
hands: I did therefore advise to have this my letter with the included
copies to be ready to attend your first arrivall, in gratulation of the
safetie thereof, which hath bene long desired. Wherein, as I strive
to performe a particular duetie to your Lordship, so trust I you will
have that honourable consideration, that in the communication
thereof with others, there growe not any prejudice to me for my
presumption, in adventuring to be a reporter of that, which in the
deliverie wrought so great astonishment to all the hearers, as it exceeded the fulnes of every man's expectation: and therefore, without
some favourable construction of mine [A4] attempt, I might incurre
great blame by my slender maner of report, so to have blemished the
excellencie of her Majestie's speaches, whereof I humbly beseech your
Lordship to have favourable regard. Thus referring them to your
Lordship's disposition, and myselfe to your favourable protection,
I humbly take my leave. 25. Novemb. 1586.

                              Your Lordship's most
                              humbly in all duetie to
                              commaund.
                                   R. C. [B1]

THE BRIEFE OF THE Lorde CHANCELLER'S first *speach, at
the time when he deli*vered her most excellent MAJESTIE *a petition*

in writing, for, and in the name of the Lordes and Commons:

Which speaches were of more length then here are by me collected: but sure I am, the substance thereof is here truely expressed.

THat the Lordes and Commons having of long time to their intol-lerable griefe, found, by howe many practises the Scottish Queene had compassed the destruction of her Highnes's most Royall person (in whose safetie next under God they acknowledged their chiefe felicitie to consist) thereby not onely to bereave them of the sincere and true Religion in this Realme professed and established, but to bring backe againe this noble Realme into the thraldome of Romish tyrannie, and to overthrowe the happie estate thereof: wherein, although her High-nesse of her abundant gratious naturall clemencie and Princely mag-nanimitie, hath either lightly passed them over, or with no small indulgence tolerated, notwithstanding the often and earnest instances of her Nobilitie and Commons in [B1v] sundry Parliaments heretofore: and further hath protected her from the violent pursuite of her owne people: she yet, as a person obdurate in malice (as it appeares,) con-tinued her former practises, as had bene lately manifested by certaine wicked conspiracies plotted by one Anthonie Babington, *and diverse desperate persons, that had combined and confederated themselves by vowe and oth in a most horrible enterprise, by murther to take away the life of her Majestie: wherein the Scottish Q. did not only advise them, but also direct, comfort, and abbette them, with perswasion, counsel, promise of reward, and earnest obtestation. Whereupon, her Majestie at the earnest request of such as tendered the safetie of her royall person and the quiet of the Realme, did direct Commission under the great Seale to sundrie Lords and others of her Majestie's privie Counsel, and a great nomber of Lordes of Parliament, of the greatest and most ancient degree, assisted with some of the principall Judges of the Realme, to heare, examine and determine the same, according to a Statute in that behalfe made in the xxviii. yeere of her reigne. Who, to the nomber of 36. having attended the execution of the said Commission, and divers daies and times heard the allegations against the said Scottish Queene in her owne presence and hearing, (shee being permitted to say what shee woulde in her owne excuse,) did with one assent, finde her culpable both in privitie and consent to the saide crimes objected, and also in compassing the Queene's Majestie's death. Which sentence, by her owne directions upon the hearing of the prooves and processe in Parliament, was judged to have beene most honourable and just, and [B2] thereupon they all beseech hir Majesty, that forasmuch as the said Queene of Scots, was the very ground and onely subject, whereupon such daungerous practises and complots had bene founded, against hir Majestie's most Royall person and the Estate of this Realme for these many yeeres, to the overthrowe of sundrie of the Nobilitie of the land, and danger of Christian religion, and that they coulde see no hope of her desisting, and her adherents, but that still her Majestie's safetie must bee hazarded, and stand to the event of the like miraculous discoveries:*

Therefore, as most humble and instant suppliants, they did upon their knees at her most gratious feete, beseech and request in most earnest maner, that aswell for the continuance of God's Religion, the quiet of this kingdome, preservation of her person, and defence of them and their posterities, it woulde please hir Highnesse to take order, that the saide sentence might be published, and such further direction given, as was requisite in this so weightie a cause, according to the purport and intent of the said Statute. Wherin, if her Majestie (pursuing her wonted clemencie) should nowe be remisse, besides the imminent danger to hir person, she might by the stay thereof, procure the heavie displeasure of Almightie God, as by sundry severe examples of his Justice in the sacred Scriptures, doth appeare. And so he delivered, to her Majestie's owne handes, the petition in writing, which he said, had bene with great deliberation assented unto, by all the whole Parliament. [B2v]

A SHORT EXTRACT OF such reasons, as were delivered in speach by Master Sergeant Puckering, Speaker of the Lower House, before the Queene's most excellent Majestie in her Presence Chamber at Richmond, the xii. of November 1586. in the xxviii. yeere of her Reigne, containing divers apparant and imminent dangers, that may grow to her Majestie's most Royall person, and to her Realme from the Scottish Queene and her Adherents, if remedie be not provided.

First, touching the danger of her Majestie's person.

1 BOth this Scottish Queene and her favourers, doe thinke her to have right, not to succeed but to enjoy your Crowne in possession: and therefore as shee is a most impacient competitor, so will shee not spare any meanes whatsoever, that may bereave us of your Majestie, the onely impediment that she enjoyeth not her desire.

2 Shee is obdurate in malice against your royall person, notwith-standing you have shewed her all favour and mercie, as well in pre-serving her kingdome, as saving her life, and salving her honour. And therefore there is no place for mercie, since there is no hope that shee will desist from most wicked attempts: the rather for that her malice appeareth such, that shee maketh (as it were) her testament of the same, to be executed after her death, and appoynteth her executors to performe it. [B3]

3 Shee boldly and openly professed it lawfull for her to moove in-vasion upon you. And therefore, as of invasion victorie may ensue, and of victorie, the death of the vanquished: so did shee thereby not obscurely bewraie, that shee thought it lawfull for her to destroie your sacred person.

4 Shee thinkes it not onely lawfull, but honourable also and meritorious to take your life from you, as being alreadie deprived of your Crowne by the excommunication of the holie father. And there-fore it is like shee will (as hitherto she hath done) continually seeke it by whatsoever meanes.

5 That shee is greedie of your Majestie's death, and preferreth it before her owne life and safetie: for in her direction to one of her late Complices, she advised (under covert termes) that whatsoever should become of her, that tragicall execution should be performed upon you.

1 IT is most perillous to spare her, that continually hath sought the overthrow and suppression of true Religion, infected with Poperie from her tender youth, and being after that a Confederate in that Holy league *when she came to age, and ever since a professed enemie against the trueth.*

2 She resteth wholly upon Popish hopes to deliver and advance her, and is thereby so devoted to that profession, that aswell for satis-faction of others, as for feeding of her owne humor, she will supplant the Gospell, where, and whensoever she may: which evill is so much the greater, and the more to be avoyded, as that it stay- [B3v] *eth the very soule, and will spread itselfe not onely over England and Scot-land, but also into those partes beyond the Seas, where the Gospell of God is mainteined, the which cannot but be exceedingly weakened, by the defection of this noble Ilande.*

1 AS the Lydians saide, Vnum Regem agnoscunt Lydi, duos autem tolerare non possunt: *So wee say,* Vnicam Reginam Elizabetham agnoscunt Angli, duas autem tolerare non possunt.

2 As she hath already by her allurements brought to destruction moe Noblemen and their houses, together with a greater multitude of the Commons of this Realme, during her being here, then she should have bin able to doe, if she had bene in possession of her owne Crowne, and armed in the fielde against us: so will she still be continuall cause of the like spoyle, to the greater losse and perill of this Estate: And therefore this Realme neither can, nor may endure her.

3 Againe, she is the onely hope of all discontented subjects, she is the foundation whereon all the evill disposed do builde, she is the roote from whence all rebellions and trecheries do spring: And therefore whilest this hope lasteth, this foundation standeth, and this roote liveth, they will reteine heart, and set on foote whatsoever their devises against the Realme, which otherwise will fall away, die and come to nothing.

4 Mercie now in this case towards her, would in the ende prove crueltie against us all, Nam est quaedam crudelis misericordia, *and therefore to spare her, is to spill us.* [B4]

5 Besides this, it will exceedingly grieve and in a maner deadly wound the hearts of all the good Subjects of your land, if they shall see a conspiracie so horrible not condingly punished.

6 Thousands of your Majestie's most liege and loving Subjectes, of all sorts and degrees, that in a tender zeale of your Majestie's safetie, have most willingly both by open subscription and solemne vowe, entred into a firme and loyall association, and have thereby protested to pursue unto the death, by all forcible and possible meanes, such as she is by just sentence nowe found to be: can neither discharge their love, nor well save their othes, if your Majestie shall keepe her alive: of which burden your Majestie's Subjects are most desirous to bee relieved, as the same may be, if justice be done.

7   Lastly, your Majestie's most loving and dutiful commons doubt not, but that as your Majestie is duely exercised in reading the Booke of God, so it will please you to call to your princely remembrance, how fearefull the examples of God's vengeance bee, that are there to bee founde against King Saul *for sparing King* Agag, *and against King* Achab *for saving the life of* Benadad: *both which were by the just judgement of God deprived of their kingdoms, for sparing those wicked Princes, whome God had delivered into their handes, of purpose to be slaine by them, as by the ministers of his eternal and divine*

Justice: Wherein full wisely Salomon *proceeded to punishment, when hee tooke the life of his owne naturall and elder brother* Adonias, *for the only intention of a marriage, that gave suspition of treason against him.* [B4v]

Herein we your Majestie's most loving and obedient subjects, earnestly depend upon your princely resolution, which we assure ourselves shall be to God most acceptable, and to us no other, then the state of your Regall authoritie may afford us, and the approoved arguments of your tender care for our safetie under your charge, dooth promise to our expectation. [C1]

A REPORT OF HER MAjestie's most gratious answere, delivered by *herselfe verbally, to the first petitions of the Lords and Commons, being the Estates of Parliament, in her Chamber of Presence at Richmond, the xii. day of November 1586. at the full almost of xxviii. yeeres of her Reigne: Whereof the Reporter requireth of all that were hearers, a favourable interpretation of his intent, because he findeth that he can not expresse the same answerable to the originall, which the learned call* Prototypon.

THE bottomlesse graces and immeasurable benefits bestowed upon me by the Almightie, are, and have bene such, as I must not onely acknowledge them, but admire them, accounting them as well miracles as benefites, not so much in respect of his divine Majestie, with whome nothing is more common then to doe things rare and singular: as in regard of our weakenesse, who can not sufficiently set foorth his wonderfull workes and graces, which to mee have bene so many, so diversely folded and imbroydered one upon another, as in no sorte I am able to expresse them.

And although there liveth not any, that may more justly acknowledge themselves infinitely bounde unto God then I, whose life he hath miraculously preserved at sundry times (beyonde my merite) from a multitude of perils and dan- [C1v] gers: yet is not that the cause, for which I count myselfe the deeplyest bounde to give him my humblest thankes, or to yeelde him greatest recognition: but this which I shall tell you hereafter, which will deserve the name of wonder, if rare things and seeldom seene be worthie of accompt: Even this it is, that as I came to the Crowne with the willing hearts of my subjects, so

doe I now after xxviii. yeres Reigne, perceive in you no diminution
of good willes, which if happily I should want, well might I breath,
but never thinke I lived.

And now, albeit I finde my life hath bene full dangerously sought,
and death contrived by such as no desert procured: yet am I therein
so cleare from malice (which hath the property to make men glad at the
falles and faultes of their foes, and make them seeme to doe for other
causes, when rancor is the ground) as I protest it is and hath bene my
grievous thought, that one, not different in sexe, of like Estate, and my
neere kin, shoulde fall into so great a crime: yea, I had so litle purpose to pursue her with any colour of malice, that as it is not unknowen to some of my Lordes here, (for nowe I will play the blabbe)
I secretly wrote her a letter upon the discovery of sundry Treasons,
that if she woulde confesse them, and privately acknowledge them
by her letters to myselfe, shee never shoulde neede be called for them
into so publike question. Neither did I it of minde to circumvent her:
for then [C2] I knew as much as she could confesse, and so did I write.
And if even yet, nowe that the matter is made but to apparant, I
thought she truely would repent (as perhappes she would easily
appeare in outwarde shewe to doe) and that for her, none other would
take the matter upon them, or that we were but as two milkemaides
with pailes upon our armes, or that there were no more dependancie
upon us, but mine owne life were onely in danger, and not the whole
Estate of your Religion and well doings, I protest (wherein you may
beleeve me, for though I may have many vices, I hope I have not accustomed my tongue to be an instrument of untrueth) I would most
willingly pardon and remit this offence.

Or if by my death, other nations and Kingdomes might truely say,
that this Realme had attained an everprosperous and florishing
estate: I would (I assure you) not desire to live, but gladly give my
life, to the ende my death might procure you a better Prince.

And for your sakes it is, that I desire to live, to keepe you from a
worse. For as for me, I assure you, I finde no great cause I should be
fonde to live: I take no such pleasure in it, that I shoulde much wish
it, nor conceive such terror in death, that I should greatly feare it:
and yet I say not, but if the stroke were comming, perchance flesh
and blood would be moved with it, and seeke to shunne it.

I have had good experience and tryall of this [C2v] world: I know
what it is to be a subject, what to be a Soveraigne: what to have

good neighbors, and sometime meete evill willers. I have founde treason in trust, seene great benefits litle regarded, and instead of gratefulnes, courses of purpose to crosse.

These former remembrances, present feeling, and future expectation of evils, I say, have made me thinke, *An evill, is much the better, the lesse while it endureth:* and so, them happiest, that are soonest hence: and taught me to beare with a better minde these treasons, then is common to my sexe: yea, with a better heart perhaps, then is in some men. Which I hope you wil not meerly impute to my simplicitie or want of understanding, but rather, that I thus conceived, that had their purposes taken effect, I should not have found the blow, before I had felt it: and, though my perill should have bene great, my paine shoulde have bene but smal and short: wherein, as I would be loth to dye so bloody a death, so doubt I not, but God would have given me grace to be prepared for such an event, chance when it shall; which I referre to his good pleasure.

And now, as touching their treasons and conspiracies, together with the contriver of them, I will not so prejudicate myselfe and this my Realme, as to say or thinke, that I might not, without the last Statute, by the ancient lawes of this land, have proceeded against her, which was not made particularly to prejudice her: though [C3] perhaps it might then be suspected, in respect of the disposition of such as depend that way.

It was so farre from being intended to intrap her, that it was rather an admonition to warne the danger thereof: but sith it is made, and in the force of a Lawe, I thought good, in that which might concerne her, to proceede according thereunto, rather then by course of common Law: wherein, if you the Judges have not deceived me, or that the books you brought me were not false (which God forbid) I might as justly have tried her, by the ancient Lawes of the land.

But you Lawyers are so nice in sifting and skanning every woorde and letter, that many times you stand more upon forme then matter, upon sillables then sence of the Lawe. For in the strictnes and exact folowing of common forme, shee must have beene indited in Stafford-Shire, have holden up her hand at the Barre, and bene tried by a Jurie: A proper course forsooth, to deale in that manner with one of her Estate. I thought it better therfore, for avoiding of these and more absurdities, to commit the cause to the inquisition of a good nomber of the greatest and most noble personages of this Realme, of the Judges and others of good accompt, whose sentence I must approove: And all litle enough: For we Princes, I tel you, are set on stages, in the sight and viewe of all the world duely observed: The eies of many beholde our actions: A spot is soone espied in our garments: A blemish quickely noted in our doings. It behooveth us there- [C3v] fore, to be carefull that our proceedings bee just and honourable.

But I must tell you one thing more, that in this last Acte of Parliament you have brought me to a narowe straight, that I must give direction for her death, which cannot be to mee but a most grievous and irkesome burthen. And least you might mistake mine absence from this Parliament (which I had almost forgotten) although there be no cause why I should willingly come amongst multitudes, for that amongest many some may be evil: yet hath it not bene the doubt of any such daunger or occasion that kept me from thence, but onely the great griefe to heare this cause spoken of, especially, that such a one of State and kin, should neede so open a declaration, and that this nation should be so spotted with blots of disloialtie. Wherein the lesse is my grief, for that I hope the better part is mine, and those of the worse not much to be accompted of, for that in seeking my destruction, they might have spoiled their owne soules.

And even nowe coulde I tell you, that which woulde make you sorie. It is a secrete, and yet I will tell it you, although it is knowen, I have the propertie to keepe counsell, but too well oftentimes to mine owne perill. It is not long since mine eyes did see it written, that an othe was taken within fewe daies, either to kill mee or to be hanged themselves: and that to be performed ere one moneth were ended. Hereby I see your dan- [C4] ger in me, and neither can nor wil be so unthankfull or carelesse of your consciences, as not provide for your safetie.

I am not unmindeful of your oth made in the association, manifesting your great good wils and affections taken and entred into, upon good conscience, and true knowledge of the guilt, for safety of my person, and conservation of my life: done (I protest to God) before I heard it, or ever thought of such a matter, until a great nomber of handes with many Obligations were shewed mee, at Hampton Court, signed and subscribed with the names and seales of the greatest of this lande: which as I doe acknowledge as a perfect argument of your true heartes, and great zeale to my safetie: so shall my bonde be stronger tied to greater care for all your good.

But forasmuch as this matter is rare, waightie, and of great consequence, I thinke you doe not looke for any present Resolution: the rather, for that, as it is not my manner, in matters of far lesse moment, to give speedy answer without due consideration: so in this of such importance, I thinke it verie requisite with earnest Prayer to beseech his divine Majestie, so to illuminate my understanding, and inspire me with his grace, as I may doe and determine that, which shall serve to the establishment of his Church, preservation of your estates, and prosperitie of this commonwealth under my charge. Wherein (for that I knowe delaie is dangerous) you shal have with [C4v] all conveniencie our Resolution delivered by our message. And whatever any Prince may merite of their Subjects, for their approoved testimonie of their unfained sinceritie, eyther by governing justly, voide of all partialitie, or sufferance of any injuries done (even to the poorest) that doe I assuredly promise inviolablie to performe, for requitall of your so many desertes. [D1]

The occasions of the second accesse.

THis Answere thus made by her Majestie, the Lords and Commons were dismissed. And then her Highnesse some fewe dayes after, upon deliberation had of this Petition, being (as it appeared) of her mercifull disposition of nature, and her Princely magnanimitie, in some conflict with herselfe what to doe in a cause so weightie and important to her and the Realme, sent by the Lorde Chauncelour (as I heard) and by the mouth of an Honorable person, and a right worthy member of the lower house, this message to both houses: moving and earnestly charging them, to enter into a further consideration, whether there might not be some way of remedy, then that they had already required, so farre disagreeing from her owne naturall inclination. Whereupon, the Lords and Commons in either houses assembled, had sundry consultations, both in their severall houses generally, and by private Committees deputed specially, and after conference had betwixt the sayd Committees, it was resolved with unanimitie of consent amongst them in the lower house, and by universall concorde in the upper house, (the question there propounded to every one of the Lords) that there could be found no other sound and assured meane, in the depth of their understanding, for the continuance of the Christian religion, quiet of the Realme, and safetie of her Majestie's most Royall person, then that which was conteined in their former petition. The reasons whereof, were summarily these that followe: which are more shortly reported, then they were uttered. [D1v]

A BRIEFE REPORT OF the second accesse the 24. of November 1586. and of the answere made in the name of the Lords of Parliament, to a message sent from hir MAJESTIE by the L. Chauncelour after hir first answere.

THE Lord Chauncelour accompanied with above five or sixe and twentie Lords of Parliament, came before her Highnes in her Chamber of presence, to deliver the resolution of all the Lords of Parliament, concerning a message which he had not long before delivered from her Majestie, for further consultation, whether any other meanes could be thought of, or found out by any of them, how the Scottish Queene's life might be spared, and yet her Majestie's person saved out of perill, and the state of the Realme preserved in quiet, declared, that according to that he had received in commandement from her Majestie, he had imparted the same to the Lordes assembled in the upper house, whome he found by their generall silence much amazed at the propounding thereof, considering the same had bene before in deliberation amongst them, and resolved upon, and as appeared by their former petition exhibited to her Highnesse, wherein they had expressed the same resolution. Notwithstanding, for her Majestie's further satisfaction, they had entred into a newe consultation, and for that purpose selected a great nomber of the choysest persons of that higher house of Parliament, to conferre thereof, either privatly or together with the lower [D2] house: which also was done accordingly at several times. At all which conferences it was concluded by them all, and so afterwards by the whole assembly of both houses, that there could be no other assured meanes for the preservation of her Majestie's life, and continuance of God's Religion, and quiet of this State, then by the full execution of the sentence according to their former petition, instantly pressing her Majestie with many arguments and reasons tending thereto, all which, though by distance from his Lordship I could not wel conceive, yet this I did remember precisely and especially was one, that as it were injustice to denie execution of Law, at the suit of any-one particular, and the meanest of her people: so much more, not to

*yeelde to the earnest instance and humble prayers of all her faithful
and loving subjects. And so concluded, with earnest petition for her
Majestie's resolute determination and answere, for a present and
speedy direction by proclamation, and otherwise also, according to the
forme of the statute.* [D2v]

A SUMMARIE REPORT of the second speech, uttered by the Speaker
of the Lower House, by direction of all the Commons.

*THat if her Majestie should be safe without taking away the life of
the* Scottish Queene, *the same were most likelie and probably to grow,
by one of these meanes following.*

1 First, *that happily she might be reclaimed and become* A re-
pentant convert, *agnising her Majestie's great mercie and favours in
remitting her heynous offence, and by her loyaltie hereafter, performe the fruites of such conversion.*

2 *Or els, by a more* Strayg64 guard *be so kept, as there shoulde be
no feare of the like attempts hereafter.*

3 *Or, that good assurance might be given by* Othe, Bonds *or*
Hostages, *as cautions for her good and loyal demeanour from hence-
forth.*

4 *Or lastly, by* Banishment, *the realme might be voyded of her person, and thereby the perils further removed, that growe to her Majestie
by her presence.*

The moments wherof being duely pondered, did yet appeare so
light in all their judgements, that they durst not advise any securitie
to rest in any, no not in all of them.

For touching her conversion, *it was considered, that if pietie or
duetie could have restreined her from such hey-* [D3] *nous attempts,
there was cause abundantly ministred to her on her Majestie's behalfe,
when she not onely protected her against the violence of her own subjects, who pursued her to death by Justice, but covered her honor,
when the same by publique fame was touched, and by very heynous
and capitall crymes objected and proved against her before certeine
Commissarie delegates assigned to examine the same, more then
blemished, and spared her lyfe, when for her former conspiracies and
confederacies with the Northren Rebelles, her highnesse was with
great instance pressed by both the houses in the xiiii. yeere of her*

Majestie's reigne, to do like justice uppon her, as nowe is desired, and as her treasonable practises then, had most justly deserved.

And where the penaltie of this Acte sufficiently notified unto her, should have terrified her from so wicked attempts, she hath neverthelesse insisted in her former practises, as a person obdurate in malice against her Majestie, and irrecoverable: so as there was no probable hope of any conversion, but rather great doubt and feare of relaps and recidivation, forasmuch as she stood obstinately in the deniall of matter most evidently prooved, and now most justly sentenced against her, and was not entred into the first part of repentance, The recognition of her offence, *and so much the farther off from the true fruites that should accompany the same.*

As for a surer guard, *and more* strait imprisonment, *it was resolved, that there was no security therein, nor yet in the other two meanes propounded of* bonds *and* hostages: *forasmuch as the same meanes that shoulde bee practised to take her Majestie's life away* [D3v] *(which God forbid) would aptly serve both for the delivery of her person, and release of the* bonds *and* hostages *that should be given for cautions in that behalfe: which being unhappily atchieved, and to our irreparable losse, who shoulde sue the* bonds, *or deteine the* hostages? *or being deteined, what proportion was there in* bonds *or* hostages *whatsoever, to countervaile the value of so precious and inestimable a Jewel, as her Majestie is to this Realme, and to us all?*

But she will solemnly vowe and take an othe, that she will not attempt anything to the hurt of her Majestie's person: Shee hath already sundry times falsified her worde, her writing and her othe, and holdeth it for an article of religion, That faith is not to be holden with heretikes, *of which sort shee accompteth your Majestie, and all the professors of the Gospel to be: And therefore have we litle reason to trust her in that, wherof shee maketh so small a conscience.*

As for banishment, *that were a step* à malo in peius *to set her at libertie: a thing so greatly desired and thirsted for by her adherents, and by some Princes her Allies, who sought her enlargement chiefly, to make her a head to be set up against her Majesty, in time of invasion.*

To the which were added some fewe reasons, collected out of her owne letters and the confession of Babington, *her instrument and chiefe conspiratour: by which appeared, howe her owne conscience bewrayed what might justly fal upon her, in case any of her intended desseignements came to light: that shee might haply bee shut up in some more close and straite prison, as the* Towre of London, *if there befell her no worse thing: and in that* [D4] *she directed* Babington, *in case he failed in the action of her delivery, that he should neverthelesse proceede in the residue, which was the death of her Majestie: who also confessed, that upon assurance of her Majestie's death, or the arrivall of strangers, he intended to proclaime the Q. of Scots, and made no doubt of the desired successe: and therefore, her Majestie's death being so earnestly sought, for advancement of this competitor, her Highnes could not remaine in quietnes or securitie, if the Scottish Queene should longer continue her life.* [D4v]

THE SECOND ANSWERE *made by the Queene's Majestie, delivered by her owne mouth, to the second speeche, uttered in the names of the Lords and Commons of the Parliament.*

FUL grievous is the way, whose going on and end, breede comber for the hire of a laborious journey.

I have strived more this day then ever in my life, whether I shoulde speake, or use silence. If I speake and not complaine, I shal dissemble: if I holde my peace, your labour taken were full vayne. For mee to make my mone, were strange and rare: for I suppose you shal finde fewe, that for their owne particular, wil comber you with such a care. Yet such I protest hath bene my greedy desire and hungrie will, that of your consultation might have fallen out some other meanes to woorke my safetie joyned with your assurance, (then that for which you are become such earnest sutors) as I protest, I must needes use complaint, though not of you, but unto you, and of the cause: for that I do perceive by your advises, prayers, and desires, there falleth out this accident, that *Onely my Injurer's bane, must be my life's suertie.*

But if any there live so wicked of nature, to suppose, that I prolonged this time onely, *pro forma*, to the intent to make a shew of clemencie, thereby to set my prayses to the wyerdrawers to lengthen them the more: they doe me so great a [E1] wrong, as they can hardly recompence. Or if any person there be, that thinke or imagine, that the least vayneglorious thought hath drawen mee further herein, they doe me as open injurie as ever was done to any living creature, as he that is the maker of all thoughtes, knoweth best to be true. Or if there bee any, that thinke, that the Lords appoynted in Commission

durst do no other, as fearing thereby to displease, or els to be suspected to be of a contrary opinion to my safetie, they doe but heape
upon me injurious conceites. For either those put in trust by me to
supplie my place, have not performed their dueties towards me: or
els they have signified unto you all, that my desire was, that every
one should do according to his conscience, and in the course of his
proceedings should enjoy both freedome of voyce and libertie of
opinion: and what they would not openly declare, they might privately to myselfe have revealed. It was of a willing minde and great desire
I had, that some other means might be found out, wherein I should
have taken more comfort, then in any other thing under the Sunne.
And since nowe it is resolved, that my suretie can not bee established
without a Princesse's ende, I have just cause to complaine, that I,
who have in my time pardoned so many Rebels, winked at so many
treasons, and either not produced them, or altogether slipt them over
with silence, shoulde nowe be forced to this proceeding, against such
a person. I have besides, during [Elv] my reigne, seene and heard many
opprobrious bookes and Pamphlets against me, my Realme and State,
accusing me to be a Tyrant: I thanke them for their almes: I beleeve,
therein their meaning was to tell me newes, and newes it is to me
indeede: I would it were as strange to heare of their impietie. What
will they not now say, when it shalbe spread, That for the safety of
her life, a Mayden Queene could be content to spill the blood, even of
her owne kinsewoman? I may therfore ful wel complaine, that any
man should thinke mee given to crueltie, whereof I am so guiltlesse
and innocent, as I shoulde slaunder God, if I should say he gave me
so vile a minde: yea, I protest, I am so farre from it, that for mine owne
life I would not touche her: neither hath my care bene so much bent
howe to prolong mine, as how to preserve both, which I am right sory
is made so hard, yea, so impossible.

I am not so voide of judgement, as not to see mine owne perill: nor
yet so ignorant, as not to knowe it were in nature a foolish course, to
cherish a sworde to cutte mine owne throate: nor so carelesse, as not
to weigh that my life dayly is in hazard: but this I do consider, that
many a man would put his life in daunger for the safegarde of a King,
I doe not say that so will I: but I pray you thinke, that I have thought
upon it.

But sith so many have both written and spoken against mee, I pray
you give me leave to say somewhat for myselfe, and before you re-

turne [E2] to your countries, let you know, for what a one you have passed so careful thoughts. Wherin, as I thinke myselfe infinitely beholding unto you al, that seeke to preserve my life by al the meanes you may: so I protest unto you, that there liveth no Prince, that ever shall be more mindefull to requite so good desertes. And as I perceyve you have kept your olde wonts, in a general seeking of the lengthning of my dayes: so am I sure that I shall never requite it, unles I had as many lives as you all: but forever I will acknowledge it, while there is any breath left mee. Although I may not justifie, but may justly condemne my sundry faults and sinnes to God: yet for my care in this government, let me acquaynt you with my intents.

When first I tooke the Scepter, my title made me not forget the giver: and therefore began, as it became me, with such religion, as both I was borne in, bred in, and I trust shal die in. Although I was not so simple, as not to know what danger and perill so great an alteration might procure me: howe many great Princes of the contrary opinion woulde attempt all they might against me: and generally, what enimitie I should breede unto myselfe: which all I regarded not, knowing that he, for whose sake I did it, might, and would defend me. For which it is, that ever since I have bene so daungerously prosecuted, as I rather marvaile that I am, then muse that I should not be: if it were not God's holy hand that conti- [E2v] nueth me, beyond all other expectation.

Then entred I further into the schoole of experience, bethinking what it fitted a King to do: and there I saw, he scant was wel furnished, if either he lacked Justice, Temperance, Magnanimitie, or Judgement. As for the two latter, I wil not boaste, my sexe doeth not permit it: But for the two first, this dare I say, Amongst my subjects I never knew a difference of person, where right was one: Nor never to my knowledge preferred for favour, whome I thought not fit for worth: Nor bent my eares to credite a tale that first was tolde me: Nor was so rash, to corrupt my judgement with my censure, before I heard the cause. I wil not say, but many reports might fortune be brought mee by such as might heare the case, whose partialitie might marre sometime the matter: For wee Princes may not heare all ourselves. But this dare I boldly affirme, My verdit went ever with the trueth of my knowledge. As ful well wished Alcibiades his friende, that hee should not give any answere, till he had recited the letters of the Alphabet: so have I not used over sudden resolutions, in matters that have touched me full neere: you wil say that with me, I thinke.

And therfore, as touching your counsels and consultations, I conceive them to bee wise, honest, and conscionable: so provident and careful for the safetie of my life (which I wish no longer then may be for your good,) that though I never [E3] can yeeld you of recompence your due: yet shall I endevour myselfe to give you cause, to thinke your good wil not ill bestowed, and strive to make myselfe worthy for such subjects.

And now for your petition, I shal pray you for this present, to content yourselves with an answere without answere: Your judgement I condemne not, neither do I mistake your reasons, but pray you to accept my thankfulnesse, excuse by doutefulnesse, and take in good part my answere answerelesse: wherein I attribute not so much to mine owne judgement, but that I thinke many particular persons may go before me, though by my degree I go before them. Therefore if I should say, I would not doe what you request, it might peradventure be more then I thought: and to say I would do it, might perhaps breed perill of that you labour to preserve, being more then in your owne wisdomes and discretions would seeme convenient, circumstances of place and time being duely considered.

The miraculous victory atchieved by the English Fleete . . . Upon the Spanish huge Armada
(1598)

The Elizabethan Age is best remembered for the Spanish Armada and its defeat by the English off their coasts in the summer of 1588. For some years previous to this the Spanish had been planning invasions of England. "It would seem to be God's obvious design to bestow upon Your Majesty the crowns of these two kingdoms," Don Bernardino de Mendoza, the Spanish ambassador to Paris, wrote to Philip II of Spain in late March 1587. By that time Philip was already reflecting on two quite dissimilar plans—that of Santa Cruz, which proposed a naval invasion in the Dover Straits executed by 150 great warships, as many merchantmen, 40 hulks for provisions, and some 320 support ships; and that of Alexander Farnese, prince of Parma, who urged a land invasion by his troops, now in the Netherlands, of 30,000 infantry and 40,000 cavalry. Parma hinted at the union of both forces and after some time absorbed in various strategies, Philip determined to build on just such a combination.

In sharp contrast, much of the English planning was catch-as-catch-can. Elizabeth did not pretend to understand naval warfare, and she was continually pestered by those who did—Drake especially —and those who did not, chief among them Burghley. In fact, it was Drake, who should have been admiral of the fleet but who gracefully accepted the position of second in command under Howard, who finally persuaded the Lord High Admiral to move out of the Straits and join him at Plymouth. It was also Drake who urged Howard to run an early attack on the Spanish fleet before it left the Spanish coast and who first maneuvered the English ships to the windward side of the Spanish, thus giving them a running offensive advantage until the Spanish anchored off Calais four days later. Throughout the campaign he reaffirmed the name the Spanish had assigned him: "El Draque"—the dragon, the devil. Despite all capabilities and caution, however, both forces were essentially surprised. The English did not expect the tight crescent formation; the Spanish did not anticipate the English fleet would be so large, since they thought for some time after battles began that the ships they encountered at Plymouth were merely the early patrol for the main fleet somewhere off Dover or Margate.

Unfortunately, much of the color of this confrontation of great powers exists in letters rather than in popular pamphlets. The engagement, for example, opened with the formality of a chivalric tournament: the Spanish admiral, Medina Sidonia, raised his flag displaying Christ crucified and flanked by the Virgin Mother and Mary Magdalen, a flag consecrated by the Pope and lending the battle the overtones of a Crusade; while the English responded by bearing a personal challenge in a pinnace ironically named the *Disdain*. As for the famous crescent formation, it was, in fact, an infantry formation set on water. According to a tradition centuries-old, the main-battle advanced protected by the vanguard, which fell back to the right, the position of honor, while the rearguard advanced to the left: it was not so surprising a formation after all. Spanish impregnability came instead from their stubborn refusal to break formation and scatter their strength.

The handling of ships on both sides during the twelve days of sighting and fighting off Portland Bill, off the Isle of Wight, off Calais, and at Gravelines was skillful on both sides. Medina Sidonia managed again and again to keep his lumbering craft together until the incident of the fire ships, despite the unknown waters, the unpredictable winds, and his own inexperience. The English ships, meanwhile, in all their sweeping and semi-circular attacks, managed to keep the wind gauge for the most part, while avoiding other Spanish and English craft. Their joy in their success—and we find it years later in their discussing the carcasses of animals washed ashore after Medina Sidonia dumped horses and cattle overboard to save water all along his retreat to the north—was in good measure a justifiable pride in their skill as sailors and fighters. But their courage then against larger ships and a much larger fleet serves in some ways as a complement to the stoutness of heart of the Spanish who, after the battle, with no certainty of ever seeing land or home again, rationed themselves, regardless of rank, to eight ounces of biscuit, a pint of water and a half pint of wine daily, and sternly set out to face the bitter winds of the unknown North Sea.

There are numerous accounts of English celebrations, although there was a pause while they made certain they were free from further attack from Parma or rebels and Catholics at home. On August 20, the Lord Mayor, aldermen, and companies of London went in a body to hear the Dean of St. Paul's Cathedral speak at Paul's Cross. The greatest occasion was on Sunday, November 24. Then "the Queen, attended by her Privy Council, by the Nobility and other honourable Persons as well spiritual as temporal, in great number, the French Ambassador [who was not aware of the cause for the holiday], the Judges, the Heralds and Trumpeters all on horseback, came in a chariot supported by four pillars and drawn by two white horses to St. Paul's Church, where, alighting at the West Door, she fell on her knees, and audibly praised God for her own and the Nation's signal deliverance; and after a sermon suitable to the occasion, preached by Dr. Pierce, Bishop of Sarum, she exhorted the People in a most Royal and Christian manner, to a due Performance of the religious Duty of Thanksgiving, then going to the Bishop of London's Palace, where she dined, she returned in the same order as before, by Torchlight, to Somerset-House." So like Elizabeth: the spectacle, the appeal to God, the propaganda, the patriotism.

More Elizabethan pamphlets are extant on the Spanish Armada than on any other historic event of her reign; but with the possible exception of the account reprinted here—which is clearly by a man sympathetic to the English cause, if not always obtrusively so—all are largely propaganda or diatribe. Of these, the most famous and popular was *The Copie of A Letter Sent Out Of England To Don Bernardino Mendoza*, an anonymous work that went through three English editions and at least as many issues and was translated into French and Italian and was, for nearly ten years, considered the most "objective" account England had. The work was really state propaganda written by Burghley: the draft, found among his papers in 1956, was suspected by Sir Walter Scott and others, yet the hoax was successful for over 350 years. Since Burghley's account—presented as a Catholic's report to the former Spanish ambassador to England on the actual situation in Elizabeth's realm—was taken as true, it must have contributed widely to the increased English pride in their own invulnerability.

Briefly, Burghley centers on three issues which, according to the marginal note on C3 are *"The 3. hopes conceived against England,* [which] *are now all frustrated."* The text at this point reads: "First of the weaknes of the English Navie: for so you know you were divers waies this last yeare advertised from hence, and so also many of us here did conceive the same: wherein we see by all this yeares service with these ships, we did all notably erre. Next, of a supposed evill contentement of a number of people in this land to serve the Queene, and her Government against her enemies. Lastly, and most principally, of a great strong partie that would be found here in the favour of us for the Catholique religion, that should take armes against the Queene upon the first sight of the Catholique Navie on the coasts of England. Of all which opinions, setled in good mens minds in maner of judgements, we know that none in the world did more constantly assure the King thereof then you: which, as the matters have evil succeeded, may, I feare, bring you in danger of his indignation, although I know you meant very wel therin." The credit for the English victory is given to God (A3) who favors the English; this is seen both in their unity against the Spanish (for the rich and poor alike contributed money and provisions and offered their lives to her in service [A3v]); and in the English Catholics who, tolerated by a Queen who punished traitors to the state but not disbelievers in religion (B1v-B4), also joined her cause. Cardinal Allen (A4) and others (A3v ff.) also hurt the Spanish by publishing lies concerning English Catholics, English persecution, and Spanish military victories, all of which both angered and terrified the English and resulted in a wave of support for the fight against Spain (A3v ff.). The bulk of Burghley's work is given over to a detailed list of "voluntary" aid given the Queen and of promises of ships and forces from the Low Countries of Holland and Zeeland (C3v), Denmark (C3v), and Scotland (D4v)—good propaganda and sufficient reward for those who served. The pamphlet closes with an account of the Queen's kindly treatment of Spanish prisoners taken during the war with the Armada and the festivals in London when flags and other treasures captured from Armada ships were put on public display (E4).

Such an account is distinct from the Dutch Emanuel van Meteren's report which is given here in Hakluyt's translation from Latin in 1598, and printed first in Hakluyt's third edition of the *Voyages* published that year. The following narration is tonally fashioned by the immense lists of facts and statistics which open it; and it is therefore predictable that this comprehensive document attempting historical record will dispense with the subsequent legend that the winds of God alone destroyed the Spanish attempt to invade England. Instead, van Meteren has pointed clearly to the decisive cause of Spanish defeat as their delay in joining battle with England. Van Meteren also holds that Spanish sea forces were not good fighting forces because their ships were too unwieldy and, though armed, were supplied by too few crew to handle problems of both navigation and fighting. Because the Spanish failed to consider a number of things—the difference in the speed, maneuverability, and equipment of the English ships (Eeelv); the early attack of the English (Ddd6); the possible delay of Parma's force (Eeel); and poor weather (Ddd4v)—they handicapped their navy beyond recovery and so actually doomed the Armada before it left Spain. Van Meteren's ability to estimate fighting strength is proven by his accurate judgment (Ddd5) that the Spanish might have won if they had been willing to break formation and attack the English who were still disorganized and undermanned at their first encounter off Plymouth. Thus there is in van Meteren's work a remarkable ability to marshal facts and render sound judgments despite his English bias.

There is also more than a little wit, best seen in his selection of anecdotes. The Spanish firing on Drake's cabin but hitting no one (Eeelv), the gentleman voluntary who has his bed shot out from under him (Eeelv), the banner from the *Saint Matthew*—one of Philip's great ships of the Twelve Apostles, consecrated for the voyage—flying now in the Protestant church at Leiden (Eee2), and the horses and mules alone swimming for life (Ddd2v); all have in them insinuations of satire. Combined with the inflated Spanish statistics, in which he turns Spanish pride back on itself (Ddd2v), and his outright admiration for the English, apparent in references to Elizabeth on Ddd4-Ddd4v and Eee1 and his emphasis on the Spanish awe of English courage (Ddd5v and elsewhere), his rendering is not so impartial as he would have us believe. Nor is it quite so accurate. There is no indication that women followed Spanish ships as he claims (Ddd3); he overestimates the percentage of Spanish ships that returned to Spain (Eee2v); he is inaccurately harsh on Medina's reception in Spain (Ddd5v); and he even misidentifies Escobedo (Ddd2v). It is, in fact, an indication of van Meteren's sentiment that he chooses to conclude his work with the poem of an outspoken Calvinist—and that tonally the poem complements his narrative. Still Hakluyt was quite right in choosing this account as the most complete and reliable one published during Elizabeth's reign; and with his own translation of it he has preserved for us as for the later Elizabethans an important near-primary document of this most singular event.

TEXTUAL NOTES

[For explanatory notes for this selection see page 376.]

The miraculous victory atchieved by the English Fleete . . . Upon the Spanish huge Armada
   Reference. STC 12626; 12626a.
   Authorship and Editions. The most detailed account which the Elizabethans had of the Armada was that by Emanuel van Meteren in Latin; it was translated by Richard Hakluyt for his 1598 edition of *The Principal Navigations, Voiages, Traffiqves and Discoueries of the English Nation* (London), I,591-606, when it was considered important and commercial enough to mention on the title page: *"And lastly, the memorable defeate of the Spanish huge Armada, Anno. 1588"* (π1). A second issue with a new title-page omitting a reference to the Cadiz voyage (see page 276) is dated 1599. This large and splendid folio is beautifully set out and the composition remarkably free of error; but the typesetting for the account of the Armada is the same and the misnumbered page (p. 605 reads "608") is uncorrected. The work went

through later unchanged reprintings in 1904 (Glasgow) for the
Hakluyt Society, VI, 197-235; and in 1910 (London; as a new edition,
with addenda, although none for this text), pp. 1-19.

Because of the completeness of the account, the work has been reissued several times; and it is this text upon which most historians
rely. The Everyman Library printed a slightly modernized text in
Hakluyt's Voyages (London, n.d. [?1907]), II, 369-401 (omitting the
Latin verse, but giving the translation). Janet Hampden edited the
text for "The World's Classics" series in *Richard Hakluyt: Voyages
and Documents* (Oxford, 1958); her slightly modernized text is complete, pp. 358-398, and she provides a general glossary at the back of
the book. More popular texts have also appeared. Purchas used this
account only for the list of ships in *Hakluytus Posthumus or Purchas
His Pilgrimes* (1625), Book X, Chapter XI. A complete edition (omitting only the Latin verse) was edited by W. H. D. Rouse for "Blackie's
English Texts" in a volume titled *The Spanish Armada, The Last
Fight of the Revenge, And other Adventures of the Reign of Queen
Elizabeth* (London, Glasgow, Dublin, 1908), 37-77; here the spelling
and punctuation have been modernized and the work heavily repara-
graphed. There is a brief and barely useful glossary (p. 128). The
following year A. E. Hall edited the work for "Brill's English Texts
for Secondary Schools" in *Selections from Hakluyt's Principal Navigations* (London), 80-114; the Latin and English verses are both omitted
and again the work is modernized in spelling, punctuation, and para-
graphing; there is no commentary but a slightly more expanded glossary (beginning p. 131). A children's book of selections from Hakluyt,
"selected and arranged" by A. S. Mott (Oxford, 1929) includes a re-
telling of the Armada adventure on pp. 186-222; although this is
divided into four chapters with headnotes giving an introductory
synopsis, the text is remarkably close (if modernized) to Hakluyt's and
only the poems at the end are omitted. Mott also provides a glossary,
starting on p. 310.

Collation. Folio in sixes (three sheets each folded once). Richard
Hakluyt, *The Principal Navigations* (1598 edition, first and second
issues), *6; **6; A-Fff6; account of the Armada, Ddd2-Eee3v. *1, title-
page; *1v, blank; *2-*3v, dedication; *4-**2v, preface; **3-**3v,
dedicatory verses to the author; **4-**6v, contents; A1-Fff4, text;
Fff4v, blank; Fff5-6 wanting [probably blank; Fff4 reads, "The end of
the first volume."].

Description of Contents. Introductory matter in roman and italics;
text in black-letter. Running-heads of contents within single rules.
Paginated. Large decorative initials at the beginning of each account.
Ornaments as tail-pieces on *3v, **2v, **6v; as head-piece on **4 only
(rules serving both sides of running-head—or enclosing no words)
elsewhere. *Armada account:* Ddd2-Eee3v, pp. 591-606 [page *605* mis-

numbered p. *608*]. Heading in mixed roman and italic; text in black-letter. Special running-head, *"The Spanish Armada."* in italics on each page. Decorative initial, Ddd2, Eee3v (for first word in Beza's poem in Latin). Marginal notes frequent; they are as follows: "The preparation of the *Spanish*: King to subdue *England* and the lowe Countreys." (Ddd2v); "The number and qualitie of the ships in the *Spanish* Fleete, with the souldiers, Mariners, and pieces of Ordinance." (Ddd2v); "A description of the Galeons." (Ddd3); "A description of the Galliasses." (Ddd3); "The great Ordinance, bullets, gun-poulder, and other furniture." (Ddd3); "Their provision of victuals and other things necessary." (Ddd3); "A *Spanish terza* consisteth of *3200.* souldiers." (Ddd3); "The preparation of the duke of *Parma* to aide the *Spaniards.*" (Ddd3v); "The Popes furtherance to the conquest of *England*, and of the low Countries." (Ddd3v); "A treatie of peace, to the end that England and the vnited prouinces might be secure of inuasion." (Ddd4); "Her maiesties warlike preparation by sea." (Ddd4); "Her Maiesties land-forces." (Ddd4); "The preparation of the vnited prouinces." (Ddd-4v); "The Spanish fleete set saile vpon *the 19.* of May." (Ddd4v); "They set saile from ye Groine vpon the *11.* of Iuly." (Ddd4v); "The Spaniards come within kenning of England." (Ddd4v); "Captaine Fleming." (Ddd4v); "The L. Admirals short warning vpon the *19.* of Iuly." (Ddd4v); "The *20.* of Iuly." (Ddd4v); "The *21.* of Iuly." (Ddd5); "The *22.* of Iuly." (Ddd5); "*Don Pedro de Valdez* with his ship & company taken." (Ddd5v); "A great Biscaine ship taken by the English." (Ddd5v); "The *23.* of Iuly." (Ddd5v); "A great Venetian ship and other small ships taken by the English." (Ddd6); "The *24.* of Iuly." (Ddd6); "The *25.* of Iuly." (Ddd6); "The *26.* of Iuly.'" (Ddd6v); "The *27.* of Iuly." (Ddd6v); "The Spaniards ancre before Caleis." (Ddd6v); "The *28.* of Iuly." (Ddd6v); "The *29.* of Iuly." (Ddd6v); "The *30.* of Iuly." (Ddd6v); "The Spaniards vaine opinion concerning their own fleet." (Eee1); "The *28.* of Iuly." (Eee1); "The galliasse of *Hugo de Moncada* cast vpon the showlds before *Caleis.*" (Eee1); "M. *Amias Preston* valiantly boordeth the galliasse." (Eee1); "The great fight before *Greueling* the *29.* of Iuly." (Eee1v); "Three Spanish shippes suncke in the fight." (Eee1v); "Two galeons taken and caried into *Zeland.*" (Eee1v); "A small shippe cast away about *Blankenberg.*" (Eee2); "The dishonourable flight of the Spanish nauy: amd the prudent aduice of the L. Admirall." (Eee2); "The English returne home from the pursute of ye Spaniards the *4* of August." (Eee2); "The Spaniards consult to saile round about *Scotland* and *Ireland*, and so to returne home." (Eee2v); "The shippewracke of the Spaniardes vpon the Irish coast." (Eee2v); "Of *134* ships of the Spanish fleet, there returned home but *53.*" (Eee2v); "New coines stamped for the memory of the Spaniards ouerthrow." (Eee3); "The people of *England* and of the vnited prouinces, pray, fast, and giue thanks vnto God." (Eee3).

License. No entry in the *Stationers' Register*; printed by the Queen's printers, George Bishop, Ralph Newberry, and Robert Barker.

Base-Copy Text. Bodleian Douce H238. For variant issue: Bodleian H.8.15 Art.

Title-heading in Full (Ddd2). / The miraculous victory atchieued by the *English* Fleete, / vnder the discreet and happy conduct of the right honourable, right pru- / dent, and valiant lord, the L. *Charles Howard*, L. high Admirall of England, &c. Vpon / the *Spanish* huge *Armada* sent in the yeere 1588. for the inuasion of *England*, toge- / ther with the woful and miserable successe of the said *Armada* afterward, vpon the / coasts of *Norway*, of the *Scottish* Western Isles, of *Ireland*, of *Spaine*, of *France*, and of / *England*, &c. Recorded in Latine by / *Emanuel van Meteran* in the / 15. booke of his / history of the low Countreys. /

Emendations. (Ddd3)weild]wield   (Ddd3v)bridges   like   wise] bridges likewise   ouens a piece]ovens apiece   (Ddd4)D. *Allen* an *English* man]D. *Allen* an *English*man in deed]indeed   *Pallas* her selfe.] *Pallas* herselfe.   (Ddd4v)state of the common wealth,]state of the commonwealth,   In the meane while]In the meanewhile   retiring her selfe]retiring herselfe   meane season]meaneseason   (Ddd5)lanterne in stead]lanterne instead   meane season]meaneseason   (Ddd5v)how the English men]how the Englishmen   (Ddd6)nauie in the meane while] navie in the meanwhile   sonne in lawe]sonne-in-lawe   In the meane while]In the meanewhile   (Ddd6v)time/over]time [given]/ over   (Eee1) meane season]meaneseason   (Eee1v)the English men would haue] the Englishmen would have   come often times very]come oftentimes very   giuing them one broad side]giving them one broadside   vntill suchtime]untill such time   the English men all that time]the Englishmen all that time   the L. Admirall]the Lord Admirall   the English men were not]the Englishmen were not   tunnes a piece,]tunnes apiece,   ship it selfe]ship itselfe   L. *Henrie Seymer*]Lord *Henrie Seymer* (Eee2v)touching no where]touching nowhere   vpon the maine land,] upon the maineland,   (Eee3)such like coines,]suchlike coines,   Like wise such solemn]Likewise such solemne   Like wise, the Queenes] Likewise, the Queene's

The miraculous victory atchieved by the English Fleete, under the discreet and happy conduct of the right honourable, right, prudent, and valiant lord, the L. Charles Howard, L. high Admirall of England, &c. Upon the Spanish huge Armada sent in the yeere 1588. for the invasion of England, together with the wofull and miserable successe of the said Armada afterward, upon the coasts of Norway, of the Scottish Westerne Isles, of Ireland, of Spaine, of France, and of England, &c. Recorded in Latine by Emanuel van Meteran in the 15, booke of his history of the low Countreys.

AVING IN PART declared the strange and wonderfull events of the yeere eightie eight, which hath bene so long time foretold by ancient prophesies; we will now make relation of the most notable and great enterprise of all others which were in the foresaid yeere atchieved, in order as it was done. Which exploit (although in very deed it was not performed in any part of the low Countreys) was intended for their ruine and destruction. And it was the expedition which the *Spanish* king, having a long time determined the same in his minde, and having consulted thereabout with the Pope, set foorth and undertooke against *England* and the low Countreys. To the end that he might subdue the Realme of *England*, and reduce it unto his catholique Religion, and by that meanes might be sufficiently revenged for the disgrace, contempt and dishonour, which hee (having 34. yeeres before enforced them to the Pope's obedience) had endured of the *English* nation, and for divers other injuries which had taken

deepe impression in his thoughts. And also for that hee deemed this to bee the most readie and direct course, whereby hee might recover his heredetarie possession of the lowe Countreys, having restrained the inhabitants from sayling upon the coast of *England*. [Ddd2v] Which verily, upon most weighty arguments and evident reasons, was thought would undoubtly have come to passe, considering the great aboundance and store of all things necessary wherewith those men were furnished, which had the managing of that action committed unto them. But now let us describe the matter more particularly.

The *Spanish* King having with small fruite and commoditie, for above twentie yeeres together, waged warre against the Netherlanders, after deliberation with his counsellers thereabout, thought it most convenient to assault them once againe by Sea, which had bene attempted sundry times heretofore, but not with forces sufficient. Unto the which expedition it stoode him nowe in hand to joyne great puissance, as having the *English* people his professed enemies; whose Island is so situate, that it may either greatly helpe or hinder all such as saile into those parts. For which cause hee thought good first of all to invade *England*, being perswaded by his Secretary *Escouedo*, and by divers other well experienced *Spaniards* and *Dutchmen*, and by many *English* fugitives, that the conquest of that Iland was lesse difficult then the conquest of *Holland* and *Zeland*. Moreover the *Spaniards* were of opinion, that it would bee farre more behoveful for their King to conquere *England* and the lowe Countreys all at once, then to be constrained continually to maintaine a warlike Navie to defend his East and West *Indie* Fleetes, from the *English Drake*, and from such like valiant enemies.

And for the same purpose the king Catholique had given commandement long before in *Italy* and *Spaine*, that a great quantitie of timber should be felled for the building of shippes; and had besides made great preparation of things and furniture requisite for such an expedition; as namely in founding of brasen Ordinance, in storing up of corne and victuals, in trayning of men to use warlike weapons, in leavying and mustering of souldiers: insomuch that about the beginning of the yeere *1588.* he had finished such a mightie Navie, and brought it into *Lisbon* haven, as never the like had before that time sailed upon the Ocean sea.

A very large and particular description of this Navie was put in print and published by the *Spaniards*; wherein were set downe the number, names, and burthens of the shippes, the number of Mariners and souldiers throughout the whole Fleete; likewise the quantitie of their Ordinance, of their armour, of bullets, of match, of gun-poulder, of victuals, and of all their Navall furniture was in the saide description particularized. Unto all these were added the names of the Governours, Captaines, Noblemen and gentlemen voluntaries, of whom there was so great a multitude, that scarce was there any family of accompt, or any one principall man throughout all *Spaine*, that had not a brother, sonne or kinseman in that Fleete: who all of them were in good hope to purchase unto themselves in that Navie (as they termed it) invincible, endlesse glory and renowne, and to possesse themselves of great Seigniories and riches in *England*, and in the lowe Countreys. But because the said description was translated and published out of *Spanish* into divers other languages, we will here onely make an abridgement or briefe rehearsall thereof.

Portugal furnished and set foorth under the conduct of the duke of *Medina Sidonia* generall of the Fleete, ten Galeons, two Zabraes, 1300. Mariners, 3300. souldiers, 300. great pieces, with all requisite furniture.

Biscay, under the conduct of *John Martines de Ricalde* Admiral of the whole Fleete, set forth tenne Galeons, 4. Pataches, 700. mariners, 2000. souldiers, 250. great pieces, &c.

Guipusco, under the conduct of *Michael de Oquendo,* tenne Galeons, 4. Pataches, 700. mariners, 2000. souldiers, 310. great pieces.

Italy with the *Levant* Islands, under *Maritine de Vertendona,* 10. Galeons, 800. mariners, 200. souldiers, 310. great pieces, &c.

Castile, under *Diego Flores de Valdez,* 14. Galeons, two Pataches, 1700. mariners, 2400. souldiers, and 380. great pieces, &c.

Andaluzia, under the conduct of *Petro de Valdez,* 10. Galeons, one Patache, 800. mariners, 2400. souldiers, 280. great pieces, &c.

Item, under the conduct of *John Lopez de Medina,* 23. great *Flemish* hulkes, with 700 mariners, 3200. souldiers, and 400. great pieces.

Item, under *Hugo de Moncada,* foure Galliasses containing 1200. gally-slaves, 460. mariners, 870. souldiers, 200. great pieces, &c.

Item, under *Diego de Mandrana,* foure Gallies of *Portugall,* with 888. gally-slaves, 360. mariners, 20. great pieces, and other requisite furniture.

Item, under *Anthonie de Mendoza,* 22. Pataches and Zabraes, with 574. mariners, 488. souldiers, and 193. great pieces.

Besides the ships aforementioned there were 20. caravels rowed with oares, being appointed to performe necessary services unto the greater ships: insomuch that all the ships appertayning [Ddd3] to this Navie amounted unto the summe of 150. eche one being sufficiently provided of furniture and victuals.

The number of Mariners in the saide Fleete were above 8000. of slaves 2088. of souldiers 20000. (besides noblemen and gentlemen voluntaries) of great cast pieces 2650. The foresaid ships were of an huge and incredible capacitie and receipt. For the whole Fleete was large ynough to containe the burthen of 60. thousand tunnes.

The Galeons were 64. in number, being of an huge bignesse, and very stately built, being of marveilous force also, and so high, that they resembled great castles, most fit to defend themselves and to withstand any assault, but in giving any other ships the encounter farre inferiour unto the *English* and *Dutch* ships, which can with great dexteritie wield and turne themselves at all assayes. The upperworke of the said Galeons was of thicknesse and strength sufficient to beare off musket-shot. The lower worke and the timbers thereof were out of measure strong, being framed of plankes and ribs foure or five foote in thicknesse, insomuch that no bullets could pierce them, but such as were discharged hard at hand: which afterward prooved true, for a great number of bullets were founde to sticke fast within the massie substance of those thicke plankes. Great and well pitched Cables were twined about the masts of their shippes, to strengthen them against the battery of shot.

The Galliasses were of such bignesse, that they contained within them chambers, chapels, turrets, pulpits, and other commodities of great houses. The Galliasses were rowed with great oares, there being in eche one of them 300. slaves for the same purpose, and were able to do great service with the force of their Ordinance. All these together with the residue aforenamed were furnished and beautified with trumpets, streamers, banners, warlike ensignes, and other such like ornaments.

Their pieces of brasen ordinance were 1600. and of yron a 1000.

The bullets thereto belonging were 120. thousand.

Item of gun-poulder 5600. *quintals*. Of matche 1200. *quintals*.

Of muskets and kaleivers 7000. Of haleberts and partisans 10000.

Moreover they had great store of canons, double-canons, culverings and field-pieces for land services.

Likewise they were provided of all instruments necessary on land to conveigh and transport their furniture from place to place; as namely of carts, wheeles, wagons, &c. Also they had spades, mattocks and baskets to set pioners on worke. They had in like sort great store of mules and horses, and whatsoever else was requisite for a land-armie. They were so well stored of biscuit, that for the space of halfe a yeere, they might allow eche person in the whole Fleete halfe a quintall every moneth; whereof the whole summe amounteth unto an hundreth thousand quintals.

Likewise of wine they had 147. thousand pipes, sufficient also for halfe a yeere's expedition. Of bacon 6500. quintals. Of cheese three thousand quintals. Besides fish, rise, beanes, pease, oile, vinegar, &c.

Moreover they had 12000. pipes of fresh-water, and all other necessary provision, as namely candles, lanternes, lampes, sailes, hempe, oxe-hides and lead to stop holes that should be made with the battery of gunshot. To be short, they brought all things expedient either for a Fleete by sea, or for an armie by land.

This Navie (as *Diego Pimentelli* afterward confessed) was esteemed by the King himselfe to containe 32000. persons, and to cost him every day 30. thousand ducates.

There were in the said Navie five *terzaes* of *Spaniards*, (which *terzaes* the Frenchmen call Regiments) under the commaund of five governours termed by the *Spaniards*, Masters of the field, and amongst the rest there were many olde and expert souldiers chosen out of the garisons of *Sicilie, Naples*, and *Tercera*. Their Captaines or Colonels were *Diego Pimentelli, Don Francisco de Toledo, Don Alonco de Lucon, Don Nicolas de Isla, Don Augustin de Mexia*; who had eche of them 32. companies under their conduct. Besides the which companies there were many bands also of *Castilians* and *Portugals*, every one of which had their peculiar governours, captaines, officers, colours and weapons.

It was not lawfull for any man, under grievous penaltie, to cary any women or harlots in the Fleete: for which cause the women hired certaine shippes, wherein they sailed after the Navie: some of the which being driven by tempest arrived upon the coast of *France*.

The generall of this mightie Navie, was *Don Alonso Perez de Guzman* duke of *Medina Sidonia*, Lord of *S. Lucar*, and knight of the golden Fleece: by reason that the Marques of *santa Cruz* appointed for the same dignitie, deceased before the time.

John Martines de Ricalde was Admirall of the Fleete. [Ddd3v]

Francis Bovadilla was chiefe Marshall: who all of them had their officers fit and requisite for the guiding and managing of such a multitude. Likewise *Martin Alorcon* was appointed Vicar generall of the Inquisition, being accompanied with more then a hundreth Monkes, to wit, *Jesuites, Capuchines*, and friers *mendicant*. Besides whom also there were Phisitians, Chirurgians, Apothecaries, and whatsoever else perteined unto the hospitall.

Over and besides the forenamed governours and officers being men of chiefe note, there were 124. very noble and worthy Gentlemen, which went voluntarily of their owne costs and charges, to the ende they might see fashions, learne experience, and attaine unto glory. Amongst whom was the prince of *Ascoli, Alonzo de Leiva*, the marques *de Pennafiel*, the marques *de Ganes*, the marques *de Barlango*, count *de Paredes*, count *de Yelvas*, and divers other marquees and earles of the honourable families of *Mendoza*, of *Toledo*, of *Pachieco*, of *Cordova*, of *Guzman*, of *Manricques*, and a great number of others.

While the *Spaniards* were furnishing this their Navie, the duke of *Parma*, at the direction of king *Philip*, made great preparation in the low Countreys, to give ayd and assistance unto the *Spaniards*; building ships for the same purpose, and sending for Pilots and ship-wrights out of *Italy*.

In *Flanders* hee caused certaine deepe chanels to be made, and among the rest the chanell of *Yper* commonly called *Yper-lee*, employing some thousands of workemen about that service: to the end that by the said chanel he might transport ships from *Antwerp* and *Ghendt* to *Bruges*, where hee had assembled above a hundreth small ships called hoyes being well stored with victuals, which hoyes hee was determined to have brought into the sea by the way of *Sluys*, or else to have conveyed them by the saide *Yper-lee* being now of greater depth, into any port of *Flanders* whatsoever.

In the river of *Waten* he caused 70. ships with flat bottomes to be built, every one of which should serve to cary 30. horses, having eche of them bridges likewise for the horses to come on boord, or to goe foorth on land. Of the same fashion he had provided 200. other vessels at *Neiuport*, but not so great. And at *Dunkerk* hee procured 28. ships of warre, such as were there to be had, and caused a sufficient number of Mariners to be levied at *Hamburg, Breme, Emden*, and at other places. Hee put in the ballast of the said ships, great store of beames of thicke plankes, being hollow and beset with yron pikes beneath, but on eche side full of claspes and hookes, to joyne them together.

Hee had likewise at *Greveling* provided 20. thousand of caske, which in a short space might be compact and joyned together with nailes and cords, and reduced into the forme of a bridge. To be short, whatsoever things were requisite for the making of bridges, and for the barring and stopping up of havens' mouthes with stakes, posts, and other meanes, he commanded to be made ready. Moreover not farre from *Neiuport* haven, he had caused a great pile of wooden fagots to be layd, and other furniture to be brought for the rearing up of a mount. The most part of his ships conteined two ovens apiece to bake bread in, with a great number of sadles, bridles, and such other like apparell for horses. They had horses likewise, which after their landing should serve to convey, and draw engines, field-pieces, and other warlike provisions.

Neere unto *Neiuport* he had assembled an armie, over the which he had ordained *Camillo de Monte* to be Camp-master. This army consisted of 30. bands or ensignes of *Italians*, of tenne bands of *Wallons*, eight of *Scots*, and eight of *Burgundians*, all which together amount unto 56. bands, every band containing a hundreth persons. Neare unto *Dixmud* there were mustered 80. bands of *Dutch* men, sixtie of *Spaniards*, sixe of high *Germans*, and seven bands of *English* fugitives, under the conduct of sir *William Stanlie* an English knight.

In the suburbes of *Cortreight* there were 4000. horsemen together with their horses in a readinesse: and at *Waten* 900. horses, with the troupe of the Marques *del Gwasto* Captaine generall of the horsemen.

Unto this famous expedition and presupposed victorie, many potentates, princes, and honourable personages hied themselves: out of *Spaine* the prince of *Melito* called the duke of *Pastrana* and taken to be the sonne of one *Ruygomes de Silva*, but in very deed accompted among the number of king *Philip's* base sonnes. Also the Marques of *Burgrave*, one of the sonnes of Archduke *Ferdinand* and *Philippa Welsera. Vespasian Gonsaga* of the family of *Mantua*, being for chivalry a man of great renowne, and heretofore Vice-roy in *Spaine.* Item *John Medices* base sonne unto the duke of *Florence.* And *Amadas* of *Savoy*, the duke of *Savoy* his base sonne, with many others of inferiour degrees.

Likewise Pope *Sixtus quintus* for the setting forth of the foresaid expedition, as they use to do against *Turkes* and infidels, published a *Cruzado*, with most ample indulgences which printed in great numbers. These vaine buls the *English* and *Dutchmen* deriding, sayd that the devill at [Ddd4] all passages lay in ambush like a thiefe, no whit regarding such letters of safe conduct. Some there be which affirme that the Pope had bestowed the realme of *England* with the title of *Defensor fidei*, upon the king of *Spaine*, giving him charge to invade it upon this condition, that hee should enjoy the conquered realm, as a vassal and tributarie, in that regard, unto the sea of *Rome*. To this purpose the said Pope proffered a million of gold, the one halfe thereof to be paied in readie money, and the other halfe when the realme of *England* or any famous port thereof were subdued. And for the greater furtherance of the whole businesse, he dispatched one D. *Allen* an *English*man (whom hee had made Cardinall for the same ende and purpose) into the Low countries, unto whom he committed the administration of all matters ecclesiasticall throughout *England*. This *Allen* being enraged against his owne native countrey, caused the Pope's bull to be translated into *English*, meaning upon the arrival of the *Spanish* fleete, to have it so published in *England*. By which Bull the excommunications of the two former Popes were confirmed, and the Queene's most sacred Majestie was by them most unjustly deprived of all princely titles and dignities, her subjects being enjoined to performe obedience unto the duke of *Parma*, and unto the Pope's Legate.

But that all matters might be performed with greater secrecie, and that the whole expedition might seeme rather to be intended against the Low countries, then against *England*, and that the English people might be perswaded that all was but bare words and threatnings, and that nought would come to effect, there was a solemne meeting appointed at *Borborch* in *Flanders* for a treatie of peace betweene her majestie and the Spanish king.

Against which treatie the united provinces making open protestation, used all meanes possible to hinder it, alleaging that it was more requisite to consult how the enemie now pressing upon them might be repelled from off their frontiers. Howbeit some there were in *England* that greatly urged and prosecuted this league, saying, that it would be very commodious unto the state of the realme, as well in regard of traffique and navigation, as for the avoiding of great expenses to maintaine the warres, affirming also, that at the same time peace might easily and upon reasonable conditions be obtained of the

Spaniard. Others thought by this meanes to divert some other way, or to keepe backe the navy now comming upon them, and so to escape the danger of that tempest. Howsoever it was, the duke of *Parma* by these wiles enchanted and dazeled the eyes of many *English* and *Dutch* men that were desirous of peace: whereupon it came to passe, that *England* and the united provinces prepared indeed some defence to withstand that dreadfull expedition and huge Armada, but nothing in comparison of the great danger which was to be feared, albeit the constant report of the whole expedition had continued rife among them for a long time before. Howbeit they gave eare unto the relation of certaine that sayd, that this navie was provided to conduct and waft over the *Indian* Fleets: which seemed the more probable because the *Spaniards* were deemed not to be men of so small discretion as to adventure those huge and monstrous ships upon the shallow and dangerous chanel of *England.*

At length when as the *French* king about the end of May signified unto her Majestie in plaine termes that she should stand upon her guard, because he was now most certainly enformed, that there was so dangerous an invasion imminent upon her realme, that he feared much least all her land and sea-forces would be sufficient to withstand it, &c. then began the Queen's Majestie more carefully to gather her forces together, and to furnish her own ships of warre, and the principall ships of her subjects with souldiers, weapons, and other necessary provision. The greatest and strongest ships of the whole navy she sent unto *Plimmouth* under the conduct of the right honorable Lord *Charles Howard*, lord high Admirall of *England*, &c. Under whom the renoumed Knight Sir *Francis Drake* was appointed Vice-admiral. The number of these ships was about an hundreth. The lesser ships being 30. or 40. in number, and under the conduct of the lord *Henry Seimer* were commanded to lie between *Dover* and *Caleis.*

On land likewise throughout the whole realme, souldiers were mustered and trained in all places, and were committed unto the most resolute and faithfull captaines. And whereas it was commonly given out that the *Spaniard* having once united himselfe unto the duke of *Parma*, ment to invade by the river of Thames, there was at Tilburie in Essex over-against Gravesend, a mightie army encamped, and on both sides of the river fortifications were erected, according to the prescription of *Frederike Genebelli* an *Italian* enginier. Likewise there were certaine ships brought to make a bridge, though it were very late first. Unto the sayd army came in proper person the Queen's most roiall Majestie, representing *Tomyris* that Scythian warlike princesse, or rather divine *Pallas* herselfe. Also there were other such armies levied in *England*.

The principall catholique Recusants (least they should stirre up any tumult in the time of the *Spanish* invasion) were sent to remaine at certaine convenient places, as namely in the Isle of [Ddd4v] *Ely* and at *Wisbich*. And some of them were sent unto other places, to wit, unto sundry bishops and noblemen, where they were kept from endangering the state of the commonwealth, and of her sacred Majestie, who of her most gracious clemencie gave expresse commandement, that they should be intreated with all humanitie and friendship.

The provinces of *Holland* and *Zeland*, &c. giving credite unto their intelligence out of *Spain*, made preparation to defend themselves: but because the *Spanish* ships were described unto them to be so huge, they relied partly upon the shallow and dangerous seas all along their coasts. Wherfore they stood most in doubt of the duke of *Parma* his small and flat-bottomed ships. Howbeit they had all their ships of warre to the number of 90. and above, in a readinesse for all assayes: the greater part whereof were of a small burthen, as being more meete to saile upon their rivers and shallow seas: and with these ships they besieged all the havens in *Flanders*, beginning at the mouth of *Scheld*, or from the towne of *Lillo*, and holding on to *Greveling* and almost unto *Caleis*, and fortified all their sea-townes with strong garrisons.

Against the *Spanish* fleet's arrivall, they had provided 25. or 30. good ships, committing the government of them unto Admirall *Lonck*, whom they commanded to joine himselfe unto the lord *Henry Seymer*, lying betweene *Dover* and *Cales*. And when as the foresaid ships, (whereof the greater part besieged the haven of *Dunkerke*) were driven by tempest into *Zeland*, *Justin* of *Nassau* the Admiral of *Zeland* supplied that squadron with 35. ships being of no great burthen, but excellently furnished with gunnes, mariners and souldiers in great abundance, and especially with 1200. brave Musquetiers, having bene accustomed unto sea-fights, and being chosen out of all their companies for the same purpose: and so the said *Justin* of *Nassau* kept such diligent ward in that Station that the duke of *Parma* could not issue foorth with his navy into the sea out of any part of *Flanders*.

In the meanewhile the *Spanish Armada* set saile out of the haven of *Lisbon* upon the 19. of May, *An. Dom.* 1588. under the conduct of

the duke of *Medina Sidonia*, directing their course for the Baie of
Curunna, alias the *Groine* in *Gallicia*, where they tooke in souldiers
and warlike provision, this port being in *Spaine* the neerest unto
England. As they were sailing along, there arose such a mightie tempest, that the whole Fleete was dispersed, so that when the duke was
returned unto his company, he could not escry above 80. ships in all,
whereunto the residue by litle and litle joyned themselves, except
eight which had their mastes blowen over-boord. One of the foure
gallies of *Portingal* escaped very hardly, retiring herselfe into the
haven. The other three were upon the coast of *Baion* in *France*, by
the assistance and courage of one *David Gwin* an English captive
(whom the *French* and *Turkish* slaves aided in the same enterprise)
utterly disabled and vanquished: one of the three being first overcome, which conquered the two other, with the slaughter of their
governours and souldiers, and among the rest of *Don Diego de
Mandrana* with sundry others: and so those slaves arriving in *France*
with the three Gallies, set themselves at libertie.

The navy having refreshed themselves at the *Groine*, and receiving
daily commandement from the king to hasten their journey, hoised
up sailes the 11. day of July, and so holding on their course till the
19. of the same moneth, they came then unto the mouth of the narow
seas or English chanel. From whence (striking their sailes in the meaneseason) they dispatched certaine of their smal ships unto the duke of
Parma. At the same time the *Spanish* Fleete was escried by an English
pinasse, captaine whereof was M. *Thomas Fleming*, after they had
bene advertised of the *Spaniards'* expedition by their scoutes and
espials, which having ranged along the coast of *Spaine*, were lately
returned home into *Plimmouth* for a new supply of victuals and other
necessaries, who considering the foresayd tempest, were of opinion
that the navy being of late dispersed and tossed up and downe the maine
Ocean, was by no means able to performe their intended voiage.

Moreover, the L. *Charles Howard* L. high admiral of *England*
had received letters from the court, signifying unto him that her
Majestie was advertised that the *Spanish* Fleete would not come foorth,
nor was to be any longer expected for, and therefore, that upon her
Majestie's commandement he must send backe foure of her tallest and
strongest ships unto Chattam.

The lord high Admiral of *England* being thus on the sudden,
namely upon the 19. of July about foure of the clocke in the afternoone,

enformed by the pinasse of captaine *Fleming* aforesaid, of the *Span-iards'* approch, with all speed and diligence possible he warped his ships, and caused his mariners and souldiers (the greater part of whom was absent for the cause aforesayd) to come on boord, and that with great trouble and difficultie, insomuch that the lord Admiral himselfe was faine to lie without in the road with six ships onely all that night, after the which many others came foorth of the haven. The very next day being the 20. of July about high noone, was the *Spanish* Fleete escried by the English, which with a Southwest wind came sailing along, and [Ddd5] passed by *Plimmouth:* in which regard (according to the judgement of many skilful navigators) they greatly overshot themselves, whereas it had bene more commodious for them to have staied themselves there, considering that the Englishmen being as yet unprovided, greatly relied upon their owne forces, and knew not the estate of the Spanish navy. Moreover, this was the most convenient port of all others, where they might with greater securitie have bene advertised of the English forces, and how the commons of the land stood affected, and might have stirred up some mutinie, so that hither they should have bent all their puissance, and from hence the duke of *Parma* might more easily have conveied his ships.

But this they were prohibited to doe by the king and his counsell, and were expressely commanded to unite themselves unto the souldiers and ships of the said duke of *Parma,* and so to bring their purpose to effect. Which was thought to be the most easie and direct course, for that they imagined that the English and Dutch men would be utterly daunted and dismaied thereat, and would each man of them retire unto his owne Province and Porte for the defence thereof, and transporting the armie of the duke under the protection of their huge navy, they might invade *England.*

It is reported that the chiefe commanders in the navy, and those which were more skilfull in navigation, to wit, *John Martines de Ricalde, Diego Flores de Valdez,* and divers others found fault that they were bound unto so strict directions and instructions, because that in such a case many particular accidents ought to concurre and to be respected at one and the same instant, that is to say, the opportunitie of the wind, weather, time, tide, and ebbe, wherein they might saile from *Flanders* to *England.* Oftentimes also the darkenesse and light, the situation of places, the depths and shoulds were to be considered: all which especially depended upon the conveniencie of the windes, and were by so much the more dangerous.

But it seemeth that they were enjoined by their commission to ancre neere unto, or about *Caleis*, whither the duke of *Parma* with his ships and all his warrelike provision was to resort, and while the English and Spanish great ships were in the midst of their conflict, to passe by, and to land his souldiers upon the Downes.

The Spanish captives reported that they were determined first to have entred the river of Thames, and thereupon to have passed with small ships up to London, supposing that they might easily winne that rich and flourishing Citie being but meanely fortified and inhabited with Citizens not accustomed to the warres, who durst not withstand their first encounter, hoping moreover to finde many rebels against her Majestie and popish catholiques, or some favourers of the Scottish queene (which was not long before most justly beheaded) who might be instruments of sedition.

Thus often advertising the duke of *Parma* of their approch, the 20. of July they passed by Plimmouth, which the English ships pursuing and getting the wind of them, gave them the chase and the encounter, and so both Fleets frankly exchanged their bullets.

The day following which was the 21. of July, the English ships approched within musquet shot of the Spanish: at what time the lorde *Charles Howard* most hotly and valiantly discharged his Ordinance upon the Spanish Vice-admirall. The Spaniards then well perceiving the nimblenesse of the English ships in discharging upon the enimie on all sides, gathered themselves close into the forme of an halfe moone, and slackened their sailes, least they should outgoe any of their companie. And while they were proceeding on in this maner, one of their great Galliasses was so furiously battered with shot, that the whole navy was faine to come up rounder together for the safeguard thereof: whereby it came to passe that the principall Galleon of *Sivill* (wherein *Don Pedro de Valdez, Vasques de Silva, Alonzao de Sayas*, and other noble men were embarqued) falling foule of another shippe, had her fore-mast broken, and by that meanes was not able to keepe way with the Spanish Fleete, neither would the sayde Fleete stay to succour it, but left the distressed Galeon behind. The lord Admirall of *England* when he saw this ship of *Valdez*, and thought she had bene voyd of Mariners and Souldiers, taking with him as many shippes as he could, passed by it, that he might not loose sight of the Spanish Fleet that night. For sir *Francis Drake* (who was notwithstanding appointed to beare out his lanterne that night) was giving of chase unto five great Hulkes which had separated themselves from the Spanish Fleete: but finding them to be Easterlings, he dismissed them. The lord Admirall all that night following the Spanish lanterne instead of the English, found himselfe in the morning to be in the midst of his enimie's Fleete, but when he perceived it, hee cleanly conveyed himselfe out of that great danger.

The day folowing, which was the two and twentie of July, Sir *Francis Drake* espied *Valdez* his shippe, whereunto hee sent foorth his pinnasse, and being advertised that *Valdez* him- [Ddd5v] selfe was there, and 450. persons with him, he sent him word that he should yeeld himselfe. *Valdez* for his honor's sake caused certaine conditions to be propounded unto *Drake:* who answered *Valdez* that he was not now at laisure to make any long *parle*, but if he would yeeld himselfe, he should find him friendly and tractable: howbeit if he had resolved to die in fight, he should proove *Drake* to be no dastard.

Upon which answere *Valdez* and his company understanding that they were fallen into the hands of fortunate *Drake*, being mooved with the renoume and celebritie of his name, with one consent yeelded themselves, and found him very favourable unto them. Then *Valdez* with 40. or 50. noblemen and gentlemen pertaining unto him, came on boord sir *Francis Drake's* ship. The residue of his company were caried unto *Plimmouth*, where they were detained a yere and an halfe for their ransome.

Valdez comming unto *Drake* and humbly kissing his hand protested unto him, that he and his had resolved to die in battell, had they not by good fortune fallen into his power, whom they knew to be right curteous and gentle, and whom they had heard by generall report to bee most favourable unto his vanquished foe: insomuch that he sayd it was to bee doubted whether his enimies had more cause to admire and love him for his great, valiant, and prosperous exploites, or to dread him for his singular felicitie and wisedom, which ever attended upon him in the warres, and by the which hee had attained unto so great honour. With that *Drake* embraced him and gave him very honourable entertainement, feeding him at his owne table, and lodging him in his cabbin.

Here *Valdez* began to recount unto *Drake* the forces of all the Spanish Fleet, and how foure mightie Gallies were separated by tempest from them: and also how they were determined first to have put into *Plimmouth* haven, not expecting to bee repelled thence by the English ships which they thought could by no meanes withstand their impregnable forces, perswading themselves that by means of their huge Fleete, they were become lords and commaunders of the maine Ocean. For which cause they marveled much how the Englishmen in their small ships durst approch within musket shot of the Spaniards' mightie woodden castles, gathering the wind of them with many other such like attempts.

Immediately after, *Valdez* and his company, being a man of principal authoritie in the Spanish Fleete, and being descended of one and the same familie with that *Valdez*, which in the yeere 1574. besieged *Leiden* in Holland, were sent captives into *England*. There were in the sayd ship 55. thousand ducates in ready money of the Spanish king's gold, which the souldiers merily shared among themselves.

The same day was set on fire one of their greatest shippes, being Admirall of the squadron of *Guipusco*, and being the shippe of *Michael de Oquendo* Vice-admirall of the whole Fleete, which contained great store of gunnepowder and other warrelike provision. The upper part onely of this shippe was burnt, and all the persons therein contained (except a very few) were consumed with fire. And thereupon it was taken by the English, and brought into *England* with a number of miserable burnt and skorched Spaniards. Howbeit the gunpowder (to the great admiration of all men) remained whole and unconsumed.

In the meaneseason the lord Admirall of *England* in his ship called the *Arke-royall*, all that night pursued the Spaniards so neere, that in the morning hee was almost left alone in the enimie's Fleete, and it was foure of the clocke at afternoone before the residue of the English Fleet could overtake him.

At the same time *Hugo de Moncada* governour of the foure Galliasses, made humble sute unto the Duke of *Medina* that he might be licenced to encounter the Admirall of *England:* which libertie the duke thought not good to permit unto him, because hee was loth to exceed the limites of his commission and charge.

Upon Tuesday which was the three and twentie of July, the navy being come over aginst *Portland*, the wind began to turne Northerly, insomuch that the Spaniards had a fortunate and fit gale to invade the English. But the Englishmen having lesser and nimbler Ships, recovered againe the vantage of the winde from the Spaniards, whereat the Spaniards seemed to bee more incensed to fight then before. But when the English Fleete had continually and without intermission from morning to night, beaten and battered them with all their shot both great and small: the Spaniardes uniting themselves, gathered their whole Fleete close together into a roundell, so that it was apparant that they ment not as yet to invade others, but onely to defend themselves and to make hast unto the place prescribed unto them, which was neere unto *Dunkerk*, that they might joine forces with the duke of *Parma*, who was determined to have proceeded secretly with his small shippes under the shadow [Ddd6] and protection of the great ones, and so had intended circumpsectly to performe the whole expedition.

This was the most furious and bloodie skirmish of all, in which the lord Admirall of *England* continued fighting amidst his enimie's Fleete, and seeing one of his Captaines afarre off, hee spake unto him in these wordes: Oh *George* what doest thou? Wilt thou nowe frustrate my hope and opinion conceived of thee? Wilt thou forsake mee nowe? With which wordes hee being enflamed, approched foorthwith, encountered the enemie, and did the part of a most valiant Captaine. His name was *George Fenner*, a man that had bene conversant in many Sea-fights.

In this conflict there was a certaine great *Venetian* ship with other small ships surprised and taken by the English.

The English navie in the meanewhile increased, whereunto out of all Havens of the Realme resorted ships and men: for they all with one accord came flocking thither as unto a set field, where immortall fame and glory was to be attained, and faithfull service to bee performed unto their prince and countrey.

In which number there were many great and honourable personages, as namely, the Erles of *Oxford*, of *Northumberland*, of *Cumberland*, &c. with many Knights and Gentlemen: to wit, Sir *Thomas Cecill*, Sir *Robert Cecill*, Sir *Walter Raleigh*, Sir *William Hatton*, Sir *Horatio Palavicini*, Sir *Henry Brooke*, Sir *Robert Carew*, Sir *Charles Blunt*, Master *Ambrose Willoughbie*, Master *Henry Nowell*, Master *Thomas Gerard*, Master *Henry Dudley*, Master *Edward Darcie*, Master *Arthur Gorge*, Master *Thomas Woodhouse*, Master *William Harvie*, &c. And so it came to passe that the number of the English shippes amounted unto an hundreth: which when they were come before Dover, were increased to an hundred and thirtie, being notwithstanding of no proportionable bignesse to encounter with the Spaniards, except two or three and twentie of the Queene's greater shippes, which onely, by reason of their presence, bred an opinion in the Spaniardes' mindes concerning the power of the English Fleet: the mariners and souldiers whereof were esteemed to be twelve thousand.

The foure and twentie of July when as the sea was calme, and no winde stirring, the fight was onely betweene the foure great Galleasses and the English shippes, which being rowed with Oares, had great vauntage of the sayde English shippes, which notwithstanding for all that would not bee forced to yeeld, but discharged their chaine-shot to cut asunder their Cables and Cordage of the Galleasses, with many other such Stratagemes. They were nowe constrained to send their men on land for a newe supplie of Gunne-powder, whereof they were in great skarcitie, by reason they had so frankely spent the greater part in the former conflicts.

The same day, a Counsell being assembled, it was decreed that the English Fleete should bee devided into foure squadrons: the principall whereof was committed unto the lord Admirall: the second, to Sir *Francis Drake*: the third, to Captaine *Hawkins*: the fourth, to Captaine *Frobisher*.

The Spaniards in their sailing observed very diligent and good order, sayling three and foure, and somtimes more ships in a ranke, and folowing close up one after another, and the stronger and greater ships protecting the lesser.

The five and twentie of July when the Spaniardes were come over-against the Isle of *Wight*, the lord Admirall of *England* being accompanied with his best ships, (namely the Lion, Captaine whereof was the lord *Thomas Howard:* The *Elizabeth Jonas* under the commandement of Sir *Robert Southwel* sonne-in-lawe unto the lord Admirall: the *Beare* under the lord *Sheffield* nephew unto the lord Admirall: the *Victorie* under Captaine *Barker*: and the *Galeon Leicester* under the forenamed Captaine *George Fenner*) with great valour and dreadfull thundering of shot, encountered the Spanish Admiral being in the very midst of all his Fleet. Which when the Spaniard perceived, being assisted with his strongest ships, he came forth and entered a terrible combate with the English: for they bestowed each on other the broad sides, and mutually discharged all their Ordinance, being within one hundred, or an hundred and twentie yards one of another.

At length the Spaniardes hoised up their sayles, and againe gathered themselves up close into the forme of a roundel. In the meanewhile Captaine *Frobisher* had engaged himselfe into a most dangerous conflict. Whereupon the lord Admirall comming to succour him, found that hee had valiantly and discreetly behaved himselfe, and that hee had wisely and in good time [Ddd6v] [given] over the fight, because that after so great a batterie he had sustained no damage.

For which cause the day following, being the sixe and twentie of July, the lord Admirall rewarded him with the order of knighthood, together with the lord *Thomas Howard*, the lord *Sheffield*, M. *John Hawkins* and others.

The same day the lord Admirall received intelligence from Newhaven in *France*, by certaine of his Pinnasses, that all things were quiet in *France*, and that there was no preparation of sending aide unto the Spaniards, which was greatly feared from the *Guisan* faction, and from the Leaguers: but there was a false rumour spread all about, that the *Spaniards* had conquered *England*.

The seven and twentie of July, the *Spaniards* about the sunnesetting were come over-against Dover, and rode at ancre within the sight of *Caleis*, intending to hold on for *Dunkerk*, expecting there to joyne with the duke of *Parma* his forces, without which they were able to doe litle or nothing.

Likewise the English Fleete following up hard upon them, ancred just by them within culvering-shot. And here the lord *Henry Seymer* united himselfe unto the lord Admiral with his fleete of 30. ships which road before the mouth of Thames.

As the Spanish navie therefore lay at ancre, the duke of *Medina* sent certaine messengers unto the duke of *Parma*, with whom upon that occasion many Noblemen and Gentlemen went to refresh themselves on land: and amongst the rest of the prince of *Ascoli*, being accounted the king's base sonne, and a very proper and towardly yong gentleman, to his great good, went on shore, who was by so much the more fortunate, in that hee had not opportunitie to returne on boord the same ship, out of which he was departed, because that in returning home it was cast away upon the Irish coast, with all the persons contained therein.

The duke of *Parma* being advertised of the Spanish Fleet's arrivall upon the coast of *England*, made all the haste hee could to bee present himselfe in this expedition for the performance of his charge: vainely perswading himselfe that nowe by the meanes of Cardinall *Allen*, hee should be crowned king of *England*, and for that cause hee had resigned the governement of the Lowe countries unto Count *Mansfeld* the elder. And having made his vowes unto S. *Mary* of *Hall* in *Henault* (whom he went to visite for his blind devotion's sake) hee returned toward *Bruges* the 28. of July.

The next day travelling to *Dunkerk* hee heard the thundering Ordinance of either Fleet: and the same evening being come to *Dix-mud*, hee was given to understand the hard successe of the Spanish Fleete.

Upon Tuesday which was the thirtieth of July, about high noone, hee came to *Dunkerk*, when as all the Spanish Fleete was now passed by: neither durst any of his ships in the meane space come foorth to assist the sayd Spanish Fleete for feare of five and thirtie warrelike ships of *Holland* and *Zeland*, which there kept watch and warde under the conduct of the Admirall *Justin* of *Nassau*.

The foresayd five and thirtie shippes were furnished with most cunning mariners and olde expert souldiers, amongst the which were twelve hundred Musketiers, whom the States had chosen out of all their garisons, and whom they knew to have bene heretofore experienced in sea-fights.

This navie was given especially in charge not to suffer any shippe to come out of the Haven, nor to permit any Zabraes, Pataches or other small vessels of the Spanish Fleete (which were more likely to aide the *Dunkerkers*) to enter thereinto, for the greater ships were not to be feared by reason of the shallow sea in that place. Howbeit the prince of *Parma* his forces being as yet unreadie, were not come on boord his shippes, onely the English Fugitives being seven hundred in number under the conduct of Sir *William Stanley*, came in fit time to have bene embarked, because they hoped to give the first assault against *England*. The residue shewd themselves unwilling and loath to depart, because they sawe but a few mariners, who were by contraint drawne into this expedition, and also because they had very bare provision of bread, drinke, and other necessary victuals.

Moreover, the shippes of *Holland* and *Zeland* stood continually in their sight, threatening shot and powder, and many inconveniences unto them: for feare of which shippes, the Mariners and Sea-men secretly withdrew themselves both day and night, least that the duke of *Parma* his souldiers should compell them by maine force to goe on boord, and to breake through the *Hollander's* Fleete, which all of them judged to bee impossible by reason of the straightnesse of the Haven. [Eeel]

But it seemeth that the Duke of *Parma* and the Spaniards grounded

upon a vaine and presumptuous expectation, that all the ships of
England and of the Low countreys would at the first sight of the
Spanish and *Dunkerk* Navie have betaken themselves to flight, yeelding them sea roome, and endevouring onely to defend themselves, their
havens, and sea coasts from invasion. Wherefore their intent and purpose was, that the Duke of *Parma* in his small and flat-bottomed
shippes, should as it were under the shadow and wings of the Spanish
fleet, cónvey over all his troupes, armour, and warlike provision, and
with their forces so united, should invade *England*; or while the
English fleet were busied in fight against the Spanish, should enter
upon any part of the coast, which he thought to be most convenient.
Which invasion (as the captives afterward confessed) the Duke of
Parma thought first to have attempted by the river of *Thames*; upon
the bankes whereof having at his first arrivall landed twenty or thirty
thousand of his principall souldiers, he supposed that he might
easily have woonne the Citie of *London*; both because his small
shippes should have followed and assisted his land-forces, and also for
that the Citie it-selfe was but meanely fortified and easie to overcome,
by reason of the Citizens' delicacie and discontinuance from the warres,
who with continuall and constant labour might be vanquished, if
they yeelded not at the first assault. They were in good hope also to
have mette with some rebels against her Majestie, and such as were
discontented with the present state, as Papists, and others. Likewise
they looked for ayde from the favourers of the Scottish Queene, who
was not long before put to death; all which they thought would have
stirred up seditions and factions.

Whenas therefore the Spanish fleet rode at anker before *Caleis*, to
the end they might consult with the Duke of *Parma* what was best
to be done according to the King's commandement, and the present
estate of their affaires, and had now (as we will afterward declare)
purposed upon the second of August being Friday, with one power
and consent to have put their intended business in practise; the L.
Admirall of *England* being admonished by her Majestie's letters from
the Court, thought it most expedient either to drive the Spanish fleet
from that place, or at leastwise to give them the encounter: and for
that cause (according to her Majestie's prescription) he tooke forthwith
eight of his woorst and basest ships which came next to hand, and
disburthening them of all things which seemed to be of any value, filled
them with gun-powder, pitch, brimstone, and with other combustible

and firy matter; and charging all their ordinance with powder, bullets, and stones, he sent the sayd ships upon the 28 of July being Sunday, about two of the clocke after midnight, with the winde and tide against the Spanish fleet: which when they had proceeded a good space, being forsaken of the Pilots, and set on fire, were directly carried upon the King of *Spaine's* Navie: which fire in the dead of the night put the Spaniards into such a perplexity and horrour (for they feared lest they were like unto those terrible ships, which *Frederic Jenebelli* three yeeres before, at the siege of *Antwerpe,* had furnished with gunpowder, stones, and dreadfull engines, for the dissolution of the Duke of *Parma* his bridge, built upon the river of *Scheld*) that cutting their cables whereon their ankers were fastened, and hoising up their sailes, they betooke themselves very confusedly unto the maine sea.

In this sudden confusion, the principall and greatest of the foure galliasses falling fowle of another ship, lost her rudder: for which cause when she could not be guided any longer, she was by the force of the tide cast into a certaine showld upon the shore of *Caleis,* where she was immediatly assaulted by divers English pinasses, hoyes, and drumblers.

And as they lay battering of her with their ordinance, and durst not boord her, the L. Admirall sent thither his long boat with an hundreth choise souldiers under the command of Captaine *Amias Preston.* Upon whose approch their fellowes being more emboldened, did offer to boord the galliasse: against whom the governour thereof and Captaine of all the foure galliasses, *Hugo de Moncada,* stoutly opposed himselfe, fighting by so much the more valiantly, in that he hoped presently to be succoured by the Duke of *Parma.* In the meaneseason, *Moncada,* after he had endured the conflict a good while, being hitte on the head with a bullet, fell downe starke dead, and a great number of Spaniards also were slaine in his company. The greater part of the residue leaping over-boord into the sea, to save themselves by swimming, were most of them drowned. Howbeit there escaped among others *Don Anthonio de Manriques,* a principall officer in the Spanish fleet (called by them their *Veador* generall) together with a few Spaniards besides: which *Anthonio* was the first man that carried certaine newes of the successe of their fleet into *Spaine.*

This huge and monstrous galliasse, wherein were contained three hundred slaves to lug at the oares, and foure hundred souldiers, was in the space of three houres rifled in the same place; and there were found amongst divers other commodities 50000 ducats of the Spanish king's treasure. [Eeelv] At length when the slaves were released out of their fetters, the Englishmen would have set the sayd ship on fire, which *Monsieur Gourdon* the governor of *Caleis*, for feare of the damage which might thereupon ensue to the Towne and Haven, would not permit them to do, but drave them from thence with his great ordinance.

Upon the 29 of July in the morning, the Spanish Fleet after the foresayd tumult, having arranged themselves againe into order, were, within sight of *Greveling*, most bravely and furiously encountered by the English; where they once againe got the winde of the Spaniards: who suffered themselves to be deprived of the commodity of the place in *Caleis* rode, and of the advantage of the winde neere unto *Dunkerk*, rather then they would change their array or separate their forces now conjoyned and united together, standing onely upon their defence.

And albeit there were many excellent and warlike ships in the English fleet, yet scarse were there 22 or 23 among them all which matched 90 of the Spanish ships in bignesse, or could conveniently assault them. Wherefore the English shippes using their prerogative of nimble stirrage, whereby they could turne and wield themselves with the winde which way they listed, came oftentimes very neere upon the Spaniards, and charged them so sore, that now and then they were but a pike's length asunder: and so continually giving them one broadside after another, they discharged all their shot both great and small upon them, spending one whole day from morning till night in that violent kinde of conflict, untill such time as powder and bullets failed them. In regard of which want they thought it convenient not to pursue the Spaniards any longer, because they had many great vantages of the English, namely for the extraordinary bignesse of their ships, and also for that they were so neerely conjoyned, and kept together in so good array, that they could by no meanes be fought withall one to one. The English thought therefore, that they had right well acquited themselves, in chasing the Spaniards first from *Caleis*, and then from *Dunkerk*, and by that meanes to have hindered them from joyning with the Duke of *Parma* his forces, and getting the winde of them, to have driven them from their owne coasts.

The Spaniards that day sustained great losse and damage having many of their shippes shot thorow and thorow, and they discharged likewise great store of ordinance against the English; who indeed sustained some hinderance, but not comparable to the Spaniards' losse: for they lost not any one shippe or person of account. For very diligent inquisition being made, the Englishmen all that time wherein the Spanish Navy sayled upon their seas, are not found to have wanted above one hundreth of their people: albeit Sir *Francis Drake's* shippe was pierced with shot above forty times, and his very cabben was twise shot thorow, and about the conclusion of the fight, the bedde of a certaine gentleman lying weary thereupon, was taken quite from under him with the force of a bullet. Likewise, as the Earle of *Northumberland* and Sir *Charles Blunt* were at dinner upon a time, the bullet of a demi-culvering brake thorow the middest of their cabbin, touched their feet, and strooke downe two of the standers-by, with many such accidents befalling the English shippes, which it were tedious to rehearse. Whereupon it is most apparant, that God miraculously preserved the English nation. For the Lord Admirall wrote unto her Majestie that in all humane reason, and according to the judgement of all men (every circumstance being duly considered) the Englishmen were not of any such force, whereby they might, without a miracle, dare once to approch within sight of the Spanish Fleet: insomuch that they freely ascribed all the honour of their victory unto God, who had confounded the enemy, and had brought his counsels to none effect.

The same day the Spanish ships were so battered with English shot, that that very night and the day following, two or three of them suncke right downe: and among the rest a certaine great ship of *Biscay*, which Captaine *Crosse* assaulted, which perished even in the time of the conflict, so that very few therein escaped drowning; who reported that the governours of the same shippe slew one another upon the occasion following: one of them which would have yeelded the shippe was suddenly slaine; the brother of the slaine party in revenge of his death slew the murtherer, and in the meanewhile the ship suncke.

The same night two *Portugall* galeons of the burthen of seven or eight hundreth tunnes apiece, to wit the Saint *Philip* and the Saint *Matthew*, were forsaken of the Spanish Fleet, for they were so torne with shotte, that the water entered into them on all sides. In the galeon of Saint *Philip* was *Francis de Toledo*, brother unto the *Count de Orgas*, being Colonell over two and thirty bands: besides other gentlemen; who seeing their mast broken with shotte, they shaped their

course, aswell as they could, for the coast of *Flanders:* whither when
they could not attaine, the principall men in the ship committing
themselves to their skiffe, arrived at the next towne, which was *Ostend*;
and the ship itselfe being left behinde with the residue of their company, was taken by the Ulishingers. [Eee2]

In the other galeon, called the S. *Matthew,* was embarked *Don Diego
Pimentelli* another camp-master and colonell of 32 bands, being brother
unto the marques of *Tamnares,* with many other gentlemen and captaines. Their ship was not very great, but exceeding strong, for of a
great number of bullets which had batterd her, there were scarse 20
wherewith she was pierced or hurt: her upper worke was of force sufficient to beare off a musket shot: this shippe was shot thorow and
pierced in the fight before *Greveling*; insomuch that the leakage of the
water could not be stopped: whereupon the duke of *Medina* sent his
great skiffe unto the governour thereof, that he might save himselfe
and the principal persons that were in his ship: which he, upon a
hault courage, refused to do: wherefore the Duke charged him to saile
next unto himselfe: which the night following he could not performe,
by reason of the great abundance of water which entered his ship on all
sides; for the avoiding wherof, and to save his ship from sincking, he
caused 50 men continually to labor at the pumpe, though it were to
small purpose. And seeing himselfe thus forsaken and separated from
his admirall, he endevored what he could to attaine unto the coast of
Flanders: where, being espied by 4 or 5 men of warre, which had their
station assigned them upon the same coast, he was admonished to
yeeld himselfe unto them. Which he refusing to do, was strongly assaulted by them altogether, and his ship being pierced with many
bullets, was brought into farre worse case then before, and 40 of his
souldiers were slaine. By which extremity he was enforced at length
to yeeld himselfe unto *Peter Banderduess* and other captaines, which
brought him and his ship into *Zeland*; and that other ship also last
before mentioned: which both of them, immediatly after the greater
and better part of their goods were unladen, suncke right downe.

For the memory of this exploit, the foresayd captaine *Banderduess* caused the banner of one of these shippes to be set up in the
great Church of *Leiden* in *Holland*, which is of so great a length, that
being fastened to the very roofe, it reached downe to the ground.

About the same time another small ship being by necessity driven
upon the coast of *Flanders*, about *Blankenberg*, was cast away upon

the sands, the people therein being saved. Thus almighty God would have the Spaniards' huge ships to be presented, not onely to the view of the English, but also of the Zelanders; that at the sight of them they might acknowledge of what small ability they had beene to resist such impregnable forces, had not God endued them with courage, providence, and fortitude, yea, and fought for them in many places with his owne arme.

The 29 of July the Spanish fleet being encountered by the English (as is aforesayd) and lying close together under their fighting sailes, with a Southwest winde sailed past *Dunkerk*, the English ships stil following the chase. Of whom the day following when the Spaniards had got sea roome, they cut their maine sailes; whereby they sufficiently declared that they meant no longer to fight but to flie. For which cause the L. Admirall of *England* dispatched the Lord *Henrie Seymer* with his squadron of small ships unto the coast of *Flanders*, where, with the helpe of the Dutch ships, he might stop the prince of *Parma* his passage, if perhaps he should attempt to issue forth with his army. And he himselfe in the meane space pursued the Spanish fleet untill the second of August, because he thought they had set saile for *Scotland*. And albeit he followed them very neere, yet did he not assault them any more, for want of powder and bullets. But upon the fourth of August, the winde arising, when as the Spaniards had spread all their sailes, betaking themselves wholly to flight, and leaving *Scotland* on the left hand, trended toward *Norway*, (whereby they sufficiently declared that their whole intent was to save themselves by flight, attempting for that purpose, with their battered and crazed ships, the most dangerous navigation of the Northren seas) the English seeing that they were now proceeded unto the latitude of 57 degrees, and being unwilling to participate that danger whereinto the Spaniards plunged themselves, and because they wanted things necessary, and especially powder and shot, returned backe for *England*; leaving behinde them certaine pinasses onely, which they enjoyned to follow the Spaniards aloofe, and to observe their course. And so it came to passe that the fourth of August, with great danger and industry, the English arrived at *Harwich*: for they had bene tossed up and downe with a mighty tempest for the space of two or three dayes together, which it is likely did great hurt unto the Spanish fleet, being (as I sayd before) so maimed and battered. The English now going on shore, provided themselves foorthwith of victuals, gunne-powder, and other things expedient, that they might be ready at all assayes to entertaine the Spanish fleet, if it chanced any more to returne. But being afterward more certainely informed of the Spaniards' course, they thought it best to leave them unto those boisterous and uncouth Northren seas, and not there to hunt after them.

The Spaniards seeing now that they wanted foure or five thousand of their people and having divers maimed and sicke persons, and likewise háving lost 10 or 12 of their principall ships, they consulted among themselves, what they were best to doe, being now escaped out of the hands of [Eee2v] the English, because their victuals failed them in like sort, and they began also to want cables, cordage, ankers, masts, sailes, and other naval furniture, and utterly despaired of the Duke of *Parma* his assistance (who verily hoping and undoubtedly expecting the returne of the Spanish Fleet, was continually occupied about his great preparation, commanding abundance of ankers to be made, and other necessary furniture for a Navy to be provided) they thought it good at length, so soone as the winde should serve them, to fetch a compasse about *Scotland* and *Ireland*, and so to returne for *Spaine*.

For they well understood, that commandement was given thorowout all *Scotland*, that they should not have any succour or assistance there. Neither yet could they in *Norway* supply their wants. Wherefore, having taken certaine Scotish and other fisherboats, they brought the men on boord their owne ships, to the end they might be their guides and Pilots. Fearing also least their fresh water should faile them, they cast all their horses and mules over-boord: and so touching nowhere upon the coast of *Scotland*, but being carried with a fresh gale betweene the *Orcades* and *Faar-Isles*, they proceeded farre North, even unto 61 degrees of latitude, being distant from any land at the least 40 leagues. Heere the Duke of *Medina* generall of the Fleet commanded all his followers to shape their course for *Biscay*: and he himselfe with twenty or five and twenty of his ships which were best provided of fresh water and other necessaries, holding on his course over the maine Ocean, returned safely home. The residue of his ships being about forty in number, and committed unto his Vice-admirall, fell neerer with the coast of *Ireland*, intending their course for Cape *Clare*, because they hoped there to get fresh water, and to refresh themselves on land. But after they were driven with many contrary windes, at length, upon the second of September, they were cast by a tempest arising from the Southwest upon divers parts of *Ireland*, where many of their ships perished. And amongst others, the shippe of

Michael de Oquendo, which was one of the great Galliasses: and two great ships of *Venice* also, namely, *la Ratta* and *Belanzara,* with other 36 or 38 ships more, which perished in sundry tempests, together with most of the persons contained in them.

Likewise some of the Spanish ships were the second time carried with a strong West winde into the chanell of *England,* whereof some were taken by the English upon their coast, and others by the men of *Rochel* upon the coast of *France.*

Moreover, there arrived at *Newhaven* in *Normandy,* being by tempest inforced so to doe, one of the foure great Galliasses, where they found the ships with the Spanish women which followed the Fleet at their setting forth. Two ships also were cast away upon the coast of *Norway,* one of them being of a great burthen; howbeit all the persons in the sayd great ship were saved: insomuch that of 134 ships, which set saile out of *Portugall,* there returned home 53 onely small and great: namely of the foure galliasses but one, and but one of the foure gallies. Of the 91 great galleons and hulks there were missing 58, and 33 returned: of the pataches and zabraes 17 were missing, and 18 returned home. In briefe, there were missing 81 ships, in which number were galliasses, gallies, galeons, and other vessels both great and small. And amongst the 53 ships remaining, those also are reckoned which returned home before they came into the English chanell. Two galeons of those which were returned, were by misfortune burnt as they rode in the haven; and such like mishaps did many others undergo. Of 30000 persons which went in this expedition, there perished (according to the number and proportion of the ships) the greater and better part; and many of them which came home, by reason of the toiles and inconveniences which they sustained in this voyage, died not long after their arrivall. The Duke of *Medina* immediatly upon his returne was deposed from his authority, commanded to his private house, and forbidden to repaire unto the Court; where he could hardly satisfie or yeeld a reason unto his malicious enemies and backbiters. Many honourable personages and men of great renowme deceased soone after their returne; as namely *John Martines de Ricalde,* with divers others. A great part also of the Spanish Nobility and Gentry employed in this expedition perished either by fight, diseases, or drowning, before their arrival; and among the rest *Thomas Perenot* of *Granduell* a Dutchman, being earle of *Cantebroi,* and sonne unto Cardinall *Granduell* his brother.

Upon the coast of *Zeland Don Diego de Pimentell,* brother unto the

Marques *de Tamnares,* and kinseman unto the earle of *Beneventum* and *Calva,* and Colonell over 32 bands with many other in the same ship was taken and detained as prisoner in *Zeland.*

Into *England* (as we sayd before) *Don Pedro de Valdez,* a man of singular experience, and greatly honoured in his countrey, was led captive, being accompanied with *Don Vasquez de Silva, Don Alonzo de Sayas,* and others.

Likewise upon the Scotish Westerne Isles of *Lewis,* and *Ila,* and about Cape *Cantyre* upon the maineland, there were cast away certaine Spanish shippes, out of which were saved di- [Eee3] vers Captaines and Gentlemen, and almost foure hundred souldiers, who for the most part, after their shipwracke, were brought unto *Edenborough* in *Scotland,* and being miserably needy and naked, were there clothed at the liberality of the King and the Marchants, and afterward were secretly shipped for *Spaine;* but the Scotish Fleet wherein they passed touching at *Yarmouth* on the coast of *Norfolke,* were there stayed for a time untill the Councel's pleasure was knowen; who in regard of their manifolde miseries, though they were enemies, wincked at their passage.

Upon the Irish coast many of their Noblemen and Gentlemen were drowned; and divers slaine by the barbarous and wilde Irish. Howbeit there was brought prisoner out of *Ireland, Don Alonzo de Lucon,* Colonell of two and thirtie bandes, commonly called a *terza* of *Naples;* together with *Rodorigo de Lasso,* and two others of the family of *Cordova,* who were committed unto the custodie of Sir *Horatio Palavicini,* that *Monsieur de Teligny* the sonne of *Monsieur de la Noue* (who being taken in fight neere *Antwerpe,* was detained prisoner in the Castle of *Turney*) might be raunsomed for them by way of exchange. To conclude, there was no famous nor woorthy family in all *Spaine,* which in this expeiditon lost not a sonne, a brother, or a kinseman.

For the perpetuall memorie of this matter, the Zelanders caused newe coine of Silver and brasse to be stamped: which on the one side contained the armes of *Zeland,* with this inscription: *GLORY TO GOD ONELY:* and on the other side, the pictures of certeine great ships, with these words: *THE SPANISH FLEET:* and in the circumference about the ships: *IT CAME, WENT, AND WAS. Anno* 1588. That is to say, the Spanish fleet came, went, and was vanquished this yere; for which, glory be given to God onely.

Likewise they coined another kinde of money; upon the one side whereof was represented a ship fleeing, and a ship sincking: on the other side foure men making prayers and giving thanks unto God upon their knees; with this sentence: *Man purposeth; God disposeth*, 1588. Also, for the lasting memory of the same matter, they have stamped in *Holland* divers suchlike coines, according to the custome of the ancient Romans.

While this woonderfull and puissant Navie was sayling along the English coastes, and all men did now plainely see and heare that which before they would not be perswaded of, all people thorowout *England* prostrated themselves with humble prayers and supplications unto God: but especially the outlandish Churches (who had greatest cause to feare, and against whom by name, the Spaniards had threatened most grievous torments) enjoyned to their people continuall fastings and supplications, that they might turne away God's wrath and fury now imminent upon them for their sinnes: knowing right well, that prayer was the onely refuge against all enemies, calamities, and necessities, and that it was the onely solace and reliefe for mankinde, being visited with affliction and misery. Likewise such solemne dayes of supplication were observed thorowout the united Provinces.

Also a while after the Spanish Fleet was departed, there was in *England,* by the commandement of her Majestie, and in the united Provinces, by the direction of the States, a solemne festivall day publikely appointed, wherein all persons were enjoyned to resort unto the Church, and there to render thanks and praises unto God: and the Preachers were commanded to exhort the people thereunto. The foresayd solemnity was observed upon the 29 of November; which day was wholly spent in fasting, prayer, and giving of thanks.

Likewise, the Queene's Majestie herselfe, imitating the ancient Romans, rode into *London* in triumph, in regard of her owne and her subjects' glorious deliverance. For being attended upon very solemnely by all the principall estates and officers of her Realme, she was carried thorow her sayd City of *London* in a tryumphant chariot, and in robes of triumph, from her Palace unto the Cathedrall Church of Saint *Paul,* out of the which the ensignes and colours of the vanquished Spaniards hung displayed. And all the Citizens of *London* in their Liveries stood on either side the street, by their severall Companies, with their ensignes and banners: and the streets were hanged on both sides with Blew cloth, which, together with the foresayd banners, yeelded a very stately and gallant prospect. Her Majestie being entered into the Church, together with her Clergie and Nobles gave thanks unto God, and caused a publike Sermon to be preached before her at Paul's crosse; wherein none other argument was handled, but that praise, honour, and glory might be rendered unto God, and that God's name might be extolled by thanksgiving. And with her owne princely voice she most Christianly exhorted the people to doe the same: whereupon the people with a loud acclamation wished her a most long and happy life, to the confusion of her foes. [Eee3v]

Thus the magnificent, huge, and mighty fleet of the Spaniards (which themselves termed in all places invincible) such as sayled not upon the Ocean sea many hundreth yeeres before, in the yeere 1588 vanished into smoake; to the great confusion and discouragement of the authours thereof. In regard of which her Majestie's happy suc-cesse all her neighbours and friends congratulated with her, and many verses were penned to the honour of her Majesty by learned men, whereof some which came to our hands we will here annexe.

AD SERENISSIMAM ELIZABETHAM ANGLIAE REGINAM THEODOR. BEZA.

STrauerat innumeris Hispanus nauibus aequor,
  Regnis iuncturus sceptra Britanna suis.
Tanti huius, rogitas, quae motus causa? superbos
  Impulit Ambitio, vexit Auaritia.
Quàm bene te ambitio mersit vanissima ventus?
  Et tumidos tumidae, vos superastis aquae!
Quàm bene totius raptores orbis auaros,
  Hausit inexhausti iusta vorago maris!
At tu, cui venti, cui totum militat aequor,
  Regina, ô mundi totius vna, decus,
Sic regnare Deo perge, ambitione remota,
  Prodiga sic opibus perge iuuare pios,
Vt te Angli longùm, longùm Anglis ipsa fruaris,
  Quàm dilecta bonis, tam metuenda malis.

The same in English.

THe Spanish Fleet did flote in narrow Seas,
  And bend her ships against the English shore,
With so great rage as nothing could appease,
And with such strength as never seene before:
    And all to joyne the kingdome of that land
    Unto the kingdomes that he had in hand.
Now if you aske what set this king on fire,
To practise warre when he of peace did treat,
It was his *Pride*, and never quencht desire,
To spoile that Island's wealth, by peace made great:
    His *Pride* which farre above the heavens did swell,
    And his desire as unsuffic'd as hell.
But well have windes his proud blasts overblowen,
And swelling waves alayd his swelling heart,
Well hath the Sea with greedie gulfs unknowen,
Devoured the devourer to his smart:
    And made his ships a pray unto the sand,
    That meant to pray upon another's land.
And now, O *Queene*, above all others blest,
For whom both windes and waves are prest to fight,
So rule your owne, so succour friends opprest,
(As farre from pride, as ready to do right)
    That *England* you, you *England* long enjoy,
No lesse your friends' delight, then foes annoy.

The Honorable voyage unto Cadiz, 1596 (1598)

Despite John Hawkins's strategy of preying on Spanish treasure ships and depleting the Spanish King's coffers while replenishing the English Queen's, the war with Spain which dragged on for eighteen years was very costly to Elizabeth. She could not balance her budget, especially since she was also supporting an army which she had dispatched to France to support Henry of Navarre in his struggle against the Catholic League. Not until 1596 could she manage to pull together sufficient supplies for another major naval expedition: and if it proved to be less successful than she had hoped, she nevertheless found in Roger Marbeck's meticulous and colorful tribute of the voyage, reprinted below, adequate register of state propaganda for an uneven mission.

This Cadiz adventure—destined to be in many ways the most extraordinary military defeat of the Spanish after the Armada—began with the gathering of troops and equipment about April 28 or 29 in Plymouth. From the start preparations were hindered by resentment, jealousy, and debate among those appointed leaders of the mission. Sir Walter Ralegh, the vice admiral, and Sir Francis Vere, marshal of the army, quarrelled frequently over precedence and at one dinner, where they found unusually enthusiastic support from their partisans, things became so troublesome that Arthur Throckmorton, Ralegh's brother-in-law, had to be ordered from table. Howard and Essex were both in turn suspicious of Ralegh for they heard he tried to persuade Elizabeth to give him command of the expedition; but this only temporarily distracted them from their dislike of each other: Essex disliked Howard because at 60 he was growing too old and conservative, and Howard found Essex difficult because, not yet 30, this young court favorite was too reckless. Howard was especially angered when Essex was made his joint commander—he, the high lord admiral, not in full charge of this major naval assault—and when Essex signed his name in a report to the Queen over Howard's own signature, the lord admiral whipped out his knife and sliced the offensive name away because he "would have none so high as himself."

To counter these corroding relationships, unusual order and system were commanded. There was set forth first of all a "Declaration of the causes moving the queen's majesty to prepare and send a navy to the seas for defense of her realms against the king of Spain's forces," the nearest Elizabeth ever came to a declaration of war against Spain. The final document may have been drawn up by Burghley despite his age; but a draft exists in the Queen's handwriting; and the proclamation was printed in French, Italian, Dutch, and Spanish and circulated as far as the city squares of Venice. The Queen declared in this public testimonial that she was sending out a fleet only in defense of her realm and as a safeguard against a rumored Spanish invasion; that her men were ordered to harm only the Spanish or those supporting Spain; and that all those in Christendom were urged for their own protection to remove their ships from Spanish and Portuguese ports to seek safety in their own or English harbors. A second proclamation defined the duties and rights of each of her offices of the army and of the field— drawn up by Essex with the advice of Vere, this would prevent battlefield confusion and bickering. Still a third document provided rules for the general discipline of the fleet and was prepared by the old sea captain John Young. Thus the orderliness stressed in the following first-hand account by one of the participants, Roger Marbeck, chief of the royal physicians, only reflects the sense of planning which saturated Plymouth during the busy days of May 1596. The Queen herself contributed a prayer (which Marbeck quotes and translates below, Ee4v), a work Burghley saw and thought "divinely conceived . . . in the depths of her sacred heart . . . an invocation unto the Lord purposely indicted [endited] by His spirit in His annointed queen."

Still at the last moment the Queen characteristically wavered: the money, the ships, and the lives of Howard and Essex seemed too great to gamble. She countermanded her orders; and to reinstate himself and the others Essex wrote a most politic message—not to her, but to the Privy Council—using all the arguments he knew would appeal to her, for she would hear of them. He urged the Council to restore the original directives, since the English could not afford to waste the investments they had now made, the support of harbor towns that had furnished ships, or a chance to embarrass Spain and so aid the Low Countries and prevent further Spanish expansion and rebellion in Ireland. The Queen yielded and Sir Fulke Greville came to Plymouth with a letter giving Howard and Essex the necessary license to embark. Embark they did, and the sight must have been glorious: the English Armada, the country's greatest naval expedition, left with nearly 120 ships, including 15 to 17 of the Queen's own, two of Howard's, 75 or so furnished by London and other port towns, and nearly 30 sent over from the Netherlands; and together they carried more than 10,000 men. The master gunner fired the signal to depart the morning of June 1.

The Spanish, meantime, fortified Lisbon and braced themselves

generally. This time the English shrouded their destination in nearly
absolute secrecy, not even telling their own men; and when an Irish
bark confirmed their hunch that Cadiz was ripe for the taking, they
headed to that unsuspecting port which was now harboring treasure
ships of Spain. On Sunday morning June 20, while the people of
Cadiz flocked to the Sabbath mass, the English first spotted Philip's
entire West Indian fleet at anchor guarded only by four huge galleons
(four of Philip's Twelve Apostles) and a flotilla of galleys. Two of the
galleons, moreover, were among those which had attacked Grenville
at the Azores and Ralegh shouted his resolve to "be revenged for the
Revenge or to second her with mine own life." The outer harbor of
Cadiz lay slightly inland from the city; the inner harbor of Port Royal
was another six miles away and made secure by an escape canal leading
out into the sea ten miles below Cadiz. When the English appeared,
the 36 smaller ships of the loaded merchantmen scampered to safety
in Port Royal; the four Apostles and the galleys, along with the larger
merchantmen, strung themselves stem to stern across the narrow entrance to the outer harbor. But there was no immediate attack. Instead,
the English spent the entire day discussing—despite their elaborate
directions—who would lead the offensive. Ralegh for some time had
the edge, since Elizabeth had instructed them that Essex should not be
allowed to take unnecessary risks and her favorite was unwilling to
allow Howard to win glory that he could not. To prevent any of these
men from leading the attack, and thus to break the deadlock among
them, Thomas Howard finally persuaded them at a council of war that,
since he outranked Ralegh, he would lead them all in.

On Monday June 21, the English attacked; Ralegh ordered his
trumpeters to herald each salvo with a blast from their trumpets. All
the leaders were soon vying to get close to the prize galleons; and the
lord admiral and his son William, temporarily squeezed out of position,
took themselves into the fray in a longboat. The Spanish cut their
cables to slip into the inner harbor, but so distressed were they by wind,
tide, fire, and panic that the four giant galleons, the Apostles, ran
aground. Two were captured by the English and two went up in
flames; the horrified Drake later wrote that "if any man had a desire to
see Hell itself, it was then most lively figured." The greatness of
Philip's fleet was conquered at the outset.

Once the galleons were routed, Howard approved of a scheme by
Essex to land men and take the town, and for joy Essex threw his hat
into the water with grand shouts. He ordered his own troops ashore
on barges, beating time for them on a drum. But two of his barges
swamped—a contemporary Puritan account holds this was because the
English had first attacked on the Sabbath—and while the Dutch took
the outlying fort of Puntal, two miles away from the town, Essex
led 2,000 of his own men across three miles of soft sand to the city
walls. When they reached Cadiz, they found huge piles of debris

piled against the city walls for the purpose of repairing them, and these mounds of rubble enabled Essex and 300 of his men to climb over the walls to meet Vere's forces, coming in the city gates, and with them force the Spanish from the citadel of Fort San Felipe. By nightfall the town, save for the castle, belonged to the English. Only Ralegh was missing—during the naval battle some shot had sent splinters into his leg and, unable to walk, he had stayed aboard ship.

At a conference Tuesday morning, Howard's and Essex's forces agreed to ransom the lives of all the townspeople, holding 50 of the principal men as hostages, and giving the Spanish twelve days to collect the money. The remaining people of the town were transported peacefully to the mainland or allowed to go there by way of the bridge. Throughout, the English maintained excellent discipline, in full obedience to the Queen's original proclamation; only the Dutch seem to have been at all savage. But together English and Dutch pillaged the town randomly. They seized diamonds, jewelry, gold, silks, whatever they could find. Some later spoke of wine, oil, almonds, raisins, olives, and spices trampled in every highway; and sugar, hides, steel, Spanish iron, tin, lead, armor, quicksilver, wine, tapestries, and even churchbells were stuffed into the holds of their ships. Ralegh claimed a chest of books after being carried briefly ashore; Captain Edward Wilton acknowledged taking a library of volumes on civil law. There is some humor in this plundering: Arthur Savage, who took possession of a physician's house (and its contents) bemoaned the fact that "no one asked for" it and so let it all go for £65 and eight small pieces of plate. But they probably also missed much: rumor had it that £11,000 was left behind in the fortress and great personal fortunes were overlooked elsewhere.

Aboard his ship for most of the time, Ralegh alone seems to have thought of the forgotten Spanish treasure ships while the land raids went on. Finally he persuaded Howard to attack them. But before he could do so, Medina Sidonia, now the governor of Andalusia, with a splendid disregard for their value, had them all burned in a contemptuous effort to save their cargo from English hands. Besides this bitter vengeance, the Spanish had one other stroke of luck. They received news that all their galleys had escaped safely to the inner harbor and that an English guard had been set on the bridge linking the promontory of Cadiz with the mainland. They learned further that the English officers had slipped off to sack the city and the remaining soldiers were drunk on the wine they had plundered. Spaniards attacked these hapless few, cut all their throats, and then destroyed their own bridge so that their galleys could escape to the open sea to harry the English fleet when it disembarked.

The once colorful harbor of Cadiz was now quiet and nearly deserted. Empty English ships stood along the shore; in the distance there was the wreckage of Spanish ships, skeletons of boats still smoldering; and fragments of the broken bridge jutted from the water. Inside the city, at the week's end, the near-empty town broke silence with a celebration in which Essex knighted 31 men, against the Queen's express wishes, and Howard, not to be outdone, helped to dub 31 more. On Saturday, June 26, the conquerors buried their only casualty, Sir John Wingfield, with all the honors of war, the drummers and trumpeters playing, the generals dropping their handkerchiefs, "wet from their eyes," into his grave.

For a while Essex developed a plan whereby some of them would remain, garrisoning a strong and strategic position in Spain; but when he announced that he also wished to be governor of the city, Howard called a council of war and Essex was outvoted. They decided instead to burn the city as Medina had burned the ships, but so anxious were they to leave that they did not do a thorough job: two weeks later, a Spanish commission reported that 328 buildings were again inhabited, 685 more undamaged, and only 290 burned, the stone construction of which Marbeck admiringly speaks below having also helped to preserve them. In disgust, Essex managed to be the last one to leave shore. All in all, the victors took with them in money and goods a total of 621,500 ducats or £170,000.

Following this dramatic attack on Cadiz, detailed splendidly in the narration which follows, the remainder of the voyage was anticlimactic. At Faro the English took a little wine and fruit, and six or eight brass cannon. At Cape St. Vincent a strong wind from eastward drove them 80 leagues out to sea and they sent Sir Arthur Savage to England to place an interim report on their movements. They went on to Cape Roca for revictualling and there decided, against Essex's advice, to return home: they just missed the arrival of a Spanish treasure fleet from the West Indies by two days. Sailing along the coast of Spain, they stopped briefly at Ferrol and Corunna and so came on back to Plymouth.

Howard arrived first—docking two months and two days after his departure—and so received the brunt of the Queen's anger: they had brought back too little plunder, they had missed the West Indian fleet worth twenty million ducats, they had cheapened English knighthood by making more than 60 new knights, they had cost her a great deal of money after the raid on Cadiz without performing any more feats worthy of mention. Most of this was true—and to it were added rumors all about London and Plymouth of unreported plunder, reducing the Queen's profits still more. There seems in fact to have been much embezzlement: one great diamond, it was learned, had been broken up and distributed to a number of London jewelers. In the end, the best the Queen could do was charge her commanders and send her own agent, Sir Anthony Ashley, whose job it had been to look after her interests, off to Fleet Prison. If the men had become heroes, the Queen herself had precious little to show for such a grand adventure.

Essex tried to capitalize on the expedition for his own reputation—already spreading among the Spanish since he had been so modest with the nuns of Cadiz, they reported, so gentle with their ladies, and so willing to talk, unarmed, with the merchants in the city's central square—and he rushed to London his "True Relation" of the voyage by way of his secretary Henry Cuffe who swore not to admit the work was one of self-aggrandizement. But Cuffe fell sick; another secretary told both the Privy Council and the Queen, in separate sessions on July 31, of Essex's intended report glamorizing the expedition; and the Queen forbade all London printers to publish it without her approval on pain of death. It never appeared. Elizabeth's anger took some time to subside. But she might have had other feelings—mixed feelings, perhaps, of pride and anxiety—had she learned that the losses at Cadiz brought further bankruptcy to the King of Spain, who was now unable to repay money he had borrowed in Florence and so initiated a second armada against England launched in 1597.

Of all the reports that have come down to us, the most detailed and accurate is that by Roger Marbeck included here. It was, moreover, the only one circulated in English at the time. Although Marbeck is somewhat learned and often cautious in this narrative, he is also, predictably enough, highly prejudicial. His treatment of the Queen's prayer (Eee4v), the miraculous flying fishes (Eee4v) and the appearance of the doves (Eee5v) as the omens of God, culminate in his final allusion to the protective "holy hand" (Fff3v) which gives this work its providential edge. His repeated praise given the English treatment of the citizens of Cadiz—which they in fact were most grateful for—and his encomia of Howard, Ralegh and Essex (Eee6) are unhappily juxtaposed here to the description of razing a fine port city and the wanton destroying of property which was too unmanageable to claim or plunder. Indeed, Marbeck at times shows surprisingly little appreciation of this gem of Spanish civilization; rather, his attention, unconscious though it may be, on the actual piracy of the mission—beginning tellingly enough with the attack on the three German ships, here handled with unexpected equanimity and even commendation (Eee5)—suggests a universal acceptance among the crew of the Queen's views that any provocative act against the Spanish could only be construed as an act of necessary self-defense. There is an implicit crudeness here, too, adumbrated in the elemental justice at Plymouth (Eee4), to which this usually sensitive author is apparently blind. Throughout, the tone is respectful, even adulatory, although the stunning success of the mission is at times adequately restrained by Marbeck's self-conscious adherence to detail. Thus the fulsome description which follows accurately reproduces not only fact but feeling, and in the patriotic sentiments which cast this act of plundering into an event of unmitigated success there is, honestly and innocently enough, yet another kind of Elizabethan propaganda.

TEXTUAL NOTES

[For explanatory notes for this selection see page 381.]

The Honorable voyage unto Cadiz, 1596.
   Reference. STC 12626, 12626a.
   Authorship and Editions. A manuscript note by P. B. (Rev. Philip
Bliss, 1787-1857, Bodleian under-librarian) bound into a Bodleian
copy (H.8.15Art.) of Hakluyt's *Principal Navigations* identifies this
account of Cadiz as a copy of a MS "by Doctor [Roger] Marbeck
[1536-1605]," provost of Oriel College, Oxford, chief of the royal
physicians, and, according to Marbeck's title, "attending vpon the
person of the Right honorable Lord Admirall of England, all the tyme
of the saide Action." The title of this account in MS is "A Briefe and a
true discourse of the late honorable voyage vnto Spaine, and of the
wynning sacking and burning of the famous Towne of Cadiz there,
and of the miraculous ouerthrowe of the Spanish Navie at that tyme,
with a report of all other accidentes thereunto appertaying" (*sic*);
according to Rev. Bliss, "The alteration in the readings of the MS from
those of the printed copy are unworthy of particular notice." Hakluyt's
publication of this narrative—the only one made—is anonymous; but
the tone is literate and the report obviously an eye-witness one; moreover, the ease of humility suggests a learned but not titled person.
The evidence thus supports Bliss, and the DNB also credits Marbeck
with this work. The MS Bliss alludes to is in the British Museum.
   The present text is taken from the 1598 edition of *The Principal
Navigations, Voiages, Traffiqves And Discoueries of the English
Nation* compiled by Richard Hakluyt, I, 607-619; and was considered
important enough to advertise on the title-page. In part, the title-page
reads, "the famous victorie atchieued at the citie of *Cadiz*, 1596." An
order of the Queen suppressed this account of Essex's heroism after
his public disgrace, however, and the title-page was reset (STC 12626a)
omitting the reference to this pamphlet, and the account itself was
deleted. The 1599 issue exists in two typesettings, distinguished on
p. 607 by 53 lines of type divided into eight paragraphs and reset (sometime after 1603) as 63 lines of type divided into ten paragraphs (both
states are at the New York Public Library). The Cadiz account concludes the first volume of Hakluyt's *Navigations* for 1598 and the work
was therefore easily deleted, but there are a number of mixed copies of
1599 extant which still contain the account (e.g., Bodleian H.8.15Art.).
Subsequent printings also contain the work, including a London reprint of the 1599 issue (1810), pp. 19-33, and one by the Hakluyt Society
(Glasgow, 1904), IV, 236-268. Both editions are unchanged and published without notes or commentary added. Purchas used this narrative as a major source for his own more extended account in *Hakluytus
Posthumus or Purchas His Pilgrimes* (1625), Book X, Chapter XIII.

Collation. Folio in sixes (three sheets each folded once); for a full collation, see p. 241 above. The Cadiz account appears on Eee4-Fff4, pp. 607-619.

Description of Contents. For a description of Hakluyt's volume, see p. 241-2 above. For this account: Eee4-Fff4, pp. 607-619; p. *608* misnumbered *605.* Heading in mixed roman and italics; text in blackletter; subheadings in italics. Special running-head *"The honor. voyage to Cadiz."* in italics on each page. Decorative initial, Eee4. Type ornament as tail-piece (ending volume), Fff4, following the words (in roman) "The end of the first volume." Two marginal notes, on Fff2v, reading "Iune 21.22" and "27."

License. No entry in the *Stationers' Register*; printed by the Queen's printers, George Bishop, Ralph Newberry, and Robert Barker.

Base-Copy Text. Bodleian Douce H238. For variant issue: Bodleian H.8.15 Art.

Title-heading in Full (Eee4). / A briefe and true report of the Honorable voyage vnto / *Cadiz,* 1596. *of the ouerthrow of the kings Fleet, and of the winning,* / sacking, and burning of the Citie, with all other accidents of / moment, thereunto appertaining.

Emendations. [Throughout work, the author uses *L.* for *Lord, LL.* for *Lords,* and *D.* for *Duke.*] (Eee4)Regiment, an other]Regiment, another for euer afterwards]forever afterwards (Eee5) (as often times . . .)](as oftentimes . . .) cause an other]cause another one to an other:]one to another: I assure my selfe]I assure myselfe in the meane time]in the meanetime (Eee5v)all my life time]all my lifetime or there about,]or thereabout, fish it selfe]fish itselfe a fisher man] a fisherman L. returne]L.'s returne Irish man,]Irishman, presented our selues]presented ourselves an other more conuenient] another more convenient maine yard]maineyard presented her self] presented herselfe selfe same]selfe-same presented our selues,]presented ourselves, (Eee6)the Bay it selfe,]the Bay itselfe, the very Bay it selfe]the very Bay itselfe there abouts,]thereabouts, Port S. *Mary*] Port S. *Mary's* a shoare]ashoare with an other might great ship,] with another mighty great ship, (Eee6v)running in deede]running indeede (Fff1)in the night time]in the nighttime honoulable wisedomes.]honorable wisedomes. In the meane while]In the meanewhile (Fff1v)Towne of it selfe]Towne of itselfe vpon the house top,]upon the housetop, lower out roomes]lower outroomes (Fff2) penny, or penny worth.]penny, or pennyworth. common high way,] common highway, all that meane while]all that meanewhile liues of euery one]lives of everyone The twenty seuenth day]The twenty-seventh day (Fff2v)place of it selfe]place of itselfe (Fff3v)K. vse]King's use (Fff4)arme our selues]arme ourselves common wealth]commonwealth as my selfe was not,]as myselfe was not,

A briefe and true report of the Honorable voyage unto Cadiz, *1596.* of the overthrow of the king's Fleet, and of the winning, *sacking, and burning of the Citie, with all other accidents of moment, thereunto appertaining*

FTER THAT the two most Noble and Renowmed Lords Generals: The L. *Robert* Earle of *Essex,* and the L. *Charles Howard* L. High Admirall of *England,* were come unto *Plymmouth* (which was about the beginning of May last, 1596.) being there accompanied with divers other noble Peeres, as the Earle of Sussex, the L. *Thomas Howard,* the L. *Harbert,* the L. *Warden* Sir *Walter Raleigh:* the L. *Marshall* Sir *Francis Vere:* the L. *Burk, Don Christopher* young Prince of *Portingall,* young *Count Lodovick* of *Nassaw,* and the Admirall of the Hollanders, Sir *John Vanderfoord:* besides many other most worthy Knights and Gentlemen of great woorth attending upon this most honorable Action: It pleased them, there to make their abode for the time of that moneth, as well for the new furnishing and revictualing of her Majestie's Royall Navie: as also for the expecting of some other ships, which were to come from divers places of the Realme, and were as yet wanting: making that place as it should seeme the *Rendevous* for all the whole Fleete, there to complete the full number of al such companies both for sea and land: as was in their noble and deepe wisedomes thought meete and agreed upon.

All the time of this their abode there, there was a most zealous and diligent care had for the holy service of God, dayly and reverently to be frequented: and also for other good and civill orders of militarie discipline to be observed, to the exceeding great comfort and rejoycing of all the hearts of the godly and well disposed.

And for that it might the better appeare, that there was small hope of pardon to be expected of the offenders, if they did at any time neglect their duties, about due observation of matters of importance: Their orders, lawes, and decrees being once published: about the 8. or 9. of the same moneth, there were two offenders executed a little without the towne, in a very fayre pleasant greene, called the *Ho*: the one for beginning of a muteny in his company, the other for running away from his Colours.

And about the same time in the Dutch Regiment, another for murthering of one of his companions, about a quarrell betweene themselves, rising as it was supposed, upon their drinke, was by order of Martiall law, presently tyed to the partie so murthered, and foorthwith both of them so cast into the sea.

Moreover, about the 28. of the same moneth, a certaine Lieutenant (whose name I will forbeare) was by sound of Drumme publikely in all the streetes disgraced, or rather after a sort disgraded, and cashierd for bearing any farther Office at that time, for the taking of money by way of corruption, of certaine prest souldiers in the Countrey, and for placing of others in their roomes, more unfit for service, and of lesse sufficiency and abilitie. This severe executing of justice at the very first did breed such a deepe terror in the hearts of the whole armie, that it seemed to cut off all occasion of the like disorder forever afterwards to be attempted.

And here before their departure from *Plymmouth,* it pleased their Lordships to publish in print, and make knowen to all the world, especially to such as whom it concerned, and that both in the Latine, French, Dutch, English and Spanish tongue, what were the true, just, and urgent causes, that at this time provoked her Majestie, to undertake the preparing and setting forth of this so great a Navie, annexing thereunto a full declaration, what was their good will and pleasure should be done and performed of all them that ment not to incurre their owne private present daungers, or else were willing to avoyde her Majestie's future indignation and displeasure.

Likewise now, at the same instant, their owne most provident and godly decrees, which they had devised for the honest cariage of every particular person in their degrees and vocation, were made knowen to all men, and published in sundry writings, with divers great punishments, set downe and appointed for the wilfull offenders and breakers of the same.

Thus then, all things being in very good order and well appointed, the most holy name of our Omnipotent God being most religiously and devoutly called upon, and his blessed and sacred Communion being divers times most reverently and publikely celebrated: These two most noble personages, with all their honorable Associats, and most famous worthy Knights, Gentlemen, Captaines, Leaders, and very willing and expert Souldiers, and Mariners, being furnished with 150. good sayle of shippes or thereabout: In the name of the most High and everliving [Eee 4v] God, and with all true and faithful obedience, to her sacred Majesty, to the infinite good and tranqillitie of our Countrey, and to the perpetuall glory, and triumphant renowme of the eternall memory of their honorable names to all posterity, the first day of June embarked themselves, weighed Ancre, and hoysed up sayle, and put to sea onward their journey from the Sownds of *Plymmouth.*

The winde, at the first setting foorth, seemed very favourable: but yet in the evening growing very scant, and all that night falling more and more against us, and we having sayled no further then to a certaine place called *Dodman head:* we were constrained the next day, to make our returne to the road of *Plymmouth* againe, and there in the Sownds to lie at ancre for that night.

About this time, and in this very place, by good fortune there came to my handes a prayer in English, touching this present Action, and made by her Majestie, as it was voyced: The prayer seemed to me to be most excellent, aswell for the matter, as also for the manner, and therefore for certaine divers good motives which then presently came to my minde, and whereof hereafter in his more convenient time and place, I will make farther mention, I presumed at that very instant to translate it into Latine.

The Prayer is thus.

MOst Omnipotent maker and guide of all our world's masse, that onely searchest and fadomest the bottome of all our hearts' conceits, and in them seest the true originals of all our actions intended: thou that by thy foresight doest truely discerne, how no malice of revenge, nor quittance of injury, nor desire of bloodshed, nor greedinesse of lucre hath bred the resolution of our now set out Army, but a heedfull care, and wary watch, that no neglect of foes, nor over-suretie of harme might breed either daunger to us, or glory to them: these being the grounds wherewith thou doest enspire the mind, we humbly beseech thee with bended knees, prosper the worke, and with best forewindes guide the journey, speed the victory, and make the returne the advancement of thy glory, the tryumph of their fame, and surety to the Realme, with the least losse of the English blood. To these devout petitions Lord give thou thy blessed grant.

My homely translation is thus.

SVmme praepotens Deus, immensae huius totius nostri mundi molis fabricator et Rector, qui solus perscrutaris intimos cordis nostri sensus, et ad sundum vsq; nostrarum cogitationum explorando penetras, ac in eis, quid verè, et ex animo cogitemus, et quae sint actionum nostrarum rationes, ac fundamenta, cognoscis:Tu, qui ea, quae in te est, ab omni aeternitate praescientia, vides, quòd nec aliqua vlciscendi malitiosa cupiditas, nec iniuriarum referendarum desiderium, nec sanguinis effundendi sitis, nec alicuius lucri, quaestusue auiditas ad istam classem praeparandam, et emittendam nos commouerit: sed potiùs, quòd prouida quaedam cura, solersquè vigilantia huc nos impulerit: ne vel inimicorum nostrorum neglectus, vel status nostri firmitatis nimium secura cogitatio, aut illis gloriam et honorem, aut nobis damnum et periculum pariat: Cum, in quam, haec sint nostri, quicquid attentatur, negotii fundamenta: cumque tu hunc nobis animum, mentemque; inieceris, vt istud aggrederemur: curuatis genibus a te humillimè petimus, vt velis hoc nostrum incoeptum secundissimè fortunare, totum iter prosperrimis flatibus dirigere, celerem et expeditam victoriam nobis concedere, reditumque; talem nostris militibus elargiri, qualis et nomini tuo incrementum gloriae, et illis famae, laudisque triumphum, et Regno nostro firmam tranquillitatem possit apportare: idque cumminimo Anglorum sanguinis dispendio. His nostris religiosis petitionibus concede, Domine, sacrosanctam et annuentem voluntatem tuam.

After that we had anchored at *Plymmouth* that night, as I have said, the third of June very early in the morning, having a reasonable fresh gale of winde, we set sayle, and kept our course againe, and the ninth of the same moneth comming something neere to the North cape, in a maner in the same altitude, or not much differing, which was about xliii. degrees, and something more, yet bearing so, as it was impossible to bee descried from the land: There it pleased the Lords to call a select Councell, which was alwayes done by hanging out of a flagge of the armes of *England*, and shooting off of a great warning peece.

Of this select or privie Councell, were no moe then these: The two
Lords Generall, the Lord *Thomas Howard,* the Lorde *Warden* Sir
Walter Raleigh, the Lord Martiall Sir *Francis Vere,* Sir *George Cary*
master of the Ordinance, Sir *Coniers Clifford,* and Sir *Anthony Ashley,*
Clarke of the sayde]Eee5] Counsell. And when it pleased the Lords
Generall to call a common Counsell (as oftentimes they did upon
weightie matters best knowen to their honours) then they would cause
another kinde of flagge to be hanged out, which was the Redcrosse of
S. *George,* and was very easie to be discerned from the other that
appertained onely to the select Counsell, and so often as this flagge of
Saint *George* was hanged out, then came all the Masters and Captaines
of all the ships, whose opinions were to be demaunded, in such matters
as appertayned unto this sayd select Counsell: It was presently
concluded, that our course in sayling should foorthwith be altered,
and that we should beare more into the West, for some purposes to
them best knowen.

At that very instant many letters of instructions were addressed
and sent to every particular Master and Captaine of the Ships: What
the contentes of those letters of instructions were it was not as yet
knowne unto any, neither was it held meet to be enquired or knowen
of any of us. But under the titles and superscriptions of every man's
particuler letter these words were endorsed. Open not these letters
on pain of your lives, unles we chance to be scattered by tempest, and
in that case open them, and execute the contents thereof: but if by
mishap you fall into your enemie's hand, then in any case cast them
into the sea, sealed as they are. It should seeme that these letters did
conteine in them the principall place and meaning of this entended
action, which was hitherto by their deepe foresights kept so secret,
as no man to my knowledge either did, or coulde so much as suspect
it, more than themselves, who had the onely managing thereof. A
conceite in my judgement of greatest moment in the world, to effect
any matter of importance. I meane, to entertaine those two vertues,
Fidem, and *Taciturnitatem:* so much commended by the old writers.
And if there was ever any great designement, in this our age, and
memorie, discreetly, faithfully, and closely caried, I assure myselfe
it was this, and though it were but in respect of that poynt onely:
yet for such faithfull secrecie, it deserveth immortall praise.

All this while, our ships, God be thanked, kept in a most excellent
good order, being devided into five squadrons: that is to say, The

Earle of *Essex*, the Lord Admirall, the Lord *Thomas Howard*, the Lord Warden Sir *Walter Raleigh*, and the Admirall of the Hollanders. All which squadrons, albeit they did every day separate themselves of purpose, by the distance of certaine leagues, as well to looke out for such shippes as were happily under sayle, as also for the better procuring of sea-roome: yet alwayes commonly eyther that day, or the next day, towarde evening, they came all together, with friendly salutations and gratulations one to another: which they terme by the name of Hayling: a ceremonie done solemnly, and in verie good order, with sound of Trumpets and noyse of cheerefull voyces: and in such sort performed as was no small encouragement one to the other, beside a true report of all such accidents, as had happened in their squadrons.

Hitherto, as I sayde, our journey was most prosperous, and all our shippes in very good plight, more then that the Mary Rose, by some mischance, either sprang or spent her foreyarde, and two dayes after Sir *Robert Crosse* had in a manner the like mischance.

Nowe being thus betweene the North cape, and cape S. *Vincent,* and yet keeping such a course aloofe, that by no meanes, those from the shoare might be able to descrie us: The tenth of June, a French Barke, and a Fleming comming from the coast of *Barbarie* were brought in by some of our companie: but they were both of them very honourably and well used by the Lords Generall: and so after a fewe dayes tarrying, were peaceably sent away, after that they had conferred with them about such matters, as was thought good in their honorable wisedomes.

The twelfth of the same moneth, Sir *Richard Levison* Knight, assisted with Sir *Christopher Blunt,* fought with three Hamburgers, and in that fight slewe two of them, and hurt eleven, and in the ende brought them all three in: and this was the very first hansell and maydenhead (as it were) of any matter of importance, or exployt woorthy observation that was done in the way outward of this honorable voyage, and was so well perfourmed of those most worthy Gentlemen, as every man highly commended them for their great valure, and discretion, and no lesse rejoyced at this their fortunate successe.

The next day after, Sir *Richard Weston* meeting with a Flemming, who refused to vale his foretoppe, with the like good courage and resolution, attempted to bring him in. The fight continued very hot betweene them, for a good space: in the end the *Swan,* wherein the

sayd Sir *Richard* was, had her forebeake strooken off: and having
spent before in fight the one side of her tire of Ordinance, while she
prepared to cast about, and to bestow on him the other side, in the
meanetime the Fleming taking this opportunity, did get almost halfe
a league from him: and so for that time made his escape. And yet the
next day after, the sayd Flemming being in a maner got to the very
mouth of the River up to *Lisbone,* was taken, and brought in by M.
Dorrell, [Eee5v] being Captaine of the *John* and *Francis* of *London.*
Thus by deviding their squadrons, and spreading the whole sea over
a mighty way, there could not so much as the least pinke passe but
she was espied and brought in.

The 13. 14. and 15. dayes, certaine little stragling Caravels were
taken by certaine of the Fleete, and in one of them a young beggarly
Fryer utterly unlearned, with a great packet of letters for *Lisbon:*
the poore wretches were marvellously well used by the Lords Generall,
and that Caravel, and the like still as they were taken were commaunded to give their attendance, and their Honors did understand what
they might of these poore men, of the estate of *Spaine* for that present.

About this time and in this place it was, that first in all my lifetime
I did see the flying fishes, who when they are hardly pinched and
chased by the Bonitoes and other great fishes, then to avoyde the
daunger, they presently mount up, and forsake the water, and betake
themselves to the benefite of their winges and make their flight,
which commonly is not above five or sixe score, or thereabout, and
then they are constrayned to fall downe into the water againe, and
it is the Mariners' opinion that they can fly no longer then their
wings be wet. The fish itselfe is about the bignesse of a Mackrell or
a great white Hearing, and much of that colour and making, with
two large wings shaped of nature very cunningly, and with great
delight to behold, in all the world much like to our Gentlewomen's
dutch Fans, that are made either of paper, or parchment, or silke, or
other stuffe, which will with certaine pleights easily runne and fold
themselves together. One of these flying fishes was presented to my
L. Admirall by a fisherman, and newly taken in his L.'s returne from
Cadiz, and then I had good leasure and opportunitie to view it.

The 18. day early in the morning wee tooke an Irishman, and
he came directly from *Cadiz,* having beene there but the day before
at twelve of the clocke at high noone. This man being examined,
told truely that there was now great store of shipping at *Cadiz,* and

with them xviii. or xix. gallies in a readinesse, and that among those ships there were divers of the king's best: and namely, that the *Philip* of *Spaine* was amongst them, but what their intent was, hee could not tell. This man was commanded also to give his attendance.

The 20. of June being Sunday, we came before *Cadiz* very early in the morning, and in all this time as yet, the whole Navy had not lost either by sicknesse or by any other maner of wayes sixe men to my knowledge: as for the Dutch company, I am not able precisely to say what happened there, for that they were no part of our charge to be looked unto, but were a regiment entire of themselves, and by themselves to be provided for, either for their diet, or for the preservation of their healths by phisicke.

Thus then I say, being all in good plight and strong, the 20. of June wee came to *Cadiz*, and there very earely in the morning presented ourselves before the Towne, ryding about a league or something lesse, from it. The sea at that instant went marvelous high, and the winde was exceeding large. Notwithstanding, a Councell being called, our Lords Generall foorthwith attempted with all expedition to land some certaine companies of their men at the West side of the Towne, by certaine long boats, light horsemen, pynnesses, and barges made for the purpose, but could not compasse it, and in the attempting thereof, they chanced to sinke one of their Barges, with some foure score good souldiers well appointed in her, and yet by good hap and great care, the men were all saved excepting viii. And therefore they were constrayned to put off their landing till another more convenient time.

That morning very timely, there lighted a very faire dove upon the maineyard of the L. Admiral's ship, and there she sate very quietly for the space of 3. or 4. houres, being nothing dismayed all that while, every man gazed and looked much upon her, and spake their minds and opinions, yet all concluding by no meanes to disquiet her: I for my part, tooke it for a very good *omen* and boading, as in trueth (God be thanked) there fell out nothing in the end to the contrary. And as at our very first comming to *Cadiz* this chanced, so likewise on the very last day of our departing from the same towne, another Dove presented herselfe in the selfe-same order into the same ship, and presently grew wonderfull tame and familiar to us all, and did so still keepe us company, even till our arrivall here in *England*.

We no sooner presented ourselves, but presently a goodly sort of tall Spanish ships came out of the mouth of the Bay of *Cadiz,* the Gallies accompanying them in such good order, and so placed as all of them might well succour each other, and therewithall kept themselves very close to their towne, the castle, and the forts, for their better guard and defence, abiding there still, and expecting our farther determination. All that day passed, being very rough and boysterous, and litle or nothing could be done, more then that about the evening there passed some friendly and kinde [Eee6] salutations sent one from the other in warlike maner, by discharging certain great peeces, but to my knowledge no hurt done at all, or else very litle.

A carefull and diligent watch was had all that night thoroughout the whole armie, and on monday morning being the 21. day, the winde and weather being become moderate and favourable, betweene five and sixe of the clocke in the morning, our ships in the name of almightie God, and in defence of the honour of *England,* without any farther delay, with all speed, courage, and alacritie, did set upon the Spanish ships, being then under sayle, and making out of the mouth of the Bay of *Cadiz,* up toward *Puente de Suaço* on *Granada* side, being in number lix. tall ships, with xix. or xx. Gallies attending upon them, sorted in such good order, and reasonable distance as they might still annoy us, and alwayes relieve themselves interchangeably: having likewise the Castle, Forts, and Towne, continually to assist them and theirs, and always readie to play upon us and ours.

In most men's opinions it seemed that the enemy had a wonderful advantage of us, all circumstances being well weighed, but especially the straightnesse of the place, and the naturall forme and situation of the Bay itselfe, being rightly considered. For albeit the very Bay itselfe is very large and exceeding beautifull, so that from *Cadiz* to Port S. *Mary,* is some vi. or vii. English miles over or thereabouts, yet be there many rockes, shelves, sands and shallowes in it, so that the very chanell and place for sea roome, is not above 2. or 3. miles, yea and in some places, not so much, for the ships of any great burthen, to make way in, but that they must either be set on ground or else constrained to run fowle one on another. All this notwithstanding, with great and invincible courage, the Lords generall presently set upon them, and sorting out some such convenient ships, as to their honorable wisedomes seemed fittest for that time's service, they were driven to take some other course then before had beene by them entended. Wherefore upon a grave consultation had by a select Counsell, what great dangers might ensue upon so mightie a disadvantage as appeared in all probability, if it were not by good and sound judgement prevented, and therwithall in their singular wisedomes foreseeing that some great stratageme might be practised by the enemy, either by fire-worke, or some other subtill politike devise, for the hazarding of her Majestie's ships of honor in so narrow a place, thus with al expedition they concluded that the Viceadmirall, the L. *Thomas Howard,* that most noble L. *Howard* (whose exceeding great magnanimity, courage, and wisedome, joyned with such an honorable kind of sweet courtesie, bountie, and liberalitie, as is not able by me and my weakenes to be expressed, hath wonne him all the faithfull loving hearts of as many as ever have had any maner of dealing with him), This L. *Thomas,* I say, in the *Non Pareille* for that time, and the Reare Admirall Sir *Walter Raleigh* (a man of marvelous great worth and regard, for many his exceeding singular great vertues, right fortitude and great resolutenes in all matters of importance) in the Warspight associated with divers most famous worthy knights, namely, Sir *Francis Vere* the L. Martiall in the Rainbow, Sir *George Cary* M. of the Ordinance, in the Mary rose, Sir *Robert Southwell* in the Lyon, gentlemen for all laudable good vertues, and for perfect courage and discretion in all military actions, of as great praise and good desert as any gentlemen of their degree whosoever, having with them some of the ships of *London,* and some of the Dutch squadron of reasonable burthen, should leade the dance, and give the onset, and that the two most noble Lords generall with some others of their companies, should in their convenient time and order, second the maine battell. The fight being begunne and growen very hot, the L. Generall the Earle of *Essex,* (whose infinite princely vertues, with triumphant fame, deserve to be immortalized) being on Port S. *Mary's* side, upon a sudden and unlooked for of others, thrust himselfe among the formost into the maine battell. The other most honorable L. Generall (whose singular vertues in all respects are of such an excellencie and perfection, as neither can my praise in any part increase them, nor any man's envy any whit blemish or diminish them) understanding, the most noble Earle to be in fight among them, and perceiving by the M. of his ship, the Arke royall, that for lacke of water, it was not possible, that he might put any neerer, without farther delay, called presently for his Pynnesse, and in the same Pynnesse put himselfe, and his honorable son L. *William Howard* that now is, aboord the *Honor de la mer,* and there remained in the fight till the battell was ended. The fight was very terrible, and most hideous to the beholder by the continuall discharging of those roaring thundering great peeces, on all sides, and so continued doubtful till about one or two of the clocke in the afternoone: about which time the *Philip,* whom in very truth, they had all most fancie unto, began to yeeld and give over, her men that remained alive shifting for themselves as they were able, and swimming and running ashoare with all the hast that they could possibly, and therewithall, at the very same instant themselves fired their ship, and so left her, and presently thereupon a great Argosie, with another mighty great ship, fired themselves in the like maner. Immediatly hereupon, the residue of the ships, ran themselves on ground, [Eee6v] as farre from us as they could, and therby purchased their owne safety, or rather breathing space for the time. Of them all two faire ships only were boorded and taken by our men with most part of their furniture in them, the one called S. *Matthy,* a ship by estimation of some xii. hundred tunne, and the other S. *Andrew,* being a ship of not much lesser burthen. The Gallies, seeing this suddaine great victorious overthrow, made all the hast they could toward the Bridge called *Puente de Suaço,* and there shrowded themselves in such sort as our shippes could not by any meanes possible come nigh them for lacke of water.

The Spanish ships in all were lix. and as is sayd, all tall ships and very richly furnished and well appointed, whereof some of them were bound for the *Indies,* and other fraighted and furnished for *Lisbon,* as themselves affirme: and had we not come that very time that we did, (which for my part, I do not attribute so much unto meere chance, as to some secret deepe insight and foreknowledge of the two most worthy Lords generall, who no doubt spared for no cost or labour for true intelligence) we had certainely mist of them all.

Of what great wealth and riches these ships were, that I leave to other men's judgement and report, but sure I am, that themselves offered two millions and a halfe of ducats for the redemption of the goods and riches that were in them: which offer of theirs, albeit it was accepted of the Lords Generall, and should have beene received, yet we were defeated of it, as hereafter shall be more at large declared.

What maner of fight this was, and with what courage performed, and with what terror to the beholder continued, where so many thundering tearing peeces were for so long a time discharged, I leave it to the Reader to thinke and imagine. Yet such was the great mercy and goodnes of our living God, that in all this cruell terrible fight, in the end, there were not either slaine or hurt by any maner of meanes (excepting one mischance that happened, wherof I will by and by make mention) many above the number of 100. of our men: notwithstanding divers of our shippes were many times shot thorow and thorow: yea and some of them no lesse then two and twentie times, as I was enformed by credible report of the Captaines and Masters themselves. I knowe not of any other hurt done, saving onely that Sir *Robert Southwell*, who alwayes shewed himselfe a most valiant re-solute knight in all this action, making a litle too much haste with his Pinnesse to boord the *Philip*, had there his said Pinnesse burnt with the *Philip* at the same instant, and yet by good care and diligence his men were saved.

One other mischance (as I said) there happened, and it was thus: One of the Flemings' flieboats, who had, in all the conflict before, caried himselfe very well and valiantly, about ten of the clocke while the fight continued sharpest, chanced by great negligence and mis-fortune, to be fired and blowen up by his owne powder, who could not have any fewer in him, then one hundred fighting men by all supposall, and so in the very twinckling of an eye, both shippe and men were all cast away, excepting vii. or viii. which by very good fortune, and great care and diligence of some of the other ships were saved.

Immediatly upon this notable victory without any farther stay in all the world, the Lord generall the Earle of *Essex* put to shore, and landed about 3000. shot, and pikemen: of the which number the one halfe was presently dispatched to the bridge *Punete de Suaço*, under the conduct of three most famous worthy knights, Sir *Christopher Blunt,* Sir *Coniers Clifford,* and Sir *Thomas Gerard:* with the other halfe, being about fifteene hundred, the most noble Earle of *Essex* himselfe, being accompanied with divers other honorable Lords, namely the Earle of *Sussex*, the Lord *Harbert*, the Lord *Burk*, *Count Lodovick* of *Nassaw*, the Lord Martiall Sir *Francis Vere*, with many other worthy Knights, and men of great regard, who all in that daye's

service did most valiantly behave themselves, with all expedition
possible marched on foote toward the towne of *Cadiz,* which was
about three English miles' march. That time of the day was very hot
and faint, and the way was all of dry deepe slyding sand in a manner,
and beside that, very uneven, and by that meanes so tiresome and
painefull as might be. The enemie having reasonable companie
both of horse and footemen, stoode in a readinesse some good distance
without the towne to welcome us, and to encounter the Lorde Generall.
But the most famous Earle with his valiant Troopes, rather running
indeede in good order, then marching, hastened on them with such
unspeakable courage and celeritie, as within one houre's space and
lesse, the horsemen were all discomfited and put to flight, their
leader being strooken downe at the very first encounter, whereat the
footemen being wonderfully dismayed and astonished at the un-
exspected manner of the Englishmen's kinde of such fierce and resolute fight, retyred themselves with all the speede possible that they
could, to recover themselves into the Towne againe, which being done
by them, with farre swifter legges then manly courage, our men were
enforced to skale the walles: which thing in very deede, although it
was not [Fffl] without great danger and difficulty to be perfourmed:
Yet such was the invincible resolution, and the wonderfull dexterity
of the English, that in one halfe houre or thereabout, the enemie was
repulsed, and the towne wall possessed, by the noble Earle himselfe,
being in all this action, either the very first man or els in a maner
joined with the first.

The towne walles being then possessed, and the English Ensigne
being there displayed upon them, with all speede possible they proceeded on to march through the towne, making still their waie with
sworde and shot so well as they could, being still fought withall at
every turne.

Immediately upon this most famous entrie, the noble Earle, (according to their resolutions, as I take it, put downe before) was seconded
by the noble L. Admirall in person, who was accompanied, with the
noble L. *Thomas Howard,* the most worthy gentleman his sonne, now
L. Howard, Sir Robert Southwell, Sir Richard Levison, and with
divers other gentlemen, his L. followers of good account: his colours
being advanced by that valiant resolute gentleman, (a man beautified
with many excellent rare gifts, of good learning and understanding)
S. *Edward Hobby* Knight. And thus he likewise marching with al

possible speede on foote, not withstanding his L. many yeres, the Intolerable heate for the time, and the overtiring tedious deepe sands, with other many impediments: Yet in good time, joyned himselfe with the Earle and his companies, and gave them the strongest, and best assistance that he could.

Thus then the two Lords Generall with their companies being joyned together, and proceeding so farre as the market place, there they were hotly encountered, where and at what time, that worthy famous knight Sir *John Winkfield*, being sore wounded before on the thigh, at the very entry of the towne, and yet for all that no whit respecting himselfe, being caried away, with the care he had to encourage and direct his company, was with the shot of a musket in the head, most unfortunately slaine.

And thus before eight of the clocke that night were these two most noble Lords General, Masters of the market place, the forts, and the whole Towne and all, onely the Castle as yet holding out, and from time to time as they could, still annoying them, with seven battering pieces. By this time night began to grow on, and a kind of peace or intermission was obtained by them of the Castle: to whome the Lords Generall had signified: that unlesse before the next day in the morning they would absolutely render themselves, they should looke for no mercy, but should every one be put to the sword: upon which message they tooke deliberation that night: but in the morning before breake of day, they hanged out their flag of truce, and so without any further composition did yeeld themselves absolutely to their mercy, and delivered up the Castle.

And yet notwithstanding all this, in the nighttime while they had this respite to pause, and deliberate about the peacemaking, there were divers great and suddaine alarms given: which did breed some great outrages and disorder in the towne. At every which alarme, the two Lordes Generall shewed themselves marvelous ready and forward, insomuch that at the very first alarme, skant wel furnished with any more defence then their shirts, hose, and dublets, and those too altogether in a maner untied, they were abroad in the streetes themselves, to see the uttermost of it. But for that it is not as yet very well knowen (or at the least not well knowen unto me) either wherfore, or by whom these alarmes were attempted: I am therefore to intreat, that a bare report, that such a thing was done, may suffice.

These things being done, and this surrender being made, present proclamation was published, that the fury now being past, all men should surcease from all maner of blood and cruell dealing, and that there should no kind of violence or hard usage be offered to any, either man, woman or child, upon paine of death: And so permitting the spoyle of so much of the towne as was by them thought meete, to the common souldiers for some certaine dayes, they were continually in counsell about other grave directions, best knowen to their honorable wisedomes.

This honorable and mercifull Edict I am sure was streightly and religiously observed of the English: But how well it was kept by the Dutch, I will nether affirme, nor yet denie. For I perceive betweene them and the Spaniards, there is an implacable hartburning, and therefore as soone as the Dutch squadron was espied in the fight, immediatly thereupon both they of *Sivil* and S. *Lucar* and also some, of some other places did not onely arrest all such Dutch ships, as delt with them friendly by the way of traffick and Marchandise, and so confiscated their goods, but also imprisoned the Marchants and Owners of the same, and, as the report goeth, did intreat many of them with extreame cruelty thereupon.

In the meanewhile the very next day being the two and twenty day of June, all the Spanish shippes which were left on ground in the Bay of *Cadiz.* where the great overthrowe had beene but the day before, were by the Spaniards themselves there set on fire, and so from that time forward they never left burning of them, till every one of them, goods and all, as farre as wee [Ffflv] know were burnt and consumed. This their doing was much marvelled at of us, and so much the more, for that, as I sayd before, there had bene made some offer for the re-demption and saving of the goods, and it was not to them unknowen that this their offer was not misliked, but in all probabilitie should have bene accepted. The common opinion was, that this was done either by the appointment of the Duke *de Medina Sidonia,* or els by expresse commandement from the higher powers.

Not long after the same time (three dayes as I remember) the gallies that were runne on ground, did quitte themselves also out of that place, and by the bridge of the Iland called *Puente de Suaço,* made their way round about the same Iland, and so by putting themselves to the maine sea, escaped to a towne called *Rotta,* not farre off, but some-thing up towards the Towne of Saint *Lucars,* and there purchased their safety by that meanes.

Thus was this notable victorie, as well by sea as by land, both begunne and in effect perfourmed, within the compasse, in a maner, of fourteene houres: A thing in trueth so strange and admirable, as in my judgement will rather bee wondered at then beleeved of posteritie. And if ever any notable exploit in any age was comparable to *Caesar's Veni, Vidi, Vici*, certainely in my poore opinion it was this.

Here it is to be wished (and perchance of some too it is looked for) that every man's particular worthy acte in this daye's service, with the partie's, names also, should be put downe, that thereby both they and their good deserts might be registred to all posteritie: and for my part I would it were so, and wish I were able to doe it. But for that I confesse it is a matter that passeth my power, yea, and for that I thinke it also a thing impossible to be precisely perfourmed by any other, I am to crave pardon for that I rather leave it out altogether, then presume to doe it maymedly: and in this point I referre the Reader onely to the Mappe that is set foorth of this journey, where it is in some parte conveniently touched and specified.

The Towne of itselfe was a very beautifull towne, and a large, as being the chiefe See of the Bishop there, and having a goodly Cathedrall Church in it, with a right goodly Abbey, a Nunnery, and an exceeding fine College of the Jesuites, and was by natural situation, as also by very good fortification, very strong, and tenable enough in all men's opinions of the better judgement. Their building was all of a kind of hard stone, even from the very foundation to the top, and every house was in a manner a kind of fort or Castle, altogether flat-roofed in the toppe, after the Turkish manner, so that many men together, and that at ease, might walke theron: having upon the housetop, great heapes of weighty stoanes piled up in such good order, as they were ready to be throwen downe by every woman most easily upon such as passed by, and the streetes for the most part so exceeding narrow, (I thinke to avoide the intolerable great heat of the Sunne) as but two men or three at the most together, can in any reasonable sorte marche thorough them, no streete being broader commonly then I suppose Watling streete in *London* to be.

The towne is altogether without glasse, excepting the Churches, yet with faire comely windowes, and with faire grates of iron to them, and have very large folding leaves of wainscot, or the like. It hath very fewe Chimnies in it, or almost none at all: it may be some one chimney in some one or other of the lower outroomes of lest account, serving for some necessary uses, either to wash in, or the like, or els nowe and then perchance for the dressing of a dish of meate, having, as it should seeme unto me, alwayes a greater care and respect how to keepe themselves from all kind of great heat, then how to provide for any store of great roste. It had in it by report of them that should best know it, some foure thousand and moe, of very good able fighting men, and sixe hundred horsemen at the least. No question but that they were well furnished of all things appertaining thereunto, especially so many good ships lying there, and being so well stored with all manner of munition, shot, and powder, as they were.

Whether they had knowledge of our comming or no, I can say nothing to it: Themselves give it out that they understood not of it, but onely by a Caravel the Friday at evening before we came. But whether they knew it or no, thus much I dare boldly affirme, that if the English had bene possessed of that or the like Towne, and had bene but halfe so well provided as they were, they would have defended it for one two moneths at the least, against any power whatsoever in al Christendome. But surely GOD is a mighty GOD, and hath a wonderfull secret stroke in all matters, especially of weight and moment. Whether their hearts were killed at the mighty overthrow by sea, or whether they were amased at the invincible courage of the English, which was more then ordinary, caring no more for either small shot or great, then in a maner for so many hailestones, or whether the remorse of a guilty conscience toward the English nation, [Fff2] for their dishonorable and divelish practises, against her Sacred Majestie, and the Realme, (a matter that easily begetteth a faint heart in a guilty minde) or what other thing there was in it I know not, but be it spoken to their perpetuall shame and infamie, there was never thing more resolutely perfourmed of the couragious English, nor more shamefully lost of the bragging Spaniard.

Of what wealth this towne should be, I am not able to resolve the asker: for I confesse that for mine owne part, I had not so much good lucke, as to be partaker so much as of one pennie, or pennyworth. Howbeit my ill fortune maketh that towne never a whit the poorer. But as it should appeare by the great pillage by the common souldiers, and some mariners too, and by the goodly furnitures, that were defaced by the baser people, and thereby utterly lost and spoyled, as not woorth the carying away, and by the over great plenty of Wine, Oyle, Almonds, Olives, Raisins, Spices, and other rich grocery wares, that by the intemperate disorder of some of the rasher sort were knockt out, and lay trampled under feete, in every common highway, it should appeare that it was of some very mighty great wealth to the first owners, though perchance, not of any such great commoditie to the last subduers, for that I judge that the better part was most ryotously and intemperately spent and consumed. A disorder in mine opinion very much to be lamented, and if it might be by any good meanes remedied, in my conceit, it were a most honourable device.

The Wednesday, Thursday, and Friday following, the Lords Generall spent in counsell, about the disposing of all matters, aswell touching the towne and prisoners, as also concerning all other matters, thought meete of them in their honourable wisedomes, and in all that meanewhile did shew such honourable bounty and mercy, as is not able to be expressed. For not onely the lives of everyone were spared, but also there was an especial care had, that al the Religious, as wel men as women, should be well and favourably intreated, whom freely without any maner of ransome or other molestation, they caused to be safely transported over to *Port Saint Marie,* a towne in a manner as fayre as *Cadiz:* but at that time, as the case did stand, certainely knowen to be of no wealth in the world, and it was some sixe or seven miles distant over against *Cadiz,* in a maner as *Paule's* is against *Southwarke,* on the other side of the Bay, in a part of *Andaluzia,* subject to the territory of the Duke *de Medina Sidonia.*

Moreover, at the same instant they did appoint that worthy knight Sir *Amias Preston,* and some others in some convenient Barkes, to transport over to the sayd Towne safely and in good order, a hundred or moe of the better sort of ancient gentlewomen, and marchants' wives, who were suffered to put upon themselves, some of them two, yea, some three sutes of apparell, with some convenient quantitie of many Jewels, Chaines, and other ornaments belonging to their estate and degree. Such was the heroicall liberality, and exceeding great clemencie, of those most honourable Lords Generall, thereby, as it should seeme unto mee, beating downe that false surmised opinion, which hath bene hitherto commonly spread abroad, and setled among the Spaniards: which is, That the English doe trouble them and their countries, more for their golde, riches and pearle &c. then for any other just occasion. Whereas by these their honourable dealings it is manifest to all the world, that it is only in respect of a just revenge for the manifolde injuries, and most dishonourable practises that have beene from time to time attempted by them against us and our nation, and also in the defence of the true honour of *England:* which they have sought, and daylie doe seeke, by so many sinister and reprochfull devices, so much as in them lieth, to deface.

Upon Saturday being the 26. Sir *John Winkfield* knight was buried, in honourable and warlike manner, so farre foorth as the circumstances of that time and place could permit. At whose funerals the Navie discharged a great part of their Ordinance, in such order, as was thought meete and convenient by the Lords Generals' commandement.

The twenty-seventh day being Sunday, in the Abbey the divine service was had, and a learned Sermon was made there by one Master *Hopkins,* the right honourable Earle of *Essex* his Preacher, a man of good learning and sweete utterance, and even there the same day, something before the sermon was made, these worthie Gentlemen following were knighted by the Lords General. And here I am to signifie by the way that two of these were knighted three or foure dayes before, and some three or foure moe were knighted after that time, upon certaine occasions: but yet I holde it best (and I trust without offence) to recite their names in this place altogether. [Fff2v]

The names of such noble men and gentlemen, as were
knighted at Cadiz in June 1596 by the two
most honourable Lordes Generall.

SIr *Samuel Bagnol.*	Sir *John Leigh, alias Lee.*
Sir *Arthur Savage.*	Sir *Richard Weston.*
The Earle of *Sussex.*	Sir *Richard Wainman.*
The Lord *Harbert.*	Sir *James Wootton.*
The Lord *Burk.*	Sir *Richard Ruddal.*
Count Lodowick.	Sir *Robert Mansfield.*
Sir *William Howard.*	Sir *William Mounson.*
Sir *George D'Eureux.*	Sir *John Bowles.*
Sir *Henry Nevel.*	Sir *Edward Bowes.*
Sir *Edmund Rich.*	Sir *Humfrey Druel.*
Sir *Richard Leven.*	Sir *Amias Preston.*
Sir *Peter Egomort.*	Sir *Robert Remington.*
Sir *Anthonie Ashley.*	Sir *John Buck.*
Sir *Henry Leonard.*	Sir *John Morgan.*
Sir *Richard Levison.*	Sir *John Aldridg.*

Sir *Horatio Vere.*
Sir *Arthur Throckmorton.*
Sir *Miles Corbet.*
Sir *Edward Conway.*
Sir *Oliver Lambert.*
Sir *Anthony Cooke.*
Sir *John Townesend.*
Sir *Christopher Heydon.*
Sir *Francis Popham.*
Sir *Philip Woodhouse.*
Sir *Alexander Clifford.*
Sir *Maurice Barkley.*
Sir *Charles Blunt.*
Sir *George Gifford.*
Sir *Robert Crosse.*
Sir *James Escudamor.*
Sir *Urias Leigh.*

Sir *John Asshindon.*
Sir *Matthew Browne.*
Sir *John Acton.*
Sir *Thomas Gates.*
Sir *Gilly Mericke.*
Sir *Thomas Smith.*
Sir *William Pooley.*
Sir *Thomas Palmer.*
Sir *John Stafford.*
Sir *Robert Lovel.*
Sir *John Gylbert.*
Sir *William Harvie.*
Sir *John Gray.*
Don *Christ,* prince of *Portingal.*
Sir *John Vanderfoord,* Admirall
    of the Hollanders.
Sir *Robert Dudley.* 8. August.

I am not curious in placing these gentlemen, but put them downe at a venture. Only I have observed, as neere as I could, the just day and time when they were created. And I trust where the place of itselfe is so worthy and equall, there the bare naming and placing of the parties, shal breede no offence, or make a disparity. The two gentlemen that were last knighted received their knighthood in the way of our returne from *Cadiz:* the one of them upon the sea, not farre from the Bay of the *Groyne,* at what time our ships stood upon their staies for a space, while certaine Pinnasses were sent to descrie what shipping was at the *Groine:* The other at *Plimmouth* in the open streete, when the Lords Generall came from the Sermon. The one a man of long service, and good desert among the Dutch: the other of so many good parts of a worthy gentleman, as the like are seldome seene to concurre in any.

I spake in the beginning of her Majestie's praier, which I presumed (though unworthy) to translate into Latine: and nowe at this very time, there was some opportunity offered, for to make some use of that translation. For nowe being in *Cadiz,* attending upon my most honourable good Lord, I talked with certaine of the Religious men, such as I found learned, wherof indeed there were some, though not very many. I talked also with the Bishop of *Cusco* there, a grave aged comely man, and being of late chosen to that Bishopricke, he was as then to have gone to the Indies, had not we then taken him prisoner, and so stayed his journey for that time. With these men ever as occasion did serve, I did seeke nowe and then to spende some speech, and to entertaine time withall, I would breake with them of this our victorie, and of the injuries and bad dealings of their Prince and Countrey offered to her Majestie, whereby shee was provoked, and in a manner drawen to this action: though otherwise of her own most excellent [Fff3] princely good nature, she was altogether given to peace, and quietnes. And alwayes in some part of our conferences, I would shew them a copie of her Majestie's praier in Latine, which I had alwaies of purpose ready about me, wherby it might the better appeare unto them, how unwillingly, and upon how great and urgent occasions her Majesty was, as it were enforced to undertake this action: and therewithall I did use now and then to bestow upon them a copy of the same in writing. They seemed in all outward shew to allow of my speeches, and to praise her Majestie's good inclination, and earnestly to wish that there might be a firme concord and peace againe.

It pleased the Lords generall to deale exceeding favourably with this said Bishop of *Cusco:* for it was their good pleasure to give him his free passage without any ransome, and therewithal to let him to understand, that they came not to deale with Church-men, or unarmed men, or with men of peace, weaklings and children, neither was it any part of their meaning to make such a voyage for gold, silver, or any other their wealth and riches, &c. But that their only comming was to meet with their dishonorable practises, and manifold injuries, and to deale with men of warre and valour, for the defence of the true honour of *England:* and to let them to understand, that whensoever they attempted any base-conceited and dishonorable practise to their soveraigne Queene, their Mistresse, that it should be revenged to the uttermost, &c.

In this meane space, while the Lords general continued at *Cadiz,* there came to them certain poore wretched Turks, to the number of 38, that had bin a long time gally-slaves, and either at the very time of the fight by sea, or els immediately thereupon, taking the opportunity, did then make their escape, and did swim to land: yeelding themselves to the mercy of their most honorable Lordships. It pleased them with all speed to apparel them, and to furnish them with money, and all other necessaries, and bestow on them a barke, and a Pilot, to see them freely and safely conveied into *Barbary*, willing them to let the countrey understand what was done, and what they had seene. Whereby I doubt not, but as her Majesty is a most admirable Prince already, over all *Europe*, all *Africk*, and *Asia*, and throughout Christendome: so the whole worlde hereafter shall have just cause to admire her infinite Princely vertues, and thereby bee provoked to confesse, that as she hath bin mightily protected from time to time, by the powerful hand of the almighty, so undoubtedly, that she is to be judged and accounted of us, to be his most sacred handmaide, and chosen vessel. And therefore, whatsoever wicked designement shalbe conspired and plotted against her Majesty hereafter, shalbe thought to be conspired, plotted, and intended against the almighty himselfe: and for that cause, as I trust, shalbe by the infinite goodnes and mercy of that almighty, mightily frustrate and overthrowen.

The 28. day being Munday, the L. Admiral came aboord the Arke againe, minding there to remaine for a space, as indeed he did, and upon the advise of his Phisition, to deale something in physicke, for that his L. found his body something out of frame. At that time it pleased his L. to write certain letters to the Duke of *Medina Sidonia*, for the deliverance of English captives, who were remaining in the gallies. For by this time, it was reported, that the saide Duke was come downe in person with some power, and that he was either at *Port S. Mary*, or els at *Rotta*, or thereabout. His L. did endite the letters himselfe, but his pleasure was, they should be turned into Latine by another: and so to be sent (as indeed they were) in the latine tongue unto the Duke.

A copie of the Lord Admiral's letters to the Duke of Medina Sidonia.
Illustrissimo Principi Duci de Medina Sidonia.

ILlustrissime Princeps, ex nonnullis quibusdam Hispanis intelligimus, Excellentiam vestram iam nunc esse apud portum S. Mariae. Et quoniam in anno Domini 1588. id nobis tunc muneris assignatum erat à sereniss. nostra Regina domina mea, vt contra vos, vestrásque; copias, Ego solus pro eo tempore Generalis essem constitutus: Id circò non opinamur vobis ignotum esse, quàm mite quoddam, et humanum bellandi genus, tum hîc iam in hoc ipso tempore, aduersus huius loci populum atque; incolas vsurpauerimus: tum etiam saepiùs antehac quàm humaniter, benigneque; eos omnes tractauerimus, quos ex vestris iure belli capituos acceperimus. Ex quorum numero quàm multa millia, etiam gratîs, nullo accepto pretio, libertate donauerimus, id putamus omnibus esse testatius, quàm vt à quoquam denegetur. Quo circa, neque; vllo modo nobis in mentem venire potest, vt dubitemus, quin parem etiam in vobis humanitatem aduersus nostros captiuos fimus reperturi. Cùm igitur nobis compertun iam fit, habere vos in vestris galeris, ex Reginae nostre serenissimae Dominae meae subditis vnum et quinquaginta captiuōs: non equidem dubitamus, quin eos omnes fitis relaxaturi, et ad nos missuri: ea lege, ac conditione, [Fff3v] vt totidem ex vestris hic captiuis eiusdem loci atque; ordinis, melioris etiam fortassis notae, ac conditionis, homuncios, ad vos vicissim remittamus. Id quod nos facturos data fide spondemus, quàm primùm nostros captiuos ex vestris manibus acceperimus. Hac in re si nostro desiderio ac voluntati parùm satisfactum erit, aliud profectò tunc posthac belli genus ingrediemur, aliúmque; bellandi morem cogemur, etiam inuiti, et contra voluntatem prosequi. Ex Regia Anglicana classe apud Cadiz ultimo Iunij, stilo antiquo. 1596. Carolus Howard.

These letters were sent by a Spaniard, and an answere was brought from the Duke with al convenient speed, and as it should seeme by the L. Admiral's next answere returned to him in writing, which immediatly hereafter foloweth, the Duke *de Medina Sidonia* his letters were honorable, and with good regard.

A copie of my L. Admiral's second letter to the Duke of Medina Sidonia.
Illustrissimo Principi Duci de Medina Sidonia.
ILlustrissime Princeps, literas ab excellentia vestra hodiè accepimus: quae verò nostra sit ad illas responsio, nobiles isti viri, qui vestras literas ad nos pertulerunt, pleniùs declarabunt. Hoc interim cupimus esse penitùs persuasum Excellentie vestre, nos seduló operam daturos, vt in omni honorificae benignitatis humanitatisque; genere, expectationi vestrae omni ex parte respondeamus. Quod ad Anglicos nostros captiuos attinet, quos ab Excellentia vestra huc ad nos crastino die missum iri expectamus, in ea re pollicemur Excellentiae vestrae,

quòd plenius à nobis vestrae voluntati satisfactum erit: et quòd pro illis captiuis tales nos capituos vobis remittemus, quales tum ab ipso Dom. Mendoza, tum ab alijs illustrib. viris, qui à Dom. Porta Carero in illorum ad nos fauorem mittebantur, communi cum consensu erant ab ipsis approbati. Si verò quis alius iam captiuus est vel posthac futurus erit in nostra potestate, pro cuius redemptione nondum plenè conuentum est et stipulatum de certo pretio persoluendo: concedimus Excellentiae vestre, vt in hoc etiam casu vos, vestro pro arbitrio, de illis quicquid velitis, imperetis. Ex Regia classe Anglicana, apud Cadiz, 3. die Iulij stylo antiquo. 1596.

Carolus Howard.

The next day after, being the 4. of July, the LL. general caused the town of *Cadiz* to be set on fire, and rased and defaced so much as they could, the faire cathedral Church, and the religious houses only being spared, and left unblemished. And with the town al such provision for shipping, and other things, as were serviceable for the King's use, and yet were not either so convenient for us to be caried away, or els such as we stood no whit at all in need of, were likewise at the same instant consumed with fire. And presently therupon, their Lordships, with as convenient speed as they could, and the whole army in such good order and leisure, as they thought best, came aboord.

The next day being the 5. of July, the LL. general with all the armie being under saile, and now making for *England,* and but as yet passing the very mouth of the bay of *Cadiz,* a galley ful of English prisoners, with a flag of truce, met us from *Rotta,* sent by the D. of *Medina Sidonia,* and sent as it should seeme, one day later then his promise: but yet their flag being either not big enough, or not wel placed in the galley, or not wel discerned of our men, or by what other mischance I know not: but thus it was: by one of our smallest ships that sailed formost, as soone as the said galley came within gunshot, there was a great peece discharged upon her, and at that instant there was one man slaine outright, and 2. other grievously hurt. The error being espied and perceived, our ship gave over immediatly from any farther shooting. As soone as the galley came neere us, my L. Admiral caused a gracious salutation to be sounded with his trumpets, and willed the captains forthwith to come aboord his ship: which they did, and then he feasted them with a very fine and honorable banket, as the time and place might serve. And then by them understanding of that unfortunate mischance that had hapned by the shot of the said ship, he was very sory for the same, and yet such was the merciful providence of almighty God, that even in this mischance also, he did hold his holy hand over the English. And al the harme that was done did light only upon the poore Turk, and the Spaniard himselfe. When this Lorde had well banqueted them, hee presently called for his barge, and did accompany the said galley to the Lorde general the Earle of *Essex,* who then did ride with his ship a good distance off: and there they being in like maner most honorably received, and intertained, the Spanish gentlemen delivered up their prisoners the English captives, of whom some had bin there 6 yere, some 8, or ten: yea, and some 22. yeere, and upward, and some of them but lately taken in *S. Francis Drake's* last voiage to the *Indies.* The number of the prisoners delivered were but 39. and no mo, and were brought in, and delivered by *Don Antonio de Corolla* and his brother, and by *Don Pedro de Cordua,* and certaine others. If you demaund why, of one and fiftie Captives, there were no moe delivered then was, I presuppose, (and I thinke it true to) that at that time the residue were farther off in some remote places of Spaine bestowed, and so by that meanes, not able at this time to bee in a readinesse, but yet like [Fff4] enough that there is some good order taken for them hereafter, to be redeemed, and sent over into *England.*

If any man presume here so farre, as to enquire how it chanced, that the Lords generall rested so long at *Cadiz,* and went no farther, and why *Port S. Mary* being so faire a towne, and so neere to them, was forborne? and why *Sheres* alias *Xeres?* And why *Rotta* and the like? And why this or that was done? And why that or this left undone? I will not answere him with our common English proverbe, as I might, which is: That one foole may aske moe questions in one houre, then ten discrete men can wel answere in five dayes.

But that grave auncient writer, *Cornelius Tacitus,* hath a wise, briefe, pithy saying, and it is this: *Nemo tentauit inquirere in columnas Herculis, sanctiusque; ac reuerentius habitum est de factis Deorum credere, quàm scire.* Which saying, in my fancy, fitteth marveilous well for this purpose: and so much the rather, for that this *Cadiz* is that very place, (at least by the common opinion) where those said pillers of *Hercules* were thought to be placed: and, as some say, re-maine as yet not farre off to be seene. But to let that passe, the saying beareth this discrete meaning in it, albeit in a pretty kind of mystical maner uttered: That it befitteth not inferiour persons to be curious, or too inquisitive after Princes' actions, neither yet to be so sawcy and so malapert, as to seeke to dive into their secrets, but rather alwayes to have a right reverend conceite and opinion of them, and their doings: and theron so resting our inward thoughts, to seek to go no further, but so to remaine ready alwaies to arme ourselves with dutiful minds, and willing obedience, to perform and put in execution that which in their deepe insight and heroicall designements, they shall for our good, and the care of the commonwealth determine upon.

This, and much lesse to, might suffice to satisfie any honest minded man. But yet if any will needs desire to be a little farther satisfied, albeit it neede not, yet then, thus much I dare say and affirme, that upon my knowledge, the chiefest cause why *Port Saint Mary,* and the rest were left untouched, was this: For that it was most certainly knowen, that they were townes not woorth the saluting of such a royal companie, in which there was no maner of wealth in the world left, more then bare houses of stone, and standing walles, and might well have served rather as a stale, perchance, to have entrapped, then as a meanes to have enriched. And it had bin more then a suspition of follie, for such an army as this, to have sought to fight with the aire, and to have laboured with great paine and charges, yea, and with some evident danger too, to have overthrowen that, which could very litle or nothing have profited, being destroyed: and yet nowe, can doe as little harme being left, as it is, untouched.

And thus much for our journey to *Cadiz:* for the accidents that happened by the way, for the winning, spoiling, and burning of the said towne, for the overthrowe of the Spanish Fleet there, and for al other by-matters that happened, as appendances to the same, both in the time of our abode there, as also at the very last houre of our comming from thence.

As for our returne home, and our entrance into a part of *Portingal* by the way, with the taking, spoyling, and burning of the towne of *Faraon* there, and marching into the Spanish confines therabouts, &c. I minde to leave it to some other, whose chance was to be present at the action, as myselfe was not, and shalbe of more sufficient ability to performe it.

Proclamation on sending over
the Army into Ireland (1599)

Long before Elizabeth's reign and well into it, the
problem of Ireland had for England been a problem of national security,
for the Irish—divided into the four provinces of Leinster, Munster,
Connaught, and Ulster—were a quarrelsome group of strongly nationalistic and proudly clannish people living close to the Queen's shores.
Leinster, nearest the Pale, consisted of the lands of Kildare (of the house
of Fitzgerald) and of Butler and were in 1599 largely free of trouble;
the only threat of disaffection came from the wild, hilly county of
Wicklow. In Munster the O'Briens of Thomond were intermittently
loyal, the stronger Geraldines of Desmond fiercely dangerous. Connaught was wildly savage; Ulster, organized by the houses of O'Donnell (Tyrconnel) and O'Neill (in Tyrone, Fermangh, Monaghan, and
Armagh counties) was even worse. Also living in Ulster was a Scottish
clan, the MacDonalds, invaders from the Western Islands, who provided mercenary soldiers (Redshanks) under such leaders as Sorley Boy
MacDonald. These clans lived mostly by cattle raids and warfare,
ravaging the countryside and murdering its people. They did not know
Protestantism; Catholicism, which they had known partly through
Jesuit missionaries, was declining.

The Irish problem was also unavoidable because the King of England
was also Lord of Ireland: there was legal responsibility as well as legal
authority for keeping the peace which had from the time of King John
been handled rather haphazardly. By inheritance Kings of England
were titular Earls of Ulster and Lords of Meath and Connacht and other
lands, but they had to enforce their titles to make them mean anything.
The actual job of keeping peace and providing necessary security was
given to a lord deputy for the King, but the task was so difficult that
through the centuries the lord deputies had concentrated on less and
less of the country; by the sixteenth century, the only real English influence was in a lowland coastal strip between Dublin and Dundalk
and in the Pale—a narrow inland region consisting of parts of Louth,
Meath, Dublin, and Kildare counties. As the effectual rule diminished,

however, a number of Gaelic chieftains had slowly but surely rein-
stated their original power, challenging respect for the English
sovereign and building in effect a separate country with a separate
language and independent traditions.

The problem that Elizabeth inherited in Ireland when she came to the
throne in 1558 was, therefore, twofold: control over increasingly
independent Irish people and respect for her lord deputy as her
personal representative and ruler. At first, she tried to placate the Irish
with diplomacy; she invited a disputed heir of one Irish clan, Hugh
O'Neil, heir to the earldom of Tyrone, to come to England where she
saw that as a boy he was educated in English ways. This early move
was unsuccessful, partly because it was so limited; and in 1585 her lord
deputy, Sir John Perrot, tried an alternative solution first practiced
by Anthony St. Leger during the reign of Henry IV: acknowledging
the Irish custom of clan rule based on elected leadership and recogniz-
ing its basic cleavage with the English custom of obtaining influence
by ownership of land and authority by primogeniture, he persuaded
a number of Irish lords to surrender their clan-based titles, allowing
Elizabeth to regrant them as English titles with English privileges.
Perrot's negotiated treaties, executed with individual reparation and
extreme patience, were known collectively as the Composition of
Connacht. They also failed—like Elizabeth's attempt to educate the
Irish, the solution was too limited to be of much use. Now a third
solution—this one first begun under Mary Tudor—was attempted
again. Elizabeth began to settle English "plantations" in Ireland by
taking over land lost by the Irish in sporadic rebellions and selling
it cheaply to English subjects, provided they defended it in the name of
the English Crown. Early settlements by Thomas Smith in the Ards in
1572-1573 and by the earl of Essex in adjacent Clandeboyne in 1573-1575
were ill-fated, but later Burghley and Ralegh confiscated 400,000 acres
of Munster and distributed this to the English. Despite famine, disease,
and incompetence, this scheme seemed to be gaining in effectiveness,
spreading to Connaught but at the cost of reducing the landholdings
of the Irish lords and thus increasing their hatred of the English. Only
Tyrone's Ulster withstood such English infiltration. The rebels whose
lands were usurped—O'More, O'Connor, O'Neil—were active in
harrying the English settlers and, eventually, in the rebellion of 1599.

This rebellion, which really began in 1594, and was the only sizeable
and important war in the last decade of Elizabeth's reign, was led by the
English-educated Hugh O'Neil, the earl of Tyrone. He was urged on
by his ancestry, which he traced to the ancient High Kings of Ireland,
and by the memory of his grandfather, the first earl of Tyrone, who
had enjoyed much more power and freedom from English rule than
he felt. Tyrone was not a nationalist, but when a dispute between
the MacGuire clan and the lord president of Connaught, Sir Richard
Bingham, touched off a revolt, Tyrone quickly built a formidable

league of the dispossessed and dissident—including his traditional
enemy O'Donnell—and in a rebellion for Gaelic independence (but
not unity) Tyrone and O'Donnell swept down from the north,
invading the plantation of Munster and driving its inhabitants in
fear to havens along the sea. Papal support and the promise of Spanish
aid only added to Tyrone's new belligerence—he was quite willing to
play the part of a Crusader since as a nascent *realpolitik* he knew the
source of power was to align himself with either Philip or Elizabeth
against the other—and his cunning and bravery were alike aimed at
one thing: to be King.

Tyrone's first real success came in 1598 when he routed an English
army, commanded by Sir Henry Bagenal, as it was marching from
Armagh to relieve the fort at Blackwater. For the English, this was
their worst loss since Calais; and Tyrone's control spread rapidly
from Ulster to the length of Ireland. With the additional possibility
of Spanish aid or intervention, Elizabeth had no choice—however
distasteful it might be—but to send additional forces to Ireland. This
damp, disease-ridden bog of a country was known popularly in her
court as the "graveyard of reputations," but in 1599 she announced,
in the following proclamation, an expedition of an additional 16,000
foot and 1,300 horse under Essex: she had already invested 3,500 men
and more than a million pounds in the past years to no avail.

The necessity and the costs forced upon her when she was already
strapped with the wars with Spain in the Low Countries and with
civil factions in France no doubt account for the rather peevish tone
in the document which follows, in which she insists on "that fruit of
obedience which we expected": in harking back to the unnaturalness
of rebellion which has wrought "many violent outrages upon our
loyall Subjects," Elizabeth reveals the depth of her hatred for active
disobedience anywhere in her realm. Her notion that subjects should
respect their ruler because it is due "the Lawes of God and Nature"
echoes the "homily on obedience," but it is no less true for that. Still
the Queen manages to be politic: she recants her earlier use of "conquest,"
for that is too strong a word; rather, "our actions [tend] onely to reduce
a number of unnaturall and barbarous Rebels, and to roote out the
Capitall heads of the most notorious Traitours." The final, haunting
tones are those of regret and submission. Yet there is here also a voice
of firm resolve which insists with renewed—if subdued—vigor on
the preservation of those principles by which Elizabeth had directed
her life and rule: a proclamation that is also a portrait of a Queen in
her declining years.

Textual Notes

[For explanatory notes for this selection see page 384.]

Proclamation on sending over the Army into Ireland

Reference. STC 14146; Steele, II,153.

Editions. The proclamation issued by the Queen on March 31, 1599, concerning her decision to send an army into Ireland, was printed in a single edition by the official printer Christopher Barker.

Collation. 1⁰; two broadsheets (folio); unnumbered [pages are indicated by a slash (/) within the text].

Description of Contents. Heading in roman; text in black-letter; "God saue the Queene." in roman; colophon in roman and italics. Ornamental initial *A*.

License. No entry in the *Stationers' Register*.

Base-Copy Text. Bedleian Arch.G.c.6(ff. 384-385).

Emendations. our selfe,]ourselfe, euery where]everywhere our selues]ourselves which euer]whichever not withstanding]notwithstanding before hand]beforehand Highnesse]Highnesse's

By the Queene.

The Queene's Majestie's Proclamation declaring her princely resolution in sending over of her Army into the Realme of Ireland.

LTHOUGH OUR ACTIONS and carriage in the whole course of our government, ever since it pleased God to call us to the succession of this Crowne (being truely considered) may as evidently manifest to all our Subjects, as our conscience doeth clearly witnesse it to ourselfe, how earnestly wee have affected the peace and tranquilitie of the people of our Dominions, and how much we have preferred clemencie before any other respect, as a vertue both agreeable to our naturall disposition, the sinceritie of the Religion which we professe, and alwayes esteemed by us the greatest surety to our Royall State, when our Subjects' heartes are assured to us by the bond of love, rather then by forced obedience; Notwithstanding it hath fallen out to our great discontentation, that this our gracious intention in the whole scope of our government, hath not wrought in all men's mindes a like effect, nor brought forth everywhere that fruit of obedience which we expected, and namely in our kingdome and people of Ireland, where (as oftentimes heretofore, so nowe especially of late yeeres) divers of our Subjects, both of the better sort and of the meaner (abusing our lenitie to their advantage) have unnaturally and without all ground or cause offered by us, forgotten their allegeance, and (rebelliously taking Armes) have committed many bloody and violent outrages upon our loyall Subjects. And though their owne consciences can

beare them witnesse that both by us, and by our ministers there, more wayes have bene attempted to reclaime them by clemencie (for avoyding of bloodshed) then is usuall with Princes that have so good meanes to reduce them by other meanes, yet have we not thereof reaped those fruites which so great a grace hath deserved, if there had bene in them any sense of Religion, duetie, or common humanitie. This is therefore the cause that after so long patience wee have bene compelled to take resolution, to reduce that Kingdome to obedience (which by the Lawes of God and Nature is due unto us) by using an extraordinary power and force against them; Assuring ourselves so much in the justice of our cause, as we shall finde the same success (whichever it is the pleasure of God to give to Prince's rights) against unnaturall rebellions: wherein notwithstanding because we doe conceive that all our people which are at this present Actors in this Rebellion are not of one kinde, nor carried into it with one minde, but some out of sense they have of hard measures heretofore offered them by some of our ministers, some for feare of power and might which their adversse Sects and Factions have growne unto, by advantage of this loose time, and some for want of protection and defence against the wicked and barbarous Rebels, and many inveygled with superstitious impressions, wrought in them by the cunning of seditious Priestes and Seminaries (crept into them from forreine parts, suborned by those that are our enemies) and a great part out of a strong opinion put into them by the heades of this Rebellion, that wee intended an utter extirpation and rooting out of that Nation, and conquest of the Countrey.

We have therefore thought it good and answerable to that Justice and clemencie which we professe to be with us in accompt, above all other Royall vertues, to accompanie our Armie, which we send thither with this signification to our Subjects, that we are not ignorant of the divers causes that have misse-led them into these unnaturall actions, and that we both can and will make distinction of their offences. And for their better comfort touching the apprehension of Conquest, wherewith the capitall and unnaturall Traitours doe seeke to harden the hearts of those that have lesse offended us, thereby hoping to binde them faster to run their desperate fortune: We doe professe hereby to the worlde, that we are so farre from any such purpose, as the very name of Conquest in this case seemeth so absurd to us, as wee cannot imagine upon what ground it coulde enter into any man's conceite, that our actions tending onely to reduce a number of unnaturall and

barbarous Rebels, and to roote out the Capitall heads of the most
notorious Traitours, should neede any such title of Conquest, when
we have in that our kingdome (to our great contentment) the best part
of our Nobilitie, the people of all our good Townes, and divers of
our subjects so assured in their Loyaltie to us, as they give us no
suspition of falling from their dueties. Of which our true and Princely
meaning, we require all our Subjects there in generall, to take comfort,
and such as for any cause are revolted from their duetie, to bethinke
themselves betimes of the extreme miserie whereinto they shall throw
themselves, if by persisting in this rebellion, they give us cause to use
against them, the last (but worst of all remedies) the sworde, which for
repairing of our Honour, the safetie of the rest of our people, and the
assurance of the course of our Justice, wee are both forced, and so
resolved to doe to all that shall not with all expedition, penitencie,
and humilitie, prostrate themselves to our mercie, as their onely way
to redeeme themselves from the calamities and confusions, whereof
their owne heartes cannot but feele (beforehand) the horrour. For
confirmation of all which resolutions, as well howe to proceede with
the grieved and humbled hearts, as with the obstinate and obdurate: We
have made choyce of such a person to be in that Realme, the minister
both of our Justice and Mercie, whose valour, wisedome, and successe
in other publike actions, which we have committed unto him, and
the force of our good Subjects, with which he is now and shall be
furnished, as it may be just terrour to the wicked, in making them see
before their eyes, the short and desperate ende of these their barbarous
and unnaturall courses; So may this our election of a person of his
place and ranke every way, both in our Counsels and in our kingdome,
sufficiently assure our duetifull Subjects there, of the great care we
have of their preservation, of the abundance of our Clemency, and
gracious disposition to those that shall deserve mercie, and of our
resolution to make the obstinate enemies to God, and Traitours to
our Crowne and dignitie, to feele our powerfull Arme.

Given at her Majestie's Mannor of Richmond, the last day of March
1599. in the one and fourtieth yeere of her Highnesse's Reigne.

God save the Queene.
Imprinted at London by the Deputies of Christopher Barker,
Printer to the Queene's most excellent Majestie.
Anno. Dom. 1599.

Proclamation on the seizure
of the Earls of Essex, Rutland,
and others for their rebellion (1601)

Robert Devereux, earl of Essex, had all the attributes for heroism in Elizabeth's age except character. He possessed the handsome face and body and the kind of vital, magnetic charm that most attracted the Queen; and he continually recaptured royal favor after some incredible escapade or impulsive folly by fawning over her. His athletic prowess, especially at tournaments, also made him a beloved leader of the court and town. His imagination and energy led him to take extraordinary chances, especially on the battlefields where Elizabeth's gravest dangers lay—in the Netherlands, in France, on the high seas, in Ireland—and here his tendency to great risk only added to his charisma. It was beyond his capacity of understanding, however, to realize that such reckless behavior was ill advised in council chambers and that at Whitehall his wits were easily outmatched by those who also competed not simply for the Queen's good graces, but for her political favors and for positions of power. The hero would conquer all; and his pride disallowed him to see his vulnerability: that out of battle his impulsive gestures often looked like hollow vanity. But it must be noted that Elizabeth also misjudged the situation: she hoped her restraints would temper him when in fact they only bewildered and irritated him. There was even a tense moment of disagreement in 1591 when he turned his back on her, she boxed his ears—and he half-drew his sword against her.

Essex succeeded to the youngest, if poorest, earldom in England at the age of nine; when his mother remarried, he became the stepson of Sir Robert Dudley, earl of Leicester, and was his General of the Horse during the English war in the Low Countries. There he fought little, but he survived the battle of Zutphen as Philip Sidney did not. At the age of 20 Essex was made Master of the Queen's Horse, succeeding his stepfather upon his death. In 1588 Elizabeth had kept him, as she had kept Leicester, out of danger by stationing both men at Tilbury; in 1589, still pursuing the glory of adventure and war, Essex snuck off with the Portugal expedition where he challenged leaders in Lisbon

to duels; and in 1591—much to the Queen's anger—he married Philip
Sidney's widow, the Lady Frances, the daughter of Sir Francis Walsingham. Still he was able to regain the Queen's favor, and he was commanded to lead the first of the expeditions sent to France in support
of Henry VI. He was vying with young Robert Cecil as Walsingham's
successor to the principal secretaryship when Elizabeth sent him on
the voyage to Cadiz, breaking all precedent by elevating him to a
joint commandership with the lord high admiral. It is not surprising
that his head was turned, and on himself.

Now he suffered a series of setbacks. Cecil won the position while
Essex won rebuke, for the Cadiz voyage did not bring the financial
returns that Elizabeth had wished, and he had missed by two days a
valuable treasure fleet. A certain paranoia set in: Essex imagined that
the favor he curried with his Virgin Queen gained his enmity on the
Privy Council where he most needed political alliances; and there is
some reason to believe that his haughty sister Penelope Devereux, now
Mountjoy's mistress, played a Lady Macbeth to Essex's "o'ervaulting
ambition." Essex could discern that his military heroism had brought
him favor with large troops of men and great popularity with the
general populace; and when it was clear that the Irish rebel Tyrone's
power was so strong that, with or without Spanish aid, he might overthrow English rule, Essex commented in disparaging ways of the
Queen's officers in Ireland so as to suggest implicitly his own appointment as lord deputy there. The power he would inherit once freed of
the court and the enormous gamble he would take of winning greater
power while removed from the center of the conspiracy he thought
against him no doubt combined to make this position—normally a
most undesired one—especially attractive to him. There were, however,
lucid moments in which he clearly had second thoughts. In a letter
of January 4, 1599, he wrote, "I am not ignorant what are the dis-
advantages of absence; the opportunities of practising enemies when
they are neither encountered nor overlooked: the construction of
princes under whom *Magna fama* is more dangerous than *mala*,
and *successus minus quam nullus:* the difficulties of a war where the
rebel that hath been hitherto ever victorious is the least enemy that I
shall have against me; for without an enemy, the disease of that
country consumes our armies, and if they live, yet famine and naked-
ness make them lose both heart and strength. And if victuals be sent
over, yet there will be no means to carry it . . . . All these things
which I am like to see, I do foresee." And to the Council he remarked
before departing, "I provided for this service a plastion and not a
cuirass, that is, I am armed in the breast, but not on the back."

But affairs in Ireland could not have gone worse for Essex. He
suffered humiliating defeats, the more so since he went as the Queen's
first Lord-Lieutenant and Governor-General and at the head of her
largest land army. In London he had urged that the best strategy

was to aim directly at the rebel leader Tyrone; but when he arrived in Ireland, he found the weather would not allow this, and so he marched his army through Munster and Leinster, directing irrelevant skirmishes and capturing only one fairly insignificant castle: he quartered nearly three-fourths of his men in unimportant and unnecessary garrisons and the Queen complained bitterly that his "progress" was costing her £1,000 a day. The campaign was further blackened by the Curlews disaster in which Sir Conyers Clifford—heading a flank attack on forces in Ulster while Essex planned a frontal assault out of the Pale— was massacred with a large number of his men. Essex's troops were reduced to 3,500 or 4,000; and he learned to his dismay that his horse were no good in the woody, hilly reaches of Ulster while his foot-soldiers were not able to wage successful guerilla warfare with Tyrone. Through several days in early September, Essex tried valiantly to save some scrap of military success by following Tyrone's forces along Ulster's southern boundary, hoping to lure him into open plains where the English could better attack him, but the wily Irish leader was much too clever to be tricked into exposing himself. Essex had by then lost 12,000 men and spent £130,000 and in utter frustration and despair, he now agreed to a private conference and truce with Tyrone, the details of which were kept secret between them. Upon returning to his headquarters in Dublin, he learned to his surprise and anger that his successful rival Robert Cecil had now been named Master of the Wards upon his father's death—a ripe plum for personal fortune which Essex, broke and in debt, needed badly. Persuaded by his friends in Dublin and London that he must soon reappear at court if he was to replenish his authority, and privately persuaded by himself that only his charm in an interview with the Queen could restore his reputation after recent events in Ireland, he left on September 24 to see her in person, despite her command not to depart Ireland.

Essex had by then disobeyed her further—some called it treason— by dubbing some 79 knights against her express wishes, and he had a large and popular following among his soldiers: at first he was urged by them to return to court with upwards of "4,000 choice men" in order to secure his own protection; but he returned instead with 200 men and six officers, all of them personal companions. He reached London on September 28; learning that the Queen was ten miles south at Nonsuch, he left his 200 men in the city and with his six officers proceeded on. The seven men crossed the Thames by ferry, seized horses waiting for their riders on the south bank, and rode as quickly as they could, passing on the way Lord Grey, whom one of them offered to kill. At ten that morning, Essex, mud spattering his face and clothes, strode through the Queen's Presence Chamber, Privy Chamber, and found her, finally, surrounded by her waiting-women putting up her hair at the dressing table of her bedchamber. He knelt, kissed her hands, and pleaded for her mercy. Elizabeth was astounded at his sudden appearance—"By God's son," she told one of her gentlemen servants later, "That man is above me. Who gave him commandment to come here so soon?"—yet uncertain how many of his troops were with him, she received him calmly and graciously. Later that day, after consulting Cecil, she called Essex before the Privy Council for an explanation of his behavior and then made him a close prisoner of Sir Thomas Egerton at York House, next to his own Essex House on the Strand.

The Queen refused to charge Essex with treason, perhaps partly out of fear that he would be made the popular hero and martyr of all the discontent and dissident forces usually wandering about London, let alone his own 200 men just back from a discouraging term of service in Ireland. But in spite of her personal feelings for Essex, her reason prevailed. Later that fall, Essex's recurrent kidney stone gave him difficulty and for a while it appeared he might die: Elizabeth eventually sent for eight of her own physicians to hold a consultation, she sent Essex broth and a message for him to comfort himself, but she refused to see him or release him. She did, however, grant an audience to Essex's wife, who came directly from childbed—dressed in black for her husband's sake—and the Queen consented to allow Lady Essex to visit her husband daily, where she stayed from seven in the morning to six at night.

Tension did not slacken through the autumn. Angry messages attacking the Queen's Council were posted on Cecil's door and even on the doors and walls of the palace of Whitehall. On December 19, 1599, it was reported erroneously that Essex had died; churchbells were rung and preachers prayed for him at their services. Early in 1600 John Hayward's Latin *Life of Henry IV*, concentrating on the deposition of Richard II by one of his leading nobility, was printed and circulated widely: the book was dedicated to Essex. Rumors of treason were frequent. Yet the Queen appeared calm and happy; Lord Sempill said he had once looked through a window and seen her dancing a stately pavan, alone save for Lady Warwick and a man playing pipe and tabor. Platter records seeing her "alone and without escort, very straight and erect still" in her Presence Chamber.

In April Essex wrote to his old friend Sir Charles Blount, lord Mountjoy, the father of five children by his sister (although they were not married) and his successor in Ireland. A year earlier, he had discussed his misfortunes at the hands of Cecil with Mountjoy and had received his support; now he asked Mountjoy to land the English army in Wales and come to his aid. Mountjoy refused: his successful campaign against the Irish rebels had taken all his attention and energy now. In May, Elizabeth finally allowed Essex to return home, though she made him a close prisoner there; and in June, he had his formal hearing. From the beginning, Elizabeth had wanted Essex's guilt to be exposed publicly in Star Chamber, but she was finally dissuaded by members of the Privy Council who feared the wide sympathy which such a hearing would enlist. So, in June, 1600, he was given a private hearing before a commission which charged him with three offenses against the Crown: his campaign into Munster, his "dishonourable and dangerous" treaty with Tyrone, and his presumptuous leaving of Ireland. Essex was adjudged guilty of all the charges. He was deprived of most of his offices and of his position on the Privy Council: there was no promise of restoration, but the issue was deliberately left open, since Elizabeth still looked for a reformation in his behavior. In August he was given his full freedom at last except that he was no longer given access to the court.

Through the summer Essex pleaded in letters to the Queen to be given an interview; and he began gathering supporters about him once again: Puritans who disliked the Queen; Catholics who sought greater toleration; adventurers who admired his reputation; men who had fought under him or been knighted by him; wanderers and vagabonds; the poor. As his power visibly grew, so his comments to the Queen became harsher; and he set increasing store on the renewal of his monopoly on the import of sweet-wines which was due in September.

Much hung on the balance of this award. Gelly Meyrick estimated that Essex had in his lifetime paid out of his own pocket £4,000 on the campaigns in the Low Countries in 1585; £3,500 on Armada costs; £7,000 on his 1589 expedition to Lisbon; £14,000 on the siege of Rouen; and, in Ireland, £35 to £40 a day to feed and drink his own retinue and another £40 daily for his stable and the salaries and livery of his servants. He was in debt about £25,000. On August 26, Essex told Sir Charles Danvers that "at Michaelmas the lease of his wines ended, which was the greatest part of his state, that by the renewing it, or taking it from him, he should judge what was meant him; that about that time he expected there would be a Parliament; that if then he were not restored to his place and offices, of which he seemed much to doubt, he would for his own part give over the hope thereof." The answer came in September. Elizabeth withheld the renewal, though she did not give the monopoly to anyone else, hoping this would be sufficient inducement for Essex to choose new companions and mend his ways.

But Essex took her word as final. Demands on his payments of debts increased, and his fair-weather colleagues drifted away. In the fall, he said later at his trial, he was angry to hear of plans afoot to place the Spanish Infanta on the throne of England instead of James after the death of Elizabeth; and his private secretary Henry Cuffe later testified that Essex reported this belief to the Earl of Mar and through him to James. In point of fact, Cecil and others about the court had in hand pensions from the Spanish court, though no such plan could have proceeded very far, for Isabella herself did not wish to pursue it. Essex then entered into negotiations with James VI. His remarks grew wilder; and Sir John Harington noted that he said that Elizabeth, "being now an old woman, was no less crooked and distorted in mind than she was in body" and that Essex "uttered strange words bordering on such strange designs that made me hasten forth and leave his presence." Plots grew up around him, and at some point he seems to have consented to a conspiracy to march on the Queen and place himself at her mercy, so desperate was he now to gain the court. By February 4, a handful of chief conspirators—Essex was not among them—met at Drury House and plans to march on the court itself were worked out. The group also hired Shakespeare's company to perform *Richard II* at the Globe. A plan to capture the Tower and so command the city's arsenal before marching on the court was rejected because this might point to open rebellion. Throughout the autumn, the Queen continually heard that mobs gathered at Essex House, and this, coupled with plots of rebellion which reached her, made her apprehensive. On Saturday, February 7, she summoned Essex to appear before the Privy Council to pronounce such grievances as he was rumored to have. He pleaded illness and did not attend her. Frightened now that he was under suspicion and would not have much longer in which to act, he planned to march on the court on Sunday, February 8.

There seems then and later to have been considerable confusion over Essex's actual intentions and plans, but the facts concerning what happened on that fateful Sunday are essentially what are laid out in the following proclamation. Between 200 and 300 of his followers were given the signal to meet at his house in the morning; they had no sooner gathered than a delegation of four members of the Privy Council arrived. The crowd demanded their lives or their imprisonment and the intimidated Essex consented to their close confinement. He then marched with at least 200 of his men on the city, urging everyone he met to support him in his attempt to save the Queen's life which, along with his own, he insisted, had been threatened.

Elizabeth had been forewarned; and now she was forearmed. The Bishop of London, Richard Bancroft, raised troops; pikemen barred Essex's return home at Ludgate; and his friend the sheriff, upon whom he had depended for additional forces, left by his back door when he heard Essex had arrived to see him. William Cecil's son Thomas, the second lord Burghley, went about the city with the Queen's king of heralds, reading a proclamation in which the Queen declared Essex a traitor. Forced to retreat, Essex returned to his house by way of the Thames and set up barricades. He then destroyed evidence which he was carrying with him, in a black bag tied about his neck, and burned his papers. When his attackers threatened to blow up Essex House—and brought down explosives from the Tower to do it—he surrendered. Essex, Rutland, Southampton, Sandys, Cromwell— all the nobility involved—came out of the house, went to their knees, and handed up their swords. John Nichols records that the next morning Essex was led from Lambeth Palace, where he had spent the night, along the streets of the old city to his solitary rooms in the Tower, but this once popular man now "went with a swift pace, bending his face towards the earth and would not look upon any of [the people] though some of them directly spoke to him."

On Monday, February 9, the Queen published the following document. It is, all told, an astonishing proclamation because of its lucidity, its simplicity, and its dispassionate and detailed accounting of the previous day's events. At no other time in her reign had one of the Queen's favorites practiced open treachery, at no other time had there been an uprising against her life outside her very palace walls. That the woman who was affectionately disposed towards Essex could act so quickly, yet without rancor, is a true mark of her character and true measure of her royalty; the charges, as the "homily of obedience" might have made predictable, are those of shocked and thorough disapproval that any citizen did not treat her position with customary and deserved wonder and obeisance. Essex's rebellion would in a short time be a major cause of the Queen's own passing, but there is no indication of that in the clarity, concentration, and forthrightness which distinguishes the proclamation reprinted here.

TEXTUAL NOTES
[For explanatory notes for this selection see page 384.]

Proclamation on the seizure of the Earls of Essex, Rutland, and others for their rebellion

Reference. STC 8279-8281; Steele, I,913-915.

Authorship and Editions. It is not known who first drafted the Queen's proclamation on the Essex rebellion, but according to the *Calendar of State Papers, Domestic,* Robert Cecil heavily corrected it (1598-1601, p.546). The proclamation was issued on Feb. 9, 1601, by Robert Barker, the Queen's printer; the STC lists three editions, but unfortunately no trace of the third edition (which according to Steele was once privately owned by Hodgkins) now exists.

Translations. Flemish and French translations were issued in octavo in 1601 in Brussels, both printed by R. Valpius.

Collation. 1°; single broadsheet (folio).

Description of Contents. Heading in roman; text in black-letter; "God saue the Queene." in roman; colophon in roman. Large ornamental initial *W*.

License. No entry in the *Stationers' Register.*

Base-Copy Text. Bodleian Arch.G.c.6(f.409). Copy of second edition consulted: Queens College (Oxford) Sel.b.228(42).

Textual Variants. The abbreviation "ANNO" is added before the date in the second edition; in addition, there are 26 incidental variants of spelling, punctuation, and capitalization.

Emendations. our selues.]ourselves.

By the Queene

WHEREAS THE EARLE OF ESSEX, accompanied with the Earles of Rutland and Southampton, and divers other their complices, Gentlemen of birth and qualitie, knowing themselves to be discovered in divers treasonable actions, into which they have heeretofore entred, as well in our Realme of Ireland, where some of them had layed plots with the Traitour *Tirone,* as in this our Realme of England, did upon Sunday, being the eight of this Moneth, in the morning, not onely imprison our Keeper of our Great Seale of England, our Chiefe Justice of England, and others both of our Nobilitie and Councell, that were sent in our Name to his house, to perswade the sayd Earle to lay open any his petitions or complaints, with promise (if he would disperse his disordered company in his house) that all his just requests shoulde bee heard, and graciously considered: but also did (after strait order given by him to murder our sayd Counsellers and others, whensoever they should offer to stirre out of that place) traitourously issue into our City of London in armes, with great numbers, and there breaking out into open action of rebellion, devised and divulged base and foolish lies, That their lives were sought, spreading out divers strange and seditious inventions, to have drawen our people to their partie, with purpose to attempt traitourous actions, both against our Person and State, and to expose (as it now appeareth) our City and people with their goods to the spoile of a number of needy and desperate persons their adherents, continuing still in armes, and killing divers of our Subjects, after many Proclamations of rebellion made by our King of Heralds:

Forasmuch as notwithstanding (God be thanked) they have found themselves deceived of their expectation (being now all apprehended, and within our Tower of London, as well the three principal Traitorous Earles, of Essex, Rutland, and Southampton, as divers others of the principal Gentlemen their confederats) our good Subjects of our Citie, and elsewhere, having shewed themselves so constant, and unmoveable from their duties towards us, as not any one of them of any note (that we can yet heare of) did offer to assist the said Earle and his associats; Wee have bene contented, in regard of the comfort that we take to finde by so notorious evidence, the loyall disposition of our people (whereof we never doubted) not onely to make knowen to all our said Subjects of our Citie and elsewhere, in how thankefull part wee doe accept both their loyall persisting in their duetie, and stay from following the false perswasions of the Traitours, but to promise on our part, That whensoever wee shall have cause to shew it, they shall finde us more carefull over them, then for ourselves. And hereby also in regard of our gracious meaning towards our good people, to admonish them, That seeing this open Acte was so sudden, as it cannot yet be throughly looked into, how farre it stretched, and how many hearts it hath corrupted, but that it is to bee presumed by the common example of the maner of proceeding of all Rebels in like actions, that it was not without instruments and ministers dispersed in divers places, to provoke the mindes of our people, to like of their attempts, with calumniating our government, and our principall Servants and ministers thereof; That they shall doe well (and so wee charge them) to give diligent heede in all places, to the conversation of persons not well knowen for their good behaviour, and to the speaches of any that shall give out slanderous and unduetifull wordes or rumours against us and our government: And they that be in authoritie, to lay holde on such Spreaders of rumours, And such as be not in authority, to advertise those thereof that have authoritie, to the end that by the apprehension of such dangerous instruments, both the drift and purpose of evill minded persons may be discovered, their desseignes prevented, and our people conserved in such peace and tranquillitie, as heeretofore by God's favour, we have mainteined, and doe hope still to continue amongst them. Given at our Palace of Westminster the ninth day of Februarie *1600*, in the three and fortieth yeere of our reigne.

God save the Queene.

Imprinted at London by ROBERT BARKER, Printer to the Queene's most excellent Majestie.

1600.

Queene Elizabeth's Speech
to her Last Parliament (1601)

   The question of the Queen's prerogative, raised earlier in connection with the church and with the succession to the throne, was again a subject for heated debate in her last two Parliaments. This time the focus was on monopolies. These grants—which given as rewards or sold for income helped her to raise money in a period of deficit spending—took many forms. She had the power to license men to export goods otherwise forbidden by statute law; to suspend regulations governing the manufacture of certain products, such as cloth and leather; and to sell certain privileges—in 1588, for example, Ralegh was given the privilege of licensing all taverns for thirty years. The Queen might also grant or sell a monopoly in manufacturing certain articles or in importing them. With Elizabeth even the most common of products—salt, starch, vinegar—were involved; and in a decade strapped by both inflation and scarcity, these additional forms of indirect taxation used to line the pockets of court favorites, while generally raising the prices of goods, were particularly burdensome. Especially were they distasteful in a decade in which Parliament was concentrating on welfare and debating the issues of poverty, vagabondage, and poor working conditions.

  The issue of monopolies first came to a head in the Parliament of 1597 when Francis Moore, an active and influential member of that session, introduced a motion in Commons "touching sundry enormities growing by patents of privilege and the abuse of them." After three days of debate, the issue was referred to a committee chaired by Moore; a month later, the Queen avoided confrontation with Parliament by telling both houses that she intended to handle the matter herself: she would see that all monopolies were "brought to the touchstone of the law" in her courts. The committee thanked her, and presented no report.

  But Elizabeth did not keep her word. She continued to give patents as she always had and was angry to hear that on October 7, 1601, one of them was impugned in the Court of Common Pleas. She asked her

Privy Council to inhibit the judges from hearing the suit on the grounds that it was a matter for her own private courts. As usual, she had made her appropriate answer to Parliament and then done nothing; but this time Parliament was watching.

In 1601 Elizabeth called another Parliament, for she needed additional subsidies. It was not a happy occasion. To begin with, Commons found the doors accidentally locked; and from here members broke into open resentment. Lord Buckhurst had warned the Queen and had asked her shortly before the session convened to reconsider some monopolies to appease Commons—and she herself was aware of the growing public discontent, for petitions had been presented to her personally on her walks to chapel and elsewhere—but she stoutly refused. At the opening of Parliament on Wednesday, November 18, one member rose and said that too many necessary commodities were monopolized under patents, and he had a bill with a long title "Against Patents." He was interrupted by another member who had a short bill—only twelve lines long—which consisted of only its title: "An Act of Explanation of the Common Law in Certain Cases of Letters-patent." Bacon tried to forestall discussion by noting that "The Queen, as she is our sovereign, hath both an enlarging and restraining liberty of her prerogative: that is, she hath both power by her patents to set at liberty things restrained by statute-law or otherwise, and by her prerogative she may restrain things that are at liberty" and added, "The use hath been ever by petition to humble ourselves unto her Majesty and by petition desire to have our grievances redressed, especially when the remedy toucheth so nigh in point of prerogative." Bacon's talk had no effect. Disturbance about St. Stephen's Chapel, Westminster, increased as men laughed, cleared their throats, or spit on the floor to show their disapproval. The Solicitor-General noted that the Queen had been distracted with Essex's rebellion, but Sir Robert Wroth inquired pointedly, "Why not before? There was time enough ever since the last Parliament. I speak it, and I speak it boldly: these patents are worse than ever they were." He read out a list of them and was interrupted by the young lawyer William Hakewill, who shouted, "Bread? Is not bread there?" Cecil reprimanded the session for resembling a grammar-school more than a session of Parliament.

Forces against monopolies now became more organized. At the next assembly meeting, on November 23, the diarist Townsend was handed a propaganda sheet listing the taxed commodities; and at the next committee meeting lobbying began with a "multitude of people" from the city crowding the antechamber and stairs of Parliament urging "compassion of their griefs, they being spoiled, imprisoned and robbed by monopolists." The Queen had been informed throughout of this growing desire for government by the people and the next morning the Speaker reported her fulsome thanks for passing her subsidy bill— they had not even taken it up, but she was not to give in on monopolies without extracting her price—and then proceeded in her message to express her concern that monopolies had been misused and so become a hardship for her people. She promised, though "her kingly prerogative were tender," that some monopolies "should be presently repealed, some suspended, and none put in execution but such as should first have a trial according to the law for the good of her people."

Cecil held a quick, hushed discussion with Knollys and Stanhope and then stood to confirm her statements. Moreover, he named certain products. Men could "eat their meat more savourly," for the letter patent for salt would be called in; those with weak stomachs need not worry, for vinegar would be freed; "those that desire to go sprucely in their ruffs" would find "starch which hath been so much prosecuted shall now be repealed." There was immediate applause; the usually rebellious Richard Wingfield remarked, "If a sentence of everlasting happiness had been pronounced unto me, it could not have made me show more outward joy than now I do" and, says Townsend, he wept.

Three days passed, the subsidy bill was brought up and approved, and still there was no further word on monopolies. Members grew restless. Finally they inquired if the Queen meant to speak well and do nothing again; and to preclude further outburst Cecil produced a rough draft of her proclamation on which he had been working; and the next day published copies were in all their hands. "A proclamation for the reformation of many abuses and misdemeanors committed by patentees of certain privileges and licenses, to the general good of all her Majesty's loving Subjects," it divided monopolies into two groups. Those concerning salt, vinegar, alcohol and liquors containing it, salt fish, train oil, fish-livers, pots, brushes, butter and starch were voided at once, the letters patent revoked, and the patentees forbidden to enforce anything under threat of punishment as breaking the Queen's commandment. Holders of grants involving saltpeter, Irish yarn, new makes of cloth, calf-skins, pelts, cards, glasses, leather, steel, and some others were to abide by the rulings of the courts of common law without any special privilege. Elizabeth thanked Parliament for bringing the matter to her attention, but said nothing about their right to legislate on it: she had held firmly to prerogative. As usual, she preserved the principle while conceding the point.

The Queen concluded her message by inviting those who wished to thank her to come in a body—and when over a cheering hundred wished to go, she paused to find a hall large enough. At three o'clock on the afternoon of November 30, ten days after the debate had begun, she received under the cloth of state at Whitehall some 140 to 160 of them and after an effusive speech of most humble thanks by the speaker of the House—not a good orator at any time—she returned the oration reprinted here.

The remarks are the Queen's valedictory address. The speech we have is one she edited for publication: for some time, it was complained, one could not get a copy anywhere. Smith (p. 277) calls it "divinity dressed in the guise of utilitarianism." *It bears all the hallmarks of Elizabeth: the oration is at once formal and personal, deliberative and ceremonial, paradoxically politic and sincerely loving. From childhood the Queen had been taught by the best of tutors, William Grindall and Roger Ascham among them, and her ability to use high rhetoric, now mellowed with age, was never put to better use than here. She forestalls apology by sharing with her people concern for their welfare; she invites consideration for her difficult and unwanted position; she underscores her deep commitment to their prosperity: throughout, the speech transforms her *personae* in accord with shifting concepts of love; but love is maintained as the theme. There are tonal shifts, too, from graciousness to special pleading, from confession to indignation, yet it is all in a beautifully articulated lower key. For Elizabeth it is also unusually direct; and the simplicity records a rich and moving authenticity; her allegiance to the beliefs expressed here is complete. At its conclusion, Elizabeth asks her loyal burgesses to kiss the hand of a woman now 68 years old, and 44 years a Queen; as Harington remarked, "We loved her, for she said she did love us." Yet even at this moment of warmth and adoration, there is a note of leave-taking. The speech, finally, lingers gently on a growing awareness of mortality: and, in little more than a year, she was dead.

TEXTUAL NOTES
[For explanatory notes for this selection see page 384.]

Queene Elizabeth's Speech to her Last Parliament.
   Reference. STC 7579.
   Authorship and Editions. No copy of an Elizabethan printing of this work now exists. It is entirely by the Queen (see *State Papers, Domestic Elizabeth* 282/67; a MS exists in Lansdowne MS 94, fol. 123). The Queen had first given a copy to Henry Savile, Provost of Eton, but she forbade circulation of it. She apparently revised the text, giving it to the Royal Printer. It appeared as "taken verbatim in writing by A. B. as near as he could possibly set it down," but his seems to have been her subterfuge since the work is highly

propagandistic (and since the only MP with the initials A. B. was Anthony Balgrave, who had no traceable connection with the pamphlet). See J. E. Neale, *Elizabeth I and Her Parliaments* (London, 1953; 1957),II,392. Since the speech epitomizes the public character and role which Elizabeth chose to portray throughout her life, and since it contributes so readily to legends about her, the work has been widely reprinted.

Subsequent Editions. Recent research on the Queen's last speech shows that all extant quartos date from about 1628 onwards; the first typesetting(s)—there is some doubt whether it is one or two— are dated about 1628 by the revised STC and exist in many copies. In addition, the British Museum lists three mid-seventeenth century editions, two quartos (without date) as 1642 and another quarto as 1647. A fifth edition, an undated broadside (probably 1659) reprints the text here; this edition was put out by *"Tho. Milbourn,* and [his work is] to be sold at his House in *Jewen*-Street." This is the first edition to call the speech "Golden" and explains this addition in a headnote: "This Speech ought to be set in Letters of *Gold,* that aswell the Majesty, prudence and virue of this Royal Queen might in general most exquisitely appear; as also that her Religious Love, and tender respect which she particularly, and constantly did bear to her Parliament in unfeigned sincerity, might (to the shame, and perpetual disgrace and infamy of some of her Successors) be nobly and truly vindicated, and proclaimed, with all grateful recognition to God for so great a Blessing to his poor people of *England,* in vouchsafing them heretofore such a gracious Princess, and magnanimous Defendor of the Reformed Religion, and heroick Patroness of the liberty of her Subjects in the freedom and honour of their Parliaments; which have been under God, the continual Conservators of the Splendour, and wealth of this Common-wealth against Tyranny, and Oppression" (Bodleian Wood 276[112]). Reprinted as a folio folded once in 1679 as "The Last Speech and Thanks of Queen Elizabeth Of ever Blessed Memory, To Her Last Parliament, After Her Delivery From The Popish Plots, &c." (Bodleian Ashmole G.14[63]; Bodleian P1.16.Jur[20]) and included in Sir Simonds D'Ewes, *The Journals of all the Parliaments during the Reign of Queen Elizabeth* (London, 1682), pp. 659-660.

In the eighteenth century, the speech was issued as a broadside with a portrait of the Queen in 1702 ("Printed and Sold by *Jer. Wilkens,* near the *Green-Dragon-Tavern* in *Fleet-street"*) (Bodleian Firth b33[1]: Bodleian Fol.*θ* 591 [5]) following the original text printed here and titled "Queen Elizabeth Her Gracious Speech to Her Last Parliament, The 30th Day of November, 1601." An octavo appeared in 1749 printed by R. Offrey in London (BM 8122.dd.3).

The speech has also appeared in collections. It was first reprinted in the first collection of the first edition of the *Somers Tracts* (London, 1748), III, 130-132, following the text given here with modified capitalization and punctuation; after the text is this note: "N. B. Our *Historians* in abridging the foregoing *Piece,* have render'd the Sense so imperfect [i.e. the folio of 1679] that we were advis'd to insert the whole from a *Genuine Copy* in the *Collection* of The Right Rev. The Lord Bishop of BANGOR" (p. 132). This text was reprinted (again as "The golden speech") in the second edition of *Somers Tracts* (London, 1809), ed. Scott, I,244-246, with the appended note as an extract from Camden's *Annals* serving as headnote (p. 244). *The Harleian Miscellany* also reprinted this work in its first edition (London, 1744), I,366-367, where it is called the "Golden Speech" (p.366) and again, ed. William Oldys and Thomas Park (London, 1808), I,376-378, as well as in a cheaper edition, ed. J. Malham (London, 1809), II,352-355. Finally, a wholly modenized text is in George P. Rice, Jr., *The Public Speaking of Queen Elizabeth* (New York, 1951; 1966), pp. 106-109; and in Neale, *Elizabeth I and Her Parliaments,* II, 388-391; extracts are in G. R. Elton, *TC,* 168, pp. 316-317.

Collation. 4°; A⁴. A1, title-page; A1v, blank; A2-A4, text; A4v, blank.

Description of Contents. Title-page all capitals in roman and italics, but without any design or decoration; text in roman with italics heading. Head-piece, A2; no tail-piece. Large, undecorated initial *W*, A2. No running-head, no marginal notes. Unpaginated.

License. No entry in the *Stationers' Register.*

Base-Copy Text. Bodleian 4°C.80 Th (9); Hn. 81568 also consulted.

Title-page in Full. / QUEENE / ELIZABETHS / SPEECH / TO HER LAST / *PARLIAMENT.* /

Emendations. (A2)vild oppression]wild oppression (A2v)My selfe]Myselfe you wellfare.]your wellfare. (A3v)my selfe but as] myselfe but as were a Crowne]weare a Crowne for my selfe,]for myselfe, vnto my selfe,]unto myselfe, (A4) conscience]conscience's loue you bettet.]love you better.

Queene Elizabeth's Speech
to her Last Parliament

HE 30 OF NOVEMBER 1601, her Majestie being set under State in the Councell Chamber at White-hall, the Speaker, accompanied with Privy Councel-lors, besides Knights and Burgesses of the lower House to the number of eight-score, presenting them-selves at her Majestie's feet, for that so graciously and speedily she had heard and yealded to her Subjects' desires, and proclaymed the same in their hearing as followeth.

Mr. *Speaker,*

WEE perceive your comming is to present thankes unto Us, Know I accept them with no lesse joy then your loves can have desire to offer such a Present, and doe more esteeme it then any Treasure or Riches, for those Wee know how to prize, but Loyaltie, Love, and Thankes, I account them invalluable, and though God hath raysed Mee high, yet this I account the glorie of my Crowne, that I have reigned with your Loves. This makes that I doe not so much rejoyce that God hath made Mee to bee a [A2v] Queene, as to bee a Queene over so thankefull a People, and to bee the meane under God to conserve you in safetie, and preserve you from danger, yea to bee the Instrument to deliver you from dishonour, from shame, and from infamie; to keepe you from out of servitude, and from slaverie under our Enemies, and cruell tyrannie and wild oppression intended against Us: for the better withstanding wherof, Wee take verie acceptably your intended helpes, and chiefely in that it manifesteth your loves and largenesse of heart to your Soveraigne. Of Myselfe I must say this, I never was any greedy scraping grasper, nor a strickt fast-holding Prince, nor yet a waster, My heart was never set upon any worldly goods, but onely for My Subjects' good. What you doe bestow on Me, I will not hoard up, but receive it to bestow on you againe; yea Mine owne Properties I account yours to be expended for your good, and your eyes shall see the bestowing of it for your wellfare.

Mr. *Speaker*, I would wish you and the rest to stand up, for I feare I shall yet trouble you with longer speech.

Mr. *Speaker*, you give Me thankes, but I am more to thanke you, and I charge you, thanke them of the Lower-House from Me, for had I not received knowledge from you, I might a fallen into the lapse of an Error, onely for want of true information.

Since I was Queene yet did I never put My [A3] Pen to any Grant but upon pretext and semblance made Me, that it was for the good and availe of my Subjects generally, though a private profit to some of my ancient Servants who have deserved well: But that my Grants shall bee made Grievances to my People, and Oppressions, to bee priviledged under colour of Our Pattents, Our Princely Dignitie shall not suffer it.

When I heard it, I could give no rest unto my thoughts untill I had reformed it, and those Varlets, lewd persons, abusers of my bountie, shall know I will not suffer it. And Mr. *Speaker*, tell the House from mee, I take it exceeding gratefull that the knowledge of these things are come unto mee from them. And though amongst them the principall Members are such as are not touched in private, and therefore need not speake from any feeling of the griefe, yet We have heard that other Gentlemen also of the House, who stand as free, have spoken as freely in it, which gives Us to know that no respects or intersts have moved them other then the minds they beare to suffer no diminution of our Honour, and our Subjects' love unto Us. The zeale of which affection tending to ease my People, and knit their harts unto Us, I embrace with a Princely care farre above all earthly Treasures. I esteeme my Peoples' love more then which I desire not to merit; And God that gave me here to sit, and placed mee over you, knowes that I never re-[A3v] spected myselfe but as your good was concerned in mee, yet what dangers, what practises, and what perils I have passed, some, if not all of you know, but none of these things doe moove mee, or ever made me feare, but it is God that hath delivered me.

And in my governing this Land, I have ever set the last Judgement day before mine eyes, and so to rule, as I shall be Judged and answer before a higher Judge, to whose Judgement Seat I doe appeale in that never thought was cherished in my heart that tended not to my Peoples' good.

And if my Princely bountie have beene abused, and my Grants turned to the hurt of my People contrarie to my will and meaning, or if any in Authoritie under mee have neglected, or converted what I have committed unto them, I hope God will not lay their culps to my charge.

To be a King, and weare a Crowne, is a thing more glorious to them that see it, then it is pleasant to them that beare it, for myselfe, I never was so much inticed with the glorious name of a King, or the royall authoritie of a Queene, as delighted that God hath made me His Instrument to maintaine his Truth and Glorie, and to defend this Kingdome from dishonour, dammage, tyrannie, and oppression. But should I ascribe any of these things unto myselfe, or my sexly weakenesse, I were not worthy to live, and of all most unworthy [A4] of the mercies I have received at God's hands, but to God onely and wholly all is given and ascribed.

The cares and trouble of a Crowne I cannot more fitly resemble then to the Drugges of a learned Physitian, perfumed with some Aromaticall savour, or to bitter Pils guilded over, by which they are made more exceptable or lesse offencive, which indeed are bitter and unpleasant to take, and for my owne part, were it not for Conscience's sake to discharge the duetie that God hath layd upon me, and to maintaine his Glorie, and keepe you in safetie, in mine owne disposition I should bee willing to resigne the place I hold to any other, and glad to be freed of the Glory with the Labors, for it is not my desire to live nor to reigne longer then my life and reigne shall bee for your good. And though you have had and may have many mightier and wiser Princes sitting in this Seat, yet you never had nor shall have any that will love you better.

Thus Mr. *Speaker*, I commend mee to your loyall Loves, and yours to my best care and your further Councels, and I pray you Mr. *Controullor*, and Mr. *Secretarie*, and you of my Councell, that before these Gentlemen depart into their Countreys you bring them all to kisse my Hand.

FINIS.

A Letter from a Souldier of good place in Ireland
(1602)

   Elizabeth's Irish Wars were conterminous with her reign. From the day she declared the Elizabethan Settlement, which the Irish Roman Catholics refused to recognize, until the day she died, savage and crafty Irish chieftains were in rebellion. They were able to carry the intermittent warfare on as long as they did in part because until 1599 the Queen did not invest a heavy commitment in troops and money—often there were several thousand men or fewer, 20 or 30 alone holding a garrison. Then, too, the English were not as successful as the Irish in conducting a guerilla warfare amidst the woods, hills, and bogs of a foreign and primitive country; and the Irish chiefs, never successfully allied, were continually making pledges or treaties with the English—what they called "compositions"—which they broke at will. Unable to effect either a national church or a strong civil administration with English and Irish nobility, Elizabeth was constantly distressed by periodic defeats and anxious over Spanish intervention, fearing Philip II might capitalize on her insecure outposts in Ireland as she had long capitalized on his difficulties in the Netherlands.

  The long and confusing history of the wars can be understood best if seen in four stages: as the rebellion of Shane O'Neill (1559-1566), the confederacy of the Fitzmaurices in Munster (1569-1572), the Desmond rebellion (1579-1583), and the Tyrone rebellion (1594-1603). The Shane O'Neill rebellion began when Shane, the Irish chief of the Clan O'Neill, quarrelled with the English candidate for the succession, young Hugh O'Neill, whom the Queen supported for the earldom of Tyrone. Shane was primitive and forceful; but for three years Elizabeth's lord lieutenant, the earl of Sussex, held out for her claimant; in 1562 he compromised, by permitting Shane to retain the reality of power as captain of Tyrone and sending young Hugh off to England to be attached to the household of the earl of Leicester. Shane spent the next four years in bloody warfare, winning control of all Ulster. In 1566 he felt triumphant enough to proclaim himself greater than any earl; and he appealed to Rome and France for aid in establishing himself over English rule. Sir Henry Sidney, the new lord deputy of Ireland, was forced to take action against him, and in one sweeping march through Ulster with troops inferior in number but superior in organization, he destroyed Shane's power. He was aided by the hatred which Shane's barbarity had aroused and by Hugh Roe O'Donnell, who sought revenge for the treatment Shane had given earlier to the clan of Tyrconnel; and Shane was himself killed by the Antrim Scots who recalled his attack on them. The chieftaincy then passed on to Tirlagh Luineach O'Neill, a man of more limited ambition, and Ulster, if still not conquered, ceased to be an active threat.

Sidney's attention was turned south now to Munster, where the earl of Desmond was feuding with Ormond in Tipperary; he placed Desmond in the Tower and set up presidents of Munster and Connaught to break the power of the local chiefs. But before he could Anglicize either province, James Fitzmaurice Fitzgerald, in 1569, led a rebellion throughout Munster against the English. Fitzgerald also hoped for help from the continent; and when it did not come, he fell to the forces of Ormond and Humphrey Gilbert and submitted in 1572. At this point, Sidney turned his hopes not to the Anglicized earls so much as to the English colonies—or "plantations"—and he organized some, especially in Munster and Leinster, from 1568 to 1570 with the help of Sir Richard Grenville in Ulster, Thomas Smith in Ards (1572-1573), and Essex in Clandeboyne. But the latter two were wiped out by the mercenary forces of MacDonald, and intermittent brutality continued throughout Ulster. Sidney served two terms as lord deputy and at the end of his second term, early in 1575, he left behind his division of the country into the four provinces, each with its president, and a number of Irish chieftains made landowners with English titles, a beginning of legal arrangements that looked as if they might germinate.

Later in 1575 James Fitzmaurice, who fled the country for Rome and Madrid where he had received some support, returned to invade Ireland. General war now broke out: papal forces landed, the Irish took Smerwick in a slaughter; Desmond drifted into war again; but James Eustace, the Viscount Baltinglass, a supporter of the rebels, was driven out of the country; and Desmond was forced to be a "wood-kerne"—a hill outlaw. In late 1583, while the lord deputyship lay vacant, Ormond chased Desmond down; and he was finally killed in an inter-tribal feud. His lands were taken over by the English and turned into the "Munster Plantation," headed by Ralegh, a more successful colony than others, which lasted until Tyrone's major rebellion.

Peace in Ulster began deteriorating in 1593 when Hugh Roe O'Donnell, who dominated one of two chief clans there, the Tyrconnel, traditional enemies of the Tyrones, took power at the age of 19. As a boy, O'Donnell had been tricked and abducted by the English who had made him a prisoner in Dublin Castle until he managed to escape during the Christmas season of 1591. As soon as he came to power, he sought revenge by harrying English troops. In 1595 old Tirlagh Luineach, sitting in the ancient chief's stone chair in an open field at Tullaghogue, eight miles north of Dungarvan, performed clan rites which passed the rule on to Hugh O'Neill, earl of Tyrone. Hugh had returned to Ireland from England in 1585; and the English, who now thought him friendly to their cause, gave him direct control of Armagh. But Hugh retained his personal ambition to take ultimate power for himself, and he trained extensive troops in English weaponry by making frequent changes of forces among his own men. He was a good organizer, crafty yet suprisingly patient; his only fault was that he often was inclined to hesitation. He completed a secret confederacy with his old rival O'Donnell with the marriage of Hugh Roe O'Donnell to his daughter; and together the united clans of Ulster sought additional help from Irish exiles of the Desmond rebellion—James, Thomas, and Baltinglass—who were seeking support at the Spanish court. Jointly the two chiefs commanded a trained army of 6,000 men against which the lord deputy, Sir William Russell, could oppose only 1,000 or 1,100 men. The Queen dispatched additional troops under Sir John Norreys and appointed him to a special command in Ulster; but this led to a dispute between Norreys and Russell, and, in addition, he repeatedly lost skirmishes to Tyrone who knew far better than the English how to fight in the northern bogs. In May 1597 Lord Burgh replaced Russell; but in December 1597 Norreys died and in January 1598 Lord Burgh died. The 1590s were not years of English power generally: still holding to the theories of plantation and of division and conquest, Elizabeth tried to govern Ireland with 3,000 soldiers, another 3,000 colonists, and a mere handful of officials: a bleak assignment at any period. Whatever chance England had the Queen herself demolished. After the deaths of Norreys and Burgh, Ormond, again temporarily in charge, arranged a fragile truce with Tyrone—a "cessation"—and the Queen signed a pardon on May 12, 1598. But on May 31, Ormond forwarded a letter from Tyrone about his communication with Philip III; the Queen forwarded it on to Philip himself accusing him of supporting treason against her state; and Tyrone, angry at this betrayal, refused to honor further commitments with the English. Later that year he moved out to conquer all of Ulster. Ormond, to protect Dublin in the Pale as the English headquarters, sent Sir Henry Bagenal, an old personal enemy of Tyrone's, to protect the Pale at Blackwater Fort, Armagh, an outlying garrison used as protection against Ulster. Bagenal met Tyrone on August 14 at the Yellow Ford across the Callan brook, a tributary of the Blackwater where he and his forces were routed: 1,000 men and 30 officers were killed. Tyrone had in effect eliminated nearly all the English forces in Ireland; Dublin stood openly vulnerable; and panic spread among the English colonists. Tyrone marched his men within three miles of Dublin—had he attacked, he might well have annhilated the English—and then stopped to wait for the support promised by the Spanish. Philip failed him: in 1596 and 1597 Spanish fleets setting out for Ireland were dispersed by unpredictable and uncontrollable winds. Still Yellow Ford had its effects. One of the Geraldine clansmen, the "Sugane" earl of Desmond, headed a general uprising in Munster and Hugh Roe opened fighting in Connaught. Ralegh's plantation was destroyed.

Elizabeth had still failed to appoint a successor to Norreys and Burgh; and if Ormond had not been so self-possessed, she would have lost Ireland. But she perceived the seriousness of the situation—perhaps one of the reasons for her hesitation—and in April 1599 the earl of Essex arrived in Dublin as Lord-Lieutenant and Governor-General of Ireland, with more powers than a lord deputy and with a massive commitment of 16,000 foot, 1,300 horse, and £277,782. He also had great pride: "I have beaten Knollys and Montjoy in the councele and by God I will beat Tyrone in the feilde." Essex had been urged to break the rebellion by chasing down Tyrone; but he found to his dismay that there was insufficient forage for his troops and that Ulster was unmanageable in the spring of the year; and he turned instead to minor campaigns in a sweep through Munster. He gained nothing of significance when the crafty Tyrone offered a composition to which Essex agreed; and, fearful of his own loss of court position during his absence from London, Essex arranged a private conference—himself on a river bank and Tyrone on horseback in the middle of the river—in which the two agreed to a series of six-weeks' truces, from September 8, 1599, to May, 1600. Essex took the news to the Queen. Tyrone then had a force twice Essex's, and he had also gained a breathing space, time to recruit still more troops, and a delay during which the Spanish support might still arrive. Essex's force, meantime, was left behind and further reduced by sickness and poor living conditions.

This apparent English defeat had about it the paradox of the fortunate fall, however, for Essex was replaced by a courageous and determined soldier in Charles Blount, lord Mountjoy. He was an aging man, not in good health, but he had limitless energy and cool reserve; and he first surprised the Irish when, arriving in 1600, he waged winter campaigns. Not only were the Irish unprepared to face him; they also lost the months when they sowed grain, raised cattle, and so obtained needed provisions. Mountjoy's assistant, Sir George Carew, settled Munster by seducing chief after chief to return to the English: on May 24, 1600, with depleted forces, he gained the submission of Edward Fitzgibbon; at Limerick he took the castle of Lough Gur; on July 5, he and Thomond captured Glin Castle on the Shannon, and this led to the surrender of Carrigafoyle, further down the river. On May 26, 1602, the Sugane Earl's fugitive followers led the English to their leader, who was hiding out in a deep cave, apparently the one near Mitchelstown. Mountjoy, meanwhile, entered Connaught and Ulster, pushing the rebels northward and establishing a number of new small garrisons; he proceeded in part by sowing mutual mistrust among the clans by spies and counterfeit letters. Finally, Sir Henry Docwra established a new garrison at Derry, from which, aided by disaffected O'Neills and O'Donnels, he attacked and contained Tyrconnel, thus dividing the forces in Ulster. Tyrone was driven into the outer parts of the northern counties of Ulster.

Mountjoy had thus virtually eliminated all the rebellious forces when Spanish aid arrived at last. In September 1601, 33 ships with 4,000 infantry and six field cannon under Don Juan d'l'Aguila made for Cork but, the wind falling off, arrived instead at the town of Kinsale. Though the city was walled, Mountjoy added further fortifications; he garrisoned Central Park on the west bank of the Bandon; and he took the castle of Rincurren on the east side, probably to protect the harbor. Finding Mountjoy concentrating the English forces to his north, where he was ravaging the countryside of supplies for the Spanish and Irish rebels, d'l'Aguila sent messages to Tyrone encouraging him to unite with Tyrconnel, Scots mercenaries under MacDonald, and other rebels to renew an attack from the north. D'l'Aguila thus planned to open fire on the English through his own sorties from the south, trapping a depleted and exhausted English force caught between the Irish and Spanish offensives.

Mountjoy reached Cork on September 27 and two days later he reconnoitered Kinsale. Munster remained quiet, and he hoped to attack the Spanish before the Irish could arrive, so as not to expose his deficiencies. By October 3 he had assembled 6,900 foot and 611 horse and he encamped his troops on Knockrobin Hill, a half mile from Kinsale. First Mountjoy attacked Rincurren, and, with Carew laying artillery with his quadrant, Mountjoy was able to fire accurately enough to keep Spanish boats and men from defending the castle sufficiently. Rincurren was surrendered on November 1. Carew was now sent north to head off Hugh Roe O'Donnell and the Tyrconnel clan, but an unusually sharp frost allowed O'Donnell to slip away in the night and march for Kinsale. He and his men moved within reach and stopped to await Tyrone. A Spanish sortie from the south on November 10, meanwhile, revealed to d'l'Aguila that Carew's departure had seriously depleted the English forces and he established a rearward position on which the English opened attack. The Spanish retreated. Meanwhile Elizabeth had sent further English support: 1,000 foot and 100 horse under Lord Thomond, blown by mistake into Castlehaven temporarily, was on its way; and 2,000 foot arrived at Waterford. On November 12 word came of Admiral Sir Richard Leveson's arrival at Cork with ten ships of war and an additional contingent of 2,000 men, including trained gunners, and munitions. Mountjoy turned his attention to Castle Park, and joined Levenson's forces in a bombardment; and on November 20 this fort, too, surrendered. The next day Mountjoy opened fire on Kinsale itself. On November 28 he offered the Spanish terms of surrender, but the proud d'l'Aguila replied that he was holding the town for Christ, for the King of Spain next, and would defend it *contra tutti inimici.* By December 1 the English had made a breach with their three culverin and demi-culverin, but this was not yet sufficient; on December 5 Levenson sailed back to Castlehaven to meet Spanish reinforcements of six ships—four warships, a merchantman, and a carvel—under Pedro de Zubiaur. Hearing of the new Spanish support, local Irish in west Cork and Kerry surrendered to them the castle at Castlehaven, commanding the harbour, and two castles at Baltimore, as well as Dunboy Castle. Almost simultaneously, on December 6, Mountjoy heard that Tyrone had at last joined Hugh Roe O'Donnell.

The crisis was upon them: the great battle of Kinsale, which is described in excellent detail in the pamphlet reprinted here. On December 28 d'l'Aguila, annoyed by his entrapment in the insignificant town of Kinsale, reproached Tyrone and O'Donnell for not attacking the English and they arranged a secret night attack which they would signal by guns to the Spanish. Mountjoy had also waited, unwilling to commit some troops to Kinsale while the Irish were still pressing him with their presence: he had only 6,595 men not sick or deserted from his original 11,800. He did continue, however, to make further breaches in the city walls of Kinsale. Then he was aided by a stroke of good fortune: after putting off an initial Irish foray on Spittle Hill on December 21, he was approached on December 22 by a boy who wanted whiskey for one of his Irish captains, an old friend of Carew's; and the next day the captain, Brian MacHugh Oge MacMahon, returned as his thanks the battle plans of the Tyrone forces. Warned in time, the English kept surveillance and mounted an offensive described below, eventually forcing the Irish to retreat despite their superior numbers. Nearly all MacDonald's forces were killed: 31 got away out of 300. An additional 1,200 Irish dead lay about the fields. Tryone retreated to northern Ulster and O'Donnell fled to Spain where he requested further support from Philip III. The English suffered light casualties, although the fighting had been grim enough: Clanrickard's clothing was full of bullet holes and rips from pikes, though he himself was not wounded. After rounding up his troops, Mountjoy fired off a volley to celebrate his victory; and d'l'Aguila, thinking this the expected signal from the Irish, sallied out on Christmas Day to be defeated. Two further sallies, that night and the next day, resulted in a draw. Despairing of further Spanish reinforcements and angered by the Irish withdrawal, d'l' Aguila surrendered with the honors of war on January 6, 1602.

Only mopping up campaigns remained. They lingered until March 1603—nearly until the Queen's death. Captain Roger Harvey took Castlehaven peaceably on February 10; the two castles at Baltimore were handed over on February 26; but Carew had a nasty battle for Dunboy Castle on June 16, in which he massacred the 58 remaining Spaniards in the marketplace of the camp. D'l'Aguila's two contingents, meanwhile, left for the Corunna, without mishap, on February 20 and March 16. Mountjoy roamed through Ulster; he found the countryside in ruins, the old stone chair at Tullaghogue in rubble. Except for Dunboy there were no difficulties. Mountjoy and Carew remained apprehensive of further Spanish troops landing, but none did. Just before Christmas, 1602, they backed Tyrone into the lower end of the woods of Lough Erne; and he wrote Mountjoy that "without standing on any terms of conditions, I do hereby both simply and absolutely submit myself to her majesty's mercy."

Elizabeth had at first asked for Tyrone's death; but on February 17, 1603, a month before she herself died, she authorized Mountjoy to give the rebel his life, his liberty, and his pardon if certain terms were met; and Tyrone lived on to regain his rule in Ulster under James. After Elizabeth's death, Mountjoy took both Tyrone and O'Donnell to England to meet her successor. Meanwhile, as a macabre symbol to the bloodshed of rebellion, Irish corpses continued to rot throughout the land, their mouths stained green by the grass and nettles which the starving had eaten, their bodies ravaged by other rebels, animals, and birds.

I. E.'s pamphlet is noteworthy because of his intimate knowledge of the closing events of the Irish rebellion, because of his thoroughly detailed report, and because of his factual perspective which is not in the end much harmed by his bias toward English heroism (C1; D1v). It is surprising that a man at or near such scenes of battle could maintain such accuracy, but his painstaking description of the opposing forces and his list of the killed and wounded—rarely incorrect—provides a tight and controlled narrative line; and it demonstrates both his completeness and his bias, yet shows how little, in the final analysis, partiality affects his account. The nearly stereotyped Spanish pride assigned to Don Juan (C1-C2) is offset by I. E.'s report of "an unbloudie victorie of our part, most befitting a Virgine Queene, and a Bacheler Generall" (D3). Besides being impressed with the bravery of the common soldier, he is also respectful of the leniency of the Queen and Mountjoy, but no doubt it was a great relief to both of them to be rid at last of the annoying uprisings of neighbors and subjects who had harried the English since the reign of Elizabeth's grandfather, the first of the Tudors. Their defeat, which paved the way for the unification of the British Isles, was the singularly important event in the waning days of Elizabeth's reign and life.

Textual Notes

[For explanatory notes for this selection see page 385.]

A Letter from a Souldier of good place in Ireland
   Reference. STC 7434.
   Authorship and Editions. The relatively anonymous "Letter from a Souldier" ("I. E." or "J. E. [D3v]; the author has not been identified) has come down in at least two issues, and at least one mixed copy exists. Both the inner forme of sheet B and thirteen lines of C3 were reset; both make substantial corrections (see variants below). In the instance of sheet B, "postestates" of the first issue (B4) is corrected to "potentates," and the printer may have taken this opportunity to make other changes, at least half of them incidental. As for sheet C, nothing in the outer forme was changed except for thirteen lines of C3; and here the superior readings of "and the diligence," "as though this descent," "all the forces of the kingdome which could be spared," and "wants were found" identify the second issue. The only Bodleian copy with the superior states of both settings (third, not second issue?) is Wood 504(4); and this has served as the base copy-text for this collection. Each of the other Bodleian copies contains one superior setting and they are bound as follows:

	first (inferior) setting	second (superior) setting
sheet B	Wood 616(16)	Wood 504(4); 4°C16Art.BS
sheet C	4°C16Art.BS	Wood 504(4); Wood 616(16)

The considerable care exercised in the corrections and improvements here is not altogether consistent; "dedemaunde." remains uncorrected in both settings of sheet B; sheet A ends with a half-line concluding a paragraph (A4v) and B (B1) begins in the middle of a sentence. This clear evidence of two compositors working simultaneously setting two sheets causes a major error not corrected in any copy I have seen, and this may suggest that the corrections on sheets B and C were made simultaneously, the pamphlet existing in two issues and not three. But because of the nature of the corrections there is no reason to assume more than one edition. There have been so subsequent editions.
   Collation. 4°; A-D⁴. A1, blank; A2, title-page; A2v, blank; A3-D3, text; D3v, D4-D4v, blank.
   Description of Contents. Overall decoration is sparse; the pamphlet is unusually plain. Title-page is in a mixture of roman and italics; heading of text is in mixture of roman and italics; body of text is in black-letter. Paginated; text=pp. 1-25. Decorative initial *S*, A3. No running-head, no marginal notes, no head-pieces or tail-pieces or type ornaments.
   License. Registered by the Stationers' Company on March 25, 1602, and licensed to "master *waterson*" (*SR*, ed. Arber, III, 202).

Base-Copy Text. Bodleian Wood 504(4). Copy of first issue of sheet B: Bodleian Wood 616(16); copy of first issue of sheet C: Bodleian 4°C.16Art.BS.

Variants. All the changes in sheet B are as follows:

	1st issue	*2nd issue*
B1v	Towne.	Towne:
	foord.	foord:
	scituate	situate
	middest	midst
	Forces,	Forces, and
	thither. And the	thither, the
	seeing yet now	seeing it now
B2	head, which	head. Which
	Lo. Deputie, the day	L. Deputie, the day
	an Enemy thus	an enemy thus
	retiring: whereupon	retiring. Whereupon
	abide vs fight.	abide vs and fight.
B3v	captaine *Crofts*	Captaine *Crofts*
	Skowt-maister	Skowt-master
	of the rest. [ends paragraph]	of the rest. The [no paragraph]
	retriet	retriete
	knighted by the Lord Deputy,	Knighted by the Lorde Deputy,
	bodies: so did al	bodies. So did all
	victorie: a	victorie. A
B4	postestates hir	potentates, hir
	(as is sayd before.)	as is sayd before.
C3	worthie	worthy
	and diligence	and the diligence
	as when this descent	as though this descent

A Letter from a Souldier
of good place in Ireland.

TO THE RIGHT Worshipfull my especiall good friend, Sir W. D. *Knight.*

IR IN MY LAST of the 19. of December I wrote to you at large of the arrivall of the newe supplie of Spaniards at Castel-Haven, Baltemore, and Beer-haven, and of their intents and beginnings to forti-fie, in all those three important places. Likewise that Sir *Richard Levison* towing out of *Kinsale* Haven against winde and weather, fought with them within Castle Haven most valiantly, and of their ships being sixe, sunke and made unserviceable five: the men being most landed before hee could come to them, by reason of the weather, and beating upon him very danger-ously from the land with their ordinance. That they were said to be 2000. in number, with great store of ordinance and munition, and that as they reported, some thousands moe were comming after. That a great part of the Irishry of *Munster* becommen Rebels of new, were revolted to them, and received into the King of *Spaine's* pay. That *O'Donnell* with good Forces of horse and foote out of the North, by [A3v] the benefit of the then extreame and sudden frost, gat passage al-most unlooked for by himselfe, and slipping by the Lord President of *Munster* (who was sent to impeach him with such forces as could be spared from the Army) was joyned with them. That *Tyrone*, with *O'Rourck, Redman Bourck, MacGuyre, MacMahone, Randal Mac-Surley, O'Connor, Slygoe's* brother, *Tyrrel*, the Baron of *Lixenho*, and the rest of the old fugitive Rebels of *Munster*, with the greatest and choisest force that was ever amassed in *Ireland*, were drawne nere our

Camp. And that these all, together with six Ensignes of those newly arrived Spaniards, in all to the number of 6000. foote, and 500 horse, by *Powle*, were on foote ready to march towardes *Kynsale* and our Campe, with intent and most assured confident hope with helpe of them in the Town, which should have salyed out on the Campe, upon the attempt of *Tyrone* and *O'Donell*, and were above 2000. Spaniards, almost all old souldiers, aswell to releeve and rescue the Towne, as to remove our siege, and utterly to breake, dishonour, and defeate us. And truely Sir, when I did then consider, on the one side this great strength, the newly joyned men and horses to bee all fresh, vigorous, and strong, having all the Countrey open to them, abounding with victuals, forrages, armies, munition, and all furnitures: those in the Towne, the most of them experienced souldiers, well armed, and in no such want as was supposed: On the other side, our men in numbers scant equall to them, all almost tyred and wearied out with the miserie of a long Winter's siege, our horses decayed, leane and very weake, our best meanes of victuals and forrage likely to be cut from us, with many other impediments whereof I speake not; When I say, I well wayed and pondred with myselfe these poynts, and layde together withall, this one of great importance, that when we should be forced (as it [A4] was likely) to answere two forces at once, one from the Towne, another without, a great part of our men were like enough to shrink, or at least not to stick firmely to us (which by good conjectures I could make probable to you) Blame me not, if upon these considerations I wrote to you then somewhat distrustfully of our estate, as taking indeed our lives and honors, this service, and by consequence this whole Countrey likely to be put to an unequall jumpe. And so may I well say they were, although by the goodnesse of GOD especially, and by the most vigilant circumspection and valiant prowes of our worthy Generall, things out of these difficulties have now sorted to so happy successe, as by that which followeth you shall sufficiently perceive. To continue therefore my accustomed Relation to you, and to begin from that said day of the 19. of December, It may please you to knowe, that on Sunday the 20. wee still plying our attempts to the Towne, with face and shew as though we nothing cared for *Tyrone* and his companie, at night certaine intelligence was brought us, that he would bee the next night within a myle and a halfe of us, with all the above recyted Forces. And accordingly upon Munday the 21. towardes night, hee shewed himselfe with most part of his horse and foote, on a hill be-

tweene our Campe and *Corke,* a myle off us. At which time seeing two
Regiments of our foote, and some horse drawne out of our Campe,
and making a resolute march towardes him, hee fell backe to the
other side of the hill, where hee encamped that night, strengthened
with a fastnesse of wood and water. Whereby though his retyre might
bee imputed to some touch of credite, yet had hee this advantage, that
hee might keepe from our Armie all passages and meanes for forrage:
The other side over the River of *Ownibuoye* beeing wholly at his
disposition, by reason of the generall revolt of those parts. [A4v]

On Tuesday the 22. some of *Tyrone's* horse and foote made shewe
againe in the place where they had done the day before, and that
night were some of their horse, and 500. foote discovered, searching if
they might finde fit way to the Towne.

On Wednesday the 23. aswell by intelligence otherwise, as by letters
of *Don John d'l'Aquila,* Generall of the Spaniards, and Captaine of
the Towne newly intercepted, we found that he had importuned *Tyrone*
and his company very much, to give an attempt upon our Campe; in-
timating unto them his owne necessitie, and likelyhood to bee shortly
forced within the Towne, their faithfull promises to succour him, the
facilitie and undoubted successe of the enterprise, he assuring them,
that our numbers could not be but much lessened, and those that were
remaining, greatly decayed and weakened with the long winter siege,
so that it was not possible we should be able to maintaine so much
ground as we had taken when our strength was full, if they on the one
side, and he on the other put us well too it: which he for his part
promised them assuredly to doo very soundly from the Towne, whensoever they should thinke fit to doo the like from their Campe. And it
seemeth that upon this advise they tooke their determinate resolution
for this course, and to put it in execution with all speed, either that
night or the next at the furthest. Those of the Towne in the meanetime gave us alarums, made Sallies, and did by all meanes what they
could to keepe our men in continuall travell, that they might be the
lesse able for resistance when this attempt should come to be performed. The Lord Deputie till now applied himselfe in show wholly
towardes the Towne, but indeed not meaning any forceable effectuall
attempt upon it, till he sawe what would become of *Tyrone* and his
Forces[;] [B1] and therefore [we] hadde an especiall eye, by continuall
espiall, upon his moovings, and lest suddaine hurt should be taken
from him, or the Towne, if both he without, and they within should

invade at once, he made Fortes and Barracadoes, heightned the ditches, deepened the Trenches, stopped and strengthened all the Avenues to the Towne, hadde the whole Army in a readinesse uppon every suddaine warning, and kept strong and watchfull guardes alwayes in all places. And now late in the night of this Wednesday, the three and twentieth day, being assuredly enfourmed of their intent of attempt upon his Campe that night, or the morrow after, his Lord gave order to strengthen the ordinary guards, and to put the rest of his Army in readines, but not as yet into Armes: commaunding that the Regiment volant, which was a squadron of viii. Companies of foote, selected out of al the old Bands, conducted by Sir *Henry Poore*, and appointed to be alwayes in a readiness to answere all Alarames, and therefore exempted from all other duties, should draw out beyond the west parte of the Campe, and there stand in Armes, not farre from the maine guard of horse.

A litle before the breake of day Sir *Richard Greame*, who had the guard of horse that night, sent the Lord Deputie word, that the skowts had discovered the rebels' matches in great numbers, wherupon his Lord caused the Armie presently to arme, and 300. choise men to be drawne out of the quarter, where the Earle of *Thomond* and 3. other Regiments lay, to make stand betweene that quarter, and the Fort upon the west hill, himselfe with Sir *George Carow*, Lord President of *Munster*, Sir *Richard Wingfield*, marshall of *Ireland*, advanced forward towards the skowt, and having given order to Sir *Henry Davers* Liuetennant generall of the horse, for the ordering of those troopes, sent the Marshall, to take view of [B1v] the Enemy, who sent word he was advanced horse and foote neere the toppe of the hill, where the Erle of *Thomond* first quartered, within lesse then 2. musket shotte of the towne. Whereupon the Lord deputie calling to him Sir *Oliver Lambert* Governor of *Connaught*, who beeing there without Charge, was commaunded to attend his Lo. that day, made choise of a peece of ground beetweene that and the towne, of good advauntage, both to embattel, and fight, as having on the backe a Trench drawne from the Earle of *Thomond's* quarter, and so secured from the Towne: And on the front, a boggish glyn passable with horse only at one foord: The ground wheon the Enemy must have drawn in grosse to force the passage flanckfered from the Earle's quarter by the canon, and situate in the midst of all our Forces, and returned word to the Marshall, that in that place hee was resolved to give the Enemy battel, if hee came forward: commaunding further, the Regiment of Sir *H. Fol-yat* and three old Companies of the Regiment of Sir *Oliver Sainte-John* to bee brought thither, the rest of the Army being already in Armes, together with five hundred Sea-men, brought by Sir *Richard Leveson* to attend, when, and what, he should command.

But *Tirone*, whose meaning overnight, was, to have beene with us before daie, and as wee since learned, to have put al the Spaniards into the Towne, with viii. hundred of the best Irish under *Tirrell* seeing it now faire daylight, and discovering the Marshall and Sir *Henry Davers* to bee advaunced with all the horse, and Sir *Henry Poer* with his Regiment, stopt at the foote of the hill, and anon, thinking it to bee no day for him, retired the Troopes he had advanced againe, to the bodie of his Armie beyond the Foord. Presently the Marshall sent the Lord Deputie word, that the Enemy retired [B2] in some disorder, whereupon his Lord commanding the forenamed troops to folow him with al speed, advanced himselfe into the head of al, to see with his owne eie, the maner of the enemy, and in what sort thereupon he might determine to proceede. But before he could, either well view, or direct, a violent storme, during some quarter of an hower, gave the enemy oportunitie, not yet perfectly discovered, to drawe off over a plaine in three great bodies of foote, all their horse in the Rere, and the wings with all their other loose men fallen up into the head. Which the L. Deputie, the day now clearing, perceiving and discovering, by this their disorderly March, that they were in feare, being certified also, that there was not before them any place of so good advantage to make head on, as those they had passed and quited, resolved to follow, and to see what profit might be made of an enemy thus troubledly retiring. Whereupon dispatching presently Sir *George Carew*, Lord President of Munster with three cornets of horse backe to the Campe, to attend there against the Towne, and whatsoever other attempt, because he was to be the fittest Commaunder in his Lord's absence, and because there had otherwise no horses bene left in the Campe, himselfe having with him, in al, betweene three and foure hundred horse, and under 1200. foot, made after the Enimy. And advancing some mile further on, pressed him so hard, that he was forced to stand firme in three bodies upon a foorde of a bogge (which bogge to assaile them, we must of necessity passe) and in all apparance, with a Resolution there to abide us and fight. They maintained a good skirmish on our side the Bogge, with their loose wings, newly drawne out of their bodies, and hurt some of our men and horses, till with our wings they were at length beaten backe. [B2v]

The Marshall being somewhat advaunced, espied a Foord, a musket shot off on the left hand, neglected by their foote, and onely guarded by their horse: whereof advertising the Lord Deputy, with desire of leave to force them that way: the Lord Deputy approoving it, and commaunding to drawe up the foote with all expedition, the first wings of foote once arrived, seconded with sir *Henry Poer's* regiment, the Marshall, with the earle of *Clanicard*, who never ceased urging to fight, taking with them sir *Richard Greame*, and other companies of horse: with them, and those foote, forcing the enemies' horse that kept the passage, passed over, and with that advantage, finding themselves side by side with the enemies' battell, and further on then their rere, charged their battell in flanke, but finding them to stand firme, wheeled about. At which the enemies taking corage, drew on their horse, with a cry to a charge, who came on bravely within fiftie or sixtie paces of our horse, and thereafter their country fashion stopped, shaking their staves, and railingly vaunting, but durst charge no further. Which the Lord Deputy seeing, sent presently over the Foorde to them his owne cornet of horse, under sir *William Godolphin*, and the Lord President's cornet under Captaine *Minshow*, (which twoo cornets he had appoynted before, to keepe stil a grosse in the Rere, to answer all accidents) together with twoo of our three bodies of foote under sir *John Barkeley* Serjant major of the Campe. Whereupon the Marshall and Earle of *Clanrickard* seeing a second at hand, uniting themselves with Sir *Henrie Davers*, having with him Captaine *Taffe*, Captaine *Flemming*, and other companies of horse, charged againe the Enemies' horse, who not abiding the shocke, fledde. At the sight whereof, the battell dismaying, our menne thought [B3] it better to charge againe upon them, then to follow the horse, and so coragiously doing, utterly brake them. The rereward of the Enemie, in which was *Tyrrell*, and all the Spaniards, stood firme upon the bogge on the right hand, unto whom, within caliver shot, the Lorde Deputie had drawne up our Rere, which was Sir *Oliver Saint-John's* 3. companies, commanded by Captaine *Roe*, in absence of sir *Oliver*, (dispatched few days before by the Lord Deputie, and Counsaile, for speciall affaires to her Majesty) charging him first, not to stir, till he received direction from him. But seeing *Tirrell*, and the Spaniards drawing betweene our horse, beeing on the execution, and the bodies of our foote, his Lord having hitherto, by direction, set al other men's swords on work, himselfe now in the head of our said Rere, where he had before resolved to fight, charged the Enemy in flancke, and put them to a disorderly retreite after their fellows to the toppe of the next hill, where they made stand a little while. But the Irish quiting the Spaniards, the Spaniardes in short time were broken by the Lord Deputie's horse, commaunded by sir *William Godolphin,* and most of them slaine. The vantgarde of the Enemy, with all the loose wings, which were many, seeing what happened, threw away their armes (and all our men being otherwise busie) escaped. The chiefe Commaunder of the Spaniards, *Don Alonso d'Ocampo* was taken prisoner, with three Captaines, sixe Alferrez, and fortie souldiers. *Tirone,* and *O'Donnell,* with the rest of the Irish Lords, ran apace, and saved themselves. Those of the battell were almost all slaine, and there were (of the Irish Rebelles onely) found dead in the place, about twelve hundred bodies, and about eight hundred were hurt, whereof many dyed that night: and the chacc continuing almost two miles, was left off, our men [B3v] being tyred with killing. The Enemy lost two thousand Armes brought to reckning, besides great numbers imbezeled, al their powder and drummes, and ix. ensigns, whereof 6. Spanish. Those of the Irish that were taken prisoners, being brought to the Campe, though they offered ransome, were all hanged. On our side, onely one man was slaine, the Cornet of sir *Richard Greame.* Sir *Henry Davers* was hurt with a sword slightly: sir *William Godolphin* a little raced on the thigh with a holbert, Captaine *Crofts* the Skowt-master with a shot in the back, and not above sixe moe common soulders hurt. Many of our horses were killed, and moe hurt. And thus were they utterly overthrowne, who but the very night before, were so brave and confident of their owne good successe, as that they reckoned us already theirs, and as wee since have understoode, were in contention whose prisoner the Lord Deputy should be, whose the Lorde President, and so of the rest. The Earle of *Clanrickard* carried himselfe this day very valiantly, and after the retreite sounded, was Knighted by the Lorde Deputy, in the field amongst the dead bodies. So did all the rest of the Captaines, Officers, and Souldiers, named and unnamed, and especially the Lord Deputy himselfe, who brake, in person, upon the floure of the army the Spaniards, and omitted no duety of a wise diligent Conductor and valiant souldier. Upon the fight ended, he presently called together the Army, and with prayers, gave God thankes for the victorie. A victorie indeede given by the God of Hostes, and marvellous in our eyes, if all circumstances be duely considered, and of such consequence for the preservation and assuraunce to her Majestie, of this deepely endangered kingdome, as I leave to wiser consideration, contenting myselfe with this, that I see the God of power and [B4] might, disposed to protect the just cause of his servaunt, our gratious Queene *Elizabeth*, against the pride, malice, and powerful disdain of the greatest potentates, hir enemies. To him be the glorie.

After this glorious victorie thus valiantly atchieved, the Lord Deputy the same day hasted to his campe, lest anything (in his absence) might happely have beene attempted there. But, not finding the Ennemy to have made any sally, which indeede had beene but vaine for him, considering the small fruit he reaped by them heretofore, every one that he made hitherto redounding stil to his owne detriment and losse, and every place of our Camp, at this time, being so wel and sufficiently strengthened and provided for against him as is sayd before.

The next day his Lordship commaunded Captayne *Bodlegh* Trenchmaister generall of the Campe, who as well in the fight, as in the workes, had deserved speciall commendation, to see the formerly begunne Forte and platforms, to be undertaken againe, and neerer approches to be cast out towardes the towne. But after five or six dayes labour *Don John d'l'Aquila*, captaine of the Towne and Forces within, offered a parlee, sending the Drumme *major* of the Towne with a sealed letter to the Lord Deputy, by which he required, that some gentleman of speciall trust and sufficiencie might be sent into the towne from his Lordship, to conferre with him, whom he would acquaint with such conditions, as hee then stoode upon. His Request being assented unto by his Lordship, sir *William Godolphin* was imployed in the negotiation, which was carried in this sorte, word for word, as it is taken out of the originalls here, viz.

Don John tolde sir *William*, that having found the Lord Deputy (whome he termed the Viceroy) although a sharpe and powerfull, yet an honorable Enemy, and [B4v] the Irish, not onely weake and barbarous, but (as hee feared) perfidious friendes, he was so farre in his affections reconciled to the one, and distasted with the other, as did invite him to make an overture of such a composition as might be safe and profitable for the State of *England*, with least prejudice to the Crowne of *Spaine*, by delivering into the Viceroy his power, the Towne of *Kynsale*, with all other places in *Ireland*, held by the Spanish, so as they might depart on honorable termes, fitting such men of warre, as are not (by necessity) inforced to received conditions, but willingly induced, for just respects to dis-ingage themselves, and to relinquish a people, by whom their King and Master had bene so notoriously abused, (if not betrayed). That if the Viceroy liked to entertaine further parley touching this point, he would first be pleased to understand them rightly, and to make his propositions such as might be sutable, to men thorowly resolved, rather to bury themselves alive, and to endure a thousand deaths, then to give way to one Article of accord, that shuld taste of basenes or dishonour, being so confident of their present strength, and the royall Second of Spaine, that they should make no doubt of yeelding good accompt of themselves and their Interest in this Kingdome, but that a just disdaine, and spleene conceived against the nation, disswaded them from being further engaged for it, then of force they must, Sir *William Godolphin* being commaunded by the Lord Deputie onely, to receive *Don John's* propositions and demaunds. Having made his Lord and Counsel this Relation, was by them returned with the answere following. That howbeit the Lord Deputie having lately defeated their succours, didde so well understand his owne strength and their weakenesse as made him nothing doubt of forcing them within a short time, [Cl] whom he did know to be pressed with unresistable difficulties, how much soever they laboured to cover and conceale the same, yet knowing that her sacred Majestie out of her gracious and mercifull disposition would esteeme the glory of her victory to be blemished by a voluntary effusion, and an obstinate expence of Christian bloud, was content to entertaine this offer of agreement, so as it might be concluded, under such honorable articles for her highnes as the advauntage she had against them gave reason to demaund: being the same which are sette downe in the Articles of agreement following, signed by the Lord Deputie, and *Don John* and others: saving that there was in them besides, the leaving of his treasure, munition, artillery, and the Queene's naturall Subjects to her disposicion, all which points hee did peremptorely refuse, with constant asseveracion that both he and all his would rather indure the last of misery then be found guilty of so foule a Treason against the honour of his Prince and the reputacion of his profession, though hee should find himselfe unable to subsiste, much more now, when hee might not onely hope to sustaine the burden of the warre for a time, but with patience and constancie in the end to overcome it. That he tooke it so ill, to bee misunderstood in having Articles of that nature propounded unto him, as were they but once againe remembred in the Capitulacion, the Viceroy should from thencefoorth use the advantage of his sword and not the benefite of his former offers: adding, that the Viceroy might rather thinke to have made a good and profitable purchase for the Crowne of England, [C1v] if with the expence of 200,000 Duckats hee had procured *Don John* to quite his interest and footing but in Baltymore alone, to say nothing of Kynsale, Castell-haven, and Beerehaven: for (saide he) suppose that all we with the rest of our places here had perished, yet would that *Peninsula* (beyng strong in its owne nature, bettered by our arte and industrie, provided as it is of victuals, munition, and good store of Artillerie) preserve unto the King of Spaine a safe and commodious port for the arrivall of his Fleete, and be able to mayntaine itselfe against a land Armie of ten thousand, untill Spaine (being so deepely engaged) did in honour releeve them: which would drawe on a more powerfull invasion then the first, being undertaken upon false groundes, at the instance of a base and barbarous people, who in discovering their weakenes and want of power, have armed the King my Master to relie upon his owne strength, beyng tied in honour to releeve his people that are engaged, and to cancell the memory of our former disaster. But this was spoken (said he) in case the Viceroy were able to force this town, as I assure myselfe he cannot, having upon mine Honour within these wals at this instant, above two thousand fighting men, that are strong and able, besides those, which having been sicke and hurt, recover dayly: the greatest part of these, composed of old Souldiers, which fall not but by the sword, and those that were new, beyng new both trayned to their Armes and growne acquainted with the Climate, are more able to endure then at the firste: our meanes as good as they have beene any times these two monethes, such as [C2] the Spaniardes can well away withall, and therof to suffize us for three moneths more. We lodge in good warme houses, have store of munition, and (which is best of all) stand well assured that our succours wilbee shortly here. To bee playne, wee preserve our men, and reserve our strength the best wee may, hoping to front you in a breach, which if our harts fayle us not, we have hands and breasts enough to stop against treble your forces: though I will give the Viceroy this right, That his men are passing good, but spent and tyred out with the misery of a Winter siege, which he hath obstinatly maintayned beyond my expectacion, but with such caution, and upon so good guard, as having nicely watched all advauntages, I could never fasten a Sallie yet upon him, but with losse to myselfe: wherein I must acknowledge my hopes deceaved, that grounding on some errour in his approches, promised myself the defeate of at least a thousand men at one blowe. But when wee meete on the breach, I am confident on good reason, to lay five hundred of your best men on the earth, and rest hopeful that the losse of those will make a great hole in an Armie that hath already suffred so much extremitie.

But to conclude our businesse, the king my Master sent me to assist the Condees, *O'Neale* and *O'Donnell*, presuming on their promise, that I should have joined with them within few daies of the arrivall of his forces. I expected long in vaine, sustained the Viceroye's Armie, saw them drawne to the greatest head they could possibly make, lodged within two myles of Kynsale, reenforced with certaine [C2v] companies of Spanyards, every houre promising to releeve us, and beeing joyned together to force your campes, sawe them at last broken with a handfull of men, blowne asunder into divers parts of the world, *O'Donnell* in to Spaine, *O'Neale* to the furthest of the North, so as now I finde no such Condees *in rerum natura* (for those were the very wordes hee used) as I came to joyne withall, and therefore have moved this accord, the rather to disingage the King my Maister from assisting a people so unable in themselves, that the whole burden of the warre must lie upon him, and so perfidious, as perhaps might bee induced in acquitall of his favour, at last to betray him. Upon relation made by Sir *William Godolphin* to the Lord Deputie and Councell, of these offers of *Don John*, which at severall conferences had beene brought to such heads, as are spoken of before: it was thought good, for diverse important reasons, to proceed roundly to the agreement. For whereas in the propositions by him made; there was not anything that admitted exceptions on our part, but onely, that he required to carrie with him his ordinance, munition, and treasure, that beeing no way prejudiciall to the maine scope or drift of our Treatie, which cheefely respected the common good and safetie of the kingdome, deserved not almost to be thought upon. Besides that, the Treasure beeing at the first but a hundred thousand Duckats, with foure monethes' payment of so many men, and other necessarie deductions, could not but bee very neere wasted; and that little remaynder, more fit for a prey to the poore souldiour, [C3] after his tedious travell, than for a clause in the composition. Furthermore, how needfull it was to embrace this

accord, may clearely bee seene, by whosoever considereth the state of
our Armie, almost utterly tyred: how full of daunger and difficultie
it was to attempt a breach defended by so many hands: how long time
it might have cost us, if wee had lodged in the Breach, before wee
could have carried the Towne, it beeing full of strong castles: how her
Majestie's ships and others lying in the harbour, should have been
forced speedily to forsake us for want of victuals: how by a long con-
trarietie of winds, ourselves were not provided for above sixe daies, at
the time of this parley, though within fewe dayes after good store
arrived: it beeing indeed worthy of observation, that by her Majestie's
great care, and the diligence of her ministers, so good providence was
used, as though this descent of Spanyards drew into that quarter all the
forces of the kingdome which could be spared, all which were onely to
live by provision out of England; notwithstanding all the difficulties
of transportation, in so unseasonable a time, no notorious wants were
found in the Armie, but that which is unseparable from a Winter
siege, in that Climate: that we had neyther munition nor Artillerie
left but for one batterie in one place at once, five of our peeces being
before crazed: and finally, that if wee had missed of our purpose, the
whole countrey had been hazarded. Furthermore, that which seemeth
of greatest consequence to induce his Lordship to this agreement, was:
That the Spanyards to Baltymore Castle-haven and Beere- [C3v] haven,
by vertue of this contract were likewise to surrender those places, and
depart the countrey, which would have prooved a matter of more difficultie, and have drawne on a long warre in a corrupted kingdome,
to root them out, beeing strongly fortified and well stored with
victuals, munition, and artillerie, for that of necessitie the Armie for
some space, must have rested, and in the end have beene constrained
after a new supplie of al necessaries, to her Majestie's intollerable
charge, to transport themselves thither by sea, the way by land being
altogether unpassable. In which time, their succours out of Spaine in
all likelyhood, would have beene come unto them, the king being so
farre ingaged in his honour to second his enterprise, and we barred
of that prosecution of the Rebels, which now by this Agreement we
may wholly entend.

The Treatie therefore was thus concluded, as by the Articles en-
suing, signed on both parts, appeareth.

Mountjoye.

IN the town of Kynsale, in the kingdome of Ireland, the second day of the month of Januarie, *1601*, between the noble Lords, the Lord *Mountejoye*, Lord Deputie, and Generall in the kingdome of Ireland, for her Majesty the Queen of England, and *Don John d'L'Aquila*, Captaine and Campe- [C4] maister, Generall and Governour of the Armie of his Majestie the king of Spaine, the said Lord Deputie being encamped, and besieging the said towne, and the said *Don John* within it, for just respects, and to avoid shedding of blood, these conditions following were made betweene the said Lords Generals, and their campes, with the Articles which follow.

First, That the said *Don John d'L'Aquila* shall quit the places which he holds in this kingdome, as well of the towne of Kynsale, as those which are held by the soldiers under his command in Castlehaven, Baltymore, and in the castle at Beerhaven, and other parts, to the said Lord Deputie, or to whome he shall appoint: giving him safe transportation, and sufficient for the saide people, of Ships and victuals, with the which the sayd *Don John* with them may go for Spain, if he can at one time, if not, in two shippings.

Item that the Souldiers at this present being under the commaunde of *Don John*, in this Kingdome, shall not beare armes against her Majestie the Queene of England, whersoever supplies shall come from Spaine, till the said souldiers be unshipped in some of the Ports of Spaine, being dispatched as soone as may be by the Lord Deputie, as hee promiseth upon his faith and honor.

For the accomplishing whereof the Lord Deputie offereth to give free passeport to the said *Don John* and his army, aswell Spaniards as other na- [C4v] tions whatsoever that are under his commaund, and that he may depart with all the things he hath, Armes, Municions, Money, Ensignes displaied, Artillery and other whatsoever provisions of warre, and any kind of stuffe, aswell that which is in Castlehaven, as Kynsale and other parts.

Item that they shal have ships and victuals sufficient for their money, according and at the prices which here they use to give. That al the people and the said things may be shipped if it be possible at one time, if not, at two: and that to be within the time above named.

Item that if by contrary windes or by any other occasions there shal arive at any Port of these kingdomes of Ireland or England, any shippes of these in which the said men goe, they be entreated as frendes, and may ride safely in the harbor, and be victualed for their mony, and have moreover things which they shall need to furnish them to their voyage.

Item, that during the time that they shall stay for shipping, victuals shalbe given to *Don John's* people, at just and reasonable rates.

Item, that of both parts shalbe cessation of armes, and security that no wrong be offred anyone.

Item, That the Ships in which they shall goe for Spayne may passe safely by any other Ships whatsoever of her Majestie the Queene of [D1] England: and so shall they of the sayd Queene and her Subjects by those that shall goe from hence: and the sayde Shippes being arrived in *Spaine,* shall returne assoone as they have unshipped their men without any impediment given them by his Majestie, or any other person in his name, but rather they shall shewe them favour, and helpe them if they neede anythinge, and for securitie of this, they shall give into the Lord Deputie's handes Three Captaines such as hee shall choose.

For the securitie of the perfourmance of these Articles, *Don John* offereth that hee will confirme and sweare to accomplish this Agreement: and likewise some of the Captaines of his charge shall sweare and confirme the same in a severall writing.

Item that hee in person shall abide in this Kingdome where the Lord Deputie shall appoint till the last shipping upon his Lordshippe's word: and if it happen that his people be shipped all at once, the sayde *Don John* shall goe in the same Fleete without any Impediment given him. But rather the Lord Deputie shall give a good Shippe in which he may goe, and if his sayd men be sent in twoo shippinges, then he shall goe in the last.

And in like sort the saide Lord Deputie shall sweare and confirme, and give his word in the behalfe of her Majestie the Queene and his owne, to keepe and accomplish this Agreement, and joyntly the Lord President, the Lord Marshall of the [D1v] Campe, and the other of the Councell of State, and the Earles of *Thomond* and *Clanrykard* shall sweare and confirme the same in a severall writing.

George Carew.

Thomond.

Clanrikard.

R. Wingfeild.

Ro. Gardemor.

Geo. Bourcher.

Rich. Liveson.

I promise and sweare to accomplish
and keepe these Articles of Agreement,
and promise the same likewise on the
behalfe of his Majestie Catholique
the Kinge my Maister.

Don John d'lAquila.

And so is this troubled Cloud, of most likely perillous danger for this time dissolved, to her Majestie's most singuler renowme; Not so much for the glorie of the event, as for her owne Magnanimitie and Princely resolution, to leave nothing undone which might preserve that Crowne, how deare soever it cost her; to the great honour of our Generall, Leaders, and Souldiers by land and Sea Actors therein, who, if it be well considered, that after the Enemie's arrivall xxviii. Septem- [D2] ber, it was xxvi. October before they could get all things readie to sit downe nere the Towne: xxix. October before their Ordinance could play, And that by i. November. they had gotten *Ricorren* castle, And then vii. November were driven shrewdly to diminish their strength by sending the Lord President from them with two Regiments of foote and 325 horses against *O'Donnell,* That hee returned not till xxv. November, his Companies *26.* And then that the Supplyes of *Spaine* were landed. That the most of our shipping that did us speciall service were gone towardes them, That *O'Donnell* was alreadie come, *Tyrone* shortly after, and xx. December all in flight: 24 beaten: That xxxi. December the Parley begunne, ii. Januarie the Articles were sworne: ix. the Towne yeelded. These thinges (I say) considered, it cannot bee thought they spent any idle time, as by the Journals also which I sent you heretofore doth particulerly appeare. Nay, let it bee duely considered indeed, that the Towne though not regularly forti- fied after the moderne sort, yet was of strong scituation, well walled, and rampierd of the old fashion, and apt to receive fit fortification, which the Enemie by his skill and leasure had given it, both within the Towne and without, as being accounted of great knowledge in fortification, and having beene a Moneth in it before our men could come neere much to molest him. And it may rather bee marvailed, that such an Enemie with such a Companie, so provided, not beeing con- strained by sickenesse, famine, or other defect of provision, and expecting [D2v] shortly (as himselfe tearmeth it) a Royall supplie from *Spaine*, should so soone yeeld up, not only it, but the other Castles, and that of *Baltymore* especially so important, so strong, so fournished to hould so long out, as by his owne acknowledgement appeareth before. Well, going they are with the loane of ordinarie vessels which they also pay for: for whome yea and almost for any enemie of lesse qualitie than these, all auncient estate wisedome would have advised to have made and given them a goulden bridge to passe over, rather than they should have stayed longer uppon any Condition, much lesse upon doubtfull hope of a small contemptible pillage to have beene gotten of them, which must needes also have beene bought with much blood, and with what further Charge and hazard to the mayne, God knoweth. And howsoever any perticuler humour may take it, I think *Don John* (all Circumstances considered) did advisedly for his King to leave it: And for our part I take it a Service to have beene most honourably perfourmed, with singuler evident profite, and all probabilitie of certaine future securitie to our Prince and Countrey, and that otherwise it cannot bee conceaved off, of any that will indifferently judge. The proofe whereof by the fruite beginneth here presently to appeare, by the diminishing of her Majestie's Charge, daunting of the Rebels, quiet, comfort, and encouragement of the good, and before dismayed Subject, and will (I doubt not) but be generally felt with you there, by sparing your men and monneys, and putting you out of feare hereafter, of your and our, and all [D3] *England's* potent Enemie for his further attempting this way. And this for this of the late victorie and yeelding of the Towne, which is my purposed taske unto you at this time. As for that which was done from the first landing of the Spaniards till the fight, I referre you to the Journals sent you before. And for the generall course of the noble Lord Deputies whose proceedinges in this Land, since his first arrivall here, I leave it to others to bee treated of more at large hereafter, onely this I will now say in generall, let it bee but without humour judicially considered, in what estate he found this Land, and to what hee hath now brought it, and there is none so unindifferently affected, but must bee forced to confesse, *Quantum mutatus ab illo*! And heere I and my object of the fight, and yeelding of the Towne, and whole quiting of all the Invadors, with *Salmacida Spolia*, and unbloudie victorie of our part, most befitting a Virgine Queene, and a Bacheler Generall. And so doe betake you to the Almightie. At *Corcke* this *13* of *Januarie, 1601*.

Your assured at commaund. I. E.

Notes

References in running glosses to Tilley are to Morris Palmer Tilley, *A Dictionary of the Proverbs in England and in the Sixteenth and Seventeenth Centuries* (Ann Arbor, 1950).

Proclamation of Accession

About 450 extant Elizabethan proclamations—twice as many as extant for Henry VIII—remain as official statements by the Queen and her Privy Council announcing, imposing, explaining, or justifying state policies; most deal with Catholicism, the Puritan movement, or economic measures. They were printed in average editions of 500, though in some instances there were as few as 50 and on at least one occasion as many as 700, and distributed by messenger. Increasingly, they were written by the Queen's law officers.

Quene of Englande, Fraunce and Ireland hereditary title; France was added by Edward III in January 1340, Ireland by Henry V. Despite Mary Tudor's loss of France, the title was continuously used until 1801   *defendour of the fayth* bestowed first by Pope Clement VII on Henry VIII for his attack on Luther   *peax* peace   *Cum . . . solum* "With sole right to publish"

The Quene's Majestie's Passage

[A2] *towre* it was customary for the kings of England to spend one or more nights in the Tower of London before their coronation processional   [A2v] *being caried* Elizabeth was transported in a litter of yellow cloth of gold in a quilt of white damask with satin lining and eight matching cushions. Four knights carried a canopy over her and on either side marched an escort of pensioners with axes   *Hatfield* the royal palace in Hertfordshire, 19 miles nnw of London, where Mary had kept Princess Elizabeth detained in state   [A3] *Fanchurche* Fenchurch Street, a major street in Aldsgate Ward leading from the Tower   [A3v] *table* printed board   *Vrbs . . . vllum*[an accurate translation is given on A3]   [A4] *gracious streate* Gracechurch Street, a major street going n from the Thames which served as a boundary of [London] Bridge Ward Within   *arke* arch   *vawted* vaulted   *degrees* tiers   *cloth* canopy   [B1v] *prease* praise   *two houses did knit* Henry Tudor, duke of Richmond, a Lancastrian sympathsizer, married Elizabeth, eldest daughter of Edward IV, a Yorkist, in January 1486   [B2] *civill warre* War of the Roses, 1455-1485   *Hii . . . tui* [an accurate Latin translation of the first two quatrains on B1v]   [B2-B2v] *Nullae . . . &c.* "No force can subdue united souls. Those who inspire fear when united must fear when they are divided. Souls in conflict divide, united souls bind together. Small things are made greater by peace, great things fall in war. Joined hands can bear a heavier burden. Unity amongst the citizens will act as a firm defense of a kingdom. Those who fight long, mourn longer. Warring rulers are the plague of their subjects. A prince born to peace is not given to arms. Plenty is the daughter of concord, peace its granddaughter. A divided state lays itself open to its enemies. Those who hold the same thing will hold for longer. A kingdom divided against itself is easily destroyed. A united city is attacked in vain by force of arms. Concord between nations strengthens the faith." *voide* unutilized   [B3] *Cornehill* the next ward s, at the w end of Leadenhall, named for a flourishing corn market there   *conduit* fountain; Cornhill Conduit which drew sweet water in lead pipes was formerly part of a prison cistern; it was restored as a town well in 1546   *curiously* carefully   [B3v]*staieng* staying   [B4] *proper beastes* then a lion rampant and red dragon (adopted from arms borne by Henry VIII) *perles* peerless   *mone* moan   [B4v] *Quae . . . honor* "The gracious queen who sits high under the proud canopy bears the image of the holy princess who is supported by the affection of her citizens, strengthened by wisdom, famed for justice and blessed by religion. Vain superstitions and crass-seeming ignorance lie crushed by true religion. Royal love subdues unbridled and rebellious minds and rightly tramples flatterers and those who seek bribes. When a wise man rules the Empire, foolishness, and vainglory which is its God, shall sit in outer darkness." *rome* room   [Cl]*great conduit in chepe* a large fountain in the e part of the market square of West Cheaping Street which transported water from Paddington. The fountain was built in 1285 and rebuilt and enlarged in 1479.   *Soper lane* beginning at the market square of West Cheaping, this lane served as headquarters for cordwainers (shoemakers) and curriers (those who dressed and colored leather)   *S. Mathew* Matthew 5:3-10   [Clv] *smart* sorrow   [C2] *Qui . . . erit* "Those who mourn shall be made joyful; those who are of meek heart alone shall reap many fertile acres; those who hunger and thirst after righteousness shall be filled. It is right that the pure in heart shall see God. God will be merciful to him who shows mercy on others. Anyone who is a peacemaker is the son of God. Whosoever suffers for the sake of righteousness and has a humble mind, shall receive the kingdom of heaven. The Almighty promised the earth, the sea and the stars to men of this kind, each one of whom shall be blessed."   *standarde* a column next to the fountain used as a market cross and a landmark midway between the w end of the Poultry and Paul's Gate; a popular place for reading proclamations, holding executions, and burning condemned documents   *Crosse* Cheapside Cross was not part of the city's fabric, but was one of the series of memorial crosses, from Hardeby, Lincolnshire, to Westminster, which Edward I erected to mark the stages in the funeral procession of his wife, Queen Eleanor of Castile. The cross was renovated with new leadwork in the fifteenth century and gilded, burnished, and regilded in 1554   [C2v] *Saint Peter's church* in Wood Street, Cheap, near Cripplesgate   *waites* wind instrumentalists maintained by the city at the public charge   *litle conduit* in West Cheapside by Paul's Gate   *sir John Parrat* Sir John Parrot (?1527-1592), reportedly the son of Henry VIII. One of four gentlemen chosen to carry the canopy of state, he was shortly afterwards appointed vice-admiral of the seas about south Wales and keeper of the gaol at Haverfordwest   *companies* London corporations of tradesmen who produced the pageants and whose activities stopped by custom and law at the city gates [C3] *whodes* hoods *wyflers and garders* ornamental borders and trimmings *penthouses* shop canopies *markes* denominations of varying weights of gold and silver, usually 8 ounces *brethren* aldermen and city council *comminal-9 citizens below the rank of peer* ₍C3v₎ *joyntly* smoothly [C4v] *ruthfull wight* lamentable man [D1] *Paul's churchyarde* the n churchyard of St. Paul's, the city cathedral, which is connected to West Cheaping by Friday Street *Ille . . . virens* [approximate translation is given on C4v above] [D1v-D2] *Philosophus . . . Amen* "The divine philosopher Plato left this observation for posterity, amongst many wise and valuable sayings: that a state would be most fortunate if its princes should be interested in matters favorable to wisdom and conspicuous for their virtues. And if it seems to us that he was right (and he was indeed entirely right), why should Britain not rejoice? Why should the people not leap with joy and pleasure? Why should this day not be marked (as they say) with a white stone? A day when we have with us a prince whose like was never seen by our ancestors, and whose like our descendants are unlikely ever to see, most excellently endowed with all bodily and spiritual gifts. The bodily gifts are so apparent that they do not lack for description. But the spiritual gifts are so manifold and so great that they cannot possibly be expressed in words. Although she is descended from the noblest kings, in nobility of manners and mind she far surpasses her race. Her breast burns with love of Christ's religion. She will bring fame to the British people by her virtues, and still protect them with the shield of justice. She is most learned in Greek and Latin literature, and outstanding in intellectual gifts. Under her rule religion will flourish, England will prosper, the Golden Age will return. O Englishmen, who are about to receive so many benefits, attend with due honor on our most celebrated Queen Elizabeth, destined by Christ himself to rule this empire. Be her most willing subjects, and show yourselves worthy of such a prince. And since boys can show their loyalty not by their strength but by their prayers, we the pupils of this school, founded by Colet, sometime Dean of St. Paul's, raising our tender hands towards heaven will pray Christ, the Best and Mightiest, that he will cause your Highness to rule England with great honor until you reach the age of Nestor, and that he will grant you to become a joyful mother of children. Amen." [D2v] *Anglia . . . regit* "O England now rejoice, clap your hands, leap and dance; your life is at hand, and your help. Behold, your hope comes, your glory, your light, and your salvation. Now she comes who will surely bring you succour. She will help your affairs which have gone astray; she will bring back those things which were lost. All will flourish, the Golden Age returns. Good things which fell will rise again as better things. You must therefore give yourself up to her in complete trust, for by her accession you will receive so many benefits. You should therefore hail her from the depths of your heart. The merit of Elizabeth's reign is not to be doubted; she comes a virgin; may she return later accompanied by dear children, may she come as a joyful parent. May the omnipotent God, creator and ruler of both heaven and earth, grant this from highest Olympus." *Ludgate* the westernmost of the city's six gates, leading to Westminster [D3] *fletebridge* a stone bridge over Turnemill Brook (alternately Fleet Dike) which emptied into the Thames. The bridge was decorated in 1431 with the same coping of angels as Cheap Standard; the stream, however, was considerably diminished by 1559 *conduit in Fleetestrete* a cistern built by the citizens of Fleet Street at Fleet Bridge in 1478   *endomaging* impairing   [D3v] *parliament robes,* ie, royal robes as ordained by Parliament *Debora* (see Judges 4:4-5)   *Jaben* the king of Canaan who oppressed the Israelites for 20 years (Judges 4:2,3)   [D4] *Quando . . . tuis* [approximate translation of verses above on D3v]   *Temple barre* the entrance to Westminster from the Duchy of Lancaster, the area between Westminster and the old city of London   *S. Dunstone's church* St. Dunstan's in the West, a parish church extending along Fleet Street from the conduit to Fetter (Fewtars) Lane   *the hospitall* Christ Hospital, a school founded for poor boys by Henry VIII in a former Greyfriars monastery and supported by the people of London   [E1] *two ymages* according to the (legendary) history of Britain by Geoffrey of Monmouth (d. 1155), two Trojans, Corineus and Brutus, the great grandson of Aeneas, settled Britain by exterminating the giants living there. Corineus, the eponymous founder of Cornwall, destroyed the giant Goëmagot (Gogmagog), bringing order and peace to the founding of Britain (New Troy)   [E1-E1v] *Ecce . . . erunt* [the translation appears below on E1v]   [E2] *shooting* shouting   *towre streat* the main street of Tower Street Ward, at the e side of the city, running from the Tower along the Thames almost to Billingsgate   [E2-E2v] *O . . . tui* [translation of the English verses on E2 above]   [E3v] *stomacke* spirit   [E4v] *Daniel* (see Daniel 6:16-24)   *He . . . him* (Matthew 6:33; Luke 12:31)

Proclamation for Peace between England, France, and Scotland
   *J. B. Black, *The Reign of Elizabeth 1558-1603* (Oxford, 2nd ed., 1959).
intelligence understanding   *Prince Henrye* Henry II (1519-1559)   *Quene, Dolphines of Scotlande* Mary Stuart, Queen of Scots, who by marriage to Francis II, Dauphin of France, made him King of Scotland and herself Dauphiness of France   *YEVEN* given (proclaimed)   *Cum . . . Maiestatis* "With the permission of Her Royal Majesty"

Homily on Obedience
   [R4] *severall orders . . . Aungelles* cf. 1 Samuel 1:3, 11; Thess. 4:16; Romans 8:38; Ephesians 1:21; Colossians 1:16, 2:15; see also Dionysius the Areopagite, *The Celestial Hierarchy*   [R4v] *Bibilonical confusyon* see Ezekiel 23:17; Revelation 17:5, 18:10   [S1] *booke of the Proverbes* Proverbs 8:15-17   *boke of wisedom* Proverbs 6:1-3   [S1v] *Deuteronomi* Deuteronomy 32:35; cf. Romans 12:19; Hebrews 10:30   *S. Paule* see Romans 13:1-6   [S2] *chosen vessell* Acts 9:15   *S. Chrisostom* Chrysostom (Greek church father, ?345-407), *Epistulum ad Rom. Homil.* XXIII, Op IX 686B   *presidentes* appointed governors or lieutenants of provinces   [S2v] *whosoever withstandeth* Romans 13:2   *pangues* pangs   *They commytted theyr cause* 1 Peter 2:23   *Pilate* John 19:10-11 *loce* loose   [S3] *s. Peter* 1 Peter 2:18-21   *frowarde* evilly disposed   *S. David* 1 Samuel 18:20   [S3v] *into Davide's handes* 1 Samuel 24:3-7   *another time* 1 Samuel 26:7-12   *a deade sleepe* proverbial; Tilley S527   *Abisai* Abishai, nephew of Joab (2 Samuel 26:5-9)   [S4v] *he praieth so oft* cf. 1 Samuel 13:14; Acts 13:22   *another notable story* 2 Samuel 1:1-16

Amalechite one of the ancient nomadic tribes which are uniformly represented as an enemy of Israel in the Old Testament   *chaunce* good fortune   [T1] *with the Apostles* Acts 5:29   *Chore, Dathan, and Abiron* Numbers 16:1-33   *fire* Numbers 16:35   *leprosye* Numbers 12:1-10   [T1v] *serpentes* Numbers 21:5-6   *sore plagued* Numbers 16:47-49   *Absalon* he was slain with darts by Joab while hanging from an oak tree, his hair entangled (see 2 Samuel 18:9-15) *treason wil not be hid* proverbial; Tilley M1315   *Ecclesiastes* Ecclesiastes 10:20   [T2] *bewray* reveal   *successor of Chryst and Peter* (see Matthew 16:18) [T2v] *paied tribute* Matthew 17:24-27   *went to the citie of David* Luke 2:1-7 *.s. Peter* 1 Peter 2:13-15   [T3] *as S. Peter writeth* 1 Peter 2:13   *as S. Paule writeth* Romans 13:5   *by the worde of god* Romans 13:7; Matthew 22:21 *Timothie* 1 Timothy 2:1-3   [T3v] *Ezechias* Hezekiah (see 2 Kings 16, 18-20; Matthew 1:9)   *Josias* Josiah (see 2 Kings 21-23; Matthew 1:10)   *death of the crosse* Philippians 2:8

Declaration to Aid France

[178] *afflicted Estate* following religious disturbances in 1562, Francis, duke of Guise, marched into Paris to effect a *coup d'etat* as the champion of militant Catholicism; he was opposed by Huguenot leaders, notably the Prince of Condé and Admiral Coligny   *Kyng* Charles IX (1550-1574)   *Quene his Mother* Catherine de Medici (1519-1589), regent and virtual ruler even after Charles's minority   *Beginning of her Raigne* in April 1559 with the peace treaty signed at Câteau, in Cambrésis; see also the proclamation on p. 40 above *a Portion of her auncient Dominion* the port city of Calais, won by Edward III after the Battle of Crécy, 1346, and lost again to France in 1558 under Mary Tudor   *restored* in the Treaty of Câteau-Cambrésis, which also pledged that Calais would revert to England after 8 years, providing there were no acts of aggression in France or Scotland   *her nexte Neyghbours* the Scots   *open Declaration* Elizabeth warned France not to intervene in the civil war of Scotland in 1559, caused by Knox's religious rebellion; when France determined to send troops, Elizabeth sent out land forces under Norfolk (on Dec. 24, 1559) and sea forces under Winter (on Dec. 27). On Feb. 27, 1560, combined forces caused the French to withdraw and Elizabeth took over the protection of Scotland's civil and religious liberties for as long as the marriage of Mary Stuart and the Daughin of France lasted (and one month following), the Scots promising to provide an army of 2,000 foot and 1,000 horse in the event of foreign invasion   *Quene of Scottes* Mary Stuart (1542-1587)   *strayghter* [more complete]   *Kynde of Amitie* the Treaty of Edinburgh (July 6, 1560) in which England and France both declared non-intervention in Scottish affairs [179] *the Guyses* Francis, duke of Guise (1519-1563) and Charles, cardinal of Lorraine (1525-1574)   *Enterview* Mary Stuart had requested to meet with Elizabeth in Jan. 1561 and in May Elizabeth agreed to such a meeting, but fresh conflict broke out putting their meeting off until early summer 1562 *Aucthours* Francis, duke of Guise; Anne of Montmorency, the maréchal of St. André   *Ambassade* deputation   *Person of good Credite* Sir Henry Sidney (1529-1586), sent to France in April 1562   *Violence* at the Slaughter of Vassy, Mar. 1, 1562   *the one Partie* Francis, duke of Guise   *ryche Townes* Vassy, Paris, Sens, Tholose, Blois, Tours, Angers, and elsewhere; an estimated 100,000

persons were killed   *Councell* the great Parliament at Orléans, Jan. 1560
Reliefe in part of the edict of Jan. 17, 1562, which allowed Protestants to worship freely   *Ambassade* on July 26, 1562   [180]   *Excester* Exeter   *Bryttayne*
Bretagne (Brittany)   *apprehended* on Aug. 19, 1562   *Complaint was made*
on Aug. 20   *Kyng of Navarre* Anthony Bourbon (1518-1562); from 1512
Navarre was a province of Spain retaining status, institutions and law as an
independent kingdom   *diminishe the Crowne* by refusing the restitution
of Calais   [181] *put certayne Numbres of her Subjectes in Order* by the Treaty
of Richmond (Sept. 1562) Le Havre was garrisoned by 3,000 English troops
and held as a pledge until Calais was surrendered; an additional 3,000 men
were given to Condé's command for defending Dieppe and Rouen and 140,000
crowns was loaned repayable when Elizabeth had Calais restored to her
Callyce Calais; England would be deprived since she would be accused of invading France

Proclamation against Hostilities to the French
   *Wallace T. MacCaffrey, *The Shaping of the Elizabethan Regime* (Princeton,
1968).
   French Kyng Charles IX (1550-1574), for whom Catherine de Medici was
acting as regent   *Ambassadours* Sir Thomas Smith (1513-1577) and Sir
Nicholas Throckmorton (1515-1571)   *this laste warre* English forces capitulated in July 1563

Proclamation against the Traffic in Spanish Countries
   advertisementes notifications   *lowe countreys* Netherlands and present-day
Belgium and Luxembourg   *Duke of Alva* (Alba) Fernando Alvarez de Toledo
(1507-1582), governor general of the Netherlands for Spain   *kyng of Spayne*
Philip II (1527-1598, brother-in-law to Elizabeth through his marriage to her
half-sister Mary Tudor   *house of Burgondy* the ruling house of the Netherlands, beginning with Philip the Bold on Jan. 30, 1384, and passing through
succeeding generations to Charles V, Philip II's father, and thence to Philip II
(ruled 1556-1598)   *warde* guards, prison   *conversation* behavior   *West countrey* present Cornwall, Devonshire, and Somerset   *certayne portes* Plymouth,
Southampton   *Spanishe ambassadour* Don Guerau de Spes   *wolles* wool
captayne of the Isle of Wight Sir Edward Horsey (d. 1583); the Isle of Wight,
3 miles off the s coast of England in the English Channel, is mid-way between
Bournemouth and Portsmouth

*Proclamation against the Earl of Northumberland and His Accomplices in
Rebellion*
   Northumberlande Thomas Percy, seventh earl of Northumberland (1528-
1572)   *Westmerland* Charles Neville, sixth earl of Westmoreland (1543-1601)
Sussex Thomas Radcliffe, third earl of Sussex (?1526-1583), lord president
and lord lieutenant of the North   *advertisement* notification   *houses and
Churches* at Durham, Darlington, and Hartlepool (see headnote)

The Offices of Excester

[C1] *Freeman* one free to trade in city markets; the right was obtained (a) by inheritance, if eldest son of a freeman, (b) by apprenticeship of seven years and payment of a small fee, (c) by purchase—in Exeter 20 shillings for an artificer, whatever the magistrates set for a merchant; only freemen were franchised *liberties* districts beyond the city boundaries subject to city control *common counsell* the 24; see D2v below *guildhable* taxable *scots and lots* local taxes for poor relief and taxes levied by a municipal corporation in proportionate shares upon its members to defray expenses *tallages* municipal rates; tolls *loiable* loyal [C1v] *ward* prison [C2] *forestalled* bought up privately to raise prices *ingrossed* bought up wholesale, usually to regrate or retail at monopoly prices *assise of bread* standard measure or price of bread as determined by ordinance *night-watchers* loiterers *tipler* tavern-keeper *perambulations* official survey *rogation weeke* the week in which Ascension Day falls *Michelmas* the Feast of St. Michael, Sept. 20; one of the four quarter-days of the English business year *eschetor* (escheator) officer appointed to take notice of escheats, or lapsing of land to the city at the death of a tenant who has no qualified successor *socage* tenure of land by certain services other than knight-service [D1] *shambles* district where meat was slaughtered and sold [D1v] *the blacke lieger* the costumal of the City of Exeter with memoranda on the duties of city officials, copies of deeds, etc. The document is no longer extant; Hooker alludes to it in his "annals" (forming part of his MS. "Commonplace Book"), "1489 This yere were delyvered to the mayor at the daye when he was sworne to the office of the mayroltie a certeyn roll named the blacke roll and a booke yn the roll were conteyned the auncient orders pryveleges customes of the government of this Citie and yn the booke the lyke was conteynid concerninge the Citie of London and order taken that the same sholde be yerely delyvered from mayor to mayor. This roll yn the tyme of Kinge Edward the VI was by one Mr. Griffeth Ameredith delyvered to Sir William Cicell Knight then Secretary to the Kinge and never could agayne be had and what became of the booke it is not knowen" (Corp. MS. Bk. 51, f.324, *sub anno* 1489). This reference is puzzling, since Hooker seems to have seen (or at least recalled) the Black Book in writing this one and the Black roll (though perhaps not the book) was back in Exeter from at least the Town Council meeting of Feb. 1604 onwards (Corp. Act Book, VI, f.59). Perhaps the book was deteriorated and Hooker felt his own work sufficient replacement after a time, for the references in this text are the last made to it *conduicts* conduits, open fountains for water supply in the city squares [D2v] *quarter sessions* court of limited criminal and civil jurisdiction, and of appeal, held quarterly by the recorder of a borough *let* lease [E1] *set* set to sale *demise* transfer an estate by will or lease *alienate* transfer ownership to another [E1v] *waremote's inquest* meetings of the wards (wardmoots) held semi-annually by the aldermen to inquire into misdemeanors *jewrie* jury *undertenants* tenants holding land or premises from another tenant [E2] *purpestures* obstructions *pales* fences *wales* ridges of earth or stone *stales* stalls *bulkes* extra goods *backes* tubs, troughs, or vats used by brewers, dyers, and picklers *heathes* hearths *scavenger* person employed to sweep or clean the streets *crookes* long-shafted iron hooks used to pull down burning wood or thatch so as to extinguish it at ground level [E2v] *imbecilled* debilitated [F1] *engrosse* write in a large character appropriate for legal documents [F1v] *Seruientes ad clauam* sergeants at the mace *travels* travails

[G1] *privie coate* a coat of mail worn under the ordinary dress   [G1v] *ammisances* errors   *pentises* sheds erected against larger buildings   [G2v] *Perkin Warbecke* (1474-1499), pretender to the throne of Henry VII by falsely claiming to be Richard, duke of York   *Scire facias* a judicial writ requiring the sheriff to ask the party before the court to show cause why execution should not be taken against him, or why letters patent, such as charters, should not be revoked   *fieri facias* a writ whereby the sheriff causes to be made out of the goods and chattels of the defendant the sum for which judgment was given   [H1] *Magdalen* (proper name of the Exeter almshouses)   *Lazar people* lepers   [H1v] *weare* weir   [H2] *bull unbaited* common belief held that bulls baited or worried by dogs before slaughter made better eating and butchers were held liable to prosecution if they sold unbaited beef   *brenning* in heat   *tupping* in heat   *blowen* stale, tainted   *foistered* grown musty or stale-smelling   [I1] *(office of) countenance* estimation, reputation   *bull or beare baiting* the act of baiting a bull or bear with dogs in a ring was a favorite amusement   *praised* appraised   [I1v] *harnesse* armor   [I2] *balling* making noise

A discoverie of the treasons attempted by Francis Throckemorton
   [π2] *Francis Throckemorton* (1554-1584), well-known Catholic graduate of Hart Hall, Oxford, and a student at Inner Temple, London; his father, John, was knighted by Queen Elizabeth in 1566 and appointed justice of Chester; he was suspended the year before his death (1579), perhaps for maladministration, perhaps because of his sympathies for Jesuits   *conceite* understanding   [π2v] *Lion's Inn* one of 14 London schools of law; with Clements Inn and New Inn, a house of Chancery located outside Temple Bar   [A1] *proceedings* Throckmorton's hearing was on May 21, 1584   *Guildhall* home of the city's nine courts   [A1v] *the Scottish Queene* Mary Stuart (1542-1587), Elizabeth's cousin and rightful Queen of Scotland whose residence in England was a rallying point for Catholic rebels and others who wished to overthrow Elizabeth   *Levsham* Lewisham, a town 6 and a half miles se of London on the Tonbridge-Hastings road   *Poule's wharfe* a major landing, with stairs, on the Thames in London   [A2] *Secretarie hand* then the most common form of writing, developed from earlier court and manuscript-book handwritings   *Romane hand* a rounder and bolder handwriting   *petidegrees* tabular genealogies   *Bishop of Rosse* John Leslie (1527-1596), nominally Scottish ambassador to England and confidant to Mary Stuart; suspected of treason with the Ridolfi plot (1571), he was imprisoned in the Tower for 2 years, then told to leave the country. He died in Brussels; see Northumberland pamphlet, B1v (p. 171)   *Tower* Tower of London, use for solitary confinement of political prisoners   [A2v] *bewray* reveal   *Racke* Throckmorton was racked for the first time on Nov. 23, 1583   [A3] *Spaw* Spa, a town known for its mineral springs in the province of Liege, Belgium   *Sir Francis Englefield* (d. ?1596), a Catholic exile who fled abroad soon after Elizabeth's accession. He returned and, although the King of Spain pleaded for him, was convicted of high treason in Parliament in 1585, whereby he suffered forfeiture of all his manors, lands, and possessions   [A3v] *Thomas Morgan* (1543-?1606), a Catholic conspirator; Lord Shrewsbury's secretary at Tutbury where he helped the imprisoned Mary Stuart, he was caught and then freed. Morgan fled to

France where, at Elizabeth's request, he was imprisoned in the Bastille for his complicity in a plot to assassinate her *Duke of Guyse* Henry of Lorraine (1550-1588), third duke of Guise, who strengthened family ties with the Spanish and befriended Don John of Austria with whom he porposed an invasion of England in the interest of Mary Stuart (1583) *the Spanish Ambassador* Don Bernardino de Mendoza, Spanish ambassador to London from 1578 to 1584 [A4] *platte* map *Arundel in Sussex* a market town on the Arun River, 10 miles ne of Chichester and 55 miles sw of London, a short distance from the Petworth holdings of Northumberland (see the following pamphlet, B4v; p. 176) *neere cutte* (the short passage across the English Channel would land on the French coast equidistant between Cherbourg and Le Havre) *Charles Paget* (d. 1612), leader of the Scottish faction of the Catholic exiles. He went to France in 1572 and was in close association with Morgan against Archbishop Beaton, Mary's ambassador; Paget was attainted for treason by Parliament in 1587 *advertisement* announcement [B1] *Cipher* secret or disguised handwriting *Atturney* Attorney General John Popham (?1531-1607) *Sollicitor generall* Sir Thomas Egerton (?1540-1617) [B1v] *conventicles* small private assemblies [B2] *Casket* small personal jewel or letter box [B3] *William Shelley* a Catholic conspirator who was attainted on Dec. 15, 1582, for complicity in Charles Paget's treasons. He was not executed, but died on April 15, 1597 *Chester* (in the sixteenth century, the scene of heavy Spanish trade) [B4v] *L. chiefe Justice* Sir Christopher Wray (1524-1592) [C1v] *Buckstones* Bawkestones, now Buxton, Derby, a market town 159 miles nnw of London on the Derby-Manchester road [C2] *Duke of Lenox* Esmé Stuart (1542-1583); he died in Paris, falsely professing Protestantism in an attempt to return to his lands at Dumbarton, Scotland, while conspiring to convert James to Catholicism (earlier he had plotted to kill him) and place Mary Stuart on the English throne. Lennox actively dealt with Mendoza in London, but was clever enough to avoid capture by Walsingham's spy by ridding his home of incriminating evidence (see B2v, above) [C3] *Cumberland and Lancashire* northern rebellious English counties bordering on the Irish Sea just s of Scotland [C3v] *Parsons the Jesuite* Robert Parsons (1546-1610), a Jesuit missionary from England schooled in Rome and a leading Catholic conspirator; Guise sent him as messenger to Rome on Aug. 22, 1583 [C4] *Feckenham* a small parish village in Worcestershire 18 miles nnw of Stratford-on-Avon [C4v] *condemned* Throckmorton was executed at Tyburn on July 10, 1584

The Earle of Northumberland's Treasons
[A2] *Earle of Northumberlande* Henry Percy, eighth earl (?1532-1585) *Lord Chancelour* Thomas Bromley (1530-1587) *M. Attorney* John Popham (?1531-1607) *Solicitour General* Sir Thomas Egerton (?1540-1617) *Lord chiefe Baron* Roger Manwood (1525-1592) [A2v] *Master Vicechamberlaine* Christopher Hatton (1540-1591) *many men reporte* the most popular rumor was that Hatton murdered Northumberland on the Queen's behalf [A3] *William* William Cecil (1520-1598) *George* George Talbot (?1528-1590) *Henry* Henry Stanley (1531-1593) *Robert* Robert Dudley (?1532-1588) *Charles* Charles Howard (1536-1624) *Henry* Henry Carey (?1524-1596) *Sir Francis Knollis* Knollys (?1514-1596) *Sir James Crofte* (d. 1590) [B1] *the*

last rebellion the northern uprising of 1569   *the Scottish Queene* Mary
Stuart (1542-1587)   *Terme of Easter* one of four annual sessions of court
[B1v] *Markes* portions of gold or silver of varying weights, usually 8 ounces
Per . . . Recordo "Through Michaelmas 14 and 15 of Queen Elizabeth, in
the fifth roll among Queen's pleas, In agreement with the Recorder of the
Court"   *Per Io. Iue.* "Recorded by John Ive"   *Byshop of Rosse* John Leslie
(1527-1596), confidant and advisor to Mary Stuart, he was part of all conspiracies involving her. He sought diplomatic immunity as Scottish ambassador when suspected of treason in connection with the Ridolfi plot (1571),
but was nevertheless imprisoned in the Tower for two years, then sent out of
England. He died in Brussels (see preceding pamphlet, A2; p. 147)   *a newe
plotte* [described in the preceding pamphlet]   [B2] *Throckmorton* Francis
Throckmorton (1554-1584)   *Doctor Sanders* Nicholas Sanders (?1530-1581),
a Catholic priest who worked for the overthrow of Elizabeth and establishment of Mary Stuart on the English throne   *Doctor Allen* William Allen
(1532-1594), a Catholic English exile who founded the English College at
Douai in 1568 to train Catholic priests for missionary work in England, his
first graduate arriving in England in 1574. Pope Gregory XIII consulted with
Allen about founding a similar college at Rome. Allen was made a cardinal
in 1587 but later lost credit with many English Catholics because he supported
Spain's invasion of England   [B2v] *Province* Provence (erroneous; Narbonne is
in Languedoc, sw of Marseilles near the Mediterranean coast)   *Allhallowtide*
the season of All Saints' (or All hallow's) Day, Nov. 1   *Duke of Guise* Henry
of Lorraine (1550-1588), third duke of Guise, who strengthened his family
ties with the Spanish and befriended Don John of Austria with whom he proposed an invasion of England in the interest of Mary Stuart (1583); see preceding pamphlet, A3v (p. 149)   ]B3] *a great personage* Esmé Stuart, duke of
Lennox (1542-1583); see preceding pamphlet, C2 (p. 159)   *Mendoza* Spanish
ambassador to London from 1578 to 1584, when he was banished for his complicity with Francis Throckmorton; see preceding pamphlet, especially A3v ff.
(p. 149)   *plotte* platte, map   *Bartholomewtide* Aug. 24   [B3v]   *Charles
Paget* (d. 1612), leader of the Scottish faction of the Catholic exiles. He went
to France in 1572 and was in close association with Thomas Morgan (1543-
?1606) against Archbishop Beaton, Mary Stuart's ambassador; Paget was
attainted for treason by Parliament in 1587. See preceding pamphlet, A4 (p.
150)   Sussex Throckmorton suggested Arundel, Sussex, as a good haven; see
preceding pamphlet, A4 (p. 150)   *Deipe* Dieppe, a French port in Picardy
almost directly across the English Channel from Brighton, Sussex   *Normandie*
the French province directly across the English Channel from Arundel   *her
Majestie's greatest force* at Brighton and Southampton   [B4]   *Westmerland*
Charles Neville, sixth earl of Westmoreland (1543-1601)   *Dacres* Lord
Leonard Dacres (d. 1573) fought in the rebellion of 1569; he was implicated
in a plot to free Mary Stuart, fled to Scotland and then to Flanders. He received
a pension from Philip II of Spain with whom he pleaded, through Jane Dor-
mer, for decisive action concerning the invasion of England   *Pope's excom-
munication* Pius V excommunicated Elizabeth as a bastard in a bull issued on
Feb. 25, 1570, and absolved all her subjects of allegiance to her   *Petworth* the
Northumberland castle and holdings in Sussex on the Arundel-London road
[B4v] *William Davies* (d. 1593), a Catholic priest from Wales who had attended
the English College at Rheims. He was arraigned for high treason on an

unjust pretense in March 1592 and was subsequently sentenced to death and hanged, drawn, and quartered at Beaumaris on July 21, 1593. Davies lived at Patching, Sussex, where he hid Paget before Paget's meeting with Northumberland at Petworth *William Shelley* a Catholic conspirator attainted Dec. 15, 1582, for complicity in Paget's treasons; he was not executed, but died on April 15, 1597; see preceding pamphlet, B3 (p. 155) *coppice* Patching Copse *Portesmouth* a seaport on the English Channel in Hampshire, 21 miles se of Southampton, 72 miles sw of London [C2v] *advertised* informed *Trinitie Sonday* Sunday following Whit-sunday [C3] *grome* groom *Crowner* coroner [C3v] *utter* outer [C4] *Dagge* a heavy pistol or hand-gun *Owen Hopton* Lieutenant of the Tower in 1585 *Examinate* witness *Holbardes* halberds, long pointed weapons combining spear and battle-axe [C4c] *pappe* breast *viva voce* "by spoken testimony" [D1] *East Smithfield* a section of London lying e and n of the Tower, outside the city walls, known for its crowded markets [D1v] *lewde* common *attaindure* the forfeiture of all estates, real and personal, and the right to inherit; the common sentence for treason [D2] *Chine bone* spine [D2v] *his house in S. Martin's* Northumberland House, home of the Percies, was located in the parish of St. Katherine Colman on St. Martin's Lane, the main street of Aldersgate Ward *in former times* in 1571 the earl supported Mary Stuart and was suspected by Sir Ralph Sadler; he was arrested on Nov. 15, 1571, sent to the Tower for 18 months, and at a trial for treason asked the Queen for mercy and was released after payment of a fine of 5,000 marks to be confined at Petworth; suspected of complicity in the Throckmorton plot, Northumberland was arrested again in 1582 and detained a few weeks in the Tower, then released without penalty except for being deprived of the governorship of Tynemouth Castle, a loss he angrily protested [D3] *Mulcte* payment as penalty

A Declaration of the Causes to Give aide in the lowe Countries
[A3] *the lowe Countries* 17 provinces comprising the Netherlands and present-day Belgium and Luxembourg *neighbours* translations in French, Italian, Dutch, and Latin were also printed by Barker in 1585 (see textual notes, p. 194) [A3v] *strange Nations* by 1578 Spain was forcing Catholicism successfully on the southern provinces and aggressively recapturing the north under the Italian Parma; Don John of Austria gathered an army at Namur (after his great victory in 1577) of Walloons, Burgundians (the aggressive Catholic party of France) and Spaniards defeating the Netherlanders' army at Gembloux. Against this Elizabeth had sent only John Casimir (son of the Elector Palatine) with limited funds and German troops; and Anjou attempted quite unsuccessfully to aid William of Orange and the Netherlanders with his French Protestant troops, sanctioned by Catherine de Medici and Henry III *directly opposite* Dover to Gravelines, Flanders, was about 30 miles; to Dunkirk, 34 miles; to Nieuport, 44 miles; to Ostend, 50 miles. Margate to Sluys or Bruges, or to Zeeland, was perhaps 10 miles farther *a continuall traffique* Antwerp especially, and Belgium generally, constituted the heart of the English woolen trade and were basic to her economy *Countries* ie, provinces *entermariages* Burgundian rule began with Philip the Bold succeeding by the right of his wife Margaret de Male to the counties of Flanders and Artois, on

Jan. 30, 1384; later he inherited (from his wife's aunt) Brabant and Limburg.
The lands were divided between his sons, who had by 1429 added Nethers,
Rethel, Halnut, Holland, Zeeland, Frisia, and Namur by gift and inheritance,
and by 1451 Luxembourg, Chiny, Cambrai, Utrecht, and Cleves: all were
united as provinces under Philip the Good, given similar administrations, and
called together for common sessions, the first in Bruges in Jan. 1464. Philip II
inherited the Netherlands on Oct. 25, 1555, but his Spanish and Catholic backgrounds made him unpopular and his division of land into smaller units of
government allowed revolt and resentment to grow   [A4] *Comminalties* citizens below the rank of peer   *Treaties* as recently as Aug. 20, 1585, Elizabeth
had signed the Treaty of Nonsuch with the United Provinces pledging military support of 5,000 foot and 1,000 horse in return for the right to establish
English garrisons at Brill and Flushing, the likeliest ports for Spanish invasion, to support previous trade agreements   *some other Princes* at first,
Francis, duke of Alençon and of Anjou; most recently, Henry, duke of Guise
(supported by the houses of Guise and Lorraine) and Henry III of France
[A4v] *Henrie* the Anglo Burgundian alliance of Amiens in April 1423 was
supported by John VI of Brittany and Henry VI's uncle, John, duke of Bedford,
who agreed to marry Anne of Burgundy   *King Henrie the seventh* a commercial treaty between Henry and Philip the Handsome was completed in
Feb. 1496, old treaties were reconfirmed, and restrictions on commerce between the two countries removed during a meeting at Calais in 1500   *King
Henrie the eight* most notably at the conference of Calais in 1521   [B1] *King
of Spayne* Philip II, king from 1556 to 1598   *appoynt Spaniardes* (1) Fernando
Alvarez de Toledo y Pimentel, third duke of Alva (1507-1582), recalled in Oct.
1573; (2) Luis de Requesens (1528-1576), died in March; (3) Don John of
Austria (1545-1578), died Oct. 1; (4) Alexander Farnese, duke of Parma (1545-
1592)   *ancient lawes* those which provided for native rulers   *Charles* Charles
V, Holy Roman Emperor (1519-1558) and King of Spain (as Charles I, 1516-
1556), father of Philip II   *meere* absolute   *lucre* gain   [B1v] *Countie of Egmond* the fourth count of Lamoal Egmond (1522-1568), the most popular
Netherlands leader on the eve of the great revolt and the most famous victim of
Spanish oppression; he was lured to Brussels in Sept. 1567 and executed by
Alba in the main square there on June 5, 1568   *intestine* internal   *Italians*
such as Alexander Farnese, duke of Parma   *Almains* Germans (no one German distinguished himself)   *Indias* (as proverbial for wealth)   *a maner desolate* Alba's absolute tribunal, the Council of Troubles (popularly the Council
of Blood) condemned 12,302 people between 1567 and 1573, executing or
banishing 1,105 of them   [B2] *the Frenche king* Henry III (1574-1589)   *the
house of Guyse* a junior branch of the ducal house of Lorraine, conspicuous
in French politics   [B2v] *brother* as fellow monarch; he was also her brother-
in-law through Philip II's marriage to her half-sister Mary Tudor   *yeelde
themselves wholy* Elizabeth had turned down such an offer; against her
desires, Robert Dudley, earl of Leicester and the leader of the Spanish forces,
was later offered the position of absolute governor of the United Provinces
on Jan. 14, 1586; he was installed on Jan. 25   [B3] *Philip the Duke of Burgundy* Archduke Philip (1475-1506), who ruled as Philip I of Castile, 1504-
1506   *monuments* written documents   *Duke of Ascot* Duke of Aerschot, head
of the Walloon house of Croy and long a staunch supporter of Catholics in
the southern provinces   *Marques of Havery* Marquis of Le Havre who in late

summer of 1577 was sent to England to raise a loan on behalf of the Netherlands and to get a consignment of troops under Leicester; Elizabeth promised
£100,000 and 5,000 foot soldiers and 1,000 horse *prests* advances [B3v]
Naples and other countries Charles V and Philip II of Spain ruled the kingdom of Naples, the duchy of Milan, and the republics of Genoa, Mantua,
Montferrat, Florence, and Sienna; the Valois of France relinquished to Philip
in 1559 the ports of Tuscany, the Presidii *into our Realme of Ireland* Pope
Gregory XIII planned a holy war in Ireland against England; Irish forces led
by James Fitzgerald (called "Fitzmaurice"), earl of Desmond, and Gerald
Fitzgerald, 18th earl of Desmond, who succeeded Fitzmaurice in Aug. 1579
with a force of Italians and Spaniards, were decisively defeated by Lord Grey
of Wilton, English lord deputy for Ireland, and Lord Ormond at Dun an Oir,
Smerwick, County Kerry, in Nov. 1580 [B4] *our expresse messenger* William
Waad (1546-1623), a clerk of the Privy Council who had previously served as
Burghley's informant in France and Italy and undertaken missions to Paris
for Lord Cobham, to the Hanse Towns for the English merchants, and to
Denmark with Lord Willoughby [B4v] *Girald Despes* Don Guerau de Spes,
expelled from the English court in Jan. 1572 for his involvement in the Ridolfi
plot (1571) to free Mary Stuart and seize or assassinate Elizabeth *Bernardin
de Mendoza* Spanish ambassador implicated in the treasonous plot of Francis
Throckmorton (see p. 138); he was summoned before the Privy Council on
Jan. 9, 1584, and given 15 days to leave the country. Mendoza had been ambassador since 1578 *our evill disposed and seditious subjectes* Francis Throckmorton (1554-1584), Charles Paget (d. 1612), Thomas Morgan (1543-?1606)—
the latter two possibly double agents for Walsingham—and Charles Arundel
(d. 1595), a Cornish recusant exile, arrested Sept. 1584 and sent to the Tower
where he died; as well as William Allen (1532-1594), head of the English College at Rome which trained Jesuit missionaries; and countless English Catholic exiles [C1v] *invasion* the plot is described in Throckmorton's pamphlet, pp.
144-163 [C1v] *accident* event [C2] *Queene of Scots* Mary Stuart (1542-1587)
Dolphin of France Francis II (1544-1560) *power in France* the Guises signed
a secret treaty of Joinville with Spain on Dec. 31, 1584, pledging aid to the
Catholic League and an end of Protestant heresy in France in return for a
monthly payment of 50,000 escudos; in March, 1585, the Guises issued (in the
name of the cardinal of Bourbon) the declaration of Péronne, protesting
Protestant maladministration and urging Catholic revolt, a clear bid for total
French power [C2v] *our aiding then* when the French invaded Scotland in
1559 to put down Knox's uprisings, Elizabeth sent military aid, after some delay,
on Dec. 24 under Norfolk. Her admiral, Winter, sailed on Dec. 27. On Feb. 28,
1560, combined efforts of the English and Scottish forces caused the French to
withdraw and Elizabeth took over the protection of Scotland's civil and
religious liberties, as long as the marriage between Mary Stuart and the
Dauphin of France lasted and for one year following, the Scots promising to
provide an army of 2,000 foot and 1,000 horse in the event of a Spanish invasion. Later battles forced the French from Scotland, resulting in the Treaty of
Edinburgh (July 6, 1560) in which England and France both declared non-
intervention in Scottish affairs. When later Morton, as leader of the Protestant
government in Scotland, was overthrown by a new favorite of King James, Esmé
Stuart, later earl of Lennox, a French Catholic who promoted the conversion
of Scotland, Elizabeth protested treatment of Morton. But he was thrown into

prison at Dumbarton Castle and in June 1581 executed on trumped-up charges of complicity in the Darnley murder 13 years previous. Elizabeth launched a punitive force to Scotland under Lord Hunsdon. Lennox overplayed his hand; his plot fell apart; and he narrowly escaped through England and back to France in 1582. In July 1583 the Ruthven forces were overthrown and the Arran forces came to power; Elizabeth sent Walsingham to Scotland to pursue peace with James. Perhaps in part because of his apparent inheritance to the English throne, James made peace despite his mother's (Mary Stuart's) enmity towards Elizabeth *parcialities* rivalries *the yong King* James VI (later James I of England), son of Mary Stuart and Henry, lord Darnley, born in 1566 [C3] *the French kinges* (1) Henry II (king 1547-1559), with the treaty of peace of April 2, 1559; (2) Charles IX (king 1560-1574), with an alliance with England against Spain in the Netherlands in April 1572; (3) Henry III (king 1574-1589) *Guelders* Guelderland [C3v] *generall governour* Alexander Farnese, duke of Parma (1545-1592), appointed by Philip II early in 1579 [C4] *some fewe townes* Brill and Flushing [C4v] *conceits* opinions [D1] *Nuouo aduiso* "New Advice" *Archbishop of Milan* Viscount Caspar, archbishop Nov. 29, 1584-Dec. 1, 1595 *expugnation* Alexander Farnese, who served as regent in the Netherlands from 1578, sacked the town of Antwerp, and massacred thousands of the citizens following religious disturbances in 1585 *saved our life* Philip urged protection of Elizabeth from 1555 to 1558, since he preferred her succession to Mary Tudor over that of Mary Stuart's, and prevented the Pope from excommunicating Elizabeth in 1559 [D3] *Richmount* Richmond, Elizabeth's favorite palace, about 15 miles wsw of London

The Copie of a Letter to the Earle of Leycester
[A3] *Earle of Leicester* Robert Dudley (?1532-1588); appropriately enough, he first conceived of the "bond of association" (see B4) *honour you first vouchsafed me* (presumably a literary pretext) *your late voyage* Leicester was commander of Her Majesty's forces in the Low Countries (present Netherlands, Belgium, and Luxembourg); he departed England Dec. 10, 1585 *vulgar* common [A3v] *Richmond* Elizabeth's favorite palace, about 15 miles wsw of London; before she became Queen, Elizabeth had been confined there by Mary Tudor *Lord Chauncelour and Speaker* Sir Thomas Bromley, Chancellor 1579-1587, for the House of Lords and Sir John Puckering, Speaker 1584-1585 and 1586-1587, for the House of Commons; they were attended by a delegation from both houses *in the dayly expectation of your Lordship's returne* a literary pretext; Leicester returned to court at 10 p.m. on Nov. 24, 1586; this pamphlet was not issued before Dec. 11 *gratulation* appreciation *R. C.* Robert Cecil (see BM Additional MS 48027 [Yelverton 31], f. 396) [B1] *the Scottish Queene* Mary Stuart (1542-1587) (see headnote) [B1v] *sundry Parliaments* in the late spring session of 1572, 1584-1585, and the session beginning Oct. 27, 1586 *Anthonie Babington* (1561-1586), Catholic conspirator in a plot to murder Elizabeth and instate Mary Stuart; he became Mary's partisan as her page at Sheffield when she was imprisoned there by Elizabeth. His plot to have a general English Catholic uprising was discovered and he was tortured and later executed *obtestation* entreaty *direct Commission* Elizabeth appointed 36 judges, peers, and

privy councillors to meet at Fotheringay, Northamptonshire, judge her, and give their verdict to the Queen and Parliament; but Elizabeth later relented, prorogued the court before it concluded its business, and recalled the members to London *Statute* 27 Eliz. cap. 1; "An act for the provision to be made for the surety of the Queen's Majesty's most royal person and the continuance of the realm in peace"; this reads, in part, that if an act of treason occurs, "That then, by her Majesty's commission under her Great Seal, the Lords and others of her Highness's Privy Council and such other Lords of Parliament to be named by her Majesty as with the said Privy Council shall make up the number of twenty-four at the least . . . shall by virtue of this Act have authority to examine all the offences aforesaid and all circumstances thereof, and thereupon to give sentence or judgment as upon good proof the matter shall appear unto them" [B2] *sundry severe examples* as Ezekiel 45:6-8; Amos 4:1-3; Judges 4:3; 2 Kings 13:4 [B2v] *have right* as direct descendant from Henry VII (and arguing Elizabeth had no claim to the throne since she was born in bastardy) [B3] *moove invasion* in complicity with Mendoza, the Guises and Throckmorton (see pp. 148-151 above) *bewraie* reveal *excommunication* Pope Pius V excommunicated Elizabeth as a bastard in a bull issued on Feb. 25, 1570, absolving her subjects from allegiance to her *her tender youth* Mary Stuart was reared in Catholic France by the Guises *Holy league* the French League, a Catholic association dominated by the duke of Guise and determined to destroy Protestantism in alliance with Spain and to restore Catholicism to England [B3v] *Vnum . . . possunt* "The Lydians acknowledge one king, but cannot tolerate two" (a corruption of Plato's *Republic* 360; cf. Herodotus I, 13) *Vnicam . . . possunt* "The English acknowledge Elizabeth as their only rightful Queen; they cannot tolerate two queens" *Noblemen* such as Northumberland (see pp. 168-187) *her owne Crowne* Mary Stuart as Queen of Scotland following her elopement with the Earl of Bothwell, believed to be the murderer of her second husband, Henry, lord Darnley, in 1567 *Nam . . . misericordia* "For there is a certain kind of mercy which is cruel"; c.f. Guazzo, *Civile Conversation*, I, 106 (1574) [B4] *loyall assocation* the outcome of the "Bond of Association," a document circulated throughout the country organizing its signers into a sworn brotherhood of avengers. The idea was conceived by Leicester, the document written by Walsingham, and revised by Burghley; the bond pledged that members would obey the Queen against all earthly powers and exterminate those who tried to harm her *Saul* I Samuel 15 *Achab* I Kings 20 *Salomon* I Kings 2:13-25 [C1v] *my neere kin* cousin; both Elizabeth and Mary Stuart were granddaughters of Henry VII *secretly wrote her* in April, May, and June of 1583 Elizabeth offered Mary freedom if she would return to Scotland and rule there jointly with her son, James VI, as Catherine de Medici had ruled France with her sons Charles IX and Henry III; Elizabeth had at the time uncovered the treasonous activities of Don Bernardino de Mendoza, Spanish ambassador to London, and Sir Francis Throckmorton (1554-1584); see pp. 144-163 [C2v] *subject* a reference to her own imprisonment at Richmond and Hatfield by Mary Tudor who feared that Elizabeth would serve as rallying point for Protestant rebels during Mary Tudor's Catholic rule of England [C3] *indited in StaffordShire* Mary Stuart was moved to Chartley Castle, Staffordshire, in Jan. 1586 and was there in conspiracy with Babington, producing the incriminating evidence that finally gave Walsing-

ham opportunity to prosecute; Elizabeth is therefore urging the respect of the
letter of civil law (and removing herself from the responsibility for judgment
and execution)   *A spot is soone espied in our garments* proverbial; see Tilley
S781   [C3v] *absence* (see headnote)   [C4] *Hampton Court* royal palace sse of
London begun by Wolsey and taken over and refashioned by Henry VIII
[D1] *an Honorable person* Sir Christopher Hatton (1540-1591)   *right worthy
member* Puckering   [D2v] *agnising* acknowledging   [D3] *heynous and
capitall crymes* attempted treason (in the Ridolfi, Throckmorton, and Babington plots) and possibly murder (in a speech to Parliament Mildmay had accused Mary Stuart of killing her second husband)   *Northren Rebelles*
Thomas Percy, seventh earl of Northumberland (1528-1572) and Charles
Neville, sixth earl of Westmoreland (1543-1601) who led the Northern counties
in revolt in 1569 on behalf of Mary Stuart (see pp. 98-105)   [D3v] *à malo in
peius* "from bad to worse"; Tilley B27   [D4v] *comber* trouble   *mone* complaint   [E1v] *to cherish a sworde to cutte mine owne throate* proverbial; see
Tilley S1054   [E2] *countries* county seats or estates   [E2v] *to credite a tale*
proverbial; Tilley T42   *Alcibiades* Athenian general and statesman (c. 450-
404 B.C.); the tale is a distortion of Plutarch, *Life of Alcibiades* 196 (Loeb
edition, IV, 25); cf. Plutarch, "Precepts on Statecraft" in *Moralia* (Loeb X,
189); "Progress in Virtue," *Moralia* (Loeb, I, 429)

*The miraculous victory atchieved by the English Fleete . . . Upon the
Spanish huge Armada*
**from Libre Decimquintus (Book XV), *Historia Belgica Nostri Potissimvm
Temporis, Bellgii svb Qvatvor Bvrgvndis & totidem Avstriacis Principibvs
coniunctionem & gubernationem breuiter* (no city or date [but covers through
1596]), ff.Ss5-Tt6v (pp. 470-485); the translation is the literal one by Richard
Hakluyt published in England in 1598 (see textual notes, p. 241)
[Ddd2] *ancient prophesies* 1588 had been marked in popular prognostica-
tions as a period of great disaster based on the predictions of Philip Mel-
ancthon who argued that the final cycle of history since the Incarnation
would end in 1588 since that year followed Luther's defiance of the Pope by
just seven times ten years, the same period the Babylonian captivity had
lasted and the Last Judgment was at hand; and by Regiomontanus of Königs-
berg, a mathematician whose astronomical tables served Columbus, who
argued that 1588 would be a year of great upheaval and destruction because
it would be ushered in by an eclipse of the sun in February and two total
eclipses of the moon in March and August   *L. Charles Howard* (1536-1624),
baron of Effingham, earl of Nottingham   *low Countreys* 17 united
provinces now the Netherlands, Belgium, and Luxembourg   *the Spanish
king* Philip II, ruler from 1556-1598   *Pope* Sixtus V (1520-1590)   *enforced
them* through his marriage to Mary Tudor (an overstatement, since Mary had
already proclaimed the Catholic faith in England); his dishonor came when
Elizabeth refused to marry him as her half-sister had   *hereditarie possession*
as son of Charles V; he inherited the provinces on Oct. 25, 1555, but his
Spanish and Catholic backgrounds made him unpopular and his division of
land into smaller units of government caused resentment and revolt to grow
[Ddd2v] *Escouedo* Juan de Escobedo (d. 1578), rightly secretary to Don John of

Austria, not to Philip II of Spain   *Holland and Zeland* two of the low countries   *English Drake* Sir Francis Drake (?1540-1596), circumnavigator and admiral; his sea raids against Spanish treasure ships and his success against Cadiz in 1587 established his English and European reputation   *Lisbon haven* a major harbor on the w coast of Portugal about half-way (350 miles) between Cadiz and the Bay of Biscay   *Governours* company commanders in the Spanish military   *Medina Sidonia* Alonso Perez de Guzman el Bueno (d. 1619), seventh duke of Medina-Sidonia   *Galeons* Spanish ships of war, shorter but higher than galleys   *Zabraes* small vessels used by the Spanish and Portuguese for scouting (as were *fregatas* and *pataches*)   *pieces* cannon   *Biscay* (Viscaya) a Basque province of n Spain   *John Martines de Ricalde* knight of Santiago, a native of Bilbao and second-in-command of the Armada; with Oquendo and Pedro de Valdés, Medina-Sidonia's council of war. Recalde gained his reputation in 1582 as second-in-command from Don Antonio at the battle of St. Michael's and the whole of the Azores; he was known for common sense and courtesy. He died shortly after reaching Spain in Oct. 1588   *Pataches* small ships similar to pinnaces, usually equipped with oars and sails   *Guipusco* (Guipuzcoa), a province of the ne coast of Spain between Biscay and France   *Michael de Oquendo* of San Sebastian; his reputation for flamboyance stemmed from impetuosity; grieved by the defeat of the Armada, he died in Oct. 1588, shortly after returning to Spain. Like Recalde, he fought at St. Michael's, attempting to take single-handedly the flagship, vice flagship, and three other French ships   *Levant Islands* islands of the e Mediterranean   *Martine de Vertendona* (Bertendona) of Bilbao; of a second generation of seamen, his father having brought Philip to England to wed Mary Tudor. Bertendona was a trusted seaman, left to guard the main approaches to Spain and Portugal when the main forces went to the Azores in 1583. The only major veteran of the Armada, he fought Drake at the Corunna in 1589, and first attacked Grenville as captain of the *San Barnaby*; he is given credit for defeating Greville in his battle on the *Revenge* off the Azores in 1591   *Castile* the central province of Spain   *Diego Flores de Valdez* (Valdés), chief of staff for Medina-Sidonia, sharing the command; universally unpopular and singularly blamed by the Spanish for the defeat of the Armada. Highly qualified as a hydrographer and naval architect, he was impulsive and jealous; previously he had failed in a mission to guard the Straits of Magellan and had deserted an admired younger man named Sarmiento. Valdés was tried in Spain in 1589 for advising Medina to leave Don Pedro to his fate in the English Channel   *Andaluzia* (Andalusia), a s province of Spain   *Petro de Valdez* Pedro de Valdés, knight of Santiago, formerly admiral of the Galician squadron at the conquest of Portugal. Attempting a landing without leave during the Terceira campaign, he was imprisoned for a time on his return. He was the foremost advocate of greater artillery for the Armada. Arrested during the campaign, he spent four and a half years in English prison before being ransomed at £3,550   *John Lopez de Medina* captain of the *Gran Grifon*, flagship of the hulks   *hulkes* carracks; cargo vessels, usually with a length about twice their beam   *Hugo de Moncada* (d. 1588), son of the viceroy of Valencia; a veteran of long service in Flanders, his specialty was rowing, not sailing, ships and in the Armada he was therefore assigned to the galliasses. His ship was run ashore and plundered at Calais; Lord Cobham wrote Walsingham on Aug. 1, 1588, that his "ship was one of the best account of all the galleasses in the fleet." He was the only squadron commander killed in action *caravels* Portuguese ships, usually about 100 tons, with four masts, the foremast carrying square sails and the rest lateen sails [Ddd3] *yron ordnance quintals* a measure equivalent to a weight of 100 lbs. *kaleivers* (calivers), light muskets about 4 1/2 ft. long (muskets were a foot longer) *haleberts* (halberds), weapons consisting of a shaft about 6 ft. in length with a head adapted to both cutting and thrusting *partisans* broad-headed spears with a staff about 9 ft. long *canons* 60-pounder guns, about 11 ft. long *double-canons* 65-pounder guns, about 12 1/2 ft. long *culverings* (culverins), cannons the length of which ranged from 10 to 13 ft., the diameter of their bores from 5 to 5 1/2 in. *pioners* foot-soldiers who marched with or in advance of an army or regiment as engineers *pipes* large casks equivalent to half a ton *Diego Pimentelli* (Pimentel), *maestro de campo* (colonel) of an infantry brigade (*tercio*), who later attacked and was imprisoned by the Dutch between Ostend and Sluys. Pimentel and the other four colonels were directly responsible to Major-General Don Francisco de Bobadilla; when his ship, the *San Martin*, was damaged, he refused to leave it *ducates* gold coins of varying value, perhaps equivalent then to 9 shillings *Tercera* (Terceira), an island of the central group in the Azores *Don Francisco de Toledo* of the *San Felipe*; he and his crew were rescued by pinnaces when the ship was beached between Nieuport and Ostend; he was later imprisoned in Holland *women hired certaine shippes* an unfounded embellishment *the golden Fleece* the secular order founded by Philip the Good, duke of Burgundy, in 1430 to uphold the Catholic religion and the usages of chivalry; at the death of Emperor Charles V, the grand mastership devolved to Philip II of Spain, his son *Marques of santa Cruz* Alvaro de Bazán (1526-1588), first marquis, who originally suggested the Armada to Philip II in 1583 [Ddd3v] *Francis Bovadilla* Francisco de Bobadilla, commander-in-chief of land forces; after Medina-Sidonia gave up in despair in August, Bobadilla succeeded him. Before the Armada sailed, Bobadilla warned Philip that heavy supplies would render the ships useless after 4 days of fighting *friers mendicant* begging monks, those supported wholly by alms *Chirurgions* surgeons *duke of Parma* Alexander Farnese (1545-1592), duke of Parma from 1586 and regent in the Netherlands *Yper* Ypres, Flanders *Antwerp* principal trading city on the Scheldt River *Ghendt* city at the junction of the Lys and Scheldt Rivers, Flanders *Bruges* city in Flanders 8 miles s of Dunkirk *hoyes* flat-bottomed sailing vessels, often carrying as much as 300 tons *Sluys* Sluis; inland city near the Western Scheldt *Waten* a river emptying at the port city of Watten near Dunkirk; Watten mountain se of the city was a Roman fortress still used to defend the town *Neiuport* port on the coast of Flanders about 70 miles along the coast nne of Calais *Dunkerk* port on the coast of Flanders about 35 miles along the coast nne of Calais *Hamburg* a major port and trading center on the Elbe River in nc Germany *Breme* Bremen, an inland trading center on the Weser River in nw Germany *Emden* an inland trading center in nw Germany 10 miles from the Netherlands; in 1564 this became the staple town for the English Merchant Adventurers when they were barred from Antwerp *Greveling* Gravelines, a city in Flanders near the English Channel about 10 miles ne of Calais *Wallons* (Walloons), inhabitants of the se provinces of Belgium who were of Gaullist origin and who spoke

a French dialect *Burgundians* troops from the duchy of Burgundy who re-
mained Catholic supporters of the Holy League and loyal to Philip II *Dix-mud* (Dixmude), a city in w Flanders about 30 miles inland from Dunkirk
William Stanlie (1548-1630), Catholic adventurer, eldest son of Sir Rowland
Stanley of Cheshire; falling under Jesuit influence while serving Elizabeth, he
surrendered the town of Deventer to the Spanish in 1587, joined Parma, and in
July 1588 headed 700 men called the English Legion ready to join the Armada
Cortreight Courtrai, on the Lys in w Flanders *the Marques of Burgrave*
Daniel de Burchgrave; Paul Knibbe wrote Walsingham on July 17, 1588, that
he was thought to head four regiments of Germans who were to join Spanish
ships landing on Flanders *John Medices* Don Juan de Medici, brother of
Ferdinand I, grand duke of Tuscany *Amadas of Savoy* Amadise Amadeo of
Savoy, natural son of Emmanuel Philibert *published a Cruzado* proclaimed
a crusade or holy war [Ddd4] *D. Allen* Cardinal (Doctor) William Allen
(1532-1594), Catholic exile who founded the English college at Douai in 1568
to train priests for missionary work in England, the first priests beginning
their work in 1574; Pope Gregory XIII consulted with Allen about the foundation of a similar college in Rome *Pope's bull* the bull issued on Feb. 25, 1570,
by Pius V excommunicating Elizabeth as a bastard and absolving her citizens
of any allegiance to her *two former Popes* Pius V, Gregory XIII *Borborch*
Bourbourg, a town 10 miles sw of Dunkirk and 8 miles se of Gravelines
united provinces the Protestant northern confederation of provinces in the Low
Countries, Holland and Zeeland being chief among them *the French king*
Henry III (reigned 1574-1589) *Plimmouth* Plymouth, a major port in sw
England, on the Channel *lord Henry Seimer* (Seymour), commander of the
*Bonaventure and cousin to Lord Howard. After fighting at Gravelines, he
was sent to the Downs and directed to prevent Parma's forces from crossing
while the main English fleet engaged the Armada* *Dover* port city in se England on the Channel closest to France *Caleis* Calais, on the ne coast of France
22 miles across the English Channel (the narrowest point) from Dover *Til-burie* now West Tilbury, a town on the Thames River across from Gravesend
(which provides entry into Kent), the site of a fort built as a blockhouse by
Henry VIII *Frederike Genebelli* Fedrigo Giambelli, Italian engineer who
produced "hell-burners," fireships acting as huge bombs, since they were
stuffed with explosives; he sent them into the enemy in an earlier engagement
at Antwerp. During the Armada the Spanish rightly learned that Giambelli
was constructing a bridge to transport soldiers over the Thames from a major
camp at West Tilbury to the s bank at Gravesend (see Eeel below) *in proper
person* the Queen came by barge in military dress to inspect her troops at
West Tilbury where she gave a stirring speech on Aug. 18, 1588 [Ddd4v] *Isle
of Ely* an island and city in the English fens 67 miles ne of London *Wisbich*
Wisbech, a seaport and market town on the Isle of Ely 94 miles ne of London
Scheld an estuary and river emptying into the North Sea *Lillo* also the site of
a fort at the mouth of the Scheldt estuary *Admirall Lonck* Cornelius van
Roozendael Lonck, admiral of Flushing *Justin of Nassau* lieutenant-admir-
al, admiral, and vice-admiral of Zeeland, who blockaded Parma and protected
Dunkirk and Neiuport; he successfully took the *San Mateo* *Baie of Corunna*
on the n coast of Spain *Gallicia* French *Baion* Bayonne, a city a few miles
inland from the Bay of Biscay and 10 miles n of Spain *David Gwin* a Welsh
prisoner-of-war aboard the galley *Diana*; legend holds that when the *Diana*

was stranded, Gwynn freed himself and the other slaves, exterminated the Spanish crew, and successfully captured three other damaged Spanish galleys which had proven too heavy and awkward for battle   *pinasse* (pinace) small boat usually equipped with both oars and sails   *M. Thomas Fleming* captain of the *Golden Hind* and an experienced seaman; according to a story traced back to 1624, Fleming found Drake bowling on Plymouth Hoe and told him of the approaching Spanish, an important factor in the English victory (the story also holds that Drake finished his game before he set out to meet the enemy fleet)   *Chattam* (Chatham), a port on the right bank of the River Medway about 30 miles from London   *warped* cast forward   [Ddd5] *the Downes* the name of a roadstead in the English Channel off Deal between the North and South Foreland   *the Scottish queene* Mary Stuart (1542-1587) (see preceding pamphlet)   *Vice-admirall* the ship commanded by Oquendo   *to beare out his lanterne* to lead the fleet through the night (a privilege)   *Easterlings* ships of Germany or the Baltic countries   [Ddd5v] *Arke-royall* Lord Howard of Effingham's flagship; it was built in 1587 at Deptford by Richard Chapman, shipwright, for the government. She was about 700 tons burden, with a keel about 100 ft. long and a beam of about 37 ft.; she carried a crew of 400, including 100 soldiers and 32 gunners   *Portland* the port and island in Dorset 3 miles ssw of Weymouth; besides other forts, Henry VIII built a castle there for defense   *roundell* a circle formed as a battle rather than as a sailing formation [Ddd6] *Oxford* Edward de Vere, 17th earl (1550-1604)   *Northumberland* Henry Percy, 9th earl (1564-1632)   *Cumberland* George Clifford, 3rd earl (1588-1605), naval commander   *Sir Thomas Cecill* first earl of Exeter, 2d lord Burghley (1542-1623)   *Sir Robert Cecill* first earl of Salisbury and first viscount Cranborne (?1563-1612)   *Sir Walter Ralegh* (?1552-1618)   *Sir William Hatton* (d. 1597), husband of William Cecil's, lord Burghley's, granddaughter *Sir Horatio Palavicini* (d. 1600), an exiled Genoese financier whose fortune was made through confiscating papal taxes collected under Mary Tudor; he volunteered his services against the Armada but, like so many of the nobility, did not captain his own ship; his "Narrative of the Voyage of the Spanish Armada" appears in the *Calendar of State Papers, Foreign*, under Aug. 1588 but it is often erroneous   *Sir Henry Brooke* eighth lord Cobham (d. 1619) *Sir Robert Carew* (Carey), a young relative of the Queen's   *Sir Charles Blunt* earl of Devonshire, and 8th Lord Mountjoy (1563-1606)   *Master Thomas Gerard* (c. 1560-1618), captain of the Isle of Man; later knight marshal of the royal household (1597), lord president of Wales   *Master Henry Nowell* Henry Neville (d. 1617), ambassador to France 1598-1600, knighted 1599, later imprisoned for complicity in Essex's treason   *Master Edward Darcie* (d. 1612), later a member of the Queen's Privy Council   *Master Arthur Gorge* Sir Arthur Gorges (d. 1625)   *Master William Harvie* (Hervey) baron Hervey of Kidbrooke (d. 1642)   *chaine-shot* shot formed by two balls or half-balls, connected by a chain, and chiefly used to destroy masts, rigging, and sails   *Captaine Hawkins* Sir John Hawkins (1532-1595); he, not Barker, commanded the *Victory*   *Captaine Frobisher* Sir Martin Frobisher (?1535-1594), commander of the *Triumph*   *Isle of Wight* island lying off the s coast of England separated from the mainland by the Solent   *lord Thomas Howard* (1562-1626), volunteer   *Sir Robert Southwel* (d. Nov. 1598), from Woodrising, Norfolk; he also participated in the English mission against Cadiz (see pp. 276-309)   *lord Sheffield* Edmund Sheffield, first earl of Mulgrave (1564-1646), commander of the *White Bear*   [Ddd6v] *Newhaven in France* then the common English

name for Le Havre   *Guisian faction* supporters of the House of Guise and
Francis, third duke of Guise, a strong Catholic   *Leaguers* members of the
French League or Catholic league headed by Charles, cardinal of Lorraine
and the duke of Guise's brother   *road* rode, sailed   *prince of Ascoli* Philip
II's natural son; made a messenger on the night of the fireships, he instead
landed at Dunkirk and left the field of battle (his excuse is given above)
Henault Hainault, a Catholic province of the low countries   *straightnesse*
narrowness   [Eee1] *drumblers* small, fast vessels used as transports as well as
in war   *Amias Preston* Sir Amyas Preston (d. ?1617); later, as vice-admiral of
the fleet with Sir Robert Mansfeld, he captured 6 easterlings of spice and bullion from the Spanish in 1601   *Veador generall* a general vested with in-
specting and controlling powers   [Eee1v] *Monsieur Gourdon* Sngr. de Girault
de Mauléon Gourdan, governor of Calais, believed to be sympathetic with the
Holy League. Not wanting the English under Howard anchored at his harbor,
he sent word that the anchorage was dangerous and exposed; meanwhile he
offered Medina-Sidonia whatever food his men needed to purchase. When
the English conquered Moncada's ship the *San Lorenzo* in Calais harbor, M.
Gourdan agreed to their plundering it, but reminded them that by rights he
now owned the ship and its rigging and when he thought the English would
also damage that, he opened fire, killing 50 men   *listed* pleased   *pike's
length asunder* 10 to 15 ft. apart   *demi-culvering* a nine-pounder gun about
12 ft. in length   *Captaine Crosse* Robert Crosse, Drake's rear-admiral and
veteran seaman; in 1592 he captured the Spanish treasure ship Madre de Dios
Ostend a major port in Flanders 60 miles along the coast nne of Dunkirk
Ulishingers men of Flushing   [Eee2] *hault* (haught) high-minded   *Blankenberg* a port city on the North Sea 10 miles nne of Ostend   *crazed* damaged,
destroyed   *aloofe* at a distance   *Harwich* a port and market town in Essex
42 miles ene of Chelmsford and 72 miles ene of London   [Eee2v] *not have
any succour* Scotland was an ally of England, especially since the young
Scottish King James VI might inherit Elizabeth's throne   *Orcades* Orkney
Islands, in the North Sea between 30 and 60 miles nne off the coast of Scotland   *Faar-Isles* Faeroe Islands, in the Atlantic 300 miles nnw off the coast of
Scotland   *leagues* units of measure equivalent to 3 nautical miles   *Cape
Clare* Cape Clear, on the ssw coast of Ireland   *Rochel* LaRochelle   *Isles
of Lewis, and Ila* two islands of the Hebrides in the North Sea, about 40 miles
wnw off the coast of Scotland   *Cape Cantyre* promontory bordering Canty
Bay 2 1/2 miles e of North Berwick, East Loathing, on the e coast of Scotland
at the se end of the Firth of Forth   [Eee3] *Yarmouth* Great Yarmouth, a seaport in Norfolk 22 miles se of Norwich and 123 miles ne of London; in 1588
the English placed fire beacons of warning on the four towers of a castle
built there by Henry III   *Man purposeth: God disposeth* proverbial; see Tilley
M298   *outlandish* foreign   *Pauls crosse* an outside pulpit in the churchyard of St. Paul's Cathedral often used for sermons ordered by the Queen or the
Bishop of London [Eee3v] *Theodor.* Beza (1519-1605), French Protestant theo-
logian and heir to Calvin at Geneva where he was rector of the Academy.

The Honorable voyage unto Cadiz, 1596
  [Eee4] *Cadiz* wealthy port on Spain's s coast, then a base for her treasure
fleets   *king's* Philip II of Spain (ruled 1556-1598)   *Robert Earle of Essex*

Robert Devereux (1566-1601), with Howard joint commander of the expedition on which he based his later popularity and martial reputation *L. Charles Howard* (1536-1624), baron of Effingham and earl of Nottingham *Plymmouth* a major seaport in Devon on the English Channel 44 miles sw of Exeter and 215 miles wsw of London *Earle of Sussex* Robert Radcliffe (?1569-1629), 5th earl, served on this expedition as a colonel of a regiment of foot *L. Thomas Howard* (1561-1626), appointed commander of a squadron which attacked Spanish treasure ships off the Azores in 1591; he volunteered for the Armada and later was marshall of the force which besieged Essex at Essex House in Feb. 1601; on this expedition, he served as admiral of the third squadron *the L. Herbert* Henry Herbert, second earl of Pembroke (?1534-1601), brother of Catherine Parr, who in 1595 fortified Milford Haven *Sir Walter Raleigh* (?1552-1618), rear admiral and member of the councils of war because of his commission as a general officer *Sir Francis Vere* (1560-1609), lord marshall, lieutenant-general and one of 6 members of Essex's council of war *Count Lodovick of Nassaw* Louis, former troop leader under Coligny when he headed Protestant forces in the Netherlands [Eee4v] *Dodman head* Dodman Point, 5 miles off the coast of England in the English Channel and about 10 miles ssw of Plymouth *quittance* retaliation *North cape* a site of many sea battles on sw extremity of Portugal 60 miles west of Faro *Sir George Cary* George Carew (1555-1629); as lieutenant-general of the ordnance of England, he fought also in the battle off the Azores in 1591 *Sir Coniers Clifford* (d. 1599), serjeant-major of the troops *Sir Anthony Ashley* (1551-1628), secretary for war [Eee5] *S. George* legendary patron saint of England, who from the twelfth century was pictured as a youth wearing knight's armor with a scarlet cross *Fidem, and Taciturnitatem* "Faith and Discretion" *leagues* units equivalent to 3 nautical miles *sprang or spent her foreyarde* bent or snapped the lowest spar (yard) on the foremast *Sir Robert Crosse* a long-standing member of Elizabeth's armed forces, fighting at Le Havre and in Ireland and Scotland where he helped to take Edinburgh Castle; in Armada year he was Drake's rear-admiral in the western squadron and in 1592 he helped to capture the Spanish treasure ship *Madre de Dios* *cape S. Vincent* at the Straits of Gilbraltar *Barbarie* the n and nw coasts of Africa *Sir Richard Levison* (1570-1605), commander of a ship for this expedition, later vice-admiral of England *Sir Christopher Blunt* Blount (?1565-1601), colonel of the land force and afterwards campmaster *Hamburgers* ships from Hamburg, a major port and trading center on the Elbe River in nc Germany *hansell* taste *Flemming* ship of Flanders *vale his foretoppe* lower his foremast in greeting *tire* tier *Lisbone* a major harbour on the w coast of Portugal about half-way (350 miles) between Cadiz and the Bay of Biscay *M. Dorrell* Marmaduke Dorrell, commissary-general for victuals; previously he had served as assistant surveyor (of naval provisions) during the Armada [Eee5v] *pinke* small fishing boat *Caravels* Portuguese ships, usually about 100 tons, with 4 masts, the foremast carrying square sails and the rest lateen sails *Bonitoes* striped tunnies, which prey on flying fish *pleights* pleats *gallies* low flat-built vessels with one deck, equipped with both sails and oars *pynnesses* pinnaces, small boats or ships usually equipped with oars as well as sails [Eee6] *Puente de Suaço* El Puerto de Ste Marie, the sw central port of the Island of Cadiz joining the island to the mainland of Spain *Granada side* ie, the coast along the e and se of the Gulf of Cadiz *Port S. Mary* Spanish seacoast town 4 miles nnw of Cadiz *Sir Robert Southwell* son-in-law of

Lord Charles Howard, baron of Effingham, by marriage to his daughter Frances; formerly commander of the *Jonas*, a vessel of from 850 to 1,000 tons, against the Armada   *the Arke royall* Lord Howard of Effingham's flagship against the Armada, built at Deptford in 1587 by Richard Chapman, shipwright, for the government. She was about 700 tons burden, with a keel about 100 feet long and a beam of about 37 feet; she carried a crew of 400, including 100 soldiers and 32 gunners   *L. William Howard* (1577-1615), 3rd lord Effingham   *Argosie* carack, a merchant-vessel of the largest size and burden [Eee6v] *ducats* gold coins of varying value, perhaps equivalent to 9 shillings *flieboats* fast-sailing vessels   *pikemen* infantry armed with pikes   *Sir Thomas Gerard* (1560-1618), formerly captain of the Isle of Man, later knight marshal of the royal household (1597) and lord president of Wales   [Fff1] *S. Edward Hoby* Edward Hoby (1560-1617), nephew of William Cecil, lord Burghley, he married the daughter of Henry Carey, lord Hunsdon; the Queen visited him in 1592 and 1594 and thought highly enough of him to grant him the letter patent for buying and providing wool for sale in England for ten years   *Sir John Winkfield* Wingfield (d. 1596), colonel and campmaster of the *Vanguard*   *Sivil* Seville, a large Spanish city 60 miles inland ene of Cadiz *S. Lucar* San Lucar, Spanish seacoast town 20 miles nnw of Cadiz   [Fff1v] *Duke de Medina Sidonia* Alonzo Perez de Guzmán el Bueno (d. 1619), defeated admiral of the Armada of 1588   *Rotta* Rota, a port town on the Gulf of Cadiz 10 miles directly n of Cadiz on the n coast of the bay   *Veni, Vidi, Vici* "I came, I saw, I conquered"; Caesar's boast after defeating Pharnaces of Bosporus at Zela in Asia Minor in 47 B.C. (Seutonius I,37)   *Watling streete* an average street distinguished as the home of the city's wealthy drapers   [Fff2] *Paules is against Southwarke* St. Paul's Cathedral, London, looked out on Southwark, but was separated from that borough by most of the old city of London and the Thames, a distance of perhaps 2 miles   *Andaluzia* (Andalusia), a s province of Spain   *Sir Amias Preston* Sir Amyas Preston (d. ?1617), naval commander; later, as vice-admiral of the fleet with Sir Robert Mansfeld, he captured 6 easterlings of spice and bullion from the Spanish in 1601   [Fff2v] *curious* attentive   *Bay of the Groyne* Bay of Corunna, Groin of Galicia on the n coast of Spain, the closest Spanish port to England   *Bishop of Cusco* (Cuzco), Antonio de la Roya, bishop 1595-1606   [Fff3v] *S. Francis Drake* with Capt. John Hawkins, Drake (?1540-1596) left Plymouth in Aug. 1595 with 6 royal ships, 11 other ships, and 2,500 men in an offensive expedition against Spain. His mission was to capture and plunder the principal galleon of the Spanish thought to have a cargo worth over £600,000, damaged and undergoing repairs in the harbor of San Juan, Puerto Rico. Hawkins died early on the trip and disaster then hounded them: unable to take the fortifications at San Juan, Drake plundered and burned Rio de la Hacha and Nombre de Dios, but plunder was slight. Drake and Baskerville (now second in command), discontented, attempted to march troops across the Isthmus of Panama but were met by Spanish forces. Here Drake lost many men and retreated; shortly after, he took dysentery on Escudo and died in Porto Bello. Baskerville limped home with the remaining troops in the spring of 1596   [Fff4] *one foole . . . five dayes* proverbial; see Tilley F468   *Tacitus* from *Germania* 34 *malapert* impudent   *stale* decoy   *Faraon* Faro, a town just off the s coast of Portugal 2 miles nnw of Cabo de Santa Martia and 120 coastline miles nnw of Cadiz

Proclamation on sending over the Army into Ireland
    Sects and Factions most notably those of O'Donnell and Tyrone   *seditious*
Priestes and Seminaries Jesuit missionaries trained in the English College at
Douai, founded by Cardinal William Allen, and at Rome to convert England,
Ireland, and Scotland / *conceite* understanding   *betimes* before it is too late
such a person Robert Devereux (1566-1601), earl of Essex, veteran of the Armada; with Charles Howard, he served as joint commander of the expedition
to Cadiz in 1596 (pp. 276-309)   *Richmond* Elizabeth's favorite palace, about
15 miles wsw of London

*Proclamation on the seizure of the Earls of Essex, Rutland, and others for their
rebellion*
    Earle of Essex Robert Devereux (1566-1601) (see headnote)   *Rutland* Roger
Manners, 5th earl (1576-1612), colonel of foot under Essex in 1599; knighted
by Essex May 30, 1599. By June, Rutland had returned to England in disgrace
with the court. On Feb. 8, 1601, he conspired with Essex and was captured
at Essex House. In the Tower he wrote penitently, was examined by the council, fined £30,000 and released   *Southampton* Henry Wriothesley, 3rd earl
(1573-1624), accompanied Essex to Cadiz and to the Azores in 1596, but fell
out of favor with the Queen when he returned from Paris in 1598 to marry her
lady-in-waiting, Elizabeth Vernon, pregnant by him. Both bride and groom
were arrested but subsequently released. In autumn 1599 Southampton became friendly with Rutland and was drawn by him into the Essex conspiracy.
After the abortive rebellion, Southampton was tried and convicted to death
with Essex, but Robert Cecil intervened and his sentence was commuted to
life imprisonment   *complices* Sir John Davies, Sir Ferdinand Gorges, Sir
Charles Danvers, Sir Christopher Blount, Sir Gilly Meyrick, and Owel Salis-
burie   *Tirone* Hugh O'Neill (?1540-1616), leader of the Irish rebellion   *Keeper of our Great Seale of England, our Chiefe Justice of England, and others*
Lord Keeper Thomas Egerton (?1540-1617), Chief Justice Sir John Popham
(?1531-1607), the earl of Worcester (1553-1628), and Sir William Knollys
(1547-1632)

Queene Elizabeth's Speech to her Last Parliament
    *Lacey Baldwin Smith, The Elizabethan World (Boston, 1967).
    [A2] *her Last Parliament* the Parliament of 1601   *under State* on a throne
under the state canopy   *Whitehall* the Queen's principal palace, originally
York Place, then just outside London   *the Speaker* John Croke (1553-1620)
[A3] *Grant* special patents (see headnote)   *lewd* low   [A3v] *culps* faults   [A4]
Mr. Controullor Sir William Knollys, earl of Banbury (1547-1632)   *Mr.
Secretarie* Robert Cecil, first earl of Salisbury (1563-1612)   *Countreys* ie,
districts

A Letter from a Souldier of good place in Ireland

[A3] *December*, ie, Dec. 1601 *Castel-Haven* port on the s coast of Munster, 30 miles w of Kinsale Harbor; the Irish handed over the castle here to the Spanish as well as two castles covering the entry to the harbor at Baltimore *Baltemore* a village and seaport in Munster about 9 miles from Cape Clear Island and less than 3 miles from Castlehaven; in 1602 Sir Fineen O'Driscoll surrendered the castle there to the forces of Don Juan d'l'Aguila who stored artillery and ammunition there until his defeat at Kinsale *Beerhaven* Berehaven; the channel between Bere Island and the mainland, sw of County Cork, guarded by Dunboy Castle *Sir Richard Levison* (1570-1605); in Oct. 1601 he was appointed captain-general and admiral of certain ships to serve against the Spaniards lately landed in Ireland; on Dec. 5 he forced his way into Castlehaven Harbor and in severe action sank one Spanish ship and drove another ashore (the text here is mistaken) *Kinsale* a seacoast town in sw Ireland in the province of Munster, a port of some 200 houses *against winde and weather* proverbial; see Tilley W446 *said to be 2000*. (Spanish forces under Pedro de Zubiaur there actually numbered 829) *Munster* southernmost province of Ireland *King of Spaine* Philip III (reigned 1598-1621) *O'Donnell* Hugh Roe O'Donnell (?1571-1602), Irish rebel leader who with Tyrone determined to starve the English and wait them out; the greater part of his army did not engage in the action described here [A3v] *Lord President of Munster* Sir George Carew (Carey) (1555-1629), baron Carew of Clopton and earl of Totnes, a good friend of Essex; he was named lord president on Jan. 27, 1600; his support enabled Lord Deputy Mountjoy to suppress the great rebellion *Tyrone* Hugh O'Neill (?1540-1616); known as the "great earl," he was reared in London, returning to Ireland in 1567. With O'Donnell he championed religious and political liberty for Ireland *O'Rourck* Brian Oge or Brian-Na-Samhthach O'Rourke (d. 1604); he contributed to the defeat of Conyers Clifford (see below) in 1599 and served under O'Donnell at the siege of Kinsale *Redman Bourck* possibly of the Burkes of Connaught *MacGuyre* Connor Roe MacGuire, a rival chief of Fermangh *MacMahone* Brian Mac-Hugh Oge MacMahon, of Monaghan, a son-in-law of Tyrone, formerly a friend of the English whose son had gone to England as Sir George Carew's page *Randal Mac Surley* Randal MacSorley MacDonald, "Sorley Boy" MacDonald, leader of the mercenaries (Redshanks) who had obtained release from the English commander and governor of Carrickfergus, Sir Arthur Chichester, in order to accompany Tryone to Kinsale *O'Connor* Dermot O'Connor, rebel leader of Ulster and Connaught; formerly a mercenary captain, he married the sister of the earl of Desmond *Tyrrel* Richard Tyrrell, former captain of mercenaries for Elizabeth, leader of a flank troop at Kinsale *the Baron of Lixenho* Thomas Fitzmaurice (1574-1630), 18th lord Kerry and baron of Licksnaw; he was excluded from all pardons offered the Irish rebels in 1600 and fled to the north to join O'Donnell and Tyrone. The Queen offered to spare him, but only after he had raised 12 galleys and decided to fight *6000. foote* (actually, about 5,000) *Powle* head count *furnitures* supplies [A4] *jumpe* crisis *our worthy Generall* Charles Blount (1563-1606), earl of Devon and 8th lord Mountjoy (see headnote) *a hill* Spittle Hill *Corke* a seaport in Munster at the head of the inlet of Cork Harbor on the Lee River *Ownibuoye* Owyane Stream in County Cork flowing 11 miles sw to Bantry Bay [A4v] *discovered* actually, the English had been warned by Brian Mac-

Hugh MacMahan (see headnote) *Don Juan d'l'Aquila* commander of 4,500 Spanish troops sent by Philip III in 1601 to aid Tyrone; he took Kinsale but had difficulty maintaining communication with the Irish rebel leadership *travell* travail   *Lord Deputie* Charles Blount   [B1] *Barracadoes* here hastily formed ramparts of barrels, wagons, timber, stone, and household furnishings *Regiment volant* one formed for rapid and easy movement   *Sir Henry Poore* Henry Power; he fortified Mountjoy's camp on the n side by a "flying regiment" of 449 men   *Sir Richard Greame* Richard Greame, captain for Sir George Carew whom Carew called "the best horse captain in the kingdom" *Earle of Thomond* Donough O'Brien, baron of Ibrickan, 4th earl of Thomond (d. 1624), Irish loyalist who was active in repressing rebellious Irish in 1589 and in the great Tyrone rebellion of 1595-1603. He was also prominent at the siege of Kinsale to which he brought awaited reinforcements   *Sir Richard Wingfield* (d. 1634), appointed marshall of the army in Ireland in 1600, a veteran of the 1586 war in the Netherlands and the 1596 expedition to Cadiz *Sir Henry Davers* Danvers (1573-1644), earl of Derby, who had earlier served under Essex in Ireland   [B1v] *sir Oliver Lambert* Mountjoy's colonel in Hampshire in 1596 and a seasoned soldier, he first fought in Kildare, secured Sligo; admired as a fighter, he was distrusted as a politician by Mountjoy since Lambert threatened to dispossess private men from their lands and transfer the lands to the Queen   *glyn* glen   *Sir H. Folyat* Sir Henry Folliott, commander of a regiment of foot (along with Oliver St. John) who supported Powers's "flying regiment"   *Sir Oliver Saint-John* viscount Garndison and baron Tregoz (1559-1630); knighted by Mountjoy, he was given command of 200 foot. He repulsed a night attack of the Spaniards on Dec. 2 when he was wounded; shortly after, he left to carry dispatches to Elizabeth concerning affairs in Ireland   [B2] *wings* division of men to the side of the main troop *cornets* companies (of cavalry)   *a good skirmish* the charge of 100 musketeers was led by Lt. Cowel, an expert in skirmishing who wore a red cap so that his men could always locate him   [B2v] *the earle of Clanicard* Richard de Burgh; Mountjoy later knighted him for his service at the battle of Kinsale   *battell* forces   *charged their battell* the English horse charged 1,800 Irish pikemen at the odds of 1 to 6 or 7 hoping to bluff them into breaking ranks; but the Irish held their ground and the English quickly retreated   *sir William Godolphin* (d. 1613), a Cornishman; with Sir Richard Moryson and Sir Henry Danvers one of Essex's three officers in Ireland; he led Mountjoy's own troops at the battle of Kinsale   *sir John Berkeley* John Berkeley, serjeant-major of the English camp; earlier in 1601 Berkeley was deputized by Mountjoy as governor of Connaught for Sir Arthur Savage, then in England; he was killed in June 1602 by a chance shot during minor skirmishes and was succeeded by Danvers   *Captaine Taffe* Sir William Taaffe (d. 1627), a cavalryman whose gift of whiskey to MacMahon led to a warning of the Irish and Spanish assault (see headnote)   [B3] *rereward* rearward; usually a third force drawn up behind the main force   *caliver* light musket, introduced late in the sixteenth century, which could be fired without a "rest"   *vantgarde* vanguard   *Alonso d'Ocampo* Alonzo del Campo; actually, he, two captains, and 47 of his men surrendered to Mountjoy's troop of horse after the remainder of his 200 men had been killed   *Alferres* ensigns or standard bearers   [B3v] *being tyred with killing* in fact, their horses were weak from lack of forage   *Cornet* the fifth commissioned officer in a group of cavalry who carried the colors   *raced* scratched *holbert* halberd, a weapon consisting of a shaft about 6 ft. long with a head adapted to both cutting and thrusting *floure* flower (ie, choicest men) *Conductor* commander [B4] *Captayne Bodlegh* Sir James Bodley (?1550-1618), soldier and military engineer; as trench-master, he advised Mountjoy on building his camps between Thomond and Bundon in preparation for the siege on Kinsale *offered a parlee* on Dec. 31 *negotiation* as a pledge for Godolphin's security, d'l'Aguila offered and sent an officer of equal rank, Pedro Euriquez *Viceroy* Governor [B4v] *composition* agreement for submission or surrender on particular terms [C1v] *Duckats* gold or silver coins of varying amounts, roughly equivalent to 9 shillings [C2] *Condees* Spanish counts [C2v] *in rerum natura* "in the nature of things" [C3] *crazed* destroyed [C3v] *Januarie. 1601* (this date is Old Style; Jan.1602 by our reckoning) [D1] *severall* separate [D1v] *Ro. Gardemor.* Sir Robert Gardiner, chief justice of Ireland, who accompanied the troops as a representative of the Irish Council and acted as chief welfare officer [D2] *Ricorren castle* Rincurren Castle, a fort commanding the entrance to Kinsale Harbor and one of two castles (the other—Ny Park—on a peninsula in the Bandon estuary) occupied by d'l'Aguila. Carew headed the English forces that defeated the Spanish there and won a truce by offering the Spanish their lives and a return to Spain for laying down their arms *rampierd* fortified by ramparts [D2v] *proofe whereof by the fruite* Biblical and proverbial; see Tilley T498 [D3] *the first landing of the Spaniards* under Vice-Admiral Pedro de Zubiaur; with 3,814 men commanded by d'l'Aguila and sailing from Lisbon, Sept. 1, 1601 *his first arrivall here* Mountjoy left London Feb. 7, 1600, as lord deputy of Ireland, perhaps accompanied by Carew *Quantum mutatus ab illo!* "What a change [contrast] from him [that]!"

Selective Bibliography

Adamson, J. H. and H. F. Polland. *The Shepherd of the Ocean: An Account of Sir Walter Ralegh and his Times.* Boston: Gambit, Inc., 1969.

Allen, J. W. *A History of Political Thought in the Sixteenth Century.* London: Methuen and Co., 1928.

Anglo, Sydney, *Spectacle, Pageantry, and Early Tudor Policy.* Oxford: The Clarendon Press, 1969.

Baker, Herschel. *The Dignity of Man: Studies in the Persistence of an Idea.* Cambridge, Mass.: Harvard University Press, 1947.

Bergeron, David M. *English Civic Pageantry 1558-1642.* Columbia, S.C.: University of South Carolina Press, 1971.

Bindoff, S. T. *Tudor England.* London: Penguin Books, 1950; 1962.

Bindoff, S. T., J. Hurstfield, and C. H. Williams, eds. *Elizabethan Government and Society: Essays Presented to Sir John Neale.* London: The Athlone Press, 1961.

Bingham, Caroline. *The Making of a King: The Early Years of James VI and I.* Garden City: Doubleday, 1969.

Black, J. B. *The Reign of Elizabeth 1558-1603.* (Second Edition) Oxford: The Clarendon Press, 1959.

Chabod, Federico. *Machiavelli and the Renaissance,* trans. David Moore. Cambridge, Mass.: Harvard University Press, 1958.

Cheyney, Edward P. *A History of England From the Defeat of the Armada to the Death of Elizabeth.* (Two Volumes) London: Longmans, Green and Co., 1926.

Elliott, J. H. *Europe Divided, 1559-1598.* London: Collins, 1968.

_____. *Imperial Spain, 1469-1716.* London: Arnold, 1963.

Elton, G. R. *England under the Tudors.* (Third Edition) London: Methuen and Co., 1962.

_____, ed. *The Tudor Constitution: Documents and Commentary.* Cambridge: Cambridge University Press, 1968.

Falls, Cyril. *Elizabeth's Irish Wars.* London: Methuen and Co., 1950.

Fraser, Antonia. *Mary Queen of Scots.* London: Weidenfeld and Nicolson, 1969.

Handover, P. M. *The Second Cecil.* London: Eyre and Spottiswoode, 1959.

Harrison, G. B., ed. *The Letters of Queen Elizabeth.* London: Cassell and Company, Ltd., 1935; 1968.

————— . *The Life and Death of Robert Devereaux, Earl of Essex.* New York: Henry Holt and Co., 1937.

Haydn, Hiram. *The Counter-Renaissance.* New York: Charles Scribner's Sons, 1950.

Holmes, Martin. *Elizabethan London.* London: Cassell and Company, Ltd., 1969.

Hurstfield, Joel. *Elizabeth I and the Unity of England.* New York: Macmillan, 1960.

————— . *The Queen's Wards.* Cambridge, Mass.: Harvard University Press, 1958.

Jenkins, Elizabeth. *Elizabeth the Great.* London: Victor Gollancz, 1958.

Kenny, Robert W. *Elizabeth's Admiral: The Political Career of Charles Howard Earl of Nottingham, 1536-1624.* Baltimore: The Johns Hopkins Press, 1970.

Lehmberg, Stanford E. *Sir Walter Mildmay and Tudor Government.* Austin: The University of Texas Press, 1964.

Levy, F. J. *Tudor Historical Thought.* San Marino, Calif.: Huntington Library, 1967.

Lewis, Michael. *Armada Guns.* London: Allen and Unwin, 1960.

————— . *The Spanish Armada.* London: B. T. Batsford, Ltd., 1960.

Lockyer, Roger. *Tudor and Stuart Britain, 1471-1714.* London: Longmans, Green and Co., Ltd., 1964.

Lynch, John. *Spain Under the Habsburgs.* Oxford: Basil Blackwell, 1965.

MacCaffrey, Wallace. *The Shaping of the Elizabethan Regime.* Princeton: Princeton University Press, 1968.

Mattingly, Garrett. *The Defeat of the Spanish Armada.* London: Jonathan Cape, 1959.

————— . *Renaissance Diplomacy.* Boston: Houghton Mifflin Co., 1955.

Neale, J. E. *The Age of Catherine de Medici and Essays in Elizabethan History.* London: Jonathan Cape, 1958; 1965.

————— . *Elizabeth I and Her Parliaments.* (Two Volumes) London: Jonathan Cape, 1953; 1957.

————— . *The Elizabethan House of Commons.* (Revised Edition) London: Penguin Books, 1963.

————— . *Queen Elizabeth I.* London: Jonathan Cape, 1934.

Nichols, John. *The Progresses and Public Processions of Queen Elizabeth.* (Three Volumes) London, 1823.

Prothero, G. W., ed. *Select Statutes and Other Constitutional Documents Illustrative of the Reigns of Elizabeth [I] and James I.* (Fourth Edition) Oxford: The Clarendon Press, 1913; 1965.

Raleigh, Sir Walter, *et al. Shakespeare's England.* (Two Volumes) Oxford: The Clarendon Press, 1916.

Read, Conyers, ed. *Bibliography of British History: Tudor Period, 1485-1603*. Oxford: The Clarendon Press, 1933.

————— . *Lord Burghley and Queen Elizabeth*. London: Jonathan Cape, 1965.

————— . *Mr. Secretary Cecil and Queen Elizabeth*. London: Jonathan Cape, 1965.

————— . *Mr. Secretary Walsinham and the Policy of Queen Elizabeth*. (Three Volumes) Oxford: The Clarendon Press, 1924.

————— . *The Tudors: Personalities and Practical Politics in Sixteenth Century England*. New York: Henry Holt and Company, 1936.

Reese, M. M. *The Tudors and Stuarts*. London: Arnold, 1940.

Rice, George P., Jr. *The Public Speaking of Queen Elizabeth*. New York: Columbia University Press, 1951.

Robertson, A. G. *Tudor London*. London: Macdonald and Co., Ltd., 1968.

Rowse, A. L. *The England of Elizabeth: The Structure of Society*. New York: The Macmillan Company, 1950.

————— . *Sir Richard Grenville of the 'Revenge'*. London: Jonathan Cape, 1937.

Smith, Alan G. R. *The Government of Elizabethan England*. London: Arnold 1967.

Smith, Lacey Baldwin. *The Elizabethan World*. Boston: Houghton Mifflin Co., 1967.

Stevenson, David L., ed. *The Elizabethan Age*. New York: Fawcett Publications, Inc., 1966.

Stone, Lawrence. *The Crisis of the Aristocracy, 1558-1641*. Oxford: The Clarendon Press, 1965.

Tillyard, F. M. W. *The Elizabethan World Picture*. London: Macmillan, 1943.

Waldman, Milton. *Queen Elizabeth I*. London: Collins, 1952.

Wallace, Willard M. *Sir Walter Raleigh*. Princeton: Princeton University Press, 1959.

Wernham, R. B. *Before the Armada: The Emergence of the English Nation, 1485-1588*. New York: Harcourt, Brace, and World, Inc., 1966.

Williams, Neville. *Elizabeth: Queen of England*. London: Weidenfeld and Nicolson, 1967.

Williamson, James. *The Age of Drake*. London: Adam and Charles Black, 1938.

Woodward, G. W. O. *A Short History of Sixteenth-Century England*. London: Blandford Press, Ltd., 1963.

Index

(In the index boldface page numbers refer to the documents; page numbers followed by "n" refer to the textual notes found on page 361ff.; other page numbers refer to the editorial commentary immediately preceding each document.)

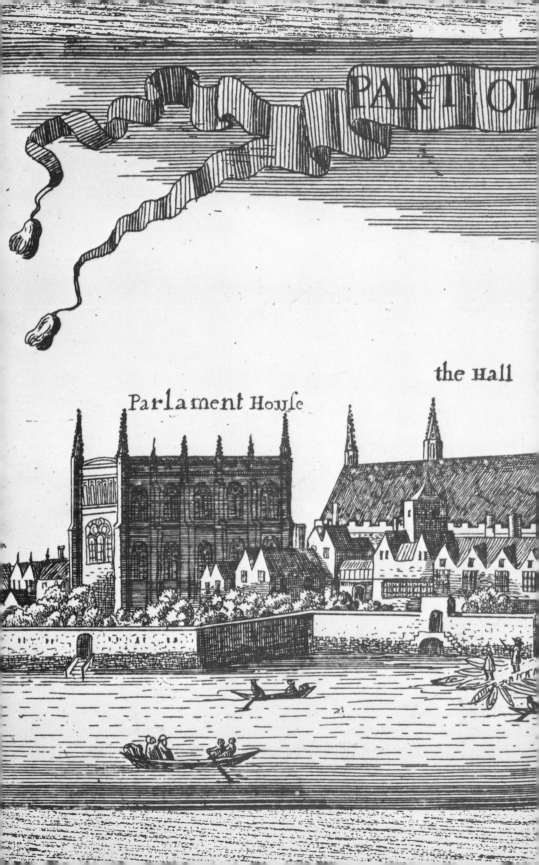